A Van Beuren Production

ALSO BY HAL ERICKSON AND FROM MCFARLAND

Any Resemblance to Actual Persons: The Real People Behind 400+ Fictional Movie Characters (2017)

From Radio to the Big Screen: Hollywood Films Featuring Broadcast Personalities and Programs (2014)

Military Comedy Films: A Critical Survey and Filmography of Hollywood Releases Since 1918 (2012)

Encyclopedia of Television Law Shows: Factual and Fictional Series About Judges, Lawyers and the Courtroom, 1948–2008 (2009)

Television Cartoon Shows: An Illustrated Encyclopedia, 1949 through 2003, 2d ed. (2005; paperback 2016)

The Baseball Filmography, 1915 through 2001, 2d ed. (2002; paperback 2010)

"From Beautiful Downtown Burbank": A Critical History of Rowan and Martin's Laugh-In, *1968–1973* (2000; paperback 2009)

Sid and Marty Krofft: A Critical Study of Saturday Morning Children's Television, 1969–1993 (1998; paperback 2007)

Syndicated Television: The First Forty Years, 1947–1987 (1989; paperback 2001)

A Van Beuren Production

*A History of the 619 Cartoons,
875 Live Action Shorts, Four
Feature Films and One Serial
of Amedee Van Beuren*

HAL ERICKSON

McFarland & Company, Inc., Publishers
Jefferson, North Carolina

ISBN (print) 978-1-4766-8027-9
ISBN (ebook) 978-1-4766-4098-3

LIBRARY OF CONGRESS AND BRITISH LIBRARY
CATALOGUING DATA ARE AVAILABLE

Library of Congress Control Number 2020041429

© 2020 Hal Erickson. All rights reserved

No part of this book may be reproduced or transmitted in any form or by any means, electronic or mechanical, including photocopying or recording, or by any information storage and retrieval system, without permission in writing from the publisher.

On the cover: Van Beuren's *Tom and Jerry* poster; opening title for 1930's *Aesop's Fables Circus Capers*

Printed in the United States of America

*McFarland & Company, Inc., Publishers
Box 611, Jefferson, North Carolina 28640
www.mcfarlandpub.com*

To my adorable grandchildren, Lorelai and Calvin.
Until they're able to read this book, they are welcome to color in it.

Table of Contents

Preface and Acknowledgments — 1

Introduction: Amedee Van Beuren (and a Cast of Thousands) — 3

1—Mr. and Mrs. Sidney Drew — 23

2—Topics of the Day — 31

3—Ernest Truex — 41

4—Animated Cartoons, Part One: Aesop's Fables — 46

5—Henry and Polly — 61

6—The Grantland Rice Sportlights — 64

7—Walter Futter's "Curiosities" — 74

8—Smitty and His Pals — 79

9—The Song Sketches — 90

10—The Vagabond Adventures — 95

11—Animated Cartoons, Part Two: Tom and Jerry, Cubby Bear, The Little King, Amos 'n' Andy — 108

12—Floyd Gibbons Supreme Thrills — 119

13—The Liberty Short Short Stories — 123

14—Frank Buck: *Bring 'Em Back Alive* (1932); *Wild Cargo* (1934); *Fang and Claw* (1935) — 127

15—The Charlie Chaplin Mutual Comedies — 142

16—*The Last Frontier* (1932) — 150

17—The Van Beuren Musical Comedies — 157

18—The Dumb-Bell Letters — 169

19—Animated Cartoons, Part Three: Burt Gillett and the Rainbow Parades — 175

20—*Adventure Girl* (1934)	185
21—Easy Aces	193
22—Struggle to Live	199
23—Sports with Bill Corum	204
24—World on Parade	209
The Van Beuren Filmography	217
Selected Bibliography	233
Index	235

Preface and Acknowledgments

Like many a child of the 1950s (yes, I'm *that* decrepit), my earliest memories of watching television include incessantly repeated viewings of the oldest talkie cartoons imaginable—foremost among these the output of Van Beuren Productions. Much of this ancient animation didn't bear the name of its production company, thanks to multitudinous reissue prints from such firms as Commonwealth and Official, where often the titles and even the character names were changed. (To avoid confusion with MGM's cat-and-mouse duo of the same name, Van Beuren's human cartoon stars Tom and Jerry were rechristened "Dick and Larry" in the Official Films reissues, while another character named "Cubby Bear" became "Brownie the Bear" for reasons unknown). However, several original theatrical prints did sneak onto the small screen, and as a result a lot of my contemporaries grew up thinking of Amedee J. Van Beuren as that obscure producer who churned out all those weird cartoons.

To this day, Van Beuren is generally mentioned only in relation to his animated manifest, leading many casual observers to assume that cartoons were his only business. Leonard Maltin's excellent chapter on Van Beuren in his landmark animation history *Of Mice and Magic* shed more light on the producer's cartoon unit than any previous volume, yet still his hundreds of live-action short subjects were ignored (understandably, given the scope and purpose of Maltin's book). So imagine my astonishment when, after compiling the information necessary for this history of the Van Beuren films, I made a tally of the 1,499 titles produced by Amedee Van Beuren (either directly or indirectly) from 1918 through 1937 and discovered that only 619 were cartoons: The remaining titles consisted of 875 live-action shorts, four full-length features and one 12-episode serial.

It was no trick to locate virtually all of Van Beuren's sound cartoons and a representative cross-section of the silent animation he oversaw as president of Paul Terry's Fables cartoon studio. Digging up the live-action material was not quite so easy. Beyond the feature films, the 1932 chapter play *The Last Frontier* and the producer's 1932–34 reissues of Charlie Chaplin's 12 Mutual silent comedies, the bulk of Van Beuren's talkie shorts—and practically all of his silent shorts—have either been scattered to the four winds or are irretrievably lost. It is with no small pride that I can lay claim to having viewed at least a dozen of Van Beuren's silents (in whole or in part) and approximately 50 of the non–Chaplin talkie shorts, but that still leaves nearly 800 live-action films that are today only "available" in the form of shooting scripts, studio synopses and contemporary reviews. So let me take this opportunity for a shout-out to fellow film historians and collectors: If you know of existing prints of any of the remaining talkies, *please* find some way to make them accessible to the rest of world (or at least to me).

In the meantime, permit me to extend thanks and appreciation to the dedicated film and animation archivists of my (social-media) acquaintance, who have either in person, via their internet sites and blogs, or by way of their painstaking restorations of surviving material have helped me fill in the gaps: Jerry Beck, Jerry Blake, Bruce Calvert, Ralph Celentano, Richard Finegan, Michael Hayde, Greg Hilbrich, Milton Knight, Richard Roberts, Bill Sprague and Steve Stanchfield.

Personal thanks for moral support and/or assistance with the preparation of this manuscript go out to Cari and David Bobke, Dale Craven, Jim Feeley, Wayne and Rita Hawk, Jane and Mark Martell, Dave Michelson, Barb Parkman, David Seebach, all my siblings and in-laws, and others within my circle of fellow community-theater participants too numerous to mention.

And especially my beloved wife Joanne, my sons Brian and Peter, my daughter-in-law Janel and my grandchildren Lorelai and Calvin. No words can express how blessed I am for their presence in my life.

Now on to the manuscript itself. After the introduction, the 24 chapters are listed in order of the first release date of the first title in the short-subject or cartoon series covered in that chapter. Likewise, the chapters on Van Beuren's feature films and the producer's one serial are listed in release order. The three chapters covering Van Beuren's animated cartoons each represent a separate development in that output.

So here we are at the *final* paragraph, and I haven't yet explained what drew me to the topic of Amedee Van Beuren and his films. I could say that I wanted to know more about the man behind the films, but since details of Van Beuren's private life are sparse beyond the public knowledge that he was twice married and twice divorced—and the fact that one of the former employees of his animation studio, legendary comedy director Frank Tashlin, was inspired to create a newspaper comic strip in the 1930s titled "Van Boring"—I'll have to let his work speak for him. When all is said and done, the real reason I tackled this book is because no one else had done it before. That, and I should probably get out of the house more often.

Introduction

Amedee Van Beuren (and a Cast of Thousands)

In most biographies of Hollywood's pioneer movie moguls, one will read gut-wrenching accounts of how these future industry Goliaths had emigrated from the dark ghettos of Europe to the Eldorado of the United States with nary a penny to their names; or, how they punched, scratched and kicked their way out of the grinding poverty of Hell's Kitchen and the Lower East Side. The life stories of these men painstakingly trace their professional progress from wretched low-wage employment as scrap-iron collectors (MGM's Louis B. Mayer), fur-factory janitors (William Fox) and seedy song-pluggers (Columbia's Harry Cohn), through their first taste of the movie business via management of—or distribution to—tumbledown neighborhood nickelodeons, and climaxing with their ultimate ascension to fame and enormous fortune running the top feature-film factories of Tinseltown. Similarly rough-and-ready are the backstories of the producers of short-subject films (generally running between one and three reels, or 14 to 42 minutes at silent-film speed). Canadian-born Mack Sennett was a boilermaker and a burlesque performer before slapping together his Keystone studio; New York native Hal Roach was a construction worker and stagecoach driver prior to going into the comedy-short business; and so on. No matter who it is or how the story is told, the alliterative designation "rags to riches" immediately comes to mind.

The life and career of short-subject producer Amedee Van Beuren is something else again. Indeed, one might summarize his story as "riches to even more riches." Van Beuren was born into wealth, carefully groomed to be a corporate executive, and a financial success long before entering the moviemaking business. And unlike those moguls mentioned in the first paragraph, who were dedicated to show business and the manufacture of motion pictures often before they were old enough to vote, Amedee Van Beuren was 39 years old when he produced his first film.

One is tempted to label Van Beuren a dilettante—but what sort of dilettante turns out nearly 1500 shorts, features, and animated cartoons over a 19-year period? One is *not* tempted to refer to Van Beuren as a creator or innovator. He brought nothing new or progressive to the art of the motion picture. The majority of the films he produced—under his own imprimatur or through one of his many colorfully named and short-lived corporations—were delivered to him fully formed by other, more adventurous filmmakers in need of an executive producer who was disinclined to interfere with the creative process as long as the cash poured in. And as you shall see in the course of this book, several of Van Beuren's most successful film projects didn't even come to him directly, but were laid in his lap by the powerful theatrical chain to whom he was beholden for well over a decade. In the latter stages of his film career, Van Beuren was inclined to repeat his own past successes to keep his plant in operation, on the theory that if they liked it once, they'd love it twice. Fortunately for him, "they" usually did.

So let us simply refer to Amedee J. Van Beuren as a very careful and very canny showman. I'm sure he could have lived with that.

He was born Amedee James Vignot in Carmel, New York, on July 10, 1879. His father Alfred Vignot was the son of prominent French winemaker and importer Amédée Vignot, whose business thrives to this day as the Clement Company. In 1877 Alfred Vignot married Marietta Ferguson; two years later Amedee James was born, the first of the Vignots' four children (two sons, two daughters). Despite his father's considerable income, Amedee earned his keep in the livery and grocery business as soon as he was old enough. In 1894, when Amedee was 14, his father died. Four years later, his mother Marietta remarried: Her new soulmate was Alfred Van Beuren, born in New York State sometime between 1839 and 1841.

Known to friends and colleagues as "Bill Poster" Van Beuren, Amedee's new father had been in the outdoor-advertising business since early adulthood. For the better part of the 19th century, the trade of posting signs and bills for commercial purposes was a hardscrabble existence in which itinerant posters, usually hired by the day at starvation wages, put up their signs wherever and whenever they could without permission. The result was usually a quick arrest from the local constabulary, or more often bloody brawls with rival posters. Attempts to organize and systemize the profession generally ended in violence, but gradually the more enterprising bill posters were able to secure exclusive contracts from the more affluent customers. In the early 1870s Alfred Van Beuren had the good fortune to make the acquaintance of E.V. Street of Street & Smith Publishing, whose flagship

Amedee J. Van Beuren in 1919, at the outset of his motion picture career.

periodical, the *New York Weekly*, was lagging behind its competition. Street engaged Van Beuren to hand out sample copies of the *Weekly* on the streets of New York's Harlem district, at the same time engaging a man named Ellsworth to post promotional material for the *Weekly*'s serialized adventure stories. In 1872, the Harlem-based firm of Ellsworth, Van Beuren & Street was born.

The synergistic relationship between publishing and advertising enabled the young company to flourish and attract new customers. Upon Ellsworth's death Van Beuren briefly shuttered the business, reopening with a dynamic new partner: Henry Munson, a former poster-hanger himself and something of a legend in the promotion business. With Munson in charge and Van Beuren as general manager, the company's name was changed to A. Van Beuren Bill Posters, maintaining offices in Harlem and Manhattan. In 1888, one year after E.V. Street's death, Samuel Pratt joined the operation, and upon Munson's exit in 1891 the company was (briefly) rechristened Van Beuren & Pratt. Even after his name was removed from the shingle in favor of A. Van Beuren & Company, Samuel Pratt proved to be an even more valuable partner than Munson. Known to the trade as the "guiding spirit" of the Van Beuren plant, it was Pratt who brokered most of the company's largest exclusivity deals with customers, notably a fat contract to handle all New York State advertising for Barnum & Bailey. It was probably also Pratt who coined the firm's bulky but effective slogan: "Bill Posters, Distributors and Tackers. Our System of Distribution Is Perfect, and We Ask No Pay If Work Is Not Properly Done." With Pratt at the helm, Alfred Van Beuren began spending less time in the office and more time at his sprawling villa in Lakewood, New York, and on overseas vacations. Meanwhile, his stepson Amedee quietly and studiously attended business college.

Before proceeding, it should be mentioned that in 1892 a man was struck and killed by a falling billboard on the streets of New York, prompting a lawsuit against A. Van Beuren & Company. It was the first time that the family name was connected with a costly courtroom litigation. It would not be the last.

By 1895 the company was earning $200,000 a year and had expanded its business to other parts of the country. Van Beuren and Pratt were universally admired for the improvements they continually made upon their operation, both technological and businesswise. To cite one example among many, *The Billboard* (a periodical for outdoor advertisers and not the entertainment trade paper of the same name) lavished praise upon Van Beuren's development of an imprint board made of blue and white enameled iron, "practically indestructible" no matter the weather. In 1896 Van Beuren laid claim to the highest posting rental in New York: $5200 for a triple-decker board measuring a total width of 279 feet, spanning the corner of 37th and Broadway. Clients for whom Samuel Pratt had secured exclusive commercial rights included the top Broadway theaters, Grumbler Cigars, Buffo Cigarettes, Pepper Whiskey, Sapolio (a popular cleansing agent), Pabst Beer and Holbrook's Sauces—the latter renting a sign described by *Billboard* in 1898 as "nearly half a mile long," clearly visible from great distances to incoming ocean liners. The cash outlay for such displays was enormous, but Alfred Van Beuren could always justify the expenditure, pointing out that the lavish signs would pay for themselves within a few months.

Though the bill-posting business had gentrified since the mid–19th century it was still hardly a place for gentlemen. Backed up by the brute strength of the mighty Showmen's Association, Alfred Van Beuren showed no mercy in smashing down any smaller company who tried to encroach upon his turf or who posted so much as a church bulletin on any of his property holdings. And while he was willing to negotiate his way out of strikes and other labor agitations, he was rumored to have a battalion of hired hoodlums at his beck and call.

Naturally there were those who resented Alfred Van Beuren's clout and fought back at every turn, notably his biggest rival, the New York Billposting Company. After several years' warfare the two companies arrived at a stalemate in June of 1905. Van Beuren then figured that the best way to beat New York Billposting was to join it. In his official capacity as Van Beuren's vice president, Samuel Pratt handled the particulars of the merger, with most of his time spent haggling with the competition's point man O.J. Gude over who should get the biggest slice of the pie. Finally a deal was struck favoring Van Beuren, with New York Billposting's president Alexander Clark signing an agreement that gave Alfred Van Beuren a 66 percent controlling interest.

What Pratt didn't know was that Van Beuren had already sold his common stock to New York Billposting's Barney Link and W.P. Fay, the result being that that their chunk of the merger was a full 34 percent interest—effectively freezing out Samuel Pratt. Barney Link took over as general manager of Van Beuren & New York Billposting Company from Alfred Van Beuren (who was now chairman of the board), while Pratt was reduced to treasurer. Before you could say "all in the family," the name of the company's new vice president was announced to the public: None other than Alfred Van Beuren's oldest stepson Amedee, who on December 30, 1906, formally changed his name to Amedee James Vignot-Van Beuren, billing himself as such for several years before eliminating the "Vignot" entirely.

This formal portrait of Amedee J. Van Beuren first appeared in *Pathé Club Yearbook* of 1927, and was used for publicity purposes for the remainder of his life.

The heir-apparent of Van Beuren & New York Billposting proved equal to his new responsibilities, combining the benefits of his expensive college education with the professional knowhow gleaned from his stepfather. But after Alfred Van Beuren's death in 1909, Amedee's thoughts began to wander. He had always been fascinated with the members of the entertainment and amusement industries who had purchased advertising from his firm. In particular he became friendly with sports promoter Dr. Harry Kelton—known as "Doc" to his cronies at the Lambs Club—who ran a number of popular amusement centers in the city and its boroughs, and also managed several top athletes.

In 1912 Amedee Van Beuren and Doc Kelton, in concert with attorney Alfred M. Barrett, incorporated the Notlek Amusement Company (Kelton spelled backwards), with Van Beuren as president. The company established headquarters on 8th Avenue and 57th Street at Van-Kelton Stadium, the largest of Kelton's many outdoor tennis and handball courts. The Van-Kelton Tennis Club, likewise at 8th and 57th, would grab a great deal of media attention as a training area for such boxing champs as Jack Dempsey, and in 1927 hosted the first U.S. Pro Tennis Championship. Another major holding, Notlek Amusement Park in the Bronx (later the Riverside Ice Rink) doubled as a tennis court in summer and (after being flooded and frozen over) an ice-skating rink in winter.

A few years before partnering with Kelton, Van Beuren had opened the Moorish Gardens at 110th Street and Riverside Drive, an "airdrome" (open-air theater) initially designed for live outdoor entertainment. After incorporating Notlek in 1912 Van Beuren forged another alliance with motion-picture distributors John R. Freuler and Harry A. Aitken, who that same year established the Mutual Film Corporation in offices located on Wall Street. This enabled Van Beuren to secure first-run rights to the Mutual product, notably the Keystone comedies produced by Mack Sennett—allowing Van Beuren to boast in later years that his was the first major New York movie house to screen Keystone's money-spinning Charlie Chaplin films (Chaplin's later independent productions under the Mutual banner would prove to be another cash cow for Van Beuren when in the early 1930s he reissued the 12 silent two-reelers with musical scores and sound effects). These films and the rest of the Mutual output played to packed houses at the Moorish Gardens, where patrons sat under the open sky in comfy wooden chairs and laughed the nights away—all the while impressing Van Beuren with the drawing power of the fledgling movie medium. "If I told you how many thousand dollars we made there the first summer you would wonder why I stuck to the billposting business," he told *Moving Picture World* in 1919, adding that he credited his ability to accurately gauge public tastes to his outdoor-advertising experience.

In 1914, the same year his mother passed away, Amedee Van Beuren resigned from the Van Beuren & New York Bill Posting Company, which subsequently merged with the Poster Advertising Company and in 1926 was swallowed up by General Outdoor Advertising. Van Beuren and Kelton had hitched their wagons to outdoor athletics and motion-picture exhibition, with Kelton overseeing the former and Van Beuren the latter, adding the Colorado Springs Theater Corporation to his acquisitions. By 1915 Kelton had stepped down as partner to become treasurer of Notlek, with Van Beuren as president and he and his first wife Blanche comprising the board of directors.

Three years later Van Beuren followed the lead of such former exhibitors as William Fox and Adolph Zukor by plunging into film production. In a 1919 profile of Van

The Moorish Gardens shown in an article in the New York–based show business publication *Reel Life*, March 1913.

Beuren, *Moving Picture World* reasoned that this was a logical progression of events, since the novice producer was already widely acknowledged for "knowing almost as much of what the public wants as the public knows itself." Van Beuren's business model was not so much William Fox, who preferred to create and nurture new movie stars for public consumption, as it was Adolph Zukor, who chose to hire established theatrical favorites for his films (it's not for nothing that Zukor named his company Famous Players). Knowing from experience how successful "tried and true" could be, Van Beuren's first film series was a group of two-reel comedies starring Mr. and Mrs. Sidney Drew, whose popularity on stage was exceeded only by their success in motion pictures. While hedging his bets with a proven commodity, Van Beuren held fast to his late stepfather's credo that it takes money to make money, telling *Motion Picture News*: "I'm in the producing end of the motion picture business, first and primarily, to build entertainment for the public, for when I do this, my success in the venture is assured, since I have always held that money is no object when one can give the public what it wants. And when the public gets what it wants it will pay for it and the man supplying the demand will not lose for his trouble."

With Doc Kelton throwing in with his partner's first stab at filmmaking, Van Beuren created V.B.K. Productions to produce the Mr. & Mrs. Drew series for release through Famous Players subsidiary Paramount Pictures. Five films had been completed and released when V.B.K. suffered a setback that at the time seemed insurmountable: The death of Sidney Drew in April of 1919. But Van Beuren calmly plucked another star from the Broadway stage, comic actor Ernest Truex, and was able to round out his commitment to Paramount. At the same time he created a new film company, with the self-aggrandizing name AyVeeBee—indicating that hereafter Doc Kelton would confine himself to the sports end of the business.

Following this flurry of activity on behalf of Paramount, Van Beuren would be most closely linked with a successful film distribution firm called Pathé Exchange. Created in France in 1900, Pathé had been releasing their films in the U.S. from the outset. This allowed the company to join the highly exclusive Motion Picture Patents Company, who permitted Pathé to use MPPC's General Film Company subsidiary to distribute their product. Pathé set up temporary production facilities in New Jersey to make serials, but when the company broke from General Film and reincorporated as Pathé Exchange in 1915, hands-on production was largely abandoned in favor of distributing product from independent producers like Hal Roach and Mack Sennett.

Van Beuren was added to the Pathé roster in 1919, not because of his somewhat sparse film track record but because he was on intimate terms with the supremely powerful theatrical circuit formed by dime-museum impresario Benjamin Franklin Keith (1846–1914) and circus promoter and troubleshooter Edward Franklin Albee (1857–1930). Keith and Albee had first joined forces in 1882 to bankroll a Boston dime museum that operated during the annual eight-month circus layoff. Albee soon emerged as the guiding force of the partnership, renovating their dingy museum and expanding it into a fabulous theatrical showcase called the Gayety (or Gaiety) Musée. From this foundation Keith and Albee were able to purchase other major theaters in Philadelphia and New York City, while erecting a fully furnished and totally modernized 3000-seat vaudeville house, the New Theater, in their home base of Boston.

As their empire expanded, B.F. Keith remained in the public eye as the nominal senior partner, a respected figurehead who'd gained favor with vaudeville patrons by promoting clean and wholesome entertainment. Meanwhile the more ambitious and less ethical Albee set about organizing and centralizing vaudeville, transforming the popular variety medium into Keith-Albee's own personal monarchy. Tightly controlling salaries and ruling over performers with an iron hand, Albee never hesitated to blacklist anyone who got on the partnership's bad side. Though E.F. Albee became the most feared and despised man in show business, his stable of talent and his luxurious theaters kept his patrons happy and coming back for more. By the end of the 19th century Keith-Albee had a stranglehold on American variety entertainment, determining which performers received playdates and where they appeared by creating the United Booking Office, and later counteracting efforts to unionize by forcing their contractees to join the anti-union National Vaudeville Artists. The partners would eventually seize control of their fiercest rival, the Orpheum circuit, which in similar dictatorial fashion had controlled virtually every top vaudeville house in the South and West while Keith-Albee engulfed the North and East.

B.F. Keith died in 1914. With the death of Keith's son Paul in the 1918 influenza epidemic, E.F. Albee officially became what he'd unofficially been all along: Sole emperor of the realm, with his trusted (by Albee if no one else) general manager John J. Murdock at his side. From existing evidence, it would seem that it was Murdock who urged Albee to get into the motion picture business. It has sometimes been claimed that the reason Keith-Albee collapsed along with the rest of vaudeville in the early 1930s was the organization's failure to recognize the popularity of movies. But as early as 1911 *Motion Picture News* was reporting that Keith-Albee "for years have been one of the country's leading exhibitors—if not THE leading exhibitor" of motion pictures. Albee (or more likely Murdock) had determined that vaudeville audiences would remain in their seats between acts if good short films were run in the intervals. But *only* if the films were of decent quality—and Murdock saw to that by booking the product of Pathé Exchange, especially their serials and weekly newsreels.

In 1915 Albee purchased a sizeable block of Pathé stock, agreeing to book the company's newsreels in all his stage and movie houses; other films were of course included in the set-up, especially serial chapters and comedies. Pathé would become so financially dependent upon Keith-Albee that the company agreed to bestow first-run rights upon the circuit's theaters, with non-affiliated vaudeville and movie houses forced to be satisfied with second runs. In a 1917 article in the trade publication *Motography*, Albee assured his patrons that the circuit was not switching over completely to movies, but merely offering them as a "high class feature" along with the regular live acts.

Ultimately Albee and Murdock reasoned that they could sustain the quality of the films by producing their own shorts for Pathé release—and then strong-arming their own houses into a "play or pay" policy, compelling them to purchase whatever films the circuit turned out. Keith-Albee's first celluloid effort was *Topics of the Day*, a series of half-reel "slide shows" featuring amusing headlines and articles from various newspapers and periodicals. *Topics of the Day* had earlier proven its worth when released regionally on a state's-rights basis (different distributors covering different U.S. territories), so there was little doubt that the series would go over with a typical big-market audience.

Unwilling to reveal that they were on the verge of becoming a (possibly) illegal entertainment monopoly by advertising their participation in the film series to the public in general and the showbiz trade paper *Variety*—which had long opposed E.F. Albee's gestapo tactics—in particular, Keith-Albee set up a "beard" production firm to turn out *Topics of the Day*. This being 1919, the year that Amedee Van Beuren was enthusiastically immersing himself in film production, Van Beuren was agreeable to function as producer of *Topics* on Keith-Albee's behalf. As he'd indirectly indicated to *Moving Picture World*, Van Beuren had known Albee for years: "Billposting had brought me into personal acquaintance with theatrical men of all stratas." For the purposes of his new cinematic venture, Van Beuren set up Topics of the Day Inc. in partnership with A.E. Siegel, who'd created *Topics* in 1918, along with two silent partners, unnamed at the time but later identified as E.F. Albee's son-in-law Ted Lauder and his personal attorney J. Henry Walters.

Pathé of course released *Topics of the Day* on orders from Keith-Albee, and two years later began distributing a series of animated cartoons called *Aesop's Film Fables*, produced by Paul Terry with Keith-Albee's financial backing, and designed to be run in tandem with *Topics* in all circuit theaters. The cartoons were filmed in the same Albee-owned New York building where *Topics* was headquartered and were nominally produced by Fables Pictures Inc., actually a subsidiary of Topics of the Day Inc. Both *Topics* and *Fables* earned oodles and oodles of money for Van Beuren, and though his name never appeared onscreen his executive participation was frequently cited in the trade papers. For the first half of the 1920s *Topics of the Day* and

Aesop's Fables were the sole products of Van Beuren's film operation, save for a trio of two-reelers produced by his own company AyVeeBee, released by Pathé and (again) starring Ernest Truex.

Van Beuren's marine-raiders enthusiasm for film production back in 1919 had mellowed into complacency by 1927. The expansive interviews he'd given at the

Early trade ad for *Aesop's Film Fables* and *Topics of the Day*, Van Beuren's two big screen attractions of the early 1920s.

beginning of his movie career became fewer and farther between. He would be photographed at exhibitor conventions and studio tours, but most of the trade-paper space devoted to Van Beuren focused on his social and leisure activities (his 1926 divorce from his first wife was barely mentioned at all). One can easily speculate that he would have been satisfied to continue limiting himself to *Topics* and *Fables* with no other films to his credit, were it not for the simmering corporate intrigue involving Keith-Albee and a pair of unrelated film studios—but not unrelated for long.

Back in 1923, pioneer moviemaker Cecil B. DeMille left his longtime Paramount Pictures stomping grounds and established his own independent production firm, variously known as the DeMille Corporation and Producers Distributing Corporation (PDC), setting up shop at the old Thomas Ince studios in Culver City, California. In 1926 E.F. Albee got into the act when he joined the board of directors of Cinema Corporation, PDC's holding company. Meanwhile, Albee's lieutenant J.J. Murdock had kept busy brokering all of his boss' dealings with Pathé, including a 1925 agreement to first-run the company's Hal Roach releases in the Keith-Albee houses, billing the comedy shorts as formal "acts." Through an arrangement fabricated by the Wall Street banking firm Blair & Company, which had purchased Pathé in October 1926, Pathé merged with PDC the following year, allowing the company to resume active film production at the PDC facilities. E.F. Albee by now had an even larger financial interest in Pathé, and had himself merged with Orpheum circuit to form Keith-Albee-Orpheum, or K-A-O for short (the merger was officialized on January 28, 1928). All outstanding stock of the old B.F. Keith Corporation and 90 percent of Orpheum stock were wrapped into the Pathé/PDC/K-A-O bundle. J.J. Murdock was rewarded for his role in the negotiations when in June of 1927 he was elected Pathé's president and chairman of the board.

Just prior to Murdock's ascension, K-A-O announced plans to go into film production with several short-subject projects, to be released by Pathé under the banner of Gaiety Films. Among these was a series of comedy shorts based on the newspaper humor column "The Jarr Family." Still indebted to Albee, Van Beuren was enlisted to head up Gaiety and assemble this package, but chose instead to revive an old property: *Henry and Polly*, inspired by his 1919 Mr. & Mrs. Sidney Drew comedies. Since the Drews were both dead and gone, different actors were hired for the roles, and in consequence the Drew chemistry was sorely lacking. The resulting comedies displeased the Pathé executives, who wanted to scrap the project; but Van Beuren had gone too far to pull out now. With the producer backed up by J.J. Murdock's muscle, the three completed *Henry and Polly* two-reelers were reluctantly distributed by Pathé—and as the company had feared, were flops.

Enter Joseph P. Kennedy, former bootlegger, future U.S. Ambassador to England, patriarch of a political dynasty—and, since 1926, president of Film Booking Offices (FBO), a production-distribution firm formed in 1922. Like E.F. Albee, Kennedy owned a piece of Pathé and was interested in expanding his own comparatively small-scale operation. In late February of 1928 Albee sold 200,000 shares of Pathé stock to Joe Kennedy: The benefits were instantaneous, with 18 of FBO's 30 features for 1928 purchased by the K-A-O theater circuit on a first-run basis. Later in 1928 Kennedy entered into an agreement with David Sarnoff, head of the National Broadcasting Company radio network, to turn over financial control of FBO to NBC's parent company Radio Corporation of America. Heavily invested in the impending talking-picture revolution, RCA had created RCA Photophone, a sound system that surpassed the existing Movietone and Vitaphone systems in quality and versatility. RCA Photophone was also the name bestowed upon a combination recording and film studio in New York—and, additionally, the corporate name of the organization

E.F. Albee announces his new association with Cecil B. DeMille's PDC studio (*Photoplay*, 1927).

that in October of 1928 became the holding company of FBO. Accordingly, K-A-O was now committed to the manufacture of all-talking pictures.

But Pathé wasn't, not entirely; the company still had several silent properties in their manifest, including a proposed two-reel series of "kid" comedies, intended to replace Hal Roach's popular Our Gang shorts after Roach switched distribution to MGM in 1927. This property had previously been announced in the same trade-paper articles that had heralded K-A-O's *Henry and Polly* shorts in 1927. By the following year Van Beuren, taking his marching orders from K-A-O, had purchased the film rights to Walter Berndt's widely circulated juvenile comic strip *Smitty* and was all set to begin production in rented space at Los Angeles' Tec Art Studios. Longtime Keith-Albee functionary Harry Weber was appointed supervisor of the 10 *Smitty and His Pals* comedies, released by Pathé between 1928 and 1929. This was Van Beuren's last all-silent project—and the first one packaged by his brand-new company Van Beuren Enterprises, which also controlled the two long-running series produced by Topics of the Day Inc. Before 1928 was over, the company's name was permanently changed to the Van Beuren Corporation.

Gone from the scene were Amedee Van Beuren's Albee-appointed partners Ted Lauder and J. Henry Walters, whom neither Van Beuren nor Pathé needed any more—any more than they needed their longtime benefactor E.F. Albee. What happened? Well, back at the FBO/K-A-O ranch, after decades of being the Kublai Khan of Vaudeville the much-reviled Edward F. Albee suddenly found himself odd man out. His "loyal" assistant J.J. Murdock had for years been secretly undermining his boss by tipping off Albee's movements to the producer's nemesis Sime Silverman, publisher of *Variety*. Now Murdock's duplicity was finally out in the open as he purchased the controlling stock of K-A-O and sold it to Joseph P. Kennedy—who in turn greeted Albee one morning with a cheerful "Haven't you heard, Ed? You're washed up. You're through." On October 25, 1928, Albee's initial was removed from K-A-O and replaced with the "R" of RCA Photophone, thereby giving birth to Radio-Keith-Orpheum. This was not only the new name of the theater chain but also the film division, with FBO officially rechristened RKO on January 1, 1929.

Just before this name change, Amedee Van Beuren fulfilled one last obligation to the Albee interests at FBO by wooing short-subject producer Walter Futter away from Educational Pictures (despite its name a leading purveyor of comedy and novelty shorts) and taking charge of Futter's *Curiosities* series for FBO release. Like his stepfather before him, Van Beuren had mastered the art of landing on his feet while all around him were falling on their keesters. *Variety* snarkily reported on July 18, 1928, that Amedee Van Beuren's survival after all the mergers and firings "would indicate Van Beuren has been swinging with the Kennedy-Murdock crowd."

The switchover to sound served to reinvigorate Van Beuren, who shot double-barreled into a blaze of activity. He formally announced to the trade papers that all future films from the Van Beuren Corporation would be talkies, beginning with Paul Terry's *Aesop's Fables*. Satisfied to continue grinding out silent cartoons, Terry resisted this conversion until Van Beuren forced it upon him, grafting a synchronized music- and sound-effects track onto the 1928 silent cartoon *Dinner Time*. Van Beuren also purchased Terry's Fables Pictures outright from K-A-O, renaming it the Van Beuren Studios. In dogged defiance, Terry persisted in making silent cartoons, contemptuously adding token music-and-effects tracks rather than fully commit himself to the new sound technology. The standoff ended abruptly May of 1929, when Van Beuren took time off from his honeymoon with his second wife Ethel Anderson to fire Terry in person and assume total control of the animation department. Four months later, Van Beuren Studios released their first full-fledged sound cartoon, *Jungle Fools*.

In addition to *Aesop's Fables*, Van Beuren converted virtually all his existing

Van Beuren touts the new talking-picture technology in the pages of *Exhibitors Herald*, 1929.

properties to sound: *Topics of the Day* and *Grantland Rice Sportlights* (picked up from independent Town and Country Films in 1928) for Pathé release, and Walter Futter's *Curiosities* for distribution by FBO's successor RKO. Only *Smitty and His Pals* failed to make the cut, though this was no great loss. Anxious to score points with RCA, which provided Pathé's recording equipment, in early 1929 Van Beuren shipped out a brace of one-reelers for RCA Photophone release: *The Swan*, the first (and last) in a series of "Walter Futter's Overtures"; and *Four in a Flat*, starring Robert Ober in a comedy sketch about obnoxious in-laws. *The Swan* was well received, but *Four in a Flat* was brusquely written off by *Film Daily* as "nothing worth talking about." The short was never copyrighted—and as far as this writer can determine, never officially released.

RCA Photophone's Manhattan studio was the main production center for Van Beuren's first all-talkie shorts series *Song Sketches*, wherein popular tunes were dramatized by such prominent radio vocalists as James Stanley and Frank Luther. Only six one-reelers were released by Pathé in 1930 before the series was dropped, in keeping with Van Beuren's past and future policy of cutting loose any film property that didn't immediately show "legs." Far more successful—and far longer-lasting, in active production from 1930 through 1935—was a series of one-reelers brought to Van Beuren by actor Tom Terriss, producer Alfred T. Mannon and director Elmer Clifton: *Vagabond Adventures*, one of the most popular travelogue series of the 1930s.

Both *Vagabond Adventures* and *Grantland Rice Sportlights* remained up and running after their distributor Pathé merged with RKO in 1930. Van Beuren's releasing firm would be billed variously as RKO-Pathé and Radio Pictures (RKO's main production arm at 780 Gower Street in Hollywood) until September 1932, when the RKO executives elected to confine Pathé to the production of newsreels and in-house documentaries. Also in 1930, RKO purchased a 50 percent interest in Van Beuren Productions, solidifying the producer-distributor relationship between Van Beuren and RKO long after Pathé was out of the picture. (RKO and Radio would officially incorporate as RKO-Radio Pictures in 1937, the year of Van Beuren's exit from active filmmaking).

Artist's rendering of baritone James Stanley, principal star of Van Beuren's all-talking series *Song Sketches* in *Exhibitors Herald World*, November 2, 1929.

Though dependent on his distributor to get his product into theaters, the New York–based Van Beuren was one of the few short-subject producers able to maintain control of his company after the talkie revolution, a feat matched in Hollywood only by Hal Roach, Mack Sennett and Educational Pictures' E.W. Hammons. As noted (with slight inaccuracies) in Benjamin Hampton's 1931 tome *A History of the Movies*: "In the east the only important producer who had continued from the pre-feature era, maintaining his independence of mergers and Wall Street, was Amedee J. Van Beuren. When Pathé left General Film to establish its own business, Van Beuren allied himself with Pathé as an independent producer of travels, comedies, novelties, and other short subjects. His 'animated cartoons' were successful as silent films; when talkies entered he caused his lively caricatures to talk and sing and dance, and with the addition of sound they became more popular than ever." (Hampton was either unaware of, or chose not to discuss, the important role that the Keith-Albee chain had played in the producer's career.) Van Beuren's commitment to the motion picture industry was by now a full-time effort: He would officially divest himself of all outdoor-amusement interests when he dissolved his partnership with Doc Kelton in 1932.

In addition to *Grantland Rice Sportlights* (which moved to Paramount in 1932) and *Vagabond Adventures*, Van Beuren's most successful sound-era ventures in the short subject field included *Dumb-Bell Letters* (1934–36), samples of unintentionally funny correspondence compiled by columnist Juliet Lowell; *Easy Aces* (1935–36), starring radio humorists Goodman and Jane Ace; *Struggle to Live* (1935–37), a nature series featuring the dazzling microscopic photography of Horace and Stacy Woodard; *Sports with Bill Corum* (1935–37), headlining the titular journalist-broadcaster; and *World on Parade* (1935–37), a general-interest series created by world traveller Harold McCracken and narrated by radio personality Alois Havrilla. The profits from these ventures, together with Van Beuren's widely distributed 1932–34 reissues of Charlie Chaplin's classic Mutual silent two-reelers, cushioned the producer from losses incurred by such lesser efforts as *Floyd Gibbons' Supreme Thrills* (1931), *Liberty Short Short Stories* (1931–32) and *The Van Beuren Musical Comedies* (1933–34).

While steadfastly dedicated to his avowed policy of producing quality short subjects at a time when the market for one- and two-reelers was being tightened by the burgeoning double-feature policy in American theaters, Van Beuren occasionally dabbled in extended-length properties, with variable success. His first documentary feature starring big-game hunter Frank Buck, *Bring 'Em Back Alive*, was one of RKO's biggest moneymakers of 1932. Two follow-up features with Buck, *Wild Cargo* (1934) and *Fang and Claw* (1935), played to diminishing returns, but both ended up in the black. Van Beuren's only serial, the 12-episode *The Last Frontier* (1932), did exceptionally well, but shifting policies and management shakeups at RKO precluded any future chapter plays. Conversely, the ill-advised "docudrama" *Adventure Girl* (1934), created by and starring infamous literary hoaxter Joan Lowell, was a total disaster, the worst in Van Beuren's long career but one from which he characteristically bounced back.

The backbone of Van Beuren Productions throughout the talkie era was the company's animation division. The black-and-white *Aesop's Fables*, which remained in production until 1934, would never win any awards for animation excellence, but overall were guaranteed crowd-pleasers, still highly enjoyable today if only for their zippy musical scores, oddball character design, bizarre gags and endearingly incomprehensible storylines. When Van Beuren switched from black & white to color under the guidance of former Disney director Burt Gillett, the resulting cartoons were gorgeous to behold, even when their comedy, story and character content was found wanting. Along the way the unit turned out a few bonafide classics and cult favorites like *Pencil Mania* (1932) and *The Sunshine Makers* (1935). Whether or not

The *Motion Picture Herald* ran this page announcing forthcoming RKO-Van Beuren shorts, 1932. All but the *NBC Musical Broadcasts* came to fruition.

the Van Beuren animation unit would have survived the ultimate shutdown of the company's live-action division is an exercise in useless speculation: Once RKO signed s distribution contract with rival animator Walt Disney in 1936, the doom of the Van Beuren cartoon studio was sealed.

At first unwilling to terminate his cartoon output, by April of 1936 Van Beuren was forced to throw in the towel, though he vowed publicly that his 1936–37 manifest of 32 live-action shorts would be as robust as ever. Indeed it was, with strong rental receipts from his three remaining series *Struggle to Live, Sports with Bill Corum* and *World on Parade*. Things still looked rosy when in the January 5, 1937, edition of *Film Daily* Van Beuren was listed among the industry's "History Makers of 1936," with "a bevy of outstanding shorts" to his credit. Three months later, however, the same publication noted that despite the profits accrued by his most recent shorts, Van Beuren had been obliged to cut production costs, overhead and administration by half. Without the once-dependable cash flow from his cartoons, the handwriting was on the wall for Van Beuren Productions. Add to this the producer's progressively failing health—stemming from a 1935 heart attack that confined him to a wheelchair for several months—and the headache-inducing expenses attending the breakup of his second marriage, and it hardly surprised anyone in Hollywood when in April of 1937 the ailing Van Beuren met with his board of directors, held a quick vote, and completely shut down his operation.

But as the last shorts in his final RKO contract were released between April and

The familiar Van Beuren logo, which zoomed towards the camera at the beginning of his cartoons and live-action shorts of the early 1930s.

August of 1937, Van Beuren seemed to have been rejuvenated and was busily formulating plans to re-enter film production. He turned over his remaining 50 percent interest in Van Beuren Corporation to Schuyler Securities Corporation (becoming that outfit's president in the bargain) in order to finance a new movie venture with fellow independent producer George Hirliman. Welcoming a group of movie executives to a "beef-steak party" at his sprawling New York estate Dreamworld, Van Beuren announced the formation of Condor Pictures, for the purpose of producing both shorts and features. His partner Hirliman told the industry papers: "Despite inroads made generally by duals [double features] on outlets for shorts, the Van Beuren line-up did very nicely, we can assure you, and so will the net figures of this man's corporation when all the returns are in." With Philadelphia financier Albert H. Liebman putting up capital amounting to $1,250,000, and with Van Beuren's former studio manager Frank Snell as the new company's treasurer, Condor was primed to inaugurate their 1937–38 program with the one-reel *Unusual Personalities*, an offshoot of Van Beuren's *World on Parade* series. Bill Corum, another alumnus of Van Beuren Corporation, signed on to resume his *Sports with Bill Corum* series under the aegis of Condor. George Hirliman's contribution was to be a complement of western features starring George O'Brien, in the tradition of the O'Brien vehicles Hirliman had been producing for RKO release, but this series was temporarily shelved when Hirliman dropped out of Condor and was replaced by another prolific indie producer, M.H. Hoffman. Plans were also drawn up for an ambitious "special" feature based on Drew Pearson's controversial Supreme Court novel *Nine Old Men*.

The one project that immediately came to fruition was *The Condor Musicales*, the first in a series of 13 one-reel musical comedies. Two of these shorts, *Murder in Swing* and *A Frozen Affair* were completed by August of 1937 released by Van Beuren's former distributor RKO in September. Filmed first but released second, *Murder in Swing*, an all-black musical starring Les Hite and His Orchestra, is happily still available for viewing. A brisk and breezy nugget of nonsense, the film was good enough to raise hopes that the 11 *Condor Musicales* to follow would be just as enjoyable—and maybe even succeed in putting Condor on the map.

But the Fates had other plans in mind. After a mere two months' existence Condor Films had managed to blow their entire budget, piling up debts of nearly $150,000 before making their first film. When the U.S. Securities and Exchange Commission was barraged with complaints from creditors that Amedee Van Beuren and George Hirliman had filed untrue financial statements, Van Beuren was slapped with the last in a long line of lawsuits. And in addition to their outstanding debts, the Condor executives were hit with a $50,000 damage suit.

At this point Mary Pickford's former business manager W.G. Hutchinson entered the picture, persuading Condor's creditors to accept a 15 percent payoff, the remaining 85 percent to be doled out in 10 installments from profits accrued by future productions. Attorney Edward N. Clark assumed control of Condor, renaming it Hollywood Pictures and reorganizing from top to bottom; of the original executive staff, only Van Beuren and Frank Snell remained. Now far too ill to take an active part in production, Van Beuren left that responsibility to M.H. Hoffman's replacement Lester Cowan, and was himself appointed chairman of the board. The new films were to be produced on a $2 million budget with financing by interests "formerly connected with Condor Pictures," as reported by *Variety*. The Bill Corum and George

O'Brien films were back on the docket, along with a second sports series narrated by radio announcer Don Wilson.

But after suffering a stroke in May of 1938, Van Beuren liquidated Hollywood Pictures—which had never made and would never make a single film—and retired from show business. On November 12, 1938, 59-year-old Amedee J. Van Beuren died of a heart ailment at his New York estate in Carmel, the town of his birth. The following year RKO purchased what remained of the Van Beuren Corporation holdings. And that was that.

Van Beuren's huge backlog of short subjects from 1928 through 1937 would be acquired and circulated by such reissue firms as Commonwealth, Walter O. Gutlohn Inc. and Official Films for the next several decades, before finally lapsing into public domain. Today only the Van Beuren sound cartoons and the company's Charlie Chaplin reissues are readily available to collectors, which is a shame. Though he undeniably ground out his share of stinkers, the hundreds upon hundreds of live-action shorts produced by Van Beuren yielded a great many treasures, several of them still in existence, waiting for some lucky film enthusiasts to unearth them. If this book does nothing other than inspire a full-scale revival and restoration of Amedee J. Van Beuren's vast film output, this aging writer will lie happy in his grave. The writer's grave, not Van Beuren's.

Chapter 1

Mr. and Mrs. Sidney Drew

Amedee J. Van Beuren wasn't about to take chances on unknowns or newcomers for his first foray into film production in 1918. As savvy a showman as he'd been in his exhibition days, Van Beuren pinned his cinematic hopes on a known commodity—known, in fact, throughout the world. That commodity bore the joint professional name "Mr. and Mrs. Sidney Drew."

Born at sea in 1863, Sidney Drew was the adopted son (so the official story goes) of English-born American actress Louisa Lane Drew. The foremost stage comedienne of her time, Louisa was part of an acting dynasty that included the Barrymore family; consequently, her son Sidney was the uncle of Lionel, Ethel and John Barrymore. After launching his own theatrical career in 1887 Drew formed a stage partnership with his first wife Gladys Rankin, herself from a distinguished acting family. In 1911 the couple entered films with the Kalem Company in a series of "Mr. and Mrs. Sidney Drew" one-reel comedies, though at the outset Gladys merely wrote the films while other actresses played Mrs. Drew. Finally in 1913 the Drews began appearing on camera together at the Vitagraph Company, headquartered in Brooklyn. After Gladys' death on January 9, 1914, Sidney soldiered on alone, appearing in such landmark films as Vitagraph's first 3-reel comedy *Goodness Gracious,* costarring Clara Kimball Young and directed by her husband James Young; and the gender-bending fantasy feature *A Florida Enchantment*, which Drew himself directed.

On July 25, 1914, Sidney married 24-year-old Lucille McVey, a Vitagraph scenarist who occasionally acted under the name Jane Morrow. The new "Mr. and Mrs. Sidney Drew" went on to appear in one short comedy per week, becoming filmdom's leading proponents of "polite" comedy—and if you think this means that most film comedy in 1914 was *im*polite, you're absolutely right. Sidney Drew explained his philosophy of humor in a 1917 *Moving Picture World* interview: "Humorous action does not mean gross horseplay. It does not mean the characters are to mash madly into scenes, trip over matches and fall out of the scene again. In our own comedies, Mrs. Drew and myself work to appeal to the mind as well as the eye, but to appeal to the mind through the eye."

The Drews' standard screen characters were named Henry and Polly Minor. In each of their comedies the couple gently satirized the follies and foibles of domestic life, with their mutual affection and rapport shining through every frame. Though Sidney Drew was the credited director, in contemporary interviews he acknowledged that his wife was the team's guiding creative force: Selecting story material, writing the scripts, and directing the director. Surviving examples of their vast Vitagraph output include *Fox Trot Finesse, A Safe Investment, By Might of His Right, Wanted: A*

Mr. and Mrs. Sidney Drew, circa 1917 (Library of Congress).

Nurse, How John Came Home and *Boobley's Baby*, with nary a clinker in the carload. The Drews' naturalistic underplaying remains refreshingly contemporary; one is hard pressed to accept that their films were made over a century ago. Even when the storylines veered into a broader brand of comedy—in *Mrs. Sticky-Moufie-Kiss*, Mr. Drew is driven to suicide by Mrs. Drew's incessant baby-talk—the performances keep the material grounded in reality.

In 1916 the Drews left Vitagraph to accept a $90,000 per year contract with Louis B. Mayer's Metro Pictures, turning out one reel per week without interruption until 1918. On May 19 of that year Drew's beloved son S. Rankin Drew was killed while serving with the Lafayette Flying Corps in World War I. The tragedy was a devastating blow to the actor, severely affecting both his mind and health. All that kept him going was his work; temporarily renouncing films, Drew and his wife plunged into a stage play with the ironic title *Keep Smiling*.

It was during this difficult period that aspiring filmmaker Amedee J. Van Beuren was introduced to Sidney Drew by mutual friends. Van Beuren proposed a return to films for the Drews, promising a larger salary and lighter workload. In late July of 1918 the trade papers spread the news that "bill posting magnate" A.J. Van Beuren, in association with Dr. Harry Kelton, had signed Mr. and Mrs. Drew to a long-term contract calling for 12 two-reel comedies per year, one film per month. Release arrangements were still up in the air, indicating that it would be some time before Famous Players–Lasky's Paramount Pictures division signed on as distributor. Production was slated to begin around the same time *Keep Smiling* opened in New York. There would be no changes in the established Drew format, with Sidney and Lucille resuming their familiar roles of Henry and Polly. The films would be shot during the daylight hours, leaving the Drews plenty of time for their nightly stage obligations.

Some sources claim that the Drews doubled as the producers of this new series; in fact, that responsibility was assumed by Van Beuren and to a lesser extent Doc Kelton. Early trade reports stated that the series would be produced by the partners' Notlek Amusement Corporation, but during the first week of August 1918 V.B.K. Productions was chartered for the sole purpose of filming the new comedies. Partners in this venture were Van Beuren, Kelton, and theatrical attorney Clayton J. Heermance, the son-in-law of Broadway actor Daniel Collyer. Clayton in turn was the father of Richard Heermance, who would serve as Van Beuren's production supervisor in the 1930s and later as an editor and producer at Allied Artists Pictures. Clayton J. Heermance was also the father of actors June Collyer (a.k.a. Mrs. Stuart Erwin) and Bud Collyer (radio's Superman).

In a rare in-depth interview published in *Moving Picture World* on January 18, 1919, Amedee Van Beuren noted: "The screen stole the Drews from the stage and the stage stole them back again.... I decided that the public wanted comedies; good comedies; human nature comedies and comedies with Mr. and Mrs. Sidney Drew playing them under Mrs. Drew's direction. And I decided to bring them back to the screen, if I couldn't entirely steal them away from the stage."

Van Beuren also articulated the production terms. "When I asked the Drews how long it would take, without needless hurry, to make a two-reel comedy they told me three weeks. I told them to take four weeks for perfectly good measure, and so it is that every four weeks ... there will be a new two-reel Drew marketed through Famous Player-Lasky channels. Just as we decided to take extra time in producing comedies so will we go to extra expense in advertising them. By 'extra expense' I mean that we will spend more money in helping the exhibitor sell two-reel Drew comedies to their public than has ever been spent before in promoting comedies—and considerable more, too."

And why had Van Beuren, heretofore connected with the motion picture business solely as an exhibitor, suddenly switched to active production? "I'm an exhibitor producing for exhibitors. The Drews and I are going to produce human nature comedies—'Drew comedies'—the kind that pick clean little frailties out of human life, as only Mrs. Drew can pick them, and give a comedy reflection that has the strongest of all appeals—human nature that laughs at itself and is more human because it has laughed."

Van Beuren explained why he selected the Drews for his entrée into filmmaking in the February 1, 1919, *Motion Picture News*:

> I saw in the Drews the highest type of comedy entertainers. Before I even knew them, their comedies were in my [movie] house and never have I heard a house leave without at the least one hundred patrons commenting favorably on their work. And when I didn't run their comedies, my patrons wanted to know why.
>
> Through the Paramount people, I have supplied the public with samples of the Drews' work under my management. The returns I have received have repaid me a hundredfold for the venture. And the biggest return of all and the one that means most to me, is the fact that the public likes their work and my work in production. It isn't to be assumed from my statements that I'm not expecting financial returns, I am; but first and foremost, I'm expecting satisfaction on the part of the public and I am not only prepared but willing to wait for financial returns.

> Regardless of cost, I am in the business to put the best that is possible in each and every Drew production. Expense is a minor consideration so long as something novel, something that attracts, something entertaining, something "everydayish," and above all, something that represents an event in the life of the masses, that Mary Jones, or Bill Smith can see enacted by the Drews, are the resultants of my efforts.
>
> The little things with which we are all acquainted, they are the ones that I will endeavor to make the crux of the Drew comedies. I'm not seeking to portray on the screen those events that happen but once in a lifetime, but those that are happening every day in your household and in mine. These little incidents, heightened by the Drews' inimitable humor, are to be the basis of every Drew comedy that is made under my management. This is the brand of comedy that the public wants and this is the brand that the V.B.K. Company is going to furnish in productions. If I have to spend a million dollars on one Drew I will do so, for I know that if it merits a million it will be worth more to the public.

Van Beuren never had to spend a million on one Drew comedy. Not even on two Drew comedies.

Though Paramount Pictures distributed several comedies in 1918 and 1919, the studio had no in-house comedy unit, relying instead on such independent producers as Mack Sennett and Joseph M. Schenck (who handled the Fatty Arbuckle comedies) to keep filmgoers laughing. Picking up the new V.B.K. product was a savvy business move for Paramount: The studio acquired a hot movie commodity without incurring the headaches or expenditure of production.

Shooting of the "Paramount-Drew Comedies" commenced in August 1918. A production unit was set up at the Biograph studio in the Bronx, later moving to the Drews' old stamping grounds at Vitagraph; exteriors were lensed in locations "having never been used in photoplay productions," according to *Moving Picture World*. The initial entry *Financing the Fourth* was not, however, part of the series, but rather a one-reeler produced on behalf the United States' Fourth Liberty Loan Drive (we were still at war, remember?). It was one of several similar shorts featuring popular screen personalities slated for simultaneous release in September 1918; the best known of these patriotic sketches is Charlie Chaplin's *The Bond*.

By the end of November three Mr. and Mrs. Drew two-reelers were completed: *Once a Mason* and *The Amateur Liar*, both written by Albert Payson Terhune; and *Romance and Rings* by Emma Anderson Whitman. As with most of the couple's previous efforts, Mrs. Sidney Drew served as both director and editor. Backing up Van Beuren's "money is no object" credo, Mrs. Drew told *Moving Picture World* that the first three "cost more than five times what we expended on our other productions," adding that none of the sets, props or costars had been seen in any of their Vitagraph or Metro vehicles. A minimum 100 prints of each film were struck to ensure the widest distribution possible. How sad that none of these prints is known to exist today.

Officially released February 2, 1919, the first of the series (though the third completed) was *Romance and Rings*. The plot was typical: About to be married to Polly (Mrs. Drew), a nervous Henry (Mr. Drew) absent-mindedly forgets to bring Polly's wedding ring to the ceremony, obliging him to ask his friend Jim Truesdale's wife to lend him her ring. The fun begins when Polly, not knowing that she's wearing another woman's ring, refuses to give it up. When Mrs. Truesdale presses the issue with Henry, Polly catches her new husband in what seems to be a cozy *tête-à-tête* with her best friend.

Next up in mid–March was *Once a Mason*, in which Mr. Teasdale (what happened to Truesdale?) nominates Henry for membership in a Masonic lodge. Following the secret initiation, Polly demands to know all about the ceremony. After much aggravation Henry is forced to reveal all to his wife, but only if she swears never to tell anyone. Not surprisingly, Polly blabs to Mrs. Teasdale, setting off a chain reaction of disasters culminating in a mock suicide. Mr. Cyprian C. Hunt, Illustrious

An advertisement for the initial V.B.K. "Mr. and Mrs. Sidney Drew" two-reeler, *Romance and Rings*.

Potentate of the New York Masons, heartily endorsed this little comedy, even the scene in which Henry has to undergo the traditional "riding of the goat."

The following month offered *The Amateur Liar*. This time out Henry is detained at the bank when asked to identify family friend Mrs. Grant so she can cash a check. As a result, Henry is late for a restaurant date with the impatient Polly. Fearing that his wife might misconstrue his meeting with Mrs. Grant, Henry claims his late arrival is due to an emergency involving his pal Jim Truesdale (oh, *there* he is)—who at that moment enters the restaurant with *his* wife. Henry's little white lie snowballs into a blizzard of complications, involving among other things a tortuous mustard cure for an nonexistent attack of influenza.

Fourth in the series, *Harold, Last of the Saxons* (written by Florence Ryerson) was heavier on physical humor than its predecessors, though the situation still informed the action. When the local Art League plans to stage a play on behalf of the War Fund, Polly volunteers Henry to play Saxon king Harold, costume and all. Henry reluctantly agrees, but only to keep an eye on Polly, slated to play the wife of William the Conqueror—who is to be impersonated by notorious rake Pug O'Connor. During the performance a drunken Pug makes a pass at Polly, leading to a fistic fracas that ends only when the corpulent woman cast as Boadica literally descends upon the stage. Adding to the authenticity of the rehearsal and play scenes was the decision to film on location at New York City's Punch and Judy Theater.

Written by the Drews themselves, the fifth entry *Squared* was filmed in Chicago while the team was appearing at that city's Woods Theater in *Keep Smiling*. Though still a comedy, *Squared* had more serious undertones than the previous films. Henry Minor, junior partner of a prestigious law firm, is frustrated that all his hard work and legal expertise is invariably attributed to his superiors. When one of the partners is assigned to a murder trial that should have gone to Henry, our hero is more discouraged than ever. Just as Henry is about to offer proof that he should be congratulated for the subsequent courtroom victory, the partner who ostensibly won the case returns from the World War crippled for life. His selfless decision to let the wounded man receive full credit for the case earns Henry the undying love of the firm's stenographer Polly. According to studio publicists, Mrs. Drew interviewed Chicago Superior Court Judge Hugo Pam to pick up details about courtroom procedure.

Photos taken during production of *Squared* reveal a haggard, hollow-cheeked Sidney Drew, looking far older than his 55 years. On April 9, 1919, not long after the film's completion, Drew died of uremia, though intimates attributed his death to ongoing grief over his late son. While newspapers and trade publications were generous in their eulogies for the beloved actor, no mention of Drew's death was made by the Paramount publicity campaign accompanying the posthumous release of *Squared* on April 30.

With three more films to go on the Drews' contract, Lucille McVey—who for the rest of her life would bill herself as Mrs. Sidney Drew—valiantly agreed to fulfill her legal obligation and appear solo in the remaining two-reelers. "We shall maintain the Drew standard and style of humor," Amedee Van Beuren assured *Exhibitors Herald*. "and I am sure that Paramount-Drew comedies will continue to fill the long felt want of the picture public for good, clean and wholesome films." The producer maintained as much taste and decorum as possible under the circumstances: Publicity photos of Mrs. Drew showed her dressed in mourning, while the upcoming films

After the death of Sidney Drew in May of 1919, Mrs. Drew fulfilled her V.B.K. contract with two solo comedy shorts

were rewritten so that the actress-director would play the leading man's sister rather than his wife.

Released July 13, 1919, the first post-mortem production was *Bunkered*, with Mrs. Drew still cast as "Polly" and Donald MacBride, who'd worked with the Drews at Vitagraph and who later carved out an impressive talkie career in blustery character roles (*Room Service, Here Comes Mr. Jordan* etc.), appearing as the heroine's brother Jimmy. Nell Tracy rounded out the main cast as Jimmy's sweetheart Angie. Scripted by Emma Anderson Whitman, *Bunkered* was a comedy about love on the golf course, filmed on location at Westchester's Sleepy Hollow Country Club. The next "Mrs. Sidney Drew" effort *A Sisterly Scheme*, released August 24, was likewise location-filmed, this time at Lake Placid. Nell Tracy returned as Angie, while John Cumberland, another Vitagraph alumnus, took over the role of Jimmy; Donald MacBride moved backstage as the production unit's business manager. Lucille McVey Drew elected to temporarily withdraw from acting after *Bunkered* while agreeing to script one last two-reeler on her contract: *The Night of the Dub*, which ultimately featured Van Beuren's new star Ernest Truex (see Chapter 3).

Establishing a pattern that would repeat itself throughout Amedee Van Beuren's movie career, the saga of the Drew comedies ended with legal action. As reported by *Wid's Daily* on November 17, 1919, Mrs. Sidney Drew filed suit in the New York Supreme Court against V.B.K Productions "for an accounting of sums due her as executrix under the will of her husband from films in which they appeared under a contract made with Amedee J. Van Beuren and Harry Kelton on July 15, 1918, which was assigned to the defendant corporation." According to her complaint, the Drews were to receive $1500 each for the films and 30 percent of profits after first two, in addition to their yearly salary. Mrs. Drew further claimed that the completed films' net profit was "more than $100,000" and thus the share for her husband's estate should be "at least $25,000."

However this lawsuit was resolved, Mrs. Sidney Drew was not by any means left destitute. She continued to write, direct and occasionally act in feature films for the next five years, and was poised to start a new production with herself in the cast at the time of her early death from cancer on November 3, 1925. A full assessment of the life and career of this pioneering woman filmmaker is long overdue.

Chapter 2

Topics of the Day

While Amedee Van Beuren's first film project involved a presold commodity—namely, Mr. and Mrs. Sidney Drew (see Chapter 1)—he could take pride in the fact that the purchasing, packaging and merchandising of the project originated with his own V.B.K. Film Corporation. Not so his second filmic effort, which for all intents and purposes was laid at his feet by the Keith-Albee theater chain.

To tell the whole story of *Topics of the Day* we must journey back to 1890, the year that the first issue of *The Literary Digest* hit the newsstands of America. Created by Isaac Kaufmann Funk on behalf of dictionary publisher Funk & Wagnalls, *Literary Digest* was a weekly news and general-interest magazine, largely offering abridgements of articles that had previously appeared in other periodicals. By 1916 the increasingly popular magazine had assumed a strong patriotic stance, and in that spirit solicited input from the public in the form of polls and letters to the editor. (This reliance on the *vox populi* would lead to *Literary Digest*'s demise in 1938, two years after the magazine confidentially predicted that Alf Landon would be elected president on the basis of a reader poll). The opinions of its own editorial staff appeared in a regular "Topics of the Day" section. Typical topics included prohibition, the organized-labor movement, public vs. private schools and the advisability of going to war. Ever so gradually a few humorous topics began sneaking into "Topics of the Day," along with witticisms and comic doggerel harvested from newspapers throughout the country. These niblets were listed separately within the column as "Topics in Brief."

Outside the realm of *Literary Digest*, among the more ubiquitous "between-the-acts" features of pre–1920 American vaudeville was the topical monologist, who made pithy and funny comments about the state of the world (Will Rogers was easily the best of this breed). Boston *Globe* reporter-humorist Charles Leonard Fletcher scored a great success by setting up a projector and running his own topical slides (called Fletchergrams) in theaters throughout the East, with himself as commentator. Fletcher's activities caught the eye of entrepreneur Abe E. Siegel, who reasoned that a similar weekly program of topical slides—or even films—could be profitably packaged and distributed to vaudeville and movie houses to be shown whenever they wished, without the expense of a live narrator.

Of course, the backing of a major publishing firm would sweeten the deal for prospective buyers. In a letter to Funk & Wagnalls on April 30, 1918, Siegel wrote:

> Now my proposition is as follows: I would undertake to distribute these slides throughout the United States and England at my own expense, and the cost of manufacturing these slides would also be borne by me; all advertising in the trade papers of our business would also be paid by me, and in each case the name of the *Literary Digest* would be used, with an aim to spread broadcast

your great journal, and also put forth every effort to increase the circulation of the *Literary Digest*—all at my own expense. In return for this, all that I expect to receive from the *Literary Digest* of Funk Wagnalls Company is the material printed in the above named magazine under "Topics in Brief," and any other such material that the writer would find advantageous to the Literary Digest of the Screen.

With the publisher's blessing—but with none of the publisher's cash—Siegel and his business partner Herman B. Freedman organized the Topics Slide and Film Company, soon to be known as Timely Topics Inc., for the self-distribution purposes listed above.

At the same time, Siegel had decided to forego slide presentations in favor of film, with his screen version of *Topics of the Day* promoted as the first "non-moving movie." In the spring of 1918, the first 300-foot *Topics* was screened in a handful of entertainment houses in the East. As reviewed by *Motion Picture News*, the 4-minute short subject was "a series of punch paragraphs, gathered by *The Literary Digest* and thrown on the screen one after the other. There are no pictures with these, all of them merely short paragraphs from various papers, and most of them lambasting the Kaiser, but they delight the audience and get a series of big hands." On June 29, 1918, Siegel took out full-page ads in several trade publications, almost instantly receiving three dozen letters of inquiry from interested exhibitors. Public demand for the property grew even stronger in the ensuing weeks, permitting Abe E. Siegel and Herman B. Freedman to cease issuing *Topics of the Day* by themselves and to offer the series on a state's-right basis, with regional distributors like Sol Lesser, Robertson-Cole and K.W.S. Films handling different territories throughout the country.

Topics of the Day's best customers included the Keith-Albee and Orpheum circuits, with the former in the market for a film attraction that could serve as a "headliner," or between-the-acts attraction, to buoy up their live entertainment. Having a controlling financial interest in such an attraction would enable Keith-Albee to monitor the quality of the films shown in its houses, and incidentally share the financial benefits of distribution to other venues. Once the theater people ponied up the money, *Topics* was slated to run in all of Keith-Albee's top houses (and most of the smaller ones) seven days per week every other week, alternating with Charles Leonard Fletcher's now-on-film *Fletchergrams*. The Orpheum circuit set up a similar deal blanketing the Western states.

Holding a large chunk of Class-A stock in the Pathé Exchange, Keith-Albee could count on a single, centralized distributor for *Topics of the Day*. What was needed now was a nominal producer and promoter for the property—and who better than fledgling filmmaker Amedee J. Van Beuren, a born showman with built-in exhibitor connections? So it came to pass that, with Van Beuren appointed president (a fact not publicly acknowledged for several months) and with Keith-Albee as benefactors and silent partners, Timely Films Inc. was formed in Albany, New York, during the last week of December 1918. The board of directors included Herman B. Freedman, Abe E. Siegel and Abe's wife Lena. The company's sole *raison d'être* was to continue producing *Topics of the Day*; to keep an eye on the operation, Van Beuren arranged for Timely Films and his own V.B.K. Productions to share corporate headquarters in New York City, occupying the entire fourth floor of Keith-Albee's Palace Theater annex at 1562 Broadway.

The combined ballyhoo of Van Beuren and Pathé ensured that the entire country would be primed for Pathé's first *Topics of the Day* release on May 4, 1919. Participating in the publicity blitz, *Literary Digest* not only informed its million-plus readers with colorful promos for *Topics*, but also circularized all 20,000,000 telephone subscribers in the country. Splashy advertisements for *Topics of the Day* were placed in 4,000 newspapers—nearly 300 of them already running the choicest quotes from *Topics* supplied by the publisher—while thousands of news dealers were apprised of Pathé's involvement and encouraged to tell their customers. Ad material was also sent *gratis* to movie and vaudeville theaters not affiliated with Keith-Albee. As icing on the cake, Andre Brunet, vice-president and general manager of Pathé, issued an effusive statement to the trade publications: "I am especially happy in making the announcement of Pathé releasing Topics of the Day. Impressed with the originality of the feature and the strength of its popular appeal, we have carefully watched the growth of it, its bookings in first run houses, the nature of its reception and the manner in which it 'went over.'" Brunet bolstered his words by listing the many prestigious national and international publications quoted in each edition of *Topics*, and the dozens of major theater concerns that had prospered with the property in its state's-rights days.

And what precisely were those theaters purchasing *Topics of the Day* getting for their money? In the early days of the property, Abe Siegel was sole writer-editor, contentedly cutting and pasting quotes from dozens of regional newspapers and magazines. He had no trouble gathering these quotes, keeping contributors happy by listing their names on-screen. But the pressure of coming up with 10 to 15 usable quotes per short on a 52-week-per-year basis obliged Timely Films to also supply their own material, building up a staff of nearly two dozen writers. Among them was none other than Charles Leonard Fletcher, who had shuttered his own *Fletchergrams* to work for Timely as editor-in-chief from May 1919 to January 1920. His replacement was Charles McDonald, who remained with *Topics of the Day* into the sound era.

According to publicity, each episode's "punch paragraphs" were pre-tested to make sure they'd score a laugh with an average audience. It need not be said that what was considered uproarious a century ago might not fly today, but after all the series was not titled *Topics for Eternity*. Peruse some of the material from a random 1920 *Topics* entry and judge for yourself:

> We cannot have a new world, and we will not have the old one painted red.—*Albany Journal*
>
> We remember when it was a disgrace to be drunk, but today, m'boy, it's an achievement.—*Detroit Journal*
>
> Teacher: "You've been a naughty boy. You must stay after school." "All right, Miss Jones, if you aren't afraid of the scandal I'm not!"—Jack Canuck
>
> It is time to board up the back of a woman's gown when it allows one to count down to the thirty-seventh vertebra.—Memphis *Commercial Appeal*
>
> A Kansas girl tells us she would rather wear a cow-bell than have a chaperone.—*Flint Journal*
>
> Policeman (to little boy whose mother is buying lard): "Where's your maw?" "She's inside gettin' fat."—*Philadelphia Ledger*

Here's one seen down in Kentucky: "No Man's Land—Turkish Baths for Ladies."—*Louisville Courier*

Query editor: "How can I make a dollar go as far today as before the war?" "Mail it!"—Columbus, O., *Citizen*

A 1919 magazine advertisement for *Topics of the Day*. The artist was a talented kid named Norman Rockwell.

If you can stop rolling on the floor and holding your sides, allow us to clarify that *Topics* wasn't all fun and games; occasionally a serious statement would wangle its way onscreen. In the very half-reel just quoted, the Chicago *Post* contributed these sage words: "Better pay for teachers. Our children must be educated. The teachers who give the best part of their lives must be satisfied. This is impossible when pay checks do not meet the cost of living." Van Beuren had learned from experience the wisdom of remaining in the good graces of the public by making gestures towards public service. For the Red Cross Christmas Seal Campaign of 1919, Van Beuren offered his cooperation by opening the Yuletide edition of *Topics* with a plaintive paragraph: "150,000 die of tuberculosis every year in the United States. You can help prevent this. BUY RED CROSS X'MAS SEALS—ALL THE YEAR ROUND!" The following year, Van Beuren prepared a special version of *Topics of the Day* for the vision-impaired, contributing braille transcripts of the film version to the Matilda Ziegler Magazine for the Blind and the Red Cross Institute for the Blind at Baltimore.

On at least one occasion Van Beuren's largesse was not altruistic, but designed to advance the cause of the industry that sustained him. When film director Marshall Neilan mounted an anti-censorship campaign on behalf of the Public Rights League, Van Beuren inserted a statement written by Neilan in *Topics of the Day* #112, released June 9, 1921: "The Constitution of the United States guarantees the freedom of the press. The motion picture is a development of the press, publishing stories in pictures instead of type, and is entitled to the same freedom enjoyed by the press."

As part of his administrative duties Van Beuren exercised self-censorship in *Topics of the Day*, avoiding overtly risqué material and especially toning down ethnic humor. Even so, Van Beuren publicist Don Hancock had this to say in *The Pathé Club Yearbook of 1927*: "Perhaps it is on account of [editor-in-]chief [Charles] McDonald that we have such a fine brand of Scotch jokes, which are our pride and our joy. The Scotch thrift gag is the most reliable in the fun game, because everyone laughs at it—even our victims. For, make a note of this, the Scotch are the one nation in the world to enjoy a hearty laugh at their expense. But is it at their expense? And, right down in their hearts, are they not a wee bit proud of their thrift?"

In the same article, Hancock offered another example of surefire comedy material: "The oldest joke in the world is the mother in law joke. It had been found chiseled in Egyptian hieroglyphics." The operative word here is "oldest." As early as 1922 *Topics of the Day* was relying less on up-to-date *bon mots* from contributors and more on familiar wheezes from their own staff. When such nuggets as "Take dancing lessons? I guess not! There are too many other ways by which I can make a fool of myself." "I know, dear, but have you tried all the rest?"; or "Why, Bobby, dear, did you see Santa Claus this time?" "No, Auntie; it was too dark to see him, but I heard what he said when he knocked his toe against the bedpost," no contributor credit was listed—a sure sign that these were home-grown groaners.

Literary Digest was by this time barely supplying any material to the series. Back in 1920 Funk & Wagnalls had demanded one-third of the Timely Films stock in exchange for extending its contract; Timely's directors balked, resulting in bad blood between the two concerns. Without Timely's knowledge, Funk & Wagnalls registered the designation "Topics of the Day" as a trademark of their own, then in 1923 sued Timely to prevent the use of that designation, as well as any reference to *Literary Digest*, in the opening credits of the films. The publishers succeeded on the second point but not on the first. Since Abe E. Siegel created the film series without any financial input from Funk & Wagnalls, the series could continue going out under its original name. Moreover, despite their trademark registration the publishers could not block usage of the *Topics of the Day* label *ex post facto*. On June 18, 1923, the First Assistant Commissioner of U.S. Patents ruled that Funk & Wagnalls were not "at the time they made application thereof" entitled to exclusive use of the series' title. So there.

Others beside Funk & Wagnalls were unhappy with the direction *Topics'* content had taken. *Variety*, perennial nemesis of the Keith-Albee operation, was especially brutal in assessing the humor level in the *Topics*, particularly after receiving complaints from theater owners that they were being forced to run the shorts by the management. Reviewing the new show at the Palace in the June 21, 1923, *Variety*, "Pam" remarked "'Topics of the Day' is improving. It had only two old ones. They were not alone aged, but sad." The trade paper habitually referred to the series' jokes as "Joe Millers," "old boys," "toothless and pointless" and "always stupid, bush league and obvious"; the shorts themselves were dissed as "plagues" and "the bane of the Keith house managers." What really raised *Variety*'s hackles was *Topics'* habit of lifting material from prominent stage comedians without permission. When monologist Walter C. Kelly appeared in one Keith theater he told a joke of his own invention in the first show, only to discover that the joke had already been flashed on-screen in that week's *Topics*. He ordered the pilfered gag removed from the offending reel in all subsequent performances. It was bad enough that *Topics of the Day* trafficked in stale old jokes—but when they began stealing stale old jokes from star performers, it was a Topics too far.

If Amedee Van Beuren was perturbed by any of this, you wouldn't know it from such articles published under his name as "Topics of the Day Has Confidence" (*Exhibitors Herald-World*, May 26, 1928). He continued to express just as much pride in and admiration of the property as he had way back in December 1920 when he purchased 55 percent of Timely Films' stock and folded the firm into his new corporation Topics of the Day Inc., with *Topics'* self-described "father" Abe E. Siegel as his newest partner. (Siegel's old partner Herman B. Freedman, demoted to production manager and subsequently fired in September 1921, ended up suing Siegel for conspiring with Keith-Albee to cheat him out of his holdings. The case was dismissed in 1924). Van Beuren had every right to be confident: *Topics of the Day* continued to flourish throughout the 1920s using the same format it started with, save for the addition of animated "Sketchograph" illustrations credited to Julian Ollendorf and introduced in the *Topics* edition of October 21, 1923, under the title "Presidential Possibilities." It would seem that nothing short of an apocalyptic upheaval in the movie industry could halt the progress of *Topics of the Day*. And then on October 6, 1927, Al Jolson sang "Toot Toot Tootsie" in *The Jazz Singer*. For many venerable silent-film properties, Judgment Day had arrived.

Fortunately, RCA Photophone's 1928 takeover of Keith-Albee-Orpheum meant that the newfangled talking-picture format was there for Van Beuren's asking. When in July of that year he purchased both *Topics of the Day* and the animated *Aesop's Fables* (see Chapter 4) as subsidiaries of Van Beuren Enterprises—Abe Siegel was long gone, having left to become director of motion picture activities for *Literary Digest*—there was no question that both properties would quickly transition to sound.

This photograph from *Exhibitors Herald*'s Christmas 1926 issue shows the work involved in selecting the gags for *Topics of the Day*.

But would it be practical for *Talking Topics of the Day* (its new blanket title) to retain its old words-on-the-screen format, or would it be necessary to refashion the property as a purely aural experience? Van Beuren's distributor Pathé got their answer when the first two all-talkie titles in the 1928–29 season of *Talking Topics*, filmed at New York's RCA Photophone studio under the direction of Charles D. McDonald (by now elevated to Van Beuren's general manager and vice president), were press-previewed during the last week of 1928.

The first noticeable change in the property was the decision to forego using numbers to differentiate each episode (the final silent *Topics* were labeled #1 through #9), replacing them with word titles. Reviewing the initial talkies for *Exhibitors Herald-World* on December 22, 1928, T.O. Service fretted

> I'm not so sure about the first two "Talking Topics of the Day" called *The Petters* and *Pressing His Suit*. In the new form they are no more or less than vaudeville sketches. The first has four characters in it; the second three. They consist of these characters making wise cracks, the wise cracks consisting, supposedly, of current jokes, but some of the jokes in these are not so current. If the Talking Topics of the Day are continued in the style of these first two, they will be, as I have said, nothing more than vaudeville sketches, and their success will depend upon the actors and the amount of humor in their dialogue.

Pathé was amenable to the vaudeville-sketch format, but not the clumsy version seen in *The Petters* and *Pressing His Suit*. Van Beuren was told to shelve these titles and try again. The remaining silent *Topics* were played off until February 24, 1929; by the end of March, the *re*-revamped version (no, I'm not stuttering) had gone into production with several entries completed. RCA Photophone was still the principal shooting location, with occasional jaunts to Pathé's New York facilities. Charles D. McDonald remained in the director's chair—earning the unofficial title "Heinz of the Movies" after shooting 57 separate gags in a single day—while the casts of the *Talking Topics* were recruited from the Broadway stage and voice-auditioned at the NBC radio studio in New York. Marjorie Main (two decades before Ma Kettle) and Edward J. LeSaint (best known for portraying the heroine's father in innumerable B westerns) are the most recognizable faces in the sound shorts; others in the series' stock company were Lawrence G. O'Brien, Jess Sidney, Isobel Vernon, Frank Andrews, Fary Hunt, Ruth Hunter, Rupert LaBelle, Eddie O'Connor, Ruth McNutt, George Neville and Little Eddie Wragge. Walter Strenge was principal photographer, and the series' theme music was "Sweetheart of All My Dreams" by Art and Kay Fitch and Bert Lowe.

The first official sound release *Topical Hits* was reviewed in the March 31, 1929, *Film Daily*, complete with a detailed description for the future benefit of film historians unable to obtain a viewing copy:

> They have a hit on a pip of an idea for the "Topics," and it looks as if the new treatment if followed up will make this popular series one of the highlights of the short sound field. Every gag is played individually as a separate skit. The two players putting over the gag appear in character before a black curtain and the skits follow one another in a snappy manner and with a laugh coming on each one. It has class and is strictly in line with the latest trend in sound comedy development. Recommended without any reservations.

This new format, remarkably similar to the blackouts and crossover gags seen on the much-later TV variety series *Rowan and Martin's Laugh-In*, also found favor with *Topics'* severest critic *Variety*, which rated *Topical Hits* an "immeasurable improvement over the old printed dud." Given its disdain for the property's overreliance on timeworn comedy material, *Variety*'s choice for the episode's best and most representative gag is astonishing:

> **MAN #1:** Pat, you ought to pull down the curtains when you kiss your wife.
> **MAN #2:** Why?
> **MAN #1:** I saw you kissing your wife last night.
> **MAN #2:** The laugh's on you. Ha ha! I wasn't at home last night. I went to the lodge.
> [BA-DUMP BUMP]

A later episode, *Topical Bits*, contained a lot more ethnic humor than usual for the series, with the actors dressed as Irishmen, Scotchmen, Jews, etc., depending on the sketch. "Some of the repartee is funny, but, as is usually the case with all joke books, some of the wheezes fall pretty flat." (*Motion Picture News*, April 13, 1929). Lukewarm reviews like this were regularly offset by such comparative raves as *Motion Picture News'* critique of the sixth entry *Topical Nips*: "The entertainment is varied and lively enough to get by on a program of talkies. Suitable entertainment for this toddling age of the talkies." *Film Daily* also liked this one, observing that the series "has greatly increased its popular appeal since being treated as a series of comedy sketches in character in the manner of vaude turns.... Real novelty that is crisp, clean, with up-to-date jokes that are neither too slapstick nor too subtle, but strike that middle ground which reaches the average audience with a sure touch and brings ready laughs."

Now that the updated *Topics* were scoring with audiences and the press, Van

Beuren figured he could afford a couple of strikeouts; thus the two unreleased talkie episodes from 1928 finally saw the light of a carbon arc. *Pressing His Suit* was sprung in May of 1929, while *The Petters* escaped in August. Predictably, this undynamic duo were adjudged the weakest of the current crop. Of *Pressing His Suit*, *Motion Picture Daily* said, "An average quality of jokes.... They were neither very good nor very bad and will achieve a fair amount of laughs. Program filler material." The periodical's summation of *The Petters* was equally tepid: "The jokes are strung along a parlor conversation between a girl and her sweeties and are interspersed with goo-goo talk. The verbal puns are not strong rib-ticklers..."

Misleadingly advertised onscreen as "Selected from the Press of the World," *Talking Topics of the Day* appeared to have emerged from the talkie revolution unscathed by July 6, 1929, the day *Exhibitors Herald-World* gave over a healthy portion of column space to Van Beuren's by-now-expected puffery: "[N]o expense has been spared in the production properties and settings. The editorial staff of *Topics of the Day* has been augmented by several professional readers who are continually scratching the publications of the world for the newest jokes obtainable. The finest studio equipment both in camera and recording apparatus is being used for these productions..." Van Beuren also went to the expense of having staffers clock the laughs during previews, enabling him to boast that the series served up "A Laugh Every Ten Seconds."

After Charles D. McDonald left Van Beuren in November 1929, direction of the series was taken over by Alfred T. Mannon, president of Hollywood's Tec-Art Studios; accordingly, production moved from the East Coast to the West. This meant the loss of *Talking Topics*' pool of New York actors, which probably explains why the series' format was streamlined beginning with its first 1930 release *On the Air*. The verbal gags were now dispensed by a ventriloquist called The Professor and his sarcastic dummy Nifty (How my buttons would burst had my research revealed that the Professor was played by Edgar Bergen or some other celebrated voice-thrower. But my research hasn't, so the actor will remain anonymous). This unyielding format was given a scintilla of variety by changing the setting in each episode, reflected in such titles as *In the Park, Cover Charge, What No Bait?* and *Home Sweet Home*. No one was doing handsprings over the re-re-revised format (now I *am* stuttering), least of all the trades. *Motion Picture News* wrote off *Cover Charge* with "'Topics' in their old silent form had a much better appeal. Their new form just doesn't click." As for *What No Bait?*, *Film Daily* lamented "The fun in this one doesn't get over very well. Much of its humor is pointless and a little of it not exactly new and refreshing."

Van Beuren and Pathé weren't happy with the recent string of *Talking Topics* either, and by April 1930 they were promising "an altogether different layout which has been made on the West Coast and which is now en route to the New York Van Beuren offices," according to *Film Daily*. A preview of this different layout was seen in the final *Topics* entry for the 1929–30 season. *Van Beuren News* was the title, and *Film Daily* was again on hand for the unveiling. With the headline "A Change for the Better," the publication's review for *Van Beuren News* began: "In this issue ... we see a young fellow gathering jokes in a newspaper office. As each is pasted up it is shown on the screen. This is by far the best method of presentation devised to present." The short was directed by Elmer Clifton, then also busy with Van Beuren's *Vagabond Adventure* series (see Chapter 10).

Amedee Van Beuren's follow-up announcement that there would be 26 more *Talking Topics of the Day* (or, perhaps, new editions of *Van Beuren News*) during the 1930–1931 season was nipped in the bud when Pathé ordered the series discontinued. Suddenly after 12 years, two titles and four formats, *Topics of the Day* was gone—but not forgotten, as we shall see in the upcoming chapter (#18) on Van Beuren's 1934–36 series *Dumb-Bell Letters*.

Chapter 3

Ernest Truex

Less than a week after the death of actor Sidney Drew on April 9, 1919, Amedee Van Beuren, producer of the "Mr. and Mrs. Sidney Drew" two-reelers for Famous Players-Lasky release (see Chapter 1), engaged one Harry Fields to seek out a purchaser for a proposed series of comedy shorts starring Ernest Truex. Fields didn't have to look too far: Famous Players-Lasky offered $110,000 for a group of ten Truex films. The company's decision had as much to do with the fact that Truex had made most of his previous feature films for Famous Players' Paramount Pictures division as it had with their ties to Van Beuren.

Whoa! Let's back up a bit and introduce our star. Born in Kansas City, Missouri, Ernest Truex (1889–1973) started acting at age 5 in a stage production of *Quo Vadis?* He received his theatrical training from a patient of his doctor father, as payment for outstanding medical bills. By the time he was 9, Truex was touring in his own act "The Child Wonder in Scenes from Shakespeare." After several years with stock companies he made his Broadway debut opposite the legendary Lillian Russell in 1908. His 5'2" height enabling him to play juveniles into his early 20s, he appeared as the hero's kid brother in his first film *Caprice* (1913); the star was Mary Pickford, who'd previously worked with Truex in David Belasco's Broadway hit *A Good Little Devil*. Though he continued to make occasional films, Truex' reputation as a gifted light comedian was established on stage in Jerome Kern's *Very Good Eddie*, William LeBaron's *The Very Idea* and other popular plays. Hailed as Broadway's youngest male comedy star, he was acting opposite Edith Taliaferro in *Please Get Married* at New York's Fulton Theater when he was approached by Van Beuren.

"In signing Mr. Truex to appear in two-reel comedies," Van Beuren explained in an official press statement of May 17, 1919, "I am continuing my policy established with my pictures starring Mr. and Mrs. Sidney Drew, in making refined comedies of feature quality with stars of ability and reputation. I am firmly convinced that this type of screen comedy is a favored institution in America and abroad and that there is sufficient demand for comedies of distinction to warrant the appearance of a star like Ernest Truex in two reel pictures." Van Beuren concluded by soliciting authors to send story material for Truex to V.B.K. Productions, home of the Mr. and Mrs. Drew comedies, As it turned out, the new films would be made by the producer's latest venture, the AyVeeBee Corporation—an acronymic moniker indicating that Van Beuren's business partner Doc Kelton had left the movie business to concentrate on his other amusement enterprises. Later trade reports stated that Van Beuren had insured Ernest Truex' life for $200,000, which might have been a publicity stunt but more likely was a precautionary measure in the wake of Mr. Sidney Drew's sudden and unexpected demise.

Production of the Paramount-Truex comedies began in July with *The Night of the Dub*, a title previously announced for Mrs. Sidney Drew, then fulfilling her late husband's contract with solo film appearances for Van Beuren. Mrs. Drew stayed around long enough to write the screenplay, based on a *Saturday Evening Post* short story by Albert Payton Terhune. Judging from the studio synopsis for *Night of the Dub* (the film no longer exists), Ernest Truex was cast in a role tailor-made for Sidney Drew: A lowly Wall Street clerk who poses as a captain of finance in his own home to impress his friends and family. Truex' basic character name "Ernie" would be recycled in all but one of his subsequent AyVeeBee efforts. The film was made at the Vitagraph studio in Flatbush under the direction of comedy specialist John Joseph Harvey, with David Torrence, Vallie Belasco Martin and Charles Haskins in the supporting cast.

Officially released November 30, 1919, *The Night of the Dub* made its way to New York during the week of January 25, 1920. Van Beuren's faith in Ernest Truex' drawing power was fully justified by the film's reception from the hard-boiled New York critics. The reviewer for the *Evening Herald* declared: "A remarkably clever little comedy…. Every minute is a delight in the unwinding of the two-reel feature—thanks to the art and personality of the star." The New York *Times* also enjoyed the show, or rather enjoyed the star: "Truex is one of the cleverest pantomimists of screen comedy, and the wit of his gestures and expressions makes his present play constantly amusing and often outright merry." These sentiments were echoed by the *Morning Telegraph* ("Truex is one of those comedians who never overworks his effects") and the *Evening Sun* ("The Truex picture is excellent comedy"). The manager of New York's Strand theater went so far as to write a personal congratulation to Van Beuren: "In sharing honors with [film star] Constance Talmadge on our all comedy program this week, *The Night of the Dub* was very enthusiastically received yesterday afternoon and last evening at capacity houses. It is a relief to secure pictures that have a real idea back of them." Similar hosannas came from theater owners in Pittsburgh, Boston, Washington, D.C., Providence, and Birmingham, Alabama. I guess they liked it.

Completed by early September of 1919 and released the last week of December, Truex' second AyVeeBee starrer was *Too Good to Be True*, again directed by John Joseph Harvey. The story was by veteran director and vaudeville sketch writer Kenneth Webb, who according to publicity suggested the idea to Ernest Truex at the Lamb's Club, a gathering place for Broadway actors. Mann Page adapted the story for the screen, with Truex appearing as wealthy but wussy film fan M. Anthony Biggs. Enamored of movie vamp Vera Venton (played by French actress Cyprian Giles, fresh from the internationally acclaimed Gaumont serial *Judex*), Biggs goes into raptures when Vera drops by his country club. Though embarrassed by his own gaucherie in the presence of La Venton, Biggs nonetheless summons enough courage to invite the actress to an elaborate *soiree* he's arranged at the posh Peacock Inn. Alas and alack, during the festivities Vera is distracted by Biggs' handsome rival Kirk Maxwell (Reed Hamilton), but our height-challenged hero prevails. Also in the cast was Frank Lyons in the coveted role of "A Grouchy Golfer." Greeted with an effluence of praise and laughter from filmgoers and critics, *Too Good to Be True* was successful enough for Van Beuren to promise a third Truex comedy in the immediate offing.

But it wasn't to be, thanks to another in the endless parade of legal tangles that unraveled down Van Beuren's road throughout his film career. As reported in the May 28, 1920, *Wid's Daily*, Harry Fields, the intermediary who'd arranged for Famous Players-Lasky to purchase the Truex two-reelers, filed suit in the New York Supreme Court, charging that Van Beuren had refused to pay him a promised $10,000 commission. We don't know how this wound up, though it's a verifiable fact that Famous Players cancelled the remaining eight shorts called for in the contract.

The abrupt cutoff of the "Paramount-Truex" deal did not result in the dissolution of AyVeeBee productions, nor did it cause any schism in the relationship between Van Beuren and Ernest Truex. In the fall of 1921, with Truex hotter than ever thanks to his spectacular stage success in William Anthony McGuire's comedy *Six Cylinder Love*, the actor inked a second contract with Van Beuren for another parcel of two-reelers, again filmed in New York so as not to impede the star's stage work. These comedies would be distributed by Pathé, then also handling the producer's *Topics of the Day* half-reelers (see Chapter 2) and *Aesop's Fables* cartoons (see Chapter 4). Evidently Van Beuren had been confident all along that Truex would return to the fold, else why would the producer's press release for the new Pathé series be the same one he'd shipped out two years earlier for the Famous Players series, virtually word for word?

The two Paramount-Truex shorts have long since vanished, but there's hope for the existence of the three 1921–22 Pathé releases. After their theatrical run, all three were acquired for non-theatrical 16-millimeter exhibition by the Kodascope Library, whose prints have enjoyed a healthy survival rate. It is from the Kodascope catalogue that the following synopses have been gleaned.

First out of the chute on November 20, 1921, was *Little, But Oh My!*, which introduced Ernie Dibbs (you know who) as the shortest and eagerest benchwarmer on the Calder football team. Truex' real-life wife Julia Mills, who costarred in all of his Van Beuren Pathés, played the girl Ernie adores. Unfortunately the girl's father, an ex-football star, refuses to allow her to marry anyone but a gridiron hero. During the inevitable big game between Calder and Fulton, Ernie roosts disconsolately on the "sub" bench until struck by an idea in the last ten minutes of play. Persuading the coach to put him on the field, Ernie contrives to have the ball hiked to him, whereupon his teammates lift him into the air and toss him over the heads of the opposing team. A winning touchdown and a fade-out kiss with his sweetheart are now a *fait accompli*. Accomplices in this assault on the laugh muscles were supporting actors Henry Pemberton, Wallace McCutcheon, Joseph P. Mack, Lincoln Plummer, Gilbert Douglas, Blythe Daly and Beatrice Colony.

One of the few films in which Ernest Truex capitalized on his short stature for comedy purposes, *Little, But Oh My!* was released along with some ripe and risible Pathé promotional material that must have caused the actor no little embarrassment: "The notion of the 'pint measure' stage fun-maker triumphing as the hero of the titanic game of football, as in the first picture of the series, *Little, But Oh My*, proves captivating as well as timely. Besides, Truex has achieved a wide reputation for the quality of his stage love-making. Matinee girls are said to observe his methods with intense attention to detail—perhaps in view of anticipated experiences of their own."

The film proved just as popular as those in the star's Famous Players-Paramount group. The manager of the Grand Theater in Atlanta, Georgia, spoke for the majority when he told *Exhibitors Trade Review*: "First Truex comedy and went over like a house afire, proving the real feature of the bill."

Based on a story by P.G. Wodehouse, the second Van Beuren-Pathé entry *Stick Around* premiered December 28, 1921. On this occasion "Ernie Biggs" is a detective assigned to shadow an actor in a musical-comedy troupe. The fates and the

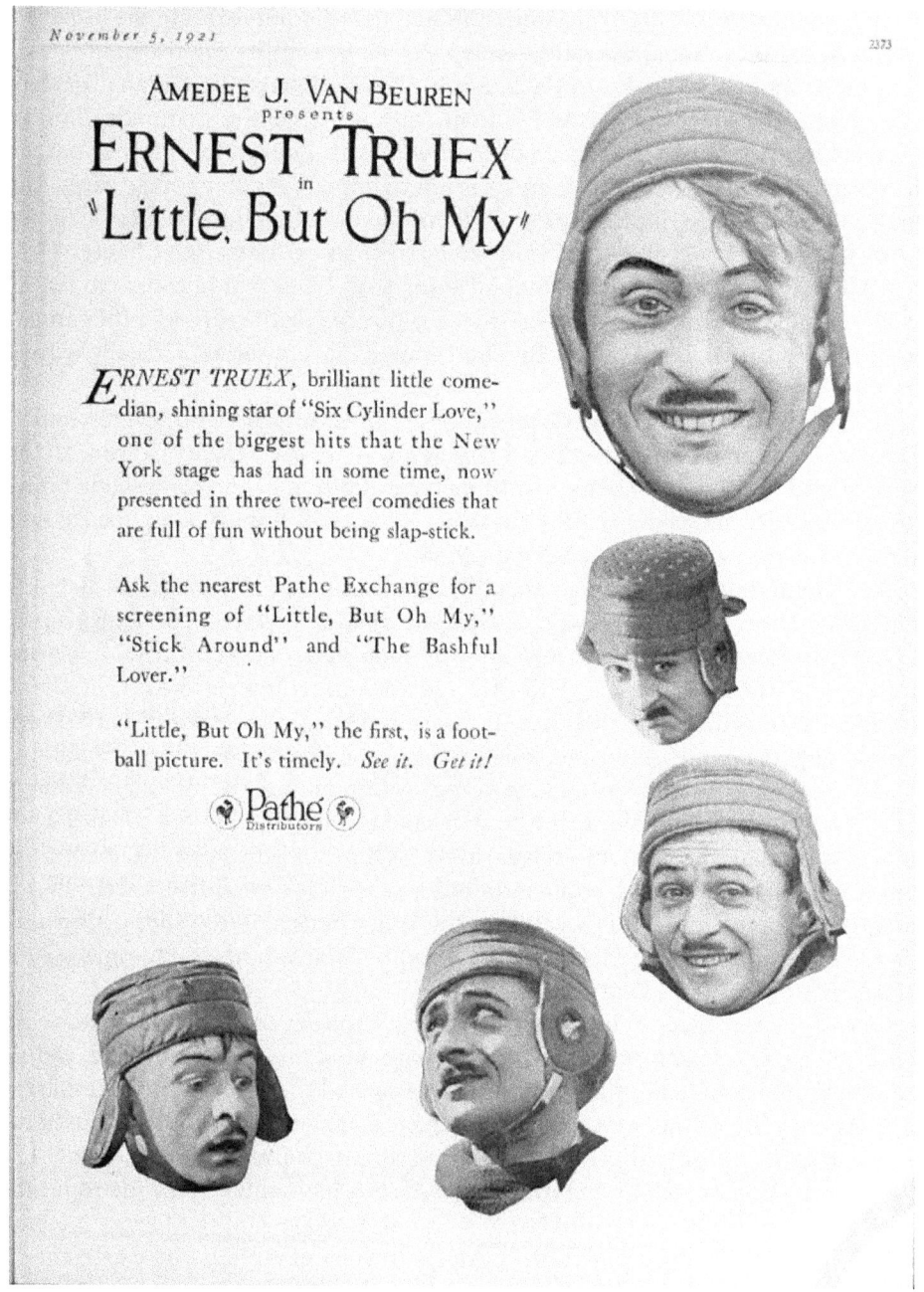

An ad for the 1921 Ernest Truex two-reeler *Little, But Oh My!*, the first of Truex's AyeVee-Bee comedies for Pathé release, in *Motion Picture News*.

scriptwriter decree that Alice Weston (Julia Mills), a chorus dancer in the troupe, is the girl Eddie worships from afar. No less prejudiced than the heroine's father in *Little, But Oh My!*, Alice won't marry anyone but a man in show business. While Ernie stands wistfully in the wings during a performance of the show, a mouse crawls up his pant leg, sending him into manic gyrations and propelling him on stage. The audience vigorously applauds Eddie's impromptu "dance act," so impressing Alice that she agrees to wed our hero even after discovering that his shimmy was both unplanned and unintentional.

Third on the roster was *The Bashful Lover*, released January 15, 1922. Ernie Biggs is now a young millionaire under the thumb of his Wagnerian aunt, who has arranged his marriage with a woman twice his size. To make sure Ernie doesn't chicken out during the backyard wedding party, Auntie locks him in his room. Thus Ernie can only stare cow-eyed out the window at his true love Betty Bliss (Julia Mills, but you already knew that), *premiere danseuse* of the troupe performing "The Spirit of Love" for the garden guests (a genuine corps de ballet was hired for this film). It goes without saying—but we will anyway—that Eddie manages to work out a complex scheme to escape his room, and the film ends with the lovers becoming man and wife in full view of the flummoxed aunt.

The Bashful Lover was not as well received as its predecessors; *Film Daily* labeled it "mild," carping "At most, the entire action ... consists of walking and running. Little attention has been paid to comedy details or attractive gags." Even so, it was probably Ernest Truex' workload on the legitimate stage rather than any loss of film popularity (or any stray lawsuits) that ended the Pathé series after three entries. Amedee Van Beuren retreated to *Topics of the Day* and *Aesop's Fables*, steering clear of live-action short comedies from 1922 to 1927.

Ernest Truex's career continued to prosper on stage and screen. The versatile actor eased into character parts in the talkie era, playing everything from boobs to businessmen in films like *The Adventures of Marco Polo* (1938), *It's a Wonderful World* (1939), *His Girl Friday* (1940), *Christmas in July* (1940) and *All Mine to Give* (1957). Truex spent his final professional years in television, with regular roles in such sitcoms as *The Ann Sothern Show* and *Pete and Gladys*, and guest spots on every major TV anthology, notably a brace of *Twilight Zone* episodes as the enigmatic peddler in "What You Need" (1960) and the disgruntled nursing-home resident in "Kick the Can" (1962). The final role for 76-year-old Ernest Truex was on the CBS sitcom *Petticoat Junction*, appearing opposite his third wife Sylvia Field (best known as Mrs. Wilson on the TV series *Dennis the Menace*) as an elderly honeymooner—a polished farceur to the last.

Chapter 4

Animated Cartoons, Part One
Aesop's Fables

When Amedee Van Beuren, Abe E. Siegel and Clayton E. Heermance chartered Topics of the Day Inc. in late December of 1920, the new firm covered not only the ongoing *Topics of the Day* half-reelers produced by Siegel's Timely Films (see Chapter 2), but also an animated cartoon studio to be named later. "Later" turned out to be a scant two weeks; in January 1921, Fables Pictures Inc. earned the distinction of being that year's first incorporation in the state of New York. Mentioned in the trade papers were Fables' board of directors: Van Beuren (also appointed president of the company), Siegel, and Timely Films director-editor Charles D. McDonald. Though it was stated that distribution plans for the cartoons under Fables' banner were "under discussion," Van Beuren's partners at Keith-Albee had already secured the services of Pathé. The names of the Keith-Albee men were not mentioned in the trades, nor was the theater circuit itself. Also unmentioned was the man responsible for Fables Pictures: A 33-year-old California boy and self-taught artist named Paul Terry (1887–1971).

While attending high school Paul Terry worked as an usher in a vaudeville house, cultivating a keen appreciation for show business, especially comedians. Following the lead of his older brother John, Paul quit school to pursue a newspaper career in San Francisco, working upward from copy boy to photographer to staff cartoonist. In 1911 Paul moved to New York, where while working at the *Evening Sun* he launched a short-lived syndicated comic strip. His career turning point came in 1914 when Terry, along with several other young artists, attended the premiere showing of Winsor McKay's landmark animated cartoon *Gertie the Dinosaur*. Sensing that his future lay in "putting a drawing in action" (as he would tell the Larchmont [NY] *Times* in 1930), Terry set up a small studio and produced his first cartoon *Little Herman*, which he sold to Thanhouser Films at a bargain rate. By 1915 he'd landed at the John R. Bray cartoon studio in New York, abandoning the matte process (combining two films to create one image) used on *Little Herman* in favor of the more efficient cel animation process (painting the moving figures on celluloid, then placing the cel over a stationary painted background) that Bray had patented in collaboration with Earl Hurd. During this period Terry also created his first true cartoon "star," the cantankerous Farmer Al Falfa. This and Terry's other characters (mostly cats and mice) were designed to streamline and speed up the animation process through compartmentalization, animating only the parts of the body that had to move rather than redraw the entire body (painted on a separate cel) for each successive movement. Terry's time- and labor-saving techniques would come in handy while turning out cartoons on an assembly-line basis a few years later.

After making instructional films for the Army Medical Corps in World War I, Terry formed an animation company with brother John and soon-to-be lifelong business partner Frank Moser, as well as John Terry's collaborator Jerry Shields and John R. Bray's former associate Earl Hurd. Once his partners had the business up and running, Terry left to form yet another studio to make cartoons for Paramount Pictures release. By 1919 Terry's two main attractions were Farmer Al Falfa and "Terry Burlesques," animated lampoons of popular Paramount feature films. Early the following year, actor-producer Howard Estabrook approached Terry with an idea to produce a new series of cartoons based on Aesop's Fables.

If we are to believe Terry's claim that up until then he'd never heard of Aesop, we must also conclude that he was raised in a vacuum bottle. Presuming he actually existed, Aesop lived in the 6th century BCE and was either the slave of a Grecian landowner or court jester for Lydian king Croesus. Either way, Aesop earned his keep by telling stories using humanized animals to illustrate a moral—in other words, fables. Passed along verbally for centuries, Aesop's Fables were not written down and published until the 14th century, gaining widespread popularity when retold and republished in 1668 by French fantasist Jean de la Fontaine. In all, 359 fables have been attributed to Aesop, enough for nearly 14 years' worth of six-minute cartoons on the standard contractual basis of 26 per year. However, Howard Estabrook insisted that he and Terry could make more money turning out modernized, "jazzed-up" fables at the rate of one cartoon *per week*. Already a proven expert at making cartoons with utmost speed and efficiency, the young and ambitious Terry agreed to these terms.

Estabrook proceeded to establish the Fables Studio, with himself as producer and Terry overseeing a three-man staff. On a weekly salary of $300 Terry made two trial cartoons while Estabrook shopped for a distributor. When none were immediately forthcoming, Terry accepted a salary reduction while Estabrook continued extending the animator's contract. Five cartoons were in the can by the time Estabrook sparked the interest of Keith-Albee, who by late 1920 were seeking out a companion piece for the *Topics of the Day* shorts. It was determined that since the 300-foot *Topics* had been successful in the Keith-Albee theaters and elsewhere, padding out each short with a six-minute cartoon, thus providing an entire reel of entertainment, would have even more audience appeal. The theater chain agreed to bankroll Fables, acquiring 90 percent of the company while Terry and Estabrook retained 10 percent. The cartoons would be shown in tandem with *Topics* in all Keith-Albee houses either as a curtain-raiser or a Second Act opener, while Pathé would distribute the shorts to movie houses as a separate entity. This connection with *Topics of the Day* resulted in Amedee Van Beuren folding *Aesop's Modernized Fables* (as the series was then known) into the same corporation handling *Topics*. Both Timely Films (*Topics*' parent company) and Fables Pictures became subsidiaries of Van Beuren's new Topics of the Day Inc.

Perhaps because of the negative publicity surrounding complaints from theater managers that Keith-Albee had grabbed up exclusive exhibition of the Pathé product in certain communities, the theater concern's name was conspicuously absent from the first trade announcements for *Aesop's Modernized Fables*. And while an occasional item in the trades would identify Van Beuren as the president of both Timely and Fables, his name was not referenced in articles specifically about the new cartoons. Further avoiding suspicion that an octopus-like cartel was determining what would and would not be shown on American theater screens, it was announced in early April of 1921 that Pathé had agreed to distribute the *Fables* solely on the basis of viewing the first five completed cartoons, just as if they *hadn't* been on the ground floor of the deal. Two weeks later, industryites were fed the "news" that Keith-Albee had contracted to run the cartoons—all because of Pathé's enthusiastic reaction to the series.

Thanks to Paul Terry's track record and saleability, most publicity and critical commentary was firmly focused on the animator as *Fables* rolled off the conveyor belt beginning with *The Goose That Laid the Golden Egg* on June 19, 1921. "Paul Terry, the cartoonist, has awakened new interest in the ancient Greek classics, by his clever animation of the Aesop's fables," observed *Exhibitors Herald*. "The first to be shown in Chicago was *The Goose That Laid the Golden Egg*, and if succeeding pictures of this series are as funny as the first, their success is assured.... Terry has taken the familiar story of the farmer and his greedy wife and with a few deftly written titles ... made as delightful a one-reel subject as has flashed across the screen in some time. The animation is good, the photography excellent, and he gets a laugh without striving for it in every scene. Let us have more of these unique cartoons." *Motion Picture News* reviewer Laurence Reid noted that Terry "has certainly evolved a highly interesting series of cartoons," adding: "By using the ancient wheezes to bring forth comparison of present day ideas—he shows there is nothing new under the sun—that what Aesop said over two thousand years ago has its moral today." Terry remained the "face" of the *Fables* well into the series' second season, as noted in a 1922 critique from *Motion Picture News*: "It is no easy task to keep these modern twists of old man Aesop up-to-date. But Paul Terry proves that his talent in this direction is no flash in the pan."

Two hallmarks of the *Fables* were established from the outset. Getting a laugh "in every scene" was far more important to Terry than characterization or story values, and frequently the biggest yocks had little or nothing to do with the fable at hand—in fact, many of the gags were downright gratuitous and not a little offensive, such as the appearance in *The Lioness and the Bugs* (1921) of a Jewish-pawnbroker stereotype named Goldbug. In the spirit of modernization, contemporary references were included in the "ancient wheezes." *The Mice in Council* (1921) features pointed questions from "The Gentleman from Missouri" at the mice's "Down with Cats" rally while anarchist agitators picket outside convention headquarters. In *The Rooster and the Eagle* (1921) the recent passage of Women's Suffrage was lampooned by the image of a female voter shapeshifting into a club in order to pummel a windbag politician into senselessness. And *The Frogs That Wanted a King* (1921) is a thinly-disguised attack on local "blue laws" which decreed that all businesses—including movie theaters—be closed on Sunday.

Still, *Aesop's Modernized Fables*—retitled *Aesop's Film Fables* once the series got under way—paid lip service to their source, using the titles of the famous fables for the cartoons (*The Ants and the Grasshopper*, *The Country Mouse and the City Mouse*, *The Hare and the Tortoise*) and ending each short with a quote from "2600 Years Ago" by Aesop himself, including such bonafide moral codas as "Conceit Only Begets Disaster," "United We Stand, Divided We Fall" and "Hospitality Is a Virtue Which Should Be Exercised Wisely." This tenuous fidelity to Aesop paid off in goodwill for

Terry as educators throughout America began sending letters of praise to the animator for providing impressionable children with important life lessons in an entertaining fashion—or as the series' unofficial motto put it, delivering "Sugar Coated Pills of Wisdom." What those educators thought of the *Fables*' constant references to such Roaring-20s byproducts as bootleg liquor, mercenary flappers and outdoor toilets has been lost to the ages.

Pathé and Keith-Albee were more than satisfied with the *Fables*, the theater people extending the property's original 12-month contract for two additional years in 1922 and 1923, increasing the annual extension to five years in 1924. Pathé treated the cartoons as respectfully as their live-action product, coming up with such business-boosters as sending out a weekly "mat" service, with illustrations from recent cartoons and appropriate verse written by "Aesop Jr.," to various newspapers as publicity for local theater owners. Pathé later promoted the *Fables* with illustrated "corner blocks" to be used for advertising in trade papers and theatrical house organs, an honor usually reserved for feature films and "live" two-reel comedies.

Throughout all this Van Beuren maintained a low profile, content to allow Terry and the distributor to take all the bows so long as money crossed his palm. Only on the occasion of the *Fables*' first anniversary in 1922 did he make a published statement in *Exhibitors Herald* confirming his association with the series:

> I have always firmly believed that the public likes cartoons. The hearty reception accorded "Aesop's Film Fables" by the theatre-going public has proved my personal belief. The animated cartoon has an exceptional audience appeal. It offers unlimited possibilities for presenting good comedy. The ingenuity of the cartoonist in drawing funny antics and comic scenes knows no limit. The cartoonist can make his characters do almost any action imaginable and the resultant laughs are abundant.

Though president of Fables Pictures, Van Beuren exercised little if any creative control over the cartoons: So long as they were delivered on time every week, he considered his obligation fulfilled. Such creative decisions as shipping out cue sheets to neighborhood-theater orchestras, with precise instructions as to which songs should be played and which sound effects performed for each cartoon, were made by either Terry, Pathé or Keith-Albee. Nor was Van Beuren concerned that Terry, under pressure to deliver 52 cartoons per year, had ceased to regard himself as an artist and coarsened into a factory foreman turning out animation by the yard. All that mattered was product assembled and delivered—and delivered it was thanks to the back-breaking efforts of an animation staff that had grown to over two dozen. By now, Terry was not only head of animation but also the series' line producer, Howard Estabrook having left Fables Pictures for other projects.

The sheer volume of *Aesop's Film Fables* was enough to secure the series' status as the leading animated commodity of the film industry. By early-1920s standards the cartoons were expertly made, and no less than Walt Disney later confessed that his fondest wish during this period was to produce cartoons on the same lofty level as the *Fables*. But though sales remained high and audiences were generally pleased, by mid-decade Terry's output began suffering in comparison with rival cartoon properties. Unlike Pat Sullivan and Otto Messmer's personality-driven *Felix the Cat*, the *Fables* lacked a strong central character. Farmer Al Falfa had been with series since *The Goose That Laid the Golden Egg*, but his tendency to alternate between hero and villain lessened his overall appeal. Of the animal characters, Milton and Mary (aka

From *Exhibitors Herald*, June 25, 1921.

Chapter 4—Animated Cartoons, Part One

What They Will Do For You

HERE'S a comedy release that will captivate everyone, young or old, as sure as shooting.

Every kid in the land knows Aesop's fables,—the hare and the tortoise, the goose that laid the golden egg, and all the rest. Grown-ups quote them; children read them and love them; all will want to see them on the screen, modernized. They've been advertised 2600 years!

Cartoonist Terry is clever; his drawings are delightful, once seen your crowd will come back for them again and again. They're a true novelty and a mighty good addition to any program.

Try them on yourself, and then count your laughs!

Cartoonist
PAUL TERRY

Rita) Mouse, Tom the Cat (later known as "Henry" and, after a 1928 radio contest, "Waffles"), Doug Dog, Andy Ant and Bess Beetle can best be described as irregulars, never showing up long enough to develop a following.

Nor could the *Fables* match the technical advances and inventiveness of Max Fleischer's *Koko the Clown* cartoons. Though some *Fables* stood out among the rest, notably whenever Terry harked back to his Paramount movie-parody days (*The Covered Push-Cart, The Last Ha-Ha*) or satirized such passing fancies as Couéism (*Day by Day—in Every Way*) and the Florida real-estate rush (*The Land Boom*), too many entries wallowed in formula and repetition, making it hard to tell the cartoons apart. Exhibitor comments like "A good short filler if not played too often" and "Good once in a while but soon grow old" began to outweigh such accolades as "Best one-reeler made" and "They please everybody." The property's biggest drawback was its mired-in-1921 animation: Though serviceable enough at the beginning of the series, the artwork seemed more and more primitive and archaic as the decade rolled on.

One consistent virtue of the *Fables* was the series' high comedy content and frequently outrageous individual gags, with scatological humor and ethnic jokes abounding. To hype the laugh quotient, the series had by 1925 forsaken the "authentic" Aesop morals in the closing footage in favor of vaudeville-style punchlines, many of them supplied by the writers of Fables' sister series *Topics of the Day*. Examples include "A monkey wrench is useless on a human nut," "He who laughs last, didn't see the joke in the first place," "The race to the altar is won in laps," and what must have been the writers' personal favorite, "A powdered nose is no guarantee of a clean neck." It was not uncommon for the closing moral to be funnier than the cartoon that preceded it—a fact recognized by Terry, who from 1921 on began building an enormous joke file, and in 1926 announced to the world that he had installed "a library of short stories by the world's leading humorists." As the producer explained to *Motion Picture News*, "Although my staff artists each enjoy a keen sense of humor and a natural gift of originality, the reading of these stories prevents them from 'getting in a rut' and keeps their minds actively engaged in enlarging upon and supplementing ideas which may be derived from the books." If only Terry had been equally concerned with the rut his animation had fallen into by 1926.

That same year the *Fables* endured two potentially lethal body blows. The first was Pathé's decision to charge a higher rental fee, resulting in the sort of reaction articulated in *Exhibitors Herald* by the manager of the Electric Theater in Browning, Missouri: "I ran [*Fables*] every Saturday for two years, but recently got a letter from the exchange that they would have to have more money for them, so I quit. Perhaps when the price of corn goes up and the crowds get larger I can stand the raise, but just now my bank account is low and I'm looking for reduction instead of increases in film rentals." Terry and Van Beuren were able to weather this storm with the ongoing financial support of Keith-Albee, who also may have shielded *Fables* from another assault mounted by the owners of the Bray-Hurd animation process. After years of ignoring unlicensed use of the process by Fables Studios, Bray-Hurd abruptly filed an infringement suit, citing exclusive ownership of *five* patents covering "all processes and methods now employed in the creation and production of animated cartoons." This legal action threatened to put Fables out of business, but as suddenly as the suit was filed, just as suddenly it was settled out of court, with Van Beuren securing a license so long as Bray-Hurd was credited on screen. *Motion Picture News* called this "something of an unusual situation" in that Bray-Hurd subsequently sued every other animation company in New York and Hollywood, with no settlements in sight. *Variety* editor Sime Silverman, longtime thorn in the side of Keith-Albee, never actually came out and said that the theater chain had wielded its power on behalf of Van Beuren to force Bray-Hurd into backing down, but the inference was there between the lines in future articles about the cartoons—especially those columns reporting that some Keith-Albee theater managers were beginning to balk at being ordered to run the increasingly unappealing *Fables* during vaudeville performances.

After Keith-Albee secured half-interest in the combined Pathé-PDC concern, merged with Orpheum circuit (which had also been running the *Fables* since their inception) and began laying the groundwork for RKO, Amedee Van Beuren was rewarded for services rendered. In June of 1928 the theater chain sold Fables Studios outright to Van Beuren, who retained Terry and agreed to pay the animator $320 per week and $400 after June 30, 1929. Outwardly the relationship between Van Beuren and Terry was copacetic, but when Keith-Albee-Orpheum aligned itself with RCA Photophone the seams began to show. Already displeased that Van Beuren's new screen credit in the *Fables'* opening titles was in letters as large as his own, Terry was in no mood to deal with Van Beuren's insistence that henceforth all cartoons would be produced with synchronized sound. Terry had been making cartoons his own way too long to adjust to so radical a change and resisted as much as he could. Finally he agreed to confer with RCA Photophone's music director Josiah Zuro to provide a synchronized score for the Fables entry *Dinner Time*, which had been completed as a silent. Having previously fitted scores to such silent features as 1927's *Wings*, Zuro knew his business, as did his associate Maurice Manne, who handled the sound effects.

Dinner Time is a pedestrian *Fables* cartoon, no better nor worse than the rest of the 1928 silent output, built around the hoary theme of Farmer Al Falfa's battles with his barnyard menagerie. There are no gags specifically designed for sound, nor any gags improved by the addition of sound. The resultant "talkie" consists of non-stop music, abrasive sound effects and occasional squawks and squeaks in lieu of dialogue. Yet with talking pictures still in swaddling clothes, the cartoon passed muster with Van Beuren and Pathé. Previewed in August of 1928, *Dinner Time* was officially released on October 14, hailed by Pathé publicists as "the world's first animated cartoon with sound." Since animators had been experimenting with primitive sound systems throughout the 1920s, Pathé's claim was no more accurate than Walt Disney's later assertion that his own *Steamboat Willie* was the first-ever sound cartoon. But inasmuch as it was released a month before *Steamboat Willie*, *Dinner Time* retains historical significance as the first theatrical cartoon with a licensed, non-experimental soundtrack. Audience and exhibitor reaction to this modest little effort was rapturous, with *Exhibitors Herald World* declaring "Paul Terry has done it again."

But Terry was demonstrably disinclined to continue "doing it." Not only was Van Beuren hogging all the credit for *Dinner Time* in interviews and press releases, but Terry was also embroiled in litigation with Keith-Albee-Orpheum's successor RKO over missing profits from his silent cartoons. Feeling cheated by RKO and browbeaten by Van Beuren, Terry told *Fables* animator Frank Moser that he wasn't about to do anything on behalf of the studio's new owner. Subsequent Terry-produced "talkie" *Fables* like *Stage Struck, Presto-Chango, Skating Hounds, Custard Pies* and

Farmer Al Falfa in *Broncho Buster* (1928).

Woodchoppers were conceived and filmed as silents, with music and effects grafted on as an afterthought. The synchronization is good as far as it goes, but the cartoons neither look nor play like full-fledged talkies, with the animators relying on such silent-film clichés as writing "Ha! Ha!" when a character laughs and drawing musical notes when a piano is played.

Van Beuren had had enough of this insubordination, and in early May of 1929 sent a letter informing Terry that his services were no longer required. On May 25, just hours after marrying his second wife, Van Beuren marched into *Fables'* New York headquarters at 318 46th Street and fired Terry in person. By June 13 longtime Terry associate Frank Moser was also gone, while most of the old *Fables* staff—notably directors John Foster, Mannie Davis and Harry Bailey—remained with Van Beuren. All hybrid-talkie cartoons left behind by Terry were in the hands of Pathé by September of 1929, whereupon the cartoon unit was officially renamed Van Beuren Studios.

Replacing Paul Terry as head animation director was John Foster (1886–1959), a New Jersey native who like Terry was a professional artist *sans* formal training. Foster joined the Raoul Barré animation studio in 1916, left to work on Charlie Bowers' *Mutt and Jeff* cartoons, then served in the U.S. military until 1919. Born with an innate sense of the absurd, he developed his peculiar comic style while employed by a Hearst-backed cartoon studio run by Paul Terry's brother John. Grotesque full-screen closeups, pointless but hilarious metamorphoses (a man, beast or plant shape-shifting into a pile of goo, a skeleton or a musical instrument), vocal trios and quartets sharing one single mouth, characters entering the frame walking sideways, the Sun and Moon developing shifty personalities with questionable motives—all these were part and parcel of Foster's repertoire by the time he joined the Fables unit in 1923. In later years colleagues Paul Terry and Mannie Davis proclaimed Foster a comic genius; it hardly mattered that he could barely draw and had the story sense of a gnat. Foster entered the sound era after years as chief director for the *Fables*, where even the weakest cartoons were bolstered by his breezy zaniness. Once Van Beuren Studios got under way Foster's imagination became even more unbridled, his belly-laugh virtuosity preventing the new *Fables* from ever descending into dullness (But don't watch a lot of them at the same sitting, or you'll see that Foster, like Terry before him, trotted out his favorite gags *ad nauseam*).

The first "official" Van Beuren cartoon *Jungle Fool* (1929) is also the first to fully justify the revised blanket title *Aesop's Sound Fables*. The music, sound effects and visuals all work together for a highly entertaining cartoon, beginning with the opening shot of a brass band marching in perspective (a device we'd see in dozens of subsequent cartoons) and the initial dialogue sequence with a speaker declaiming "We are gathered today to bid farewell to our distinguished fellow mem-bah!" in achingly perfect synchronization. Even when a character speaks in fluent sound effects—a slide whistle serves as a monkey's voice—it is obvious that the effect was planned and timed in advance and not merely transplanted onto a silent cartoon. It hardly matters that the animation and artwork are as crude and elementary as ever.

A large amount of credit for this perfect blend of sound and image must go to Van Beuren's new musical director Carl Eduoarde (1875–1932), longtime composer and orchestra leader for showman Samuel "Roxy" Rothfael. When RCA's Josiah Zuro was transferred to Hollywood in late 1929, Eduoarde joined the Manhattan-based *Fables* team in the official capacity of "synchronizer." Also added to the family was vaudeville song-and-dance man Jack Ward, who worked out the physical routines that the animators would replicate with pen and ink. The combination of John Foster's eccentric humor and Eduoarde and Ward's musical knowhow more than compensated for the patchy animation and graphics in such early Van Beuren sound cartoons as *Summer Time, Barnyard Melody* and *Night Club* (all 1929).

Though the logistics of making talkies obliged the studio to cut its yearly output from 52 to 26 reels, the workload for Van Beuren's ever-expanding animation staff was no less grueling than in the Terry years. To save time and effort, John Foster, Harry Bailey, Mannie Davis and Jack Ward developed a new process, by means of which "it will now be possible to present on screen as many as hundred different cartoon characters at the same time, each working in synchrony with the accompanying musical score" (according to *Exhibitors Herald-World*). This explains the preponderance of rhythmic crowd scenes in the early Van Beurens, but unfortunately the nature of the process was kept secret from the public. Not so an innovation developed in 1932 by recently hired animator George Rufle, who created a visual device representing a conductor's baton in various positions on the work print of each cartoon, synched with character movements so that animators could establish the proper tempo on behalf of the musicians and sound crew. Rufle would patent his process and receive on-screen credit right below the required acknowledgment of the Bray-Hurd patent.

Unlike Disney's Mickey Mouse cartoons of the same period, the Fables still had no regular "star" character. Farmer Al Falfa briefly continued popping up onscreen and in the studio's advertisements, but when Paul Terry established his new

Terrytoons studio in 1930 he claimed proprietary rights to the character. With the Farmer gone, Van Beuren focused on a "new" star who'd actually made his bow in the Terry silents, Milton Mouse. Prior to the talkie era Milton and his girlfriend Mary—or was it Rita?—looked like every other Terry mouse, with pointy snout, angular ears, black torso and (on occasion) white gloves and boots. But beginning with *A Close Call* in December 1929, Milton and his sweetie suddenly took on a rounder, cuter look, especially in the vicinity of the nose and ears. Milton also acquired a pair of white shorts while his lady friend wore a frilly white dress. When the two mice make their first appearance in *A Close Call* skipping through a field of musical flowers, one is startled by their strong resemblance to Mickey and Minnie Mouse. That resemblance would grow even stronger (inconsistent artwork notwithstanding) in such 1930 releases as *Western Whoopee, Circus Capers, Stone Age Stunts*, and especially *The Office Boy*.

It was the last-named cartoon that Walt Disney happened to catch while attending the Orpheum movie theater in Los Angeles. On April 30, 1931, Disney and his manager-brother Roy got a temporary court injunction (equity suit T-87-C, in case you're interested) against Van Beuren, charging character infringement. In the ensuing court battle Van Beuren was able to establish that Milton Mouse had been created by Terry employee William Ferguson back in 1921 and that Milton and his girlfriend had been wearing white gloves and boots all through the silent years. Disney's lawyer countered that while Milton Mouse predated Mickey, he didn't begin looking and

The opening title sequence for 1930's *Circus Capers*. The little animals swayed and rocked to the background music; the title card stood still.

dressing *exactly* like Mickey until after the latter's rise to fame. Following a second temporary injunction, Federal Judge Cosgrave issued a formal decree in August of 1931 prohibiting Van Beuren from "employing or using or displaying the pictorial representation of 'Mickey Mouse' or any variation thereof so nearly similar as to be calculated to be mistaken for or confused with said pictorial representation of 'Mickey Mouse.'" The decision didn't cost Van Beuren anything more than his pride. Interviewed years later by cartoon historian Jim Korkis, Roy Disney explained "We just stopped him. That's all we were out to do. We didn't ask any damages. We even let him finish marketing his pictures. We wanted to establish our right. That's what we were after. To establish a copyright like that is a big thing and that's an important thing to do."

Curiously, the Van Beuren staff failed to recognize the star quality of two characters right under their noses. Having gone through several shapes, sizes and name changes since the silent days, Waffles the Cat entered talkies as a tall, thin, highly neurotic humanized feline. Beginning with *The Haunted Ship* (1930), Waffles was teamed with a short, squat canine named Don Dog, a descendant of the "Doug Dog" who frequently made Farmer Al Falfa's life miserable in the silent *Fables*. Though superficially just another spinoff of the tall-small "Mutt and Jeff" combo, Waffles and Don began to develop a few appealing character traits of their own. The team's best cartoons *Jungle Jazz* and *Gypped in Egypt* (both 1930) contain the usual quota of John Foster's cherished comic non sequiturs—dancing and prancing skeletons, impromptu barbershop quartets, oddly-shaped aircraft and the like. But the biggest laughs arise from the personalities of Waffles and Don, with the hyperkinetic Waffles reacting in abject terror at the events transpiring around him while the inscrutable, Keaton-faced Don accepts everything the world throws at him without batting an eyelash, occasionally breaking into laughter over his friend's consternation. Waffles and Don could have emerged as the studio's premier attractions had John Foster been more concerned with character-driven comedy than outlandish spot gags. Certainly Foster's fellow animators George Stallings and George Rufle had an inkling of the two characters' potential when in 1931 they launched a companion cartoon series for *Fables* starring another big guy-little guy duo named Tom and Jerry (see Chapter 11), who were essentially Waffles and Don in human drag.

With the demise of *Topics of the Day* in 1930, *Aesop's Fables* became Van Beuren's longest-running film series, continuing unabated even after his distributor Pathé was absorbed by RKO. The popularity of the *Fables* was verified not only by box office returns but also such lucrative ancillary items as a line of character dolls manufactured by the W.R. Woodard Co. of Los Angeles. By this time, the series' blanket title bore no relation to the cartoons, even though RKO issued statements as late as 1932 insisting that Aesop was still the primary source. The written morals that had closed each silent cartoon were retained through 1929 and even briefly pepped up by adding animation to the "End" card, but were abandoned in early 1930. The loss of a tertiary throughline did no harm to the cartoons' profitability, with moviegoers and trade reviewers reacting more positively than they ever had in the waning days of the Terry regime. And despite a financial cutback passed down by RKO in 1933 which required Van Beuren to thin out his production staff, the producer generously moved the remaining employees out of their cramped and rundown New York headquarters and into roomier and fully modernized facilities at 729 Seventh Ave.

It cannot be denied that Van Beuren's cartoons look slapdash and shoddy compared to the talkie output of Fleischer and especially Disney. Though he paid decent salaries, Van Beuren spent as little as possible on budgets, while his staff remained bogged down in the techniques of the earliest talkies. In terms of animation and artwork, such shorts as 1932's *The Ball Game* might as well have been made in 1929. Another 1932 release, *Happy Polo*, *was* made in 1929, or perhaps even earlier; it had lain on the shelf since the Terry days, but was promoted as a "new" cartoon by virtue of freshly minted music and sound effects—and nobody noticed the difference. A few better-than-average *Fables* would crop up now and then: *Red Riding Hood* (1931), for example, features a "hotcha" grandma who after undergoing a beauty treatment inveigles the Wolf into marrying her, only to have Red stop the wedding by producing the Wolf's wife and kiddies. But other cartoons squandered their promising material, as witness the self-referential *Making 'Em Move* (1931), which starts strong with a boisterous backstage peek at the Van Beuren animators (in animal form) hard at work, only to degenerate into the sort of strapped-to-the-buzzsaw melodrama spoof that the studio had trampled to death in such earlier efforts as *A Close Call*. (In 1932, Van Beuren used the title "Making Them Move" for an article in *National Board of Review* magazine, which revealed even less "inside info" about the animation process than the earlier cartoon!)

The one saving grace of the talkie *Fables* output was manifested in the zesty musical scores arranged and synchronized by popular concert and radio orchestra leader Gene Rodemich (1890–1934), who succeeded Carl Eduoarde as Van Beuren's musical director in 1930. A onetime child prodigy who had played piano at the 1904 St. Louis World's Fair, Rodemich was known to his colleagues as "The Ragtime Paderewski." Forsaking Eduoarde's reliance on the public-domain library, Rodemich and his 25-piece studio orchestra made the most of such familiar ballads and contemporary dance tunes as "The Curse of an Aching Heart," "Oh You Beautiful Doll," "All the King's Horses, All the King's Men," "Ain't You Baby," "Kickin' the Gong Around," "Cupid on the Cake" and the deathless "The Cop on the Beat, the Man in the Moon and You." Even after his orchestra was reduced from 25 to 15, Rodemich never failed to deliver singable, danceable, laughable musical tracks, which went a long way in overcoming the general mediocrity of the animation.

Mediocrity was of minor concern to Amedee Van Beuren so long as his cartoons made money. But with exhibitors who preferred the Disney brand breathing down RKO's neck, Van Beuren decided in late 1932 to overhaul and upgrade the *Fables*. By March of 1933 John Foster had been fired and Gene Rodemich placed in charge of both the animation staff and the music department, which if nothing else assured that the cartoons would continue to *sound* good. Van Beuren also urged his directors to develop star characters that might conceivably match the popularity of Mickey Mouse—without, of course, resorting to plagiarism this time around. Director Mannie Davis came up with a Mickeyesque bruin named Cubby Bear (discussed in Chapter 11) who became the *Fables'* principal player, just as Mickey had dominated and ultimately outgrown Disney's *Silly Symphonies*. Of the 27 *Aesop's Fables* released between January of 1933 and June of 1934, all but eight would spotlight Cubby Bear.

This final batch of "generic" *Fables* showed a modest improvement in the series' animation, while the storylines were, if not compelling, at least coherent. Arguably the best of these, and one that has since become an animation-festival perennial,

Ad for Van Beuren's Christmas 1932 *Aesop's Fables* offering; the film actually came out the first week of January 1933.

is *Silvery Moon* (reissue title: *Candy Town*), planned as Van Beuren's Christmas 1932 release but not distributed nationally until January 1933. This loose remake of the 1932 *Fables* effort *Wild Goose Chase* stars Waffles the Cat, redesigned (again!) to resemble the diminutive round-headed hero of Charles Mintz' *Krazy Kat* cartoons (not *exactly* a Mickey Mouse double, but close enough). Drifting along in a canoe while singing "By the Light of the Silvery Moon," Waffles and his lady friend the Countess get into an argument over whether the Moon is made of green cheese or candy. The Moon "himself" offers to resolve the lovers' quarrel by inviting them to visit the lunar surface—and all points within and below. Turns out the Countess was right: The Moon *is* made of candy, partitioned into huge, scrumptious helpings. After gorging themselves on the gargantuan confections the two cats are pursued by a gigantic bottle of castor oil. Once safely back in their canoe, Waffles and the Countess bid farewell to the smiling Moon, who bursts into a deep-bass rendition of the 1911 hit "Goodnight Mr. Moon." Though the animation still leaves a lot to be desired, *Silvery Moon* coasts by comfortably on its sweet, infectious charm. That said, I must confess that when I first saw this cartoon in my preschool years, the enormous climactic closeup of Mr. Moon's rolling eyes and quivering lips scared the living daylights out of me.

Scarier still is the final "no-star" *Aesop's Fable*, 1933's *Rough on Rats*. The cartoon begins innocuously enough with three little kittens and their mother playfully exploring a department store, only to plunge headlong into *grand guignol* as a demonic rat prepares to decapitate one of the poor li'l kitties with a meat slicer. The other cats decimate the rat with such makeshift weapons as cigars and flypaper, and all ends happily with a jolly song. As for four-year-old me, I was already hiding under the couch.

Though *Aesop's Fables* would not officially end until the June 15, 1934, release of the Cubby Bear vehicle *Fiddlin' Fun*, we close this chapter with *Rough on Rats* as a summary of what the *Fables* had become in the thirteen years since their inception. The animation is smoother, the gags less chaotic and better integrated, and the plotline follows a steady course without the desultory detours of the pre–1932 efforts. Yet this later *Aesop's Fable* stills fall far short of the standards set in 1933 by Disney and Fleischer. With few exceptions, the Van Beuren *Aesop's Fables* remain today what they were when first released: Pleasant but forgettable time-fillers. Still, it's nice to see that even after John Foster's exit from the studio, vestiges of his gonzo approach to animation remained: In fine Foster tradition, *Rough on Rats* concludes with a bizarre, marrow-chilling closeup of a wild-eyed pussycat!

Chapter 5

Henry and Polly

Though the merger of the Keith-Albee and Orpheum theater chains had been forged in 1926, Keith-Albee-Orpheum would not legally incorporate until 1928. Even so, the new conglomerate was being abbreviated as K-A-O in trade papers as early as January of 1927. That same month, K-A-O made a public announcement of their intention to enter active filmmaking, in concert with their newly acquired PDC-Pathé studio in Culver City, California. K-A-O planned to start small with two-reel comedies, setting up a program separate from PDC but still for Pathé release.

The initial plan was to make a series based on "The Jarr Family," a newspaper-column created by humorist Roy McCardell, who among other achievements has been credited as the architect behind the very first Sunday color-comics newspaper supplement. Launched in 1907, the Jarr Family stories focused on Mr. and Mrs. Jarr, an eternally combative couple *a la* the later radio favorites *The Bickersons*. Desiring only peace and quiet after returning home from a hard day's work, Mr. Jarr would habitually get into an argument with Mrs. Jarr at the slightest provocation, usually a harmless remark he'd made that was completely (and often deliberately) misinterpreted by his wife. Eighteen one-reel "Jarr Family" comedies had been filmed by Vitagraph in 1915, with Harry Davenport (later "Dr. Meade" in *Gone with the Wind*) as director-star, Rose Tapley as Mrs. Jarr, and a young Paul Kelly as their son. Roy McCardell himself was brought to California to script the new Jarr Family two-reelers of 1927, to be filmed at Metropolitan Studios (housed on the PDC lot) under the direction of Lawrence Windom.

Inasmuch as longtime Keith-Albee obligee Amedee Van Beuren had evinced no desire to return to live-action comedies since his 1921–22 Ernest Truex series (see Chapter 3), it's safe to assume that his involvement in K-A-O's Jarr Family project was at the request (I could have chosen a less benign word) of E.F. Albee's right-hand man John J. Murdock, who happened to be a top executive at Pathé. Though still head of his own AyVeeBee Productions—at least on paper—Van Beuren took charge of K-A-O's new Gaiety Films, named for B.F Keith's first New York theater (PDC-Pathé's DeMille epic *The King of Kings* had recently been world-premiered at the Gaiety). Van Beuren's responsibilities were largely administrative, with producer-director Leander de Cordova (best known for helming the 1925 Betty Blythe version of *She*) functioning as production supervisor. Taylor Holmes, a well-known Broadway comic actor whose most popular film vehicle *Efficiency Edgar's Courtship* (1917) had also been directed by Lawrence Wisdom, was signed to a five-year contract by Gaiety to star in the new comedies. (Holmes remained in films until the 1950s, playing memorable character roles in such *noir* classics as *Kiss of Death* and *Nightmare Alley*). Though this arrangement was probably made by Murdock as well, Van Beuren took full credit in the press release: "In signing Mr. Taylor Holmes as our star, I am told I have made a master stroke in the selection of the right person to play the leading part in this series of domestic life comedies."

Selecting the right actress to play opposite Mr. Holmes wasn't quite as swift and simple. The initial choice, Clara Kimball Young, balked at being contractually tied down for five years. The offer was then extended to Leah Baird, a top star since the World War I years whose career was in the doldrums (in the talkie era Baird focused on screenwriting before retiring to family life, then un-retiring to accept bits and extra roles). As the first actress signed for pictures by the combined Pathé/K-A-O interests, Baird was heralded as "the first half-billion-dollar star"—not a reflection of her salary (there were only two zeroes), but in reference to the amount paid by K-A-O to join forces with PDC-Pathé. Another actress, former "Miss Pittsburgh" Mildred Watkins, was signed to play supporting parts in the films. She didn't get a half billion either.

"Jarr Family" creator Roy McCardell spent only a month or so in Culver City scripting the Holmes-Baird comedies before dashing back to New York. One doubts that he hit the road with a song in his heart and a smile on his lips, armed as he was with the knowledge that what he'd been hired to work on was not what was going to be filmed. Less than five weeks after the first announcement of the Jarr Family series, the trade papers were informed that Gaiety Films' maiden project would instead be based on the old Mr. & Mrs. Sidney Drew comedies produced by Vitagraph, Metro and Van Beuren from 1913 until Mr. Drew's death in 1919 (see Chapter 1). The only tangible connections between the battling Jarrs and the lovey-dovey Drews were that both series had earlier been filmed at Vitagraph and that Harry "Mr. Jarr" Davenport was Sidney Drew's brother-in-law: Otherwise, Night and Day were more similar than the two properties. Research has not determined whether John J. Murdock or Amedee J. Van Beuren ordered the format change, but my money's on Van Beuren.

To underline the similarity between the Drews of old and the current Gaiety films, the series was retitled *Henry and Polly*, the same characters played by Mr. and Mrs. Drew. But wait, it gets better: Two of the new comedies, *Should a Mason Tell?* and *King Harold*, were scene-for-scene remakes of Van Beuren's 1919 Drew starrers *Once a Mason* and *Harold, King of the Saxons*.

To summarize the end results, let us turn to the June 1, 1927, edition of *Variety*:

> The supremacy of J.J. Murdock in Pathé was demonstrated when A.J. Van Beuren screened a new comedy for the Pathé reviewing committee. It was to be the first of a series of comedies of home life like the former Mr. and Mrs. Sidney Drew stuff. The committee is said to have flatly rejected the first, made recently in California, and suggested the entire prospect of a series be given up. Van Beuren is said to have insisted the comedy be released.
>
> There was quite a to-do but finally orders came from Murdock that the stuff go on the program.... Negative cost on the first of the home life comedies panned by the committee, is said to have been $15,000. The kick on the first was that it looked out of date.

Although the Pathé publicists had exuberantly covered every aspect of the *Henry and Polly* series while it was in production, once the films were ready for public perusal the studio gave them virtually no promotion at all. Their cursory and slightly grudging mentions of the series in the Pathé trade ads for the 1927–28 season were written in the tiniest type that the composers could find. Not even Van Beuren had anything

Chapter 5—Henry and Polly

Leah Baird and Taylor Holmes in the inaugural Henry and Polly two-reeler *Should a Mason Tell?*, from the August 13, 1927, *Exhibitors Herald World*.

to say on record when the first two-reeler *Should a Mason Tell?* snuck into theaters on September 18, 1927—nor in fact would he ever publicly mention the project again.

Filmgoers and critics were equally underwhelmed by the three completed films in the series. Only the second two-reeler *Their Second Honeymoon* was greeted without indifference or hostility: *Film Daily* labeled it "A pretty comedy," which is about as a good as it got. Significantly, *Their Second Honeymoon* was the only one of the three not based on an earlier Van Beuren-Drew comedy. Otherwise, critical assessment was on a par with *Motion Picture Daily*'s pan of the final entry *King Harold* : "It is almost entirely devoid of laughs either of the gag or situation type." Exhibitors were virtually unanimous in their dislike of the series. *Should a Mason Tell?* was deemed "Not much, not even amusing" by M.G. Mundy of the Ivy Theater in New Orleans, while the manager of Lincoln, Kansas' Princess Theater grumbled "Might be comedy, but sure is deep stuff"; W.U. Selnett of the City Theater in Lafayette, Alabama, was more emphatic, exclaiming "If I am any judge, this is the poorest comedy ever made." The only exhibitor willing to cut the series some slack was the manager of the Silver Family Theater in Greenville, Michigan. "This is great," gushed Mr. Silver Family Theater about *Should a Mason a Tell?*'; "This is good. Could not help it with this pair, Holmes-Baird," he enthused about *Their Second Honeymoon*; "Funny comedy," he raved about *King Harold*. I'd venture a guess that this man's judgment was swayed by a few complimentary cases of Scotch, but that's not the hill I want to die on.

The final word on *Henry and Polly* was, predictably, a lawsuit—though this time Van Beuren was not involved. Viola Forster, who claimed to be personal representative of series star Taylor Holmes, sued the actor for not paying 10 percent commission on his weekly $600 salary. Holmes countered that he'd never signed a contract with Forster, and the case was thrown out of New York's Municipal Court. Just as *Henry and Polly* was thrown out of the collective memories of Amedee Van Beuren, Keith-Albee-Orpheum, and Pathé—and virtually every film history book except this one.

Chapter 6

The Grantland Rice Sportlights

Grantland Rice has been acknowledged as the greatest sportswriter of his time, and the yardstick by which all future members of the profession would be measured. Born in Murfreesboro, Tennessee, in 1880, "Granny" Rice excelled in baseball and football at Vanderbilt University, but his future lay in journalism. He graduated Phi Beta Kappa in 1901 with a BA in the Classics, which may account for his elegant, poetic and often purple prose once he turned to the newspaper game. After working at the Atlanta *Journal* and the Nashville *Tennessean*, he joined the New York *Tribune* (later the *Herald Tribune*) in 1914, that same year launching his daily "Sportlight" column which at its height would be syndicated throughout the English-speaking world. Quotations made famous by Rice as he chronicled the world of athletics would fill a book in themselves: The best known, written in verse, perfectly sums up his life philosophy: "For when the One Great Scorer comes to write against your name/ He writes—not that you won or lost, but how you played the game."

Winning of course meant *something* to Rice, but not everything, as he explained in an article for *The Pathé Club Yearbook of 1927*: "The true spirit of sport is an even break, a square deal, a start from scratch with 'a fair field and no favor.'" To him, the strong body and healthy mind, developed through sweat, dedication and perseverance, represented "the spirit of the game" and "self reliance and courage." So far as Rice was concerned, the realm of sports, amateur or professional, was "at its best ... a builder of bodily health and of ideals." But as much as he loved the Game, he loved the players more, and did everything he could in his literary output to lionize the cream of the crop. Rice's classic October 18, 1924, account of the Notre Dame football team not only immortalized college backfielders Stuhldreher, Miller, Crowley and Layden as "The Four Horsemen," but also elevated coach Knute Rockne to the Valhalla of sports icons.

Nor was Rockne the only hero whom Grantland Rice worshipped; Baseball stars Babe Ruth and Ty Cobb, tennis champ Bill Tilden, polo player Tommy Hitchcock, boxers Jack Dempsey and Gene Tunney, golfer Bobby Jones and football great Red Grange were deified by Rice in print, and also numbered among his closest friends. He was equally adept at creating heroes as reporting on them, following swimmer Johnny Weissmuller from his days of obscurity at the Illinois Athletic Club and carefully building the boy's legend with glowing accounts of Weissmuller's victories in the 1924 and 1928 Summer Olympics. Rice wrote in fluent superlative, calling Babe Ruth "the greatest figure the world of sport has ever known" and all-around athlete Babe Didrickson Zaharias "the most flawless section of muscle harmony, of complete mental and physical coordination, the world has ever seen." Seldom did Rice have an unkind word for anyone; he loved everybody and was universally loved in return.

Rice's entrée into the cinematic world occurred in 1916, when he wrote the scenario for the five-reel baseball epic *Somewhere in Georgia*, starring good buddy Ty Cobb. Four years later Rice was approached by film producer and theater manager Jack Eaton, who previously supervised Paramount Pictures' travelogues and had recently established his own Town and Country Films, making a group of wartime Red Cross shorts and a string of two-reelers based on the writings of "Uncle Sam" artist James Montgomery Flagg. Eaton proposed to Rice that they collaborate on a new series of sports reels, focusing not only on big events and big names but also on the recreational and non-competitive athletic pursuits of "regular" folks. Rice lent his name and reputation to the new *Sport Pictorial* films, choosing the topics, editing the scripts and composing the subtitles; Eaton took care of the production end while photography was overseen by Hartford, Connecticut, native John L. Hawkinson, described by Rice with surprising restraint as "a hard worker." The entertainment value of these one-reel entries was enhanced with slow-motion photography and special effects, though there was no trickery involved in the sports themselves. Advertised as "More lively than news reels, more interesting than scenics," the twice-monthly *Sport Pictorial* was released through independent Arrow Films and distributed on a states-rights basis, beginning in October of 1920 with coverage of the Yale Bowl opening.

Autographed postcard of Grantland Rice from the late 1930s.

The following year Rice and Eaton moved from Arrow to the Weiss Brothers' Artclass Pictures, changing the series' name to *The Sportlight* after Rice's newspaper column. Len Hammond and Ernest Corts began a long association with the unit as principal cameramen, while distribution was taken over by Goldwyn Pictures. Dedicated to "every branch of sport" (according to Louis Weiss), *The Sportlight* was an instant success, but after a single season and 26 episodes Jack Eaton temporarily dropped out of filmmaking to manage a movie palace in Detroit. In early 1923 photographer J.L. Hawkinson persuaded Rice to revive the series with Hawkinson in the producer's chair. Pathé was interested in acquiring distribution rights, but only if three sample reels were produced at Rice's expense. "The financing was my headache, including buying such new equipment as we needed for the job," recalled Rice in his autobiography *The Tumult and the Shouting*. "I had nearly reached the bottom of the barrel when we delivered the three films. They were accepted and a contract was signed." The first Pathé release of the rechristened *Grantland Rice Sportlight* was *Wild and Wooly* on December 16, 1923. To keep production funds flowing, Rice additionally edited and titled a series of celebrity two-reel comedies made by his former producer Jack Eaton, also for Pathé release.

Pathé's cozy association with the Keith-Albee circuit secured top playdates for the silent *Sportlights* throughout the 1920s. The films kept Grantland Rice's name alive for people who otherwise had no interest in sports. As he observed in his autobiography, "Whatever identity I've enjoyed from my byline, the Sportlight title board on movie shorts has given me contact with moviegoers who may not know an inning from a goal post and care less. Women particularly have been entertained by sporting action on the screen, and I believe these experiences they have shared have given them a keener appreciation of sports in general."

The myriad of mergers and takeovers that resulted in Pathé becoming an appendage of Keith-Albee-Orpheum in 1928 brought Amedee Van Beuren into the fold. Van Beuren purchased a small piece of Rice's Sports Pictorials Inc., then in collaboration with the writer created Sportlights, Inc., making himself an officer and adding the corporation to his ever-growing Van Beuren Enterprises. During the last week of May in 1928 the Hollywood trade papers announced that *Sportlights* was now in the hands of Van Beuren, with Pathé remaining as distributor. *Canned Thrills*, the first short delivered to Van Beuren on June 20, 1928, was released the 19th of August. A rapidly-paced overview of the carnival rides at Coney Island, the still-extant *Canned Thrills* was produced by J.L. Hawkinson, who stayed with the property throughout the final 25 silent episodes. These 10-minute vignettes ran the gamut of subject matter: Football, fishing, bowling, soccer, archery, rope-skipping, quail hunting, horse racing, sailboating and more, with special emphasis on training, technique and teamwork in films like *Getting Together* (1928), *Spartan Diet* (1928), *Young Hopefuls* (1929) and *Footwork* (1929).

The last-named film featured 1928 Olympic speed king Paavo Nurmi, just one of many sports luminaries who periodically popped up in the *Sportlights* as a gesture of friendship to Grantland Rice. Nor was the guest-star roster limited to athletes. Two 1929 silent shorts, *Players at Play* and *Surf and Sail*, were blatant promotional propaganda for the series' distributor Pathé, with studio contractees Robert Armstrong, Marie Prevost, Phyllis Haver and Frank Coghlan, Jr., appearing in the former film and PDC-Pathé honcho Cecil B. DeMille in the latter. *Players at Play* also attracted moviegoers with drop-in stars from other studios: Louise Fazenda, Noah Beery, Thelma Todd, Jackie Coogan and Neil Hamilton. (Later in 1929, First National starlet Alice White rode an aquaplane in *Girls Will Be Boys*).

Van Beuren's late-1920s commitment to talking pictures was shared by Grantland Rice, who looked forward to making *Sportlights* in sound. The missing ingredient in this recipe was producer J.L. Hawkinson, who at the end of 1928 decided to quit show business and return to his home town of Hartford, where he established a successful porcelain manufacturing business. Jack Eaton, latterly on the production staff of PDC-Pathé, returned to *Sportlights*, remaining with Grantland Rice for the remainder of both their film careers.

Released March 10, 1929, *Winning Patterns* was the first sound *Sportlight* to

Chapter 6—The Grantland Rice Sportlights 67

greet this public. Our initial glimpse of Grantland Rice (who generally did not appear in these films) is a pair of hands at a typewriter, tapping out the film's title. We are then offered a fuller view of Mr. Rice, smoking a pipe and observing in his avuncular Southern drawl that millions of sports spectators have become active participants in one game or another in the past several years. "And naturally," he continues,

Advertisement for the talkie Grantland Rice Sportlight entry *Gridiron Glory* **in a 1929 edition of** *Exhibitors Herald World.*

"they are much more interested in the right way of how to do a thing—and the wrong way—than they ever were before. These are not champions, but they don't want to be Mr. and Mrs. John J. Dumb all their lives!" To help us avoid this embarrassing fate, Rice proceeds to narrate a series of crisply photographed film vignettes, many in slow motion, illustrating the "winning patterns" of nonprofessional experts in the fields of golf, diving, pole vaulting and sprinting. Just before the close of the nine-minute short, the "right way" to play tennis is demonstrated by a professional, none other than Bill Tilden. *Winning Patterns* was very well received, with one exhibitor praising the audio reproduction as "clear as a bell."

In his autobiography Grantland Rice cited the second release *Three Aces* (1929) as the first talkie *Sportlight* to actually go before the cameras (albeit misnaming it *Four Aces*). It's understandable why this one would stand out in Rice's memory: Not only does he again appear as onscreen emcee, but the cast includes close friends Gene Tunney, Bobby Jones, Tommy Hitchcock, and, in a return engagement, Bill Tilden. More poignantly, *Three Aces* represents the only talkie appearance of celebrated sports promoter and longtime Gene Tunney associate Tex Rickard, who died January 6, 1929. Here Rickard and Rice offer a capsule history of Tunney's life and boxing career from his war service to the present, with tantalizingly brief stock-footage cutaways.

The continued success of the sound *Sportlights* was assured with the third entry *Crystal Champions*, one of nearly two dozen episodes filmed in Florida. Rice had been drawn to the Sunshine State during the land-boom days of the 1920s; after the boom went bust he made it his mission to salvage Florida's sagging economy by heavily promoting the town of Ocala's new tourist attraction Silver Springs, with its alligator wrestlers, snake milkers, glass-bottom-boat tours and the crystal-clear waters of Silver River. One of the last silent *Sportlight* reels *Water Wonders* had featured razor-sharp underwater photography of world crawl-stroke champion Martha Norelius, slow-motion studies of Olympic divers Helen Meany and Peter Desjardines, and the lightning-quick diving takeoffs of Rice's unofficial protégé Johnny Weissmuller.

Crystal Champions features these same four "water wonders" performing entirely different strokes and dives, as well as local swimming trainer and champion turtle-catcher Newton Perry, whom Rice would dub "the human fish" (building an entire one-reeler around Perry with that title in 1940). Ernest Corts' underwater camerawork was even more breathtaking than in the earlier short, with smooth and graceful tracking and POV shots. The addition of sound enabled RCA synchronizer Josiah Zuro to include a lush musical score. comprised largely of Tchaikovsky themes and performed by Frank Black and his orchestra. The film's offscreen narration (still a novelty in 1929) has been credited to both Rice and producer Jack Eaton, though the English-accented commentator doesn't sound like either of them; more likely it was actor Tom Terriss, soon to be associated with Van Beuren's *Vagabond Adventures* series. (It's interesting—at least to me—that the narrator pronounces Johnny Weissmuller's last name as "Vice-myooler"). *Crystal Champions* was producer-director Eaton's favorite of all his *Sportlights*, while Rice never tired of referencing its huge box-office gross. The film remained in first-run theatrical circulation for well over a year, and was given a special showcase presentation aboard the transatlantic liner S.S. *Berengaria*.

A production still from one of Grantland Rice's many Florida-filmed *Sportlights*.

In 1931 Rice and Eaton came up with a sequel of near-equal popularity, *Swim or Sink*, where in addition to Weissmuller and Newton Perry the cast includes Ross Allen, founder of the Silver Springs Reptile Institute, and comic diver Stubby Kruger, who would still be in harness in the early 1960s as a movie stuntman. (During filming Weissmuller and Kruger celebrated their burgeoning celebrity by going on a toot in Ocala, setting off all the city's fire alarms and spending the night in the slammer). As a byproduct of Rice's testimonials for Silver Springs in the *Sportlights* series, MGM later chose Silver River for the underwater sequences in the studio's *Tarzan* pictures—again featuring Johnny Weissmuller.

Before leaving Florida, we should mention that Rice also had a soft spot for Cypress Gardens in the town of Winter Haven. Two of the best extant Van Beuren-Pathé *Sportlights*, *Spills and Thrills* (1930) and *Outboard Stunting* (1931), feature a number of participants of the Cypress Garden Aquacade, a spectacle created by the attraction's founder Dick Pope. Swimming took a back seat to water skiing in these entries, with plenty of time left over for aqua-sleds, gliders, motorboats and a few side trips into the Everglades. The visuals were complemented by vivid on-location sound recording—no narration, just the squeals and giggles of enthusiastic young skiers and speedboat pilots—courtesy of *Sportlights'* own fully equipped, two-ton portable sound truck.

Though the series had occasionally deployed "live" sound during the 1928–29 season—notably in *Hook Line and Melody* (1929), where a fishing excursion in

Canada's Lake Lavieille region is punctuated by a self-styled troubadour's rendition of "Love's Old Sweet Song"—once the unit's sound truck was purchased for the 1929–30 season *Sportlight*s truly excelled with on-the-spot recording, starting with *Gridiron Glory* in October 1929. Though the football highlights in this short had been filmed silent in 1928, *Gridiron Glory*'s major selling points were the commentary by radio's Graham McNamee (obviously recorded outdoors and not in a studio), and a portfolio of college songs robustly performed by a male chorus under the direction of baritone James Stanley, star of Van Beuren's *Song Sketches* (see Chapter 9). Credited onscreen as "synchronizer" for *Gridiron Glory* was popular bandleader Eugene Rodemich, whose invaluable contributions to Van Beuren's animated-cartoon output are discussed in Chapter 4. (Rodemich appeared on-camera in the July 1929 *Sportlight* entry *Modern Rhythm*).

In the summer of 1930 Grantland Rice's sound truck, carrying Jack Eaton, recording engineer Russell T. Ervin and two cameramen, embarked on a coast-to-coast filming expedition covering 150,000 road miles. During a couple of stopovers in Wyoming and Colorado the unit filmed three one-reelers back to back—a customary timesaving procedure—for release between August and October of 1930: *Ski Hi Frolics*, *Dude Ranching*, and *Gliding*. *Ski Hi Frolics* follows a band of very vocal young adventurers as they scale Pike's Peak by train, mule and foot. For *Dude Ranching*, Van Beuren and Pathé collaborated with the Northern Pacific Railroad on a tie-in campaign, with the railroad's New York office featuring a lobby display of branding irons, stirrups, peace-pipes, axes and moccasins. In *Gliding*, the show is stolen by adorable young air-glider pilot Ruth Elder Camp, who is so giddy while describing her favorite pastime that she can barely get her words out. All three films are distinguished by superior photography and a wide variety of creative camera angles.

Here is the Van Beuren Sportlight sound truck in action in making the Grantland Rice reel for release by Pathe. Ernest Corts is getting the shots.

From *Exhibitors Herald World*, April 12, 1930.

In the tradition of the silent *Sportlights*, the talkie shorts devoted generous screen space to Rice's personal heroes. In addition to Tunney, Tilden, Weissmuller et. al., the series offered newly shot and stock-footage glimpses of heavyweight boxer Jack Dempsey, baseball legends Babe Ruth and Ty Cobb, golf champ Johnny Farrell, tennis pro Helen Wills, billiard whiz Willie Hoppe, celebrated horse trainer C.V. Whitney and fabled UCLA coach William H. Spaulding. Adding occasional comedy relief were non-sports celebrities who would either make jokes while indulging in athletics or provide contrast with the professionals via their own severely limited sports skills. Cartoonist Rube Goldberg in *Fairway Favorites* (1930) and radio star Frank Crumit in *Par and Double Par* (1930) were among the famous amateurs whose ineptitude made the pros look all the better. Occasionally the series strove too hard for laughs, as in *Cobb Goes Fishing* (1930), featuring humorist Irvin S. Cobb on an angling vacation with his pal "Granny." The anticipated humor arising from this situation was undercut by Cobb's sluggish screen personality, moving *Variety* to cluck "Attempt at philosophy and comedy is not there."

Far better represented by the series were unusual and offbeat recreational activities featuring "weekend warriors" and student athletes, with Grantland Rice's expected emphasis on the character-building merits of diligent training and rigorous exercise. Examples include the log-rolling contests of Canadian lumberjacks in *The River Drivers* (1929), Culver Military Institute students cutter-racing and playing pushball in *Body Building Stamina* (1929), pig-racing and "mule polo" in *Carolina Capers* (1929), demonstrations of jai-alai and lacrosse in *Racqueteers* (1930), fox and possum hunting in *Dixie Chase* (1930), gator-chasing in *Hunting Thrills* (1931), a re-creation of the 1869 Princeton-Rutgers game by contemporary students in *Pigskin Progress* (1931) and everything from flycasting to moose-calling in *Uncrowned Champions* (1931). Some of the more novel entries eschewed sports per se in favor of human-interest stories, notably the dog-raising and -training prowess of Margaret Kirsme in *Interesting Tails* (1929), a glee-club competition in *Campus Favorites* (1930), and the training of animal performers at Ringling Brothers' Florida winter quarters in *Dogging It* and *Big Top Champions* (both 1930).

If any overall criticism can be leveled at *Sportlights*, it would focus on the series' occasional male chauvinism. Though Rice and Eaton treated such professional female athletes as Glenna Collett, Helen Wills and Martha Norelius with utmost respect, non-pros were frequently subjected to demeaning mother-in-law, woman-driver and fat-lady jokes. Whenever the onscreen girls were unusually attractive (or even moderately pretty) the camera lingered lovingly on skimpy exercise outfits, shapely legs and round fundaments. (This of course had been going on since the silent days; *Motion Picture News*' review of 1929's *Sport Afloat* singled out the "hoard of attractive shorts" worn by the ladies). Rather than deflect accusations of objectification and male condescension, the *Sportlights* staff seemed to welcome them. When *Film Daily* reviewed the otherwise laudatory *Feminine Fitness* (1929), which zeroed in on the sports program at Wellesley College, the critic noted: "There are a lot of unintended laughs, especially in the rowing sequence where the female coach issues orders in a high pitched voice." Van Beuren and Rice were so proud of this review that it was reprinted in Pathé's official publicity packet.

In addition to his *Sportlights* duties, Grantland Rice contributed scripts, story ideas and poetry to Van Beuren's *Song Sketches* mini-musicals, as noted in Chapter 9. More characteristically, in December of 1930 Rice performed public-service duty for his distributors. As chronicled in *Exhibitor's Herald*,

> The Van Beuren company and the RKO circuit, with the cooperation of Grantland Rice, who makes the Pathé Sportlight series, and Seward Prosser, chairman of the mayor's unemployment relief committee in New York, have completed a short subject designed to strengthen public confidence in the successful outcome of the present situation regarding unemployment. The reel, which stresses the advantages of coordinated effort, opens with a review of present conditions by Rice, who compares the man without a job to the losing football team. Prosser, who is chairman of the board of the Bankers Trust Company, gives some facts and figures on the relief measures already carried through by the committee he heads, and expresses his optimistic opinion that a return to normalcy cannot be stopped and is not far ahead.

[That's what *he* thinks].

Grantland Rice's contract with Van Beuren and Pathé's successor RKO originally extended until May 1, 1933, but after Rice delivered 10 one-reelers for the 1931–32 season an item appeared in the January 25, 1932, *Film Daily*: "Grantland Rice's 'Sportlights,' pioneer sports reel, and RKO release presented by the Van Beuren Corp., will be handled by some other national distributor starting this spring, THE FILM DAILY learns. Three more issues will be made for Van Beuren by Jack Eaton, the producer. It is also learned that distribution offers have been made by several major companies for the 'Sportlight' release." On March 17, *Film Daily* had this to say: "Under the new title of 'A Sports-Eye View' as seen by Grantland Rice, the 'Grantland Rice Sportlights' ... will be released next year by Paramount. Production will continue under the direction of Jack Eaton." Why the title change? Better yet, what happened between Rice and Van Beuren in the first place?

Evidently not privy to *Film Daily*'s inside information of five days previous, *Motion Picture Herald*'s James Cunningham reported on January 30: "Grantland Rice's contractual relationship with the Van Beuren Corporation may, or may not, weather the storm in which differences between both factions have cast it. If Rice and the company are successful in patching up a tilt now current, Van Beuren will continue to make Rice's 'Sportlights' for RKO release.... On the other hand, if an amicable settlement is not made, Rice is expected to look elsewhere for distribution of the sport subjects which Jack Eaton produced." What storm? What tilt? Don't look to Rice's autobiography for the full story. With tactful brevity, he merely remarks, "Van Buren [sic] and I fell out."

Around the same time that Rice relocated to Paramount, his attorney Louis Nizer took Amedee Van Beuren and his corporation to court on behalf of Sportlights, Inc. As explained in the March 25, 1932, *New York State Exhibitor*: "Rice claims that [Van Beuren] improperly transferred $4,345.63 from one corporation to the other, as an officer of both. Claim is for the money and an accounting." Four days later, *Variety* offered more details while upping the ante: "[Paramount's deal] with Rice, arranged through Louis Nizer, his attorney, follows suit against A.J. Van Beuren for recovery of over $23,000 alleged to have been improperly paid from the 'Sportlights' Corp. into the Van Beuren Corp. Suit also asks that Van Beuren be removed as an officer of Sportlights Corp., although latter is reported holding a small financial interest in that production company" *Variety* added that the trial date had not yet been set, concluding with: "'Sportlights' terminated its releasing arrangement with Van Beuren and Pathé after an association of over six years."

Film Daily picked up the narrative on May 29: "Case of Grantland Rice Sportlights, Inc., against the Van Beuren Corp. is due for trial next fall. Plaintiff seeks an accounting in connection with a product deal. Case is pending before Supreme Court Justice Churchill." *Variety* filled in a few more blanks on May 31: "Louis Nizer, Rice's attorney, has made a motion to examine Van Beuren before trial. Justice Churchill hasn't passed on the motion yet."

Flash forward to the November 25, 1932, *State Exhibitor*:

> Amedee J. Van Beuren and the Van Beuren Corporation must show cause in New York Supreme Court, November 29, why they should not be adjudged in contempt of court. The order, on petition of attorneys for Grantland Rice, Philips and Nizer, is based on the alleged refusal of Van Beuren to continue with an examination he was undergoing with a suit filed against him by Rice. Van Beuren Corporation is also involved. Rice, in his petition, states that testimony given by Van Beuren in the examination revealed inconsistencies and contradiction with his own prior testimony. The petition asks for counsel fees entailed by the application for contempt order in addition to statutory fine.

The amount in contention had by then been modified: "Rice, in his original suit, claims Van Beuren unlawfully transferred certain monies from Grantland Rice Sportlights, Inc., into Van Beuren Corporation for the benefit of Van Beuren and the V.B. Corporation. Unlawful transfer of $13,345.65 is also claimed. Complaint asks the return of that and other monies." On December 9, *Film Daily* offered the next chapter in this thrilling adventure: "Judge Wasservogel yesterday handed down a decision denying the motion made by Grantland Rice, who sought action against Van Beuren for contempt."

Finally in early 1933, with Sportlights Inc.'s Jack Eaton and Van Beuren executive Frank Snell as court-appointed arbitrators, things were straightened out as well as they'd ever be straightened out. As reported in the February 4, 1933, *Film Daily*: "A settlement has been reached in the case of Grantland Rice against Van Beuren Corp. Phillips & Nizer represented Rice and Heermance & Hulbert were counsel for Van Beuren."

I've chosen to remain mum in the past several paragraphs to let the late-breaking news bulletins speak for themselves. Two personal observations might be worth mention, however. Throughout the litigation, Rice's new Paramount series was titled *Grantland Rice's Sports-eye View*, indicating that Van Beuren was holding fast to the original series title; it wasn't until June of 1933 that Rice legally regained the right to use the *Sportlights* label at Paramount. Under the guiding hand of faithful Jack Eaton, *Grantland Rice Sportlights* would roll along profitably until 1955—the year after Rice's death—earning an Academy Award for the 1943 one-reeler *Amphibious Fighters*.

Observation Number Two: At no time during the lawsuit did Rice ask for any extra remuneration beyond the money that Van Beuren had allegedly syphoned from Sportlights, Inc. and the court costs. I can think of a lot of people who would have demanded Van Beuren's entire fortune, to say nothing of his hide, but that wasn't Grantland Rice's style. As the great man himself once said, "Kindness in ourselves is the honey that blunts the sting of unkindness in others."

Chapter 7

Walter Futter's "Curiosities"

When Keith-Albee-Orpheum acquired a controlling interest in Joseph P. Kennedy's Film Booking Offices in May of 1928, the new owners promised a significant increase of moviemaking activity from FBO. In addition to an ambitious roster of features, FBO also bulked up their short-subject product, supplied in past seasons by independent comedy producers Larry Darmour and Joe Rock. Darmour committed himself to a second season of 12 two-reelers starring young Mickey Rooney as Fontaine Fox's scrappy comic-strip character Mickey "Himself" McGuire, and also launched three new comedy series of a dozen shorts each. Two were also comic-strip derivations: "Toots and Casper," with Thelma Hill and Bud Duncan as characters created by artist Jimmy Murphy; and "Barney Google," with Barney Hellum as Billy DeBeck's beloved bulbous-nosed hero. Darmour's third new series was "Racing Blood," based on the *Collier's* magazine short stories by H.C. Witwer and starring Al Cooke as a trouble-prone jockey. At first it was announced that Joe Rock would also come forth with his usual yearly quota of 26 two-reelers, but Rock had closed down his comedy units to concentrate on features. This left a gap in FBO's short-subject schedule that needed filling in a hurry.

We can't say for certain whether FBO or Keith-Albee-Orpheum's fair-haired boy Amedee Van Beuren first hatched the idea of acquiring *Walter Futter's Curiosities* once Futter's contract with Educational Pictures expired. But since both Van Beuren and Futter were headquartered in New York City, one could draw a logical conclusion. Whoever was responsible, FBO now had a short-subject property that cost very little but was guaranteed to clean up at the box office—and Van Beuren had staked his own claim in the bonanza with yet another producer's credit.

Born in Omaha, Nebraska, Walter Futter (1900–1958) cinched his first movie job at age 16 as an assistant film cutter. Rapidly working his way up to full editor, lab supervisor and negative checker, Futter held down all three duties at William Randolph Hearst's Cosmopolitan Pictures from 1920 to 1925. Upon leaving Hearst, Futter and his brother Fred set up Walter Futter Productions, which included an enormous stock-footage library called WAFilms. The Futter boys were not so much producers as accumulators, purchasing stock shots from a variety of active and defunct studios (including a huge cache of rare material from France's Gaumont Pictures) while also harvesting scraps of celluloid from cutting-room floors and unexposed reel ends; small wonder that Walter and Fred were known as "the junk men of filmdom." In addition to renting out his library footage, in 1926 Walter inaugurated a series of human interest one-reelers called *Curiosities*, initially released by Educational Pictures. The subject matter was gleaned from the Futters' voluminous film collection of "freaks and queer odds and ends from all corners of the world" (*Motion Picture News*, April 20, 1926)

Subtitled "The Movie Side Show," *Curiosities* trafficked in freaks of the animal world, persons who'd overcome physical handicaps in dramatic fashion (a one-armed architect, a blind lumberjack etc.), odd people in odd jobs, bizarre-looking plants and other natural phenomena, the strange customs and rituals of faraway lands, and so on. Whenever Futter lacked the necessary footage to chronicle his sideshow, he ran contests to solicit ideas and film clips from the public. If all this sounds familiar, Futter gleefully admitted that *Curiosities* was conceived in the same spirit as the long-running newspaper feature *Ripley's Believe It or Not*.

Since Futter was essentially his own financier, Educational Pictures shelled out only a fraction of what they spent on their other shorts series for the *Curiosities*. Undoubtedly this was the property's most attractive selling point when it joined the Van Beuren-FBO roster beginning with the September 16, 1928, release of "Curiosities No. 1," officially and somewhat brazenly titled *Believe It or Not*. Merritt Crawford was credited as editor-titler, replacing Futter's previous collaborator Beth Brown. Reviewing the inaugural FBO *Curiosities*, Raymond Ganley of *Motion Picture News* commented: "If all of them shape up as well as this does, then everything will be jake for all hands."

The subsequent six silent entries did their level best to "out-Barnum Barnum," to quote the FBO publicity flacks. *Pets* (1928), third in the series, featured an amiable middle-aged woman who'd domesticated a lion cub, and a dog peacefully frolicking on the grass with a baby cougar (the dog didn't look too thrilled at the prospect, but that's show biz). The highlight of "Curiosities No. 6" *Facts or Fancies* was a closeup, magnified "five million times," of the Lord's Prayer engraved on a head of the pin. Van Beuren promoted this one by sending out postcards with the Prayer engraved on a tiny corner slug, requiring an ordinary magnifying glass to read.

With Van Beuren converting all of his other properties to sound, Futter was expected to follow suit with *Curiosities*. An item by John S. Spargo in the August 10, 1928, *Exhibitors Trade Review* informed us "Walter Futter says that so far the sound reproducing companies have failed to get a true reproduction of the call of the JuJu fish to its mate for his 'Curiosities.'" It might be wise to take squibs like this with the proverbial grain of salt. From all appearances, Futter went no farther in transforming *Curiosities* into a talkie series than adding music and sound-effects tracks to his already completed silent shorts. And you can make anything sound like a JuJu fish if you try hard enough.

It is difficult to determine how many of the 18 *Curiosities* released by FBO's successor RKO between January and September of 1929 were all-talkie or all-silent. Only three of the shorts were acknowledged to have soundtracks by the trade papers, while information on the others is confusing and contradictory. The British Pathé Historical Collection website offers several *Curiosities* snippets featuring such esoterica as a petrified frog returning to life, legal cockfighting, the oldest living apple tree in America, the last town crier in Massachusetts, the winner of the Seattle balloon-blowing contest, and *ever* so much more—but the clips are all silent with subtitles. This could mean that these samples were lifted from the concurrently released silent versions of the talkie shorts, but until we can know for sure it's best not to leap to conclusions.

The earliest verified talkie *Curiosities* (Number 8) was *Seeing's Believing*, first shown in New York on January 2, 1929. The film included a musical score and an offscreen narrator—and to demonstrate that this last element was very much an innovation at the time, reviewers weren't sure how to describe the unseen commentator, with *Film Daily* calling him "a voice from a hidden speaker" and *Variety* using the appellation "lecturer." Of the four separate segments featured in *Seeing's Believing*, most critical attention was lavished upon the scenes of nearly naked Japanese women catching oysters and treating them with sand to obtain pearls. Another highlight took place in the sinister Palo Alto, California, mansion of the late Mrs. Winchester, reportedly haunted by the ghosts of people killed by her husband's rifles (yes, *that* Winchester). So labyrinthine was the mansion's interior that the narrator claimed it took the moving men seven weeks to escape the place—an example of how the visuals were "kiddingly described," as noted by *Film Daily*. More hilarity ensued in a segment filmed at a South American lake which purportedly had the power to grow hair: As the camera focused on an extremely hirsute dog, Mr. Narrator Man quipped, "This was a Mexican hairless in the morning."

Others in the series likewise poked fun at the filmed images. In *Faces* (No. 16), a study of diverse ethnic characteristics throughout the world, we are told at the beginning, "Your own face started like this," whereupon we see closeups of two stuffed crocodiles, a possum and an ape. *Here and There* (#17) is a real barrel of laughs, with pictures of Chinese loggers at work inspiring the comment that "eventually the timber will be made into mah-jong tiles," and shots of workmen salvaging Civil War–era resin from a Virginia river prompting the observation "Submerged for 68 years it hasn't changed a bit and may yet be of use to musicians, plumbers, acrobats and prize fighters." Only on rare occasions were the pictures allowed to speak for themselves, as in *Nifties* (#14), which showcases a Singapore seafood restaurant where customers fish for their own meals.

Judging by the showers of praise from reviewers and the number of bookings it received, the most popular of the sound *Curiosities* was the 18th in the 1928–29 season, *Follies of Fashion*. Using vintage clips that had previously done service in such silent *Curiosities* as 1926's *Rare-Bits*, the film compared the clothing fashions of 1904 to those of "today"—1929 today, that is. Thrown in for good measure were early-20th-century glimpses of traffic jams on old Fifth Avenue, with horses rearing at the sight of automobiles. Once again, reviewers cited "monologues spoken from the sidelines," suggesting that they were still casting about for a word like "narrator." Described by *Film Daily* as "a sure fire laugh getter," *Follies of Fashion* was first-run in New York's RKO theaters in March of 1929 before its general release on May 22.

The *Curiosities* were copyrighted by FBO rather than Van Beuren or Futter, with the exception of three 1929 releases: *Gleanings*, *Women Only*, and the still-extant (albeit in silent form) *Pedal Power*. These bore the copyright of Futter's own Record Films, a company set up for his planned entrée into feature films a few months hence. Curiously (if we may risk redundancy), no "Curiosities No. 25" was registered for copyright, which at first glance would indicate that only 25 of the contracted 26 shorts were delivered to FBO. But there might be an alternate solution to this mystery. In April of 1929 Van Beuren released a separate Walter Futter short, *The Swan*, billed onscreen as part of the "Walter Futter Overtures Series." Under the musical direction of Joseph Littau, this four-minute epic features the first talking-picture presentation of the title piece by Camille Saint-Saëns, which a printed prologue informs

Enticing advertisement for the first talking *Walter Futter's Curiosities, Seeing's Believing* (1929).

us was written in 1886 but not published until after the composer's death in 1921. The music is lovely, but the visuals of a swan and its mate gliding across a pond are sheer yawn bait (the film might have looked better in the original green-tinted prints). Possibly Walter Futter substituted *The Swan* for the 25th *Curiosities* in hopes of launching a new series for Van Beuren. Or possibly not.

Once his contract was fulfilled in mid–1929 Walter Futter parted company with Van Beuren, temporarily folding *Curiosities* in order to market a feature-length compilation of grisly World War I footage lensed by German cameramen; this was eventually released by Sono Art-World Wide as *Fighting for the Fatherland* (1929). Then in 1930 Van Beuren's *Topics of the Day* editor-director Charles D. McDonald (see Chapter 2) was hired away by Walter Futter and appointed president and general manager of Futter's operation.

Also in 1930 Futter struck pay dirt by organizing and editing a tangle of footage from Paul L. Hoefler's 1928 Serengeti expedition, filming a few linking scenes and phony animal attacks in California, then peddling the whole mélange to Columbia as the "documentary" feature *Africa Speaks*. This earned the producer a fat Columbia contract, allowing him to issue additional *Curiosities* until 1932. Thereafter he concentrated on feature films, among them a series of Hoot Gibson B-westerns for Futter's own Diversion Pictures, and the British-filmed Paul Robeson vehicle *Dark Sands* (1935). He also reissued a number of titles from other producers, including Sennett's *Tillie's Punctured Romance* and Von Stroheim's *Queen Kelly*. In the years just prior to his death Futter continued raking in bucks with his stock-footage library, adding a new enterprise to his resume by manufacturing and marketing inexpensive widescreen projection equipment and high-illumination lamps for small-town indoor and outdoor theaters.

I think we can safely conclude from all this that Walter Futter's association with Amedee Van Beuren was but a footnote in both their careers.

Chapter 8

Smitty and His Pals

Despite the crushing failure of the *Henry and Polly* two-reelers in 1927 (see Chapter 5), Van Beuren was back the following year with a new series of silent comedies for Pathé release. Having dealt almost exclusively in tried-and-true film properties when choosing his yearly short-subject lineup (Mr. & Mrs. Sidney Drew, *Topics of the Day*, Grantland Rice Sportlights, *Walter Futter's Curiosities*, et al.) Van Beuren surprised the industry by selecting a commodity that had never previously been filmed—though in common with past Van Beuren projects, this new addition was hardly an unknown quantity.

Debuting November 27, 1922, the Chicago *Tribune*-New York *Daily News* Syndicate comic strip *Smitty* was the brainchild of cartoonist Walter Berndt, inspired by his own youthful experiences as an office boy. The new strip was an outgrowth of Berndt's earlier, short-lived New York *World* effort *Bill the Office Boy*. After losing his *World* job, Berndt reported for work at the *Daily News*, where Captain Joseph Patterson signed the artist to revive *Bill the Office Boy*, at the same time demanding a new name for the 8-year-old protagonist. Berndt opened the Manhattan phone book, randomly selected "Smith" (hardly a remarkable feat) and came up with Smitty. Sporting a cap, bowtie and black shorts, the title character was employed in the office of Mr. Bailey, whose business was never specified. Little Augustus "Smitty" Smith made it his life's mission to confuse and outwit his boss, usually by wangling unauthorized days off right under Bailey's nose. The supporting cast included Smitty's parents and his prankish 4-year-old brother Herby, who as recalled by comic-strip historian Stephen Becker was drawn "wearing always the simplest of smocks, which bellied out before him like a spinnaker." *Smitty* was one part continuity strip, one part gag-a-day, with the characters growing older each year *a la* Frank King's *Gasoline Alley*, though Smitty leveled out at young adulthood long before the strip ended its run in 1974. The humor was warm, gentle and homey, just right for its target audience, and by 1928 *Smitty* enjoyed a following of 15,000,000 readers. In chronicling the history of *Smitty*, one otherwise thorough comic strip expert has written "There were no radio or film adaptations." He got that half right.

To hear Van Beuren tell it, bringing *Smitty* to the silver screen was all his doing. Here's a report in the May 26, 1928, *Exhibitors Herald-World*: "'Smitty,' the well-loved little cartoon character, and his pals will be the subject of these comedies, though the parts will be enacted by the pick of 'kid' actors. The newspapers running the cartoons will give full cooperation. This together with the fame of the comics, gives exceptional box office value.

"'Everyone loves the kids,' said Mr. Amedee J. Van Beuren, president of the

AyVeeBee Corporation of 1560 Broadway, the producers of these comedies, 'and in selecting Mr. Berndt's character "Smitty" for our new release, we do not merely believe we have hit upon a moneymaker for all concerned, but we take the privilege of making an absolute prediction that genuine success will crown our efforts. It has been the business of my organization since its inception to deal in motion pictures

Cartoonist Walter Berndt does his own ad copy for the upcoming Van Beuren *Smitty and His Pals* comedies, *Exhibitors Herald World*, 1928.

of laughter, fun and good humor. The best kid actors in the world will be our stars—youngsters who have appeal, pathos, humor and a bit of roguishness in their general appearance and actions. These pictures will be taken on the West Coast under the supervision of one of our executives and directed by one who not only thoroughly understands motion picture direction, but who also understands children. Stories will be selected with the utmost care. It is our purpose and expectation to turn out as fine a comedy release as is on the market.'"

Let us amend that ever so slightly. The producing firm for *Smitty and His Pals* was not AyVeeBee but instead the recently formed Van Beuren Enterprises. The principal backers of this operation, Keith-Albee-Orpheum, had previously instigated Van Beuren's benighted *Henry and Polly*, which began life as *The Jarr Family* in January of 1927 and was intended as the vanguard for K-A-O's entrée into active filmmaking upon its merger with PDC-Pathé. At the time, *Variety* noted that K-A-O planned two other short-comedy properties, one a "kid" series in the tradition of Hal Roach's *Our Gang*, the other based on an as-yet-undetermined comic strip. Several months later, the trades carried the news that Hal Roach had severed ties with longtime distributor Pathé and moved to MGM. Smarting over the loss of Roach's popular *Our Gang* comedies, Pathé needed a new kiddie-comedy series A.S.A.P. The distributor's other main comedy supplier Mack Sennett was also on the way out, having just signed with Educational Pictures, so that left only Van Beuren in Pathé's bullpen. The two previously announced K-A-O "kid" and "comic-strip" series were amalgamated into one, and that's how *Smitty and His Pals* was born.

Lest there be any doubt that Keith-Albee-Orpheum was the guiding hand behind this project, Van Beuren's choice as production supervisor for *Smitty and His Pals*—and by extension his entire West Coast branch—was theatrical agent Harry Weber, a well entrenched Keith-Albee functionary whose first agency had been formed in 1911 in partnership with E.F. Albee's son Reed. In his heyday, Weber booked such major acts as the Four Marx Brothers, Eva Tanguay, Julian Eltinge, Blossom Seeley & Benny Fields and Vincent Lopez for lengthy and fruitful runs on the Keith-Albee vaudeville circuit. Nor was he a stranger to the motion picture industry; he personally produced Eva Tanguay's first film, groomed stage comics Harry Langdon and Edgar Bergen for the big screen, and arranged vaudeville tours for such movie personalities as Theda Bara, Norman Kerry, Charles Ray, and former *Our Gang* members Mickey Daniels and Johnny Downs (Weber's links with Hollywood remained firm after his death in 1939; his daughter Muriel was the wife of film star Ray Milland). Weber also held executive positions with E.F. Albee's powerful and much-feared United Booking Office as well as National Vaudeville Artists, created by Albee to checkmate the Actors Equity union so that vaudeville entertainers "could be herded into an organization under the control of the vaudeville managers," according to *Equity* magazine. Consequently, Weber was not a universally beloved figure, with Groucho Marx speaking for most of his brethren by describing the agent with an obscenity that can't be reprinted in a chapter on kiddie films.

Personality flaws aside, Harry Weber should be recognized and praised for his genius in organizing performers into successful travelling units, developing and expanding the artists' appeal in specially prepared comedy sketches, one-act dramas and musical revues. It was his expertise as a "packager" that Weber brought to *Smitty and His Pals*. Setting up headquarters in Hollywood's Tec-Art Studios, Weber wasted no time assembling the "best and brightest" to work on the new two-reelers. Engaged as supervising director was Chicago native George Marshall, who after knocking around in a variety of jobs after his expulsion from college was hired by the Universal studio as an extra, stunt man and bit player, graduating to director in 1916. At first specializing in westerns starring Tom Mix and Neal Hart, Marshall turned to comedy under the tutelage of Mack Sennett. He joined the Fox Sunshine Comedy unit in 1924 and was appointed supervisor the following year. When Fox dismantled the unit in 1928 in favor of an all-Movietone talkie program, Marshall was hired by Harry Weber to shepherd the *Smitty* series, not only on the strength of the director's vast comic knowhow but also his successful wrangling of the kid-oriented *Fox Animals* series. James J. Tynan, previously employed by Mack Sennett to script the thematically similar *Smith Family* two-reelers, was appointed *Smitty*'s story editor, with seasoned gag men Clarence Hennecke, Milton Carruth and Bert Ennis on Tynan's staff. The series' cinematography was in the capable hands of James Meehan and William Williams, skilled veterans both.

Without the luxury of time to indulge in the Hal Roach procedure of casting and developing unknown children for Roach's *Our Gang*, Harry Weber selected his two principal child stars on the basis of their prior film work—and of course, their resemblance to their comic-strip counterparts. Born in in Nebraska in 1919, freckle-specked Donald Haines was visually a ideal Smitty, with an astonishingly expressive face to boot; his screen credits stretched back to 1926, mostly in comedies (Pathé publicists claimed that Haines was chosen from 1500 auditionees, but this seems unlikely given the short time-frame between casting and production). Similarly a perfect fit for Herby—especially when clad in the character's umbrella-shaped outfit—was Jackie Coombs, who according to his official biography was all of four years old. Coombs had already made a positive impression on filmgoers with his scene-snatching roles in MGM's *The Callahans and the Murphys* (1927) and especially Fox's *Straight Crooks* (1928). A third regular, introduced as Smitty's puppy-love interest, was little Vera, a character not seen in the original strip (Walter Berndt's nominal leading lady was Mr. Bailey's secretary Ginnie, whom the adult Smitty eventually married). Five-year-old Colorado girl Betty Jane Graham, who'd made her first film in 1927, was chosen for this part. Among the rest of Smitty's pals were several former and future *Our Gang* members: Eugene "Pineapple" Jackson, Artye Folz, Kendall "Breezy Brisbane" McComas and Georgie Ernest.

The adult regulars were recruited from the usual ranks of slapstick-comedy troupers. The first actor to portray Pa Smith was Joseph "Baldy" Belmont, who'd been on stage since the late 19th century and was an established film comedian and director as early as 1913, starring in his own short-subject series for Crystal-Universal before settling at Keystone. Befitting his professional nickname, Belmont wore a glaringly obvious bald wig (with tufts of hair on top and ridges on the side) to match the appearance of the comic-strip Pa. Maude Truax, familiar "fat lady" in many a short and feature of the teens and twenties, was 44 years old and slightly past her child-bearing years when selected to play Ma Smith. Both Belmont and Truax were active in films throughout the 1930s, both passing away in 1939. While in the *Smitty* shorts the hero's parents were more prominent than in the strip, the reverse was true for his boss Mr. Bailey, played by Roy Saeger, who disappeared after the first four films. The recurring cast was rounded out by a trained capuchin monkey named Jocko, who hadn't appeared in the strip and was probably penciled in because of the common movie-producer misapprehension that there's nothing funnier on earth than a scenery-wrecking, prop-smashing monkey. (I can think of at least one thing funnier: a crutch).

Though *Smitty and His Pals* was designed as a replacement for *Our Gang*, to their credit the filmmakers avoid imitating the venerable Hal Roach series, unlike such now-obscure ripoffs as *Hey Fellas* and *The McDougall Alley Kids*. At the same time, *Smitty* bears only a surface resemblance to its easygoing comic-strip counterpart, relying heavily on farce, slapstick and frenetic chases. Admittedly, this statement is made on the basis of the four known surviving *Smitty* comedies and a 37-second fragment of a fifth, but a lack of source material hasn't stopped me from expressing opinions up to now, so it won't here.

The one element that truly set this series apart from others in the kid-comedy genre was its reliance on celebrity guest stars, with the Pathé publicity team promising "big seat selling names in each comedy." Either by accident or design, this policy was carried over into Walter Berndt's comic strip, with well-known personalities showing up in caricature form from time to time. Long after the film series had ended, the *Smitty* strip featured a continuity wherein such notables as Babe Ruth, Douglas Fairbanks, Sr., and ex-president Calvin Coolidge provided readers with their genuine autographs.

Released October 7, 1928, the first *Smitty* two-reeler *No Picnic* featured an extended cameo appearance by boxing legend Jack Dempsey, who despite having lost the heavyweight title to Gene Tunney in the infamous "long count" match was still a strong drawing card. Speculation at the time that Dempsey's presence in *No Picnic* was arranged by his boxing-promoter friend Tex Rickard is easily refuted by noting that the Manassa Mauler had in 1928 been engaged for a vaudeville tour by none other than Harry Weber, who had previously arranged similar tours for such star athletes as Babe Ruth and Benny Leonard. Dempsey's face and name were prominently displayed in the advertising for *No Picnic*, and this as much as anything assured the success of the initial entry.

The film itself was no slouch either. Though the two-reeler is currently unavailable for reappraisal, we choose to take *Motion Picture News* critic Raymond Ganley at his word in his first-hand review of September 29, 1928:

> Sit up and take notice, exhibitors, for this "Smitty" comedy, the first of the series, is what the trade technically designates as a "wow." Anyone parading the rounds of the various distributors of short subjects does not come across comedies of the calibre of this one every day in the week. It is "extra good" and, if a consensus were in order on the ten best comedies released within the last six or ten months, "No Picnic" would easily be one of the leaders. It is exceptionally lively and "gaggy." The gags, be it known, are dispensed with amazing freedom and, although they are not all new, they are so numerous that they pep up the story and keep it humming. The story, by the way, is also nicely constructed and doesn't lag once.... Again we repeat this laugh two-reeler is considerably above the average short vehicle. Amedee J. Van Beuren, Harry Weber, George Marshall, James J. Tynan and everyone else ought to be congratulated because of its quality.

Plot details for *No Picnic* are sparse, though it can be assumed that much of the story took place at a fancy outdoor luncheon. The storyline of the second *Smitty* effort *No Sale* (1928) is more easily determined; all existing reports state that the humor was sparked by the Smiths' efforts to put their house up for sale, and that in one key scene a skunk appears "as himself." What makes the current unavailability of *No Sale* especially frustrating is the knowledge that its guest star (in the role of a prospective buyer) was fabled comedian Lloyd Hamilton, who though one of the biggest movie names of the 1920s is poorly represented today, thanks to a fire at the Educational Pictures warehouse which destroyed most of Hamilton's two-reelers. Happily, surviving examples like *The Movies* and *Move Along* (both 1925) permit modern film fans to see what all the shouting was about, with lovable Lloyd duck-walking his way into our hearts. As with Jack Dempsey, Hamilton was splashily advertised in the posters and trade ads for *No Sale*, prompting exhibitor complaints that the comedian was limited to approximately two minutes' screen time.

Only a fragment (restored by Robert Hoskins) remains of the third entry *Camping Out* (1928). What survives is the payoff to a gag sequence in which supporting player Otto Fries, playing a camp foreman, emerges from a tent with his face covered in welts, possibly bee stings. A prolific utility comic of the 1920s and 1930s who'd previously worked with director George Marshall at Fox, Otto Fries was not a big enough name to qualify as a guest star here, though the ads give him preferred billing. The actor is best known today for such talkie roles as the prison dentist in Laurel & Hardy's *Pardon Us* and the ship's purser who is given "one snoop-a too much" by erstwhile barbers Chico and Harpo Marx in *Monkey Business* (both 1931).

Otto Fries reappeared as a train conductor in *Smitty #4, All Aboard* (1929), listed at Internet Movie Database under its working title *No Vacation*. Betty Jane Graham took a break from the series for this one, with the role of Vera going to Helen Parrish, who grew up

Guest star Jack Dempsey (left) with Donald "Smitty" Haines from the first *Smitty and His Pals* comedy *No Picnic* (1928).

to be a secondary movie star of the 1940s—and incidentally, the wife of *You Bet Your Life* producer John Guedel. The film's plot got under way when Smitty's dad was separated from his two kids at a busy railroad station. With no prints currently available, all we can be sure of is that wackiness ensued during the subsequent train ride, mostly caused by Jocko the monk. "There is too much repetition in this one, and the comedy seems forced and mechanical," said *Film Daily* of *All Aboard*, though manager A.C. Digney of the Victoria Theater in Carberry, Manitoba told *Exhibitors Herald-World*, "This pleased everybody." Proving, I suppose, that one man's monk is another man's poison.

Fortunately a nearly complete print of the fifth two-reeler *Circus Time* (1929) has been preserved, proof incarnate that the firm directorial hand of George Marshall was at this juncture the series' greatest strength. The gags are well-paced and arise logically from the action (especially an adroitly lensed tightrope-walking bit involving Donald Haines and resident "fat boy" Tommy Hicks) and the whole enterprise benefits from Harry Weber's decision to hire a genuine circus—tents, sideshow, clowns, animals and all—for the premise-establishing first reel. Smitty's own backyard circus in Reel Two is also a treat, highlighted by the brief appearance of dwarf actor Billy Barty (who showed up in other *Smitty* films) as a pocket-sized strong man. Even the "see-it-coming-a-mile-away" climax in which Smitty mistakes a real lion for his pet dog is given a fresh coat of comic paint by the actors and the director. Best of all is the sparkling guest appearance by Sennett star Billy Bevan, playing a neighborhood cop who jovially enters into the spirit of things by helping the kids stage their circus, even performing an eccentric buck-and-wing to keep the spectators happy. As with *All Aboard*, critical reaction was mixed. Jan Olsen, manager of the Washington Theater in New Orleans, informed *Exhibitor's Herald-World*: "Kid stuff goes over big here. These comedies greatly aided by comic strip tie-up." But George J. Reddy of *Motion Picture News* didn't share Olsen's enthusiasm, expressing regret that *Circus Time* "does not perch on the same level as its predecessors. This film will unquestionably set the kids into an uproar, but it lack the appeal that others in the series have carried for both juvenile and adult audiences. Mention is made particularly of the titles in this number, which in most cases, are too sophisticated for the surrounding kid atmosphere." At least Mr. Reddy concurs with us that Billy Bevan "gets across some fun in the role of a cop."

The next entry *No Children* (1929) is hands down the best of the *Smitty* comedies presently available—and never mind that it's as far removed from the original comic strip as the planet Neptune. One imagines that director George Marshall and the crew threw up their hands and shouted, "To hell with format! To hell with characterization! Let's give 'em a good old fashioned laff riot!" This time out the Smith family is unable to get a room in a hotel because of a strict "no children" policy. There's nothing else for it but to come up with a clever subterfuge. Ma and Pa Smith pretend to be vaudevillians, with Pa as a ventriloquist and Smitty and Herby as his dummies. Every time the landlord approaches, the kids automatically freeze in position, no matter what position they happen to be in at the time, and Pa does all the talking through clenched teeth. There's a sight gag a second in this roarfest, culminating in a wild chase around the hotel and up and down a laundry chute. Whatever plot is still left at the finish is resolved by the *deux ex machina* appearance of guest star William Desmond, an extremely popular action-movie hero of the time—and incidentally, the

Tie-in merchandising from the exhibitors' pressbook for Van Beuren's *Smitty and His Pals* series.

main attraction of yet another recent vaudeville tour arranged by Harry Weber. Contributing to the hilarity are silent-comedy stalwarts George Ovey and Billy Franey, the latter soon to make a significant return appearance in the series. Long believed lost, *No Children* has been restored through funding from the Library of Congress. The film made its first public appearance in over 80 years at the 2011 Slapsticon, where it brought down the house.

After the completion of *No Children* Harry Weber made a sweeping change in the *Smitty* unit at Tec-Art Studios, dismissing everyone on the production crew except story editor James J. Tynan. No details are available as to why George Marshall was let go, though one can't help but notice that Marshall would not have another directorial credit until he took over RKO's *Nick and Tony* two-reel comedy series in 1930. He went on to direct shorts for Hal Roach and Vitaphone, helming Laurel & Hardy and ZaSu Pitts-Thelma Todd at the former studio and the star-studded Bobby Jones golf-instruction reels at the latter. Thereafter Marshall focused exclusively on features, turning out such noteworthy efforts as *You Can't Cheat an Honest Man* (1939), *Destry Rides Again* (1939), *Murder He Says* (1945), *The Blue Dahlia* (1946), *The Perils of Pauline* (1947) and *Houdini* (1953), plus several of the better Bob Hope and Glenn Ford vehicles. In 1962 he collaborated with John Ford and Henry Hathaway on the direction of the Cinerama epic *How the West Was Won* (1962). Active into his eighties, he directed episodes of such TV series as *Here's Lucy* and *The Odd Couple* right up to his retirement in 1972, three years before his death. To sum up, *Smitty* neither helped nor harmed Marshall's career, but he did the series an awful lot of good.

And speaking of awful, Marshall's replacement on *Smitty* was Harry Edwards, a prolific but undistinguished comedy director whose career began at Universal in 1914. Edwards went on to direct at Nestor and its successor Christie, megging comedy shorts that tended to be only as good as their stars. At Sennett in the 1920s he formed a tight professional and personal relationship with Harry Langdon, moving with Harry to First National where Edwards helmed the baby-faced comedian's first starring feature *Tramp Tramp Tramp* (1926); he also reportedly lent assistance to Langdon's subsequent (and unsuccessful) self-directed films. Back at Sennett in 1927 he directed the *Handy Andy* two-reelers with Johnny Burke, but was sacked after a single season. By this time Edwards was developing a reputation for unreliability, habitually going over budget and drinking his meals. But he was inexpensive and available, so Harry Weber hired him to direct the final four *Smitty* comedies when production resumed in October 1928.

Watch My Smoke (1929) was the first *Smitty* bearing the mark of Harry Edwards. Peruse this critique from *Motion Picture News* and recall that reviewer Raymond Ganley was an early champion of *Smitty*: "The series raised a pretty fine standard when 'No Picnic,' its first release, appeared, but seems to have deteriorated since then." The plot finds Smitty and his cohorts forming their own fire department, whereupon a rival gang stages a phony conflagration to make a fool of our hero. On this occasion the guest star was musclebound Bull Montana, an Italian-born former wrestler who got a lot of comic mileage in the 1920s from his mashed-in face, cauliflower ears and put-on aristocratic airs. What Signor Montana played in *Watch My Smoke* is anybody's guess, since the film is now believed to be lost.

At least one print of *Tomato Omelette* (1929) is still very much with us, though you may not be once you see it. This time Smitty gets the idea to form a junior army from tall-tale-spinning Soldier's Home resident Cpl. Winterbottom, played by guest star Richard Carle (remembered as the genially mad professor in the 1928 Laurel & Hardy comedy *Habeas Corpus*). The film exhumes the moldy kiddie-comedy premise of staging a phony war in a vacant lot, with rotten tomatoes and other vegetables as weapons of mess destruction. *Motion Picture News*' Raymond Ganley was by now rapidly losing his patience with the series: "The fun is standardized and all the comedy does is live up to the old pattern of juvenile comedy reels. Its movement is labored and certainly not spontaneous and its plot slackens so much that they've had to drag in one of those splattering, untidy fights as a finale."

The ancient-comedy-routine file had not yet been emptied when the next episode, *Puckered Success* (1929), came into view. Operating a small refreshment stand outside a high-society bazaar, Smitty and company accidentally serve up punch spiked with alum, causing everyone to speak through pursed lips—a gag that had whiskers even in 1929. Mary Carr, matronly leading lady of the classic mother-love tearjerker *Over the Hill* (1921), appeared as herself, supported by perennial Laurel & Hardy foil James Finlayson as "Mayor McSnooty." Replacing Baldy Belmont as Pa Smith was former *Circus Time* guest artist Billy Bevan.

Bevan in turn was replaced as Pa by Billy Franey, last seen in *No Children*, for the final *Smitty* comedy *Uncle's Visit* (1929). The titular uncle is a gouty old Australian millionaire who decides to visit his American relatives, the Smiths. Worried that the "old sand-crab," who allegedly hates children, will be sore annoyed by the behavior of Smitty and Herby, Ma and Pa bundle the kids off to a cheerless boarding school, there to remain until Uncle Theodore leaves. Herby manages to sneak his pet monkey Jocko into the school, and the resultant chaos allows the kids to escape into the busy downtown traffic, where they are nearly run over by a chauffeured limo bearing none other than Uncle Theodore. Not recognizing the man—and vice versa—the kids hitch a ride and befriend the golden-hearted old coot, all the while complaining about the horrible relative who's about to descend upon them. Once they're back home, Uncle reveals his identity and everyone shares a good laugh.

Uncle's Visit still exists in a one-reel abridgement, allowing us to state emphatically that the film will never be hailed as an unsung comedy classic. Most of the gags are arbitrary and forced, while a few potentially good ideas—notably Smitty's home-made airplane "The Spirit of Nitre"—go nowhere. More distressing for modern viewers are the film's ham-handed "gay" jokes, offensive even by 1929 standards. Seven-year-old Jackie Searl, soon to make a name for himself as the talkies' quintessential obnoxious brat, is here cast as stereotypical "pansy" Cecil. To remove all doubt as to his orientation, Cecil wears frilly clothing, sniffs roses and plays with dolls. When asked by his teacher what he wants to be when he when grows up, Cecil puts hand on hip and smirks, "A manicure." Good grief.

The one salvation of *Uncle's Visit* is the wonderfully overplayed performance of guest star Theodore Roberts. A longtime member of Cecil B. DeMille's stock company, Roberts is perhaps best known for his portrayal of Moses in DeMille's 1923 version of *The Ten Commandments*. Making a meal of his limited screen time in *Uncle's Visit*, the actor richly deserved the glowing notices he received from reviewers and exhibitors. Admittedly, however, some of these accolades were written out of sentiment: Theodore Roberts died on December 14, 1928, seven months before the release of *Uncle's Visit*.

With this last withering volley from the *Smitty* series, critic Raymond Ganley threw in the towel: "This 'Smitty' comedy is like the little girl of whom it was written 'when she was good, she was very, very good, but when she was bad she was horrid.' When the first 'Smitty' appeared it looked as if a lively and clever kid series had made its bow. However, succeeding comedies did not keep up to the standard set by the first and they have degenerated into a strange mixture of juvenile entertainment. Horrid certainly describes the direction of 'Uncle's Visit.' It jumps all over the landscape and continuity is sadly lacking. It's a shrunken affair when it comes to measuring off its laugh-getting tendencies." There it is, folks. "Horrid certainly describes the direction." Thank you, Harry Edwards.

Incredibly, this was not the end of Edwards' career. After laying waste to *Smitty* he joined the Universal short-comedy unit, where he survived until 1931; then it was off to Educational Pictures, wearing out his welcome in 1936. Edwards hadn't directed a film for six years when, at the insistence of his old friend Harry Langdon, he was hired by Jules White for the Columbia Pictures comedy shorts. His drinking and sloppy work habits were now so beyond control that otherwise pliable Columbia comedians like the Three Stooges and Vera Vague refused to work with him. Much to the relief of everyone Harry Edwards retired in 1946, passing away six years later at age 65.

Though *Smitty and His Pals* had effectively shot its wad after 10 comedies, Amedee Van Beuren announced plans to continue the series with sound during the 1929–30 season. These plans went no farther than adding a music and sound-effects track to *Uncle's Visit*, but were foredoomed in any event. Never one to focus on a single showbiz job for any length of time, producer Harry Weber left Van Beuren in 1929 to form the last of his many talent agencies, Weber-Simon. As for the youthful stars of *Smitty and His Pals*, Jackie "Herbie" Coombs, acknowledged by fans and reviewers as the most appealing member of the cast, curiously dropped out of movies—and out of sight—after one additional screen credit in 1934. Betty Jane Graham made her talkie bow as "Little Miss Vitaphone" in a 1930 all-star short celebrating Warner Bros.' silver anniversary; she then settled into bit roles, some at MGM, where she was reportedly the best friend of Judy Garland. After a long absence, Graham made one last unbilled appearance in Howard Hawks' *El Dorado* (1966). Her credits are often confused with those of fashion model Betty Jane Graham, who among a handful of small movie roles appeared as herself in the 1944 musical *Cover Girl*.

Faring the best of the three *Smitty* stars, at least professionally, was Smitty himself, Donald Haines. In 1929 he joined Roach's *Our Gang*, making a near-instant impression as "Speck," Jackie Cooper's bloodthirsty rival for the affections of Mary Ann Jackson in *The First Seven Years* (1930). The onscreen "feud" between Haines and Cooper would be sustained through such later features as *Skippy* (1931), *When a Feller Needs a Friend* (1932) and, to a lesser degree, *Seventeen* (1940). Haines also showed up in another long-running kid's series, enacting "Katink" in Larry Darmour's *Mickey McGuire* talkies starring Mickey Rooney. As an adult, Donald played Skinny (originally Pee-Wee) in seven of Monogram's *East Side Kids* comedy features, costarring opposite Leo Gorcey, Huntz Hall and Bobby Jordan. His film career cut short by World War II, Haines joined the Army Air Force as an aviation cadet, eventually achieving the rank of second lieutenant. Donald Haines was killed in action in 1943 while serving in North Africa; he was three months short of his 24th birthday.

Chapter 9

The Song Sketches

Song Sketches was Amedee Van Beuren's first 100 percent-all-talkie film series, with no silent episodes nor any re-edited silent versions. In the absence of contradictory evidence, it can be stated that it was also Van Beuren's first "original" series in that it did not star an established screen personality (*vide* Mr. and Mrs. Sidney Drew) and was not derived from a pretested movie property (*Aesop's Fables, Topics of the Day, Grantland Rice Sportlights*). Whether or not Van Beuren came up with the idea himself is worthy of speculation; at any rate, *Song Sketches* was designed to show off the RCA Photophone sound-on-film system used by the producer's distributor Pathé, and the series' principal singing star was then being heard over RCA's radio-network subsidiary NBC.

Predicting that the new *Song Sketches* "are certain to sweep into popularity," the distributor's house organ *Pathé Sun* devoted generous print space to the upcoming series in its issue of October 19, 1929:

> The six one-reel releases will dramatize songs and overtures that are internationally famous. Now and then features are brought to the screen based on plays, books or aspects of history and there is a great hullaballoo about the ready-made publicity. Now Pathé comes along with a series woven around the songs that have been sung time and time again by millions and are almost as well known as the ABC's.
>
> Where a popular song has been heard or sung by a million persons, the classic numbers selected by the Van Beuren Corporation have been heard or sung by a hundred million.

[Translation: They're mostly public domain tunes that won't cost us a dime.]

> Add to these numbers, highly dramatized settings and local color, prominent vocalists in the featured roles, musical accompaniment and the Van Beuren manner of presentation and you have units of class and distinction that will tone up any program in the land.
>
> In announcing the first of their latest sound featurettes, the Van Beuren Corporation believe that they have selected one of the most popular and universally loved songs, Rudyard Kipling's "Mandalay." Set to music by Oley Speaks it will usher in these new short reels and be the fore-runner of a series of popular song sketches.

Enlisted to star in the initial entry was James Stanley, popular Victor recording artist and lead singer on NBC's Sunday-night musical series *The Davey Hour*, sponsored by the Davey Tree Expert Company (would I lie to you?). Stanley fronted a male quartet, the other members identified in *What's on the Air* magazine as Henry Shope, Judson House and Walter Preston, who may very well have appeared alongside the star in the inaugural *Song Sketches* (only Stanley is billed). Again, the *Pathé Sun*: "Mr. Stanley was selected by Amedee J. Van Beuren, President of the Van Beuren Corporation, after a score or more baritones had been heard in their rendition of [the] famous song. 'It is hardly an exaggeration to say that Mr. Stanley's popular baritone voice is one of the most perfect I have ever heard over the air or by recording,' said Mr. Van Beuren, 'and I have been told by many who have heard our song sketch "Mandalay" in preview that it is one of the outstanding pieces of recording done by the RCA Photophone Studio."' While there's no denying that in Van Beuren's words "Mr. Stanley's voice is absolutely gorgeous," as a screen presence the balding, middle-aged baritone more closely resembles an investment banker than a movie star. Wisely, the *Song Sketches* never cast Stanley as a romantic lead.

For the first one-reeler *Mandalay* (copyrighted as *On the Road to Mandalay*) and all subsequent *Song Sketches*, the direction was in the hands of Oscar Lund—not to be confused with famed Swedish filmmaker Oscar A.C. Lund—whose previous credits are hard to find despite Van Beuren's assurances that Lund was a "pioneer." (One envisions him directing in a Davy Crockett cap). The lush background music was provided by Frank Black and his orchestra, heard to excellent advantage in the earlier *Grantland Rice Sportlight* episode *Crystal Champions* (see Chapter 6). Gene Rodemich handled synchronization and co-orchestrated the music with Black.

This dramatic adaptation of "Mandalay" was according to the opening credits "visualized by Grantland Rice," moonlighting from his regular duties on *Sportlights*. The film is set in an English pub, where the cockney barmaid welcomes back a group of veteran British "tommies" who have just finished a long stretch of duty in India and Burma. The boisterous boyos express gratitude that they've made it home in one piece and vow never to return to the sunny climes of the East. Enter a uniformed "freshie" who is thrilled over the prospect of his imminent mobilization to the Burmese capital of Mandalay. The others laugh derisively and invite their leader Jimmy (Stanley) to tell the rookie the awful truth about the far-off colonies. Jimmy obliges by singing all three verses of "Mandalay," where "the old flotilla lay" and "the flying fishes play," with the other tommies joining in on each chorus. The song has the opposite of its intended effect: Once Jimmy is finished with his progressively sentimental ballad, he and his comrades decide to re-enlist for another tour of duty "where the dawn comes up like thunder," bidding farewell to the barmaid and marching forth once more on the Road to Mandalay.

Ahead of its official general release date of January 5, 1930, *Mandalay* was screened at New York's Cohan Theatre on December 9, 1929, in support of the documentary feature *Hunting Tigers in India*. Having a dog (if not a tiger) in this hunt, *Pathé Sun* covered this auspicious event:

> Before a most distinguished and critical first night audience at the George M. Cohan Theatre ... the first Song Sketch "Mandalay" was shown preceding the feature picture, and was received with an ovation and tremendous applause as James Stanley, the noted baritone, brought the strains of this world beloved melody set to Rudyard Kipling's immortal poem to a close.
>
> Not only did this audience signify their approval of "Mandalay" at its finish, but throughout the showing of this picture Mr. Stanley was applauded for his excellent rendition of the respective verses.
>
> Motion picture critics representing trade and daily papers were unanimous in their complimentary criticism of "Mandalay."

Well, not entirely unanimous. Jaded *Motion Picture News* found the one-reeler "overdrawn" and "tiresome," adding, "It won't create any excitement. The famous song is submitted to a pictorial treatment as concocted by Grantland Rice, but as a producer with imagination—as witnessed herewith—Rice does much better with 'Sportlights.' ... Stanley's voice is nicely modulated and the recording job is good, but there the number ends." Other reviews were more encouraging, however, with most of the bouquets going to James Stanley's "pleasing rendition" and "fine baritone." *Mandalay* enjoyed a highly successful initial run in an abundance of theater chains throughout the nation, forcing Pathé to strike additional prints. Tom North, sales rep for Van Beuren, exulted to the trade press that copies of the film were selling "like good beer."

Good beer, however, has a tendency to go stale over time, and surviving prints of *Mandalay* demonstrate how dramatically critical standards have changed in the past 90 years. The short doesn't come off much better than the dozens of other musical reels flooding the marketplace in the early-talkie years, though in fairness the comparative novelty of bookending a popular song with a dramatic sketch places the film a notch above all those stagnant, unimaginative *Vitaphone Varieties* shorts spewed out by Warner Bros. The production values are plain and primitive; virtually the entire short is photographed from a single angle, with three camera setups and no close shots. The film's rare stylistic touches are crammed into three brief flashbacks, depicting a slinky Eurasian woman seductively smoking a cigarette in a dimly lit Mandalayan cabaret. As for James Stanley, his splendid singing just barely compensates for his nonexistent acting skills: Stiff as a starched collar throughout, he performs most of the ballad sitting rigidly in a chair, staring forward as if waiting to be embalmed. When he finally stands up for the third verse, one expects Colin Clive to pop out of the woodwork and exclaim, "It's alive! *Alive!!!*"

Filmed at the same time as *Mandalay* in the same New York Photophone facilities, the second *Song Sketches* entry *The Trumpeter* (1930) also starred James Stanley, performing another of what *Pathé Sun* described as "semi-classical ballads." This time the featured number was (what else?) "The Trumpeter," written in 1904 by J. Airlie Dix and John Francis Barron, the latter a British career soldier. All but forgotten today, "The Trumpeter" was in its time a very popular concert piece, gaining renewed popularity during and after World War I with its twin themes of comradeship in battle and the celestial rewards for those laying down their lives for their country. There are four verses with a dramatic and poignant key change in Verse Three, tailor-made for a throbbing baritone like James Stanley. Properly performed, "The Trumpeter" runs about four minutes; the film of the same name, again "visualized" by Grantland Rice, ran seven minutes, with Stanley dressed in the uniform of an AEF trooper, standing in a set representing an empty battlefield with a quartet of silhouetted actors posed in tableaux illustrating each verse. The film had even less "production" than *Mandalay*, with most of the running time consumed by stock footage from wartime newsreels and Hollywood reenactments of the Great War.

In its salutary pre-release review of December 21, 1929, *Exhibitors Herald World* rated *The Trumpeter* even higher than *Mandalay*, actually congratulating the filmmakers for the miserly budget: "The whole number is well done and, as far as could be seen, with little outlay. And that's a sensible way to make pictures." *Variety* was also impressed, complimenting the "decidedly novel way of providing a batch of government war film with continuity." In contrast, *Film Daily* looked askance at this gimmick: "A flock of stock and studio war shots tied up with James Stanley, vocalist, comprise this subject, which is mild entertainment."

James Stanley did not appear in the next two *Song Sketches*, which took a different approach to their musical material. Both *Songs of Mother* (1930) and *Love's Memories* (1930) starred handsome 30-year-old tenor Frank Luther, a former lay minister whose radio repertoire ranged from country-western ditties to big-band tunes, and who later produced the best-selling original cast album for the evergreen off-Broadway musical *The Fantasticks*. Luther's *Song Sketches* featured a variety of songs rather than a single ballad, though the dramatizations were retained.

In *Songs of Mother* Luther is seated at a piano while his angelic little children, reciting their lines "like a painfully memorized kindergarten lesson" (according to *Variety*), prompt him to warble as many mother-love songs as he can remember. While Luther soulfully trills such lugubrious pieces as "Songs My Mother Taught Me," "Oh Dry Those Tears," "Tommy Boy" and "Rock-a-Bye," we flash back to images of his dear old mama, played by contralto Elizabeth Lenox, garbed in anachronistic costumes suggesting that the youthful Mr. Luther is 90 years old if he's a day. Officially released February 2, 1930, *Songs of Mother* was held back from full national distribution so that it could be showcased as a "special" for Mother's Day Week in May, issued in tandem with the Pathé musical one-reeler *Home Sweet Home*. This cunning strategy paid off in choice bookings, excellent business and an endorsement from Anna Jarvis, who'd created Mother's Day in 1908. "I had the extreme pleasure of seeing your Song Sketch, 'Songs of Mother,' which your representative Mr. Klang so kindly arranged to show to me," Jarvis wrote in a personal letter to Amedee Van Beuren. "As the founder of 'Mother's Day' I am gratified to know that you have carried to the sound screen to millions of people in the United States the true spirit of 'Mother's Day' which caused the inspiration for my original suggestion."

Sentiment was tamped down a bit for *Love's Memories*, wherein Frank Luther's musical recollections of the great love of his life, played by soprano Lois Bennett, are bookended by the inane comments of his current dumb-dora sweetie, portrayed by future B-picture fixture Evalyn Knapp. *Film Daily* for one didn't appreciate these attempts at humor, grumbling that *Love's Memories* was "not up to the standard of the earlier Van Beuren Song Sketches. This one is burdened with some poor attempts at comedy and with some pretty bad dialogue, much of it with no point to it." Without mentioning Evalyn Knapp by name, *Motion Picture Daily* pinpointed what was regarded as the film's biggest drawback: "A sappy blonde throws cold water on what might have been ace-high entertainment. Her over-acting reaches the pinnacle of distaste." As with *Songs of Mother*, Frank Luther garnered the best reviews for his vocalizing of such tender ballads as "Auf Wiedersehen" and "Good-bye," while ample mention was made of the upgraded production values, with seven separate sets utilized in the ten-minute film.

It was back to penny-pinching for the final two *Song Sketches*, with James Stanley returning for both. To conserve time and money, director Oscar Lund and his star hitched a ride on *Grantland Rice Sportlights* producer Jack Eaton's RCA Photophone soundtrack and headed to Florida, where the next few *Sportlights* were scheduled for production. Borrowing Eaton's technicians, Lund lensed *Deep South* and *Voice of the Sea* (working title: *Homing*) in and around Jacksonville, Florida, lensing *Deep South* entirely out-of-doors in arboreal settings representing Kentucky, and shooting *Voice of the Sea* in locations resembling the coast of New England (adding stock shots of Anastasia, Ireland back in the New York editing room).

The scenario for *Deep South* was adapted by Grantland Rice from his own poem, a mood piece in which he hears the "roses calling" and sees the "mossed oak sway and stir" as he conjures up memories of his beloved Dixie. The plot can be described as *Mandalay* in reverse: Instead of the characters vowing to stay put in England only to be lured back to the excitement of the East, the father-and-daughter protagonists of *Deep South* are on the verge of moving North, electing at the last minute to remain below the Mason-Dixon line. James Stanley, playing the patriarch of a lavish plantation, has loosened up a bit acting-wise since *Mandalay*, while Lois Bennett as his daughter is beautiful and in excellent voice and that's where I'll leave it. Overstocked with such nostalgic (and royalty-free) songs as "My Old Kentucky Home" and "Carry Me Back to Old Virginia," not to mention the title poem as set to music by orchestrators Frank Black and Gene Rodemich, this slowly paced one-reeler is something of a Southern-fried sauna, briefly shaken from its cornpone lethargy with a lively soft-shoe shuffle performed by a gifted (and uncredited) black hoofer.

James Stanley was felicitously cast as an old Scotch tar in *Song Sketches'* swan song *Voice of the Sea* (1930), in which he and his screen wife, played by contralto Margaret Olson, perform beloved maritime ballads at the prodding of a group of chattering rugrats—likely the same little pests who intruded on *Songs of Mother*. The three songs herein include the ever-popular "When the Bells of the Lighthouse Ring Ding Dong," heard during the impressionistic staging of a romantic lighthouse rendezvous (singled out by reviewers as the film's highlight).

Once the six *Song Sketches* had run their course the series lapsed into instant obscurity, save for Pathé's revival of *The Trumpeter* for a November 1930 presentation to commemorate Armistice Day. It isn't clear why the series was halted after a single season, though the moviegoing public's ever-mounting weariness with musicals (resulting in wholesale cutting of songs from feature films like *Fifty Million Frenchmen* and *Reaching for the Moon*) may have been a contributing factor. Van Beuren would not re-enter the musical field until 1933, and then only with a gallery of star names and films with actual plotlines.

Chapter 10

The Vagabond Adventures

Yielding 59 one-reeler entries over a five-year period, *Vagabond Adventures* enjoyed the longest run of any "all-talkie" Van Beuren series, and after *Aesop's Fables, Topics of the Day* and *Grantland Rice Sportlights* was the fourth most prolific series in the studio's history. As was the case with those other properties, Amedee Van Beuren himself had precious little input in the creation of *Vagabond Adventures*, though he certainly reaped the benefits of the series' success.

Ever since the dawn of motion pictures there have been travelogues—tens of thousands of them. Relatively inexpensive to produce and of immense appeal to filmgoers who seldom ventured outside their own countries (not to mention their own home towns), the travelogue was a fixture of movie-house programs on both sides of the talkie revolution. Which is not to say that most of these "scenics" (as they were called in the trade papers) were in any way different from one another, nor that the bulk of them were particularly good. Monotony and mediocrity were but two of the genre's shortcomings: The third, and most injurious, was the tendency of most travelogue producers to focus on geography, architecture and unusual animal life while all but ignoring the human element. Even the most successful and enduring travelogue series of Hollywood's Golden Age, James FitzPatrick's *Traveltalks* (distributed by MGM for nearly two decades) suffered from the sterility of offering viewers pretty pictures of buildings, mountains, foliage and strange creatures while only rarely discussing (or even showing) the people who inhabited these colorful lands.

This is one accusation that could never be leveled against *Vagabond Adventures*, which from its inception lavished generous screen time on the human population at work and play in their native countries, ever striving to place these people in context with their exotic surroundings and ancient cultures. Such editorial devices as switching from a long shot of a crowded foreign marketplace to a medium closeup of a small child blissfully playing with a newly-purchased toy spoke more eloquently about the universality of mankind than any flowery subtitle or offscreen narration. Nor was *Vagabond Adventures* ever guilty of the static, locked-down camerawork that usually inflicted the *Traveltalks* and their ilk. Even when the Van Beuren series used footage that had been purchased from other producers, the editors selected the photography that exhibited the greatest amount of movement and the best and most creative camera angles.

Credit for this cinematic fluidity and concentration on bustling humanity rather than inanimate objects must be given to the three men responsible for bringing *Vagabond Adventures* to life, beginning with the man who continued to bill himself "The Vagabond Adventurer" long after he left the series. Born into a London theatrical family in 1872, Tom Terriss spent his formative years working his way throughout the British Empire as a seaman, sheep farmer, and stock exchange clerk, pausing long enough to graduate from Oxford and to organize a popular Hawaiian dance band. Making his acting debut at age 18 as Osric in *Hamlet*, Terriss spent several seasons with the Theatre Royal at Drury Lane. Once he'd established himself he began to specialize in stage and film adaptations of Charles Dickens, making the role of Ebenezer Scrooge his personal property. Terriss' American film career began in 1913, first as an actor (he can be seen as Chaplin's sleek romantic rival in 1919's *Sunnyside*) and then as producer-director for a vast array of New York and Hollywood studios. Continuing his peripatetic globetrotting whenever he had the chance, Terriss was among those present at the discovery of the tomb of Egyptian king Tutankhamen in 1922, and was never too shy to capitalize on the fact that he was one of but four survivors of the "King Tut curse" that knocked off twelve members of the expedition within seven years. By 1927 his trippingly theatrical tones could be heard on Los Angeles radio station KFI, spinning heavily romanticized yarns about his world travels.

While employed as a film director at Tiffany-Stahl Productions in 1929, Terriss hatched the idea for a series of "scenics" titled *Vagabond Adventures*. Using his radio broadcasts to test-market the concept before a vast West Coast audience, Terriss's labors were rewarded with overwhelmingly positive listener response. This did not go unnoticed by Alfred T. Mannon, the 32-year-old head of Hollywood's Tec-Art studio, home base for both Tiffany-Stahl and Van Beuren's *Topics of the Day* talkies. At the time, Mannon was Amedee Van Beuren's West Coast representative, having replaced Harry Weber (see Chapter 8) in early 1929. Mannon had also recently entered into a creative partnership with veteran director Elmer Clifton, who'd been in the movie industry since 1907.

A former assistant director to D.W. Griffith, Elmer Clifton's many solo directorial credits included the 1922 film version of Ernest Truex's Broadway hit *Six Cylinder Love* (see Chapter 3) and the 1923 seafaring epic *Down to the Sea in Ships*, in which the director gave future silent superstar Clara Bow her first big break. Clifton's career suffered a serious setback in 1923 when actress Martha Mansfield burned to death in a freak accident on the set of *The Warrens of Virginia*. Though the director was absolved of any responsibility for the tragedy he found himself grey-listed in the industry, unable to secure any worthwhile projects. Accepting whatever was offered him for the next several years, Clifton regained some of his lost stature with a pair of popular historical shorts, *Manchu Love* and *Light of India* (both 1929), filmed in color and produced independently through the facilities of Tec-Art. In collaboration with studio boss Alfred T. Mannon, Clifton went on to supervise *The Americans Come* (1930), a highly regarded patriotic short produced by Joseph M. Schenck for United Artists.

The Mannon–Clifton team's next project was Tom Terriss' *Vagabond Adventures*, and though they still shared a joint "supervisor" credit it didn't take much cogitation to figure out that Mannon functioned as producer while Clifton served as director. A more ideal choice could not have been made: In an article for *American Cinematographer* in 1932, Clifton laid out his theories on making "scenics," which were in perfect harmony with the *Vagabond Adventures* format: "[T]he pictures which our audience 'eats up' are those wherein the scenic and the commonplace are so blended that they create an illusion of real, living, breathing people set down in the midst of their proper surroundings, on whom the audience has sneaked up and is getting a forbidden glimpse at first hand." He added that interesting subjects capable of enlightening the audience were all around us, not just overseas: "All you have to do is to find out how to tell these things so that the audience will never smell the castor oil—will never suspect that it is being educated against its will."

But wait! The material used in the first batch of *Vagabond Adventures* was harvested from films that Tom Terriss himself photographed during the first of two world tours in 1930. So technically speaking, Terriss, and not Elmer Clifton, was the series' director, exactly as he billed himself onscreen. Right? Well, practically right. We haven't yet mentioned the one aspect of the series that truly set it apart from other travelogues of the era. In each of the first 15 *Vagabond Adventures*, the travel footage was linked together by a storyline in which Terriss would describe a nail-biting adventure he'd had on location. It hardly mattered that most if not all of these adventures were figments of Tom Terriss' animation: The abundance of "real" images from the four corners of the world, coupled with Terriss' dramatic narration, encouraged audiences to willingly suspend disbelief. And here's where Elmer Clifton really earned his money: The portions of the fanciful storylines that could not be acted out on location were filmed under Clifton's direction at Tec-Art in California, using professional actors. It wasn't really cheating,

Tom Terriss as Ebenezer Scrooge in *Film Daily Yearbook*, 1931, just after Terris inaugurated Van Beuren's *Vagabond Adventures.*

you understand—merely a bit of colorful embroidering to inject some extra punch into the proceedings.

Naturally, the first person to whom Alfred Mannon shopped *Vagabond Adventures* was his nominal boss Amedee Van Beuren. He in turn secured distribution through Pathé (and later RKO), initially releasing the films once every two weeks before settling upon a once-per-month schedule. Having disbanded his publicity department in early 1930, Van Beuren relied upon Pathé to advertise the series, and upon Terriss to promote the films on his NBC network radio broadcasts. Van Beuren also pumped his own money into the project, hiring a camera crew and sound truck to accompany Terriss on his second world tour. In a puff piece for the *Pathé Sun*, Terriss expounded upon the efforts of the sound technicians "to record the native tongue, weird music and incantations which go with the curious ceremonies and festivities of the many strange races who inhabit the far corners of the earth"; but seldom was the sound presented "live" on film, functioning mostly as background noise for scenes shot separately.

Released May 5, 1930, *The Golden Pagoda* (original title: *Jungle Fury*) was the first in the series, setting the factual-fictional tone for all the reels to come. Amidst engrossingly authentic glimpses of everyday life in Rangoon and surrounding regions of Burma, Tom Terriss floridly describes his "adventures" during a stopover at a fabulous pagoda encrusted with jewels and solid gold. The tour climaxes with the narrator's death-defying descent into the fabled "Cave of the Kings," all duly photographed by an equally intrepid cameraman, who despite the dangers surrounding him manages to compose and light the climactic scenes almost as if they'd been filmed in the safety of a movie studio. The music heard throughout the 11-minute film is "Mandalay," previously put to excellent use in Van Beuren's *Song Sketches* series (see Chapter 9). *Variety* greeted *The Golden Pagoda* warmly in their review of May 14, 1930: "Interesting bit of travel, with special excellence in the running talk that illuminated the scenes with excellent effect."

Streets of Mystery, the second-filmed *Vagabond Adventures*, was held back from release in favor of *The Glacier's Secret* (1930), lensed in the frigid mountains of New Zealand. Barely able to control his excitement, Terriss recalls how he followed such clues as a hat and a purse to determine the grisly fate of an unfortunate young woman who'd fallen into a glacier crevice while fleeing a lover's spat, offering as "proof" of her demise a large smudge within the glacier that *might* be a frozen body. Mockingly described in vaudeville terminology as "10–20–30" stuff by *Exhibitor's Herald World*, *The Glacier's Secret* was taken in the proper spirit by *Film Daily*: "The film conveys a feeling that is rarely identified with travel films, and contains a tender, tragic note that is genuinely touching." The *Variety* critic didn't have time to wax poetic, stating pragmatically: "Beats the average scenic through the story." The aforementioned *Streets of Mystery* ended up as third in the series and was well worth the wait, at least as far as audiences were concerned. In this one Terriss gooses up some gorgeously lensed footage of the Grand Trunk Road in India with a bit of hokum involving his search for a lost friend, finding the poor soul in the clutches of a demonic "dancing woman." For all that, the film's real highlight is the early scene of a mystic Indian girl lifting a chair—with her eyes.

Had the series' fourth episode *Land of Chang-Ow* (working title: *The Lotus Dream*) been content with merely displaying various Chinese boat dwellers, the film probably wouldn't have been held over for two weeks at New York's Strand Theater.

Chapter 10—The Vagabond Adventures

Vagabond Adventure Series

Stills that picture the thrills of the far places as brought to the screen in the sensational Pathé-Van Beuren one-reel features.

A radical movement in India as portrayed in "Streets of Mystery."

"The Golden Pagoda"—Interior view of the small Shrines surrounding the great Golden Pagoda, the Swi Dagon in Rangoon, Burma.

"The Golden Pagoda" Opens at Seattle

A telegram from Branch Manager C. L. Theuerkauf to Phil Reisman—

GOLDEN PAGODA FIRST ONE VAGABOND SERIES OPENED FOX FIFTH AVENUE THEATRE SEATTLE THURSDAY IT POSITIVELY RECEIVING UNANIMOUS APPROVAL AT EVERY PERFORMANCE AT END OF REEL SPONTANEOUS APPLAUSE EVERY SHOW IF BALANCE EQUALLY AS GOOD SHOULD BE MOST SUCCESSFUL SINGLE REEL SERIALS EVER PRODUCED.

"Streets of Mystery" Previewed at Los Angeles

And from Jesse J. Goldburg, now at Los Angeles, to Phil Reisman—

JUST PREVIEWED STREETS OF MYSTERY SECOND VAGABOND ADVENTURE PICTURE STOP AUDIENCE REACTION TREMENDOUS STOP PRODUCTION IS THE MOST INTERESTING REEL EVER MADE WITH SOUND AND EXCEEDS THE HIGH STANDARD ALREADY SET BY THE GOLDEN PAGODA STOP STARTED SHOOTING THIRD SUBJECT THE GLACIERS SECRET STOP AFTER LAYING OUT PRODUCTION PLANS FOR THE FIRST THIRTEEN RELEASES AND SCREENING THE MATERIAL I KNOW THAT THIS NEW SERIES WILL MAINTAIN PATHES REPUTATION AS THE HOUSE OF HITS.

Titles of First 13

"THE GOLDEN PAGODA"
(locale India)

"STREETS OF MYSTERY"
(locale India)

"THE GLACIER'S SECRET"
(locale South Pole)

"THE LAIR OF CHANG-OW"
(locale China)

"THE CAT GODDESS"
(locale Anghor)

"SACRED FIRES"
(locale Benares)

"VALLEY OF THE KINGS"
(locale Egypt)

"SATANS PIT"
(locale Volcanos of White Islands)

"JUNGLE FURY"
(locale Rangoon)

"THE LOTUS DREAM"
(locale Hong Kong)

"LOVE THAT KILLS"
(locale Malay Forest)

"DRUMS OF DESIRE"
(locale New Guinea)

"THE FORBIDDEN SHRINE"
(locale Arabia)

Many of the inhabitants of this floating city of the Far East never set foot on land. Here Tom Terris had one of his most thrilling adventures.

"The Golden Pagoda"—The public laundry of Rangoon, Burma. The ladies do most of the wash while papa plays. They wet the clothes, slap them down on the cement. The force of the blow splashes water and dirt in all directions.

Away from riot and revolution in a peaceful village of India. The cows are turning a grain grinding machine.

"The Glacier's Secret"—The crew watching Tom Terris making one of his high climbs in the Alps of the South Pole, on the great Tasman Glacier.

The strange devil box of the white man was a thing of never ending interest to the natives of the different countries in which Tom Terris met with adventure. This is a village along the Ganges.

The poor being fed by the rich. His Highness Maharaja Scindia in charge of the distribution of food to 26,000, all classes of Mahrattas.

The Pathé Sun takes the "hard sell" approach for Van Beuren's new talkie series, April 5, 1930. Some of the titles listed would be changed before release.

After weaving in and out of sundry exotic Hong Kong hot spots, Terriss spends the night in the Wang-Ho caves, only to find himself the prisoner of merciless Chinese pirate chieftain Chang-Ow (Spoiler alert: he escapes). Reviewers had plenty to say about this reel's dizzying serial-like thrills, *Variety* summing it all up in blunt racist terms: "Trick shots at an ominous array of Chinese knives and dirks hanging on the wall, quick glimpses of slant eyed desperadoes leering through sinister shadows, with appropriate talk to build up atmosphere." In case the title alone wasn't enough to draw crowds, Van Beuren issued a promotional "Find the lost Chinaman" puzzle concurrent with the release of *Land of Chang-Ow*.

Even when there wasn't danger and destruction lurking in every corner, Tom Terriss' passionate narration made it seem as if he was in perpetual peril. In *Mystic Isles* (1930), 15th in the series, the Vagabond Director journeys to Java in what was then known as the Dutch East Indies, plunking himself smack in the middle of the narrative by describing Javanese sedan chairs as being so tight that he risks losing the change in his pockets. Terriss proceeds to enliven some rather sedate shots of native wax molding and ornament manufacturing with zesty "Ooohs" and "Ahhhs" as if watching a fireworks display. Finally he gets to the meat of the story, visiting an ancient temple where he's heard of "strange rites" taking place. The temple exterior is the real McCoy: The temple interior is pure Tec-Art. Upon entering the building, "Oooh the temptation!" overcomes Terriss and he risks the wrath of "the spirits of the past" by sitting in a sacred chair. Suddenly one of the temple statues seems to come to life and stalks toward Terriss, forcing our hero to run like a bunny to the safety of the outdoors. He then informs us he really had nothing to fear, since the "statue" and a second sinister figure are merely peaceful worshippers offering prayers (Query: If he's narrating all this in the First Person, how would *he* know what happened in the temple after he fled? Ah, never mind).

Corny as this sounds—and plays—the *Vagabond Adventures* formula was irrefutably effective. By the time *Mystic Isles* was released in late November of 1930, the series was playing on regular contracts in 2,642 U.S. theaters. *Motion Picture News* adroitly summarized the property's appeal: "It is one of but a few groups of short subjects now on the market which may be always depended upon to hold its audience breathless while the tale of some mysterious country is unfolded colorfully by Terriss with his pleasing English accent."

And so it went, all through 1930: *Drums of Fear* highlights the cannibals and witch doctors of New Guinea, with fearful anticipation galvanizing the hapless narrator and production crew; *Temple of Silence* revolves around the search for an elusive "cat goddess" in Angkor Wat; *Sacred Fires* follows an East Indian child bride down the Ganges as she delivers the body of her elderly husband to the flames of the traditional (and, Terriss informs us, now outlawed) funeral *suttee*; *Love That Kills* uses the Malayan forest as backdrop for the tale of star-crossed love between members of different castes; *Jungle Terror* shows Terriss and his guide hanging on for dear life as the elephant they're riding on is spooked by deadly reptiles; and *Days of Solitude* manages to be on hand just in time for the rescue of an exhausted traveller by a St. Bernard in the Swiss Alps. It's safe to speculate that while audiences and critics were entertained by *Vagabond Adventures*, only the most obtuse observer took any of the plastic thrills seriously. In reviewing *Satan's Fury*, wherein Terriss and his guide are nearly boiled to death in the volcanic formations and mini-geysers of New Zealand,

Motion Picture News remarked "one wonders how the cameraman managed to keep on grinding"—though without much discernable sense of wonder.

This Barnum & Bailey baloney extended to the press releases issued by Pathé about the alleged near-death experiences of the *Vagabond Adventures* units. In August 1931 it was reported that a cameraman on location in China had been kidnapped and held for ransom by outlaws, then rescued by soldiers five days later. *Film Daily* countered this tidbit by claiming that their own correspondent "One Lung Lee" had the real lowdown: The Chinese outlaws had released their prisoner immediately upon learning his identity, "knowing it was useless to try to get ransom on film muggs."

For all its kitschiness, *Vagabond Adventures* offered plenty of authentic material, thoroughly fascinating in its own right. The scenes of Fete Day on the Grand Canal in *Venetian Nights* (1930) moved *Motion Picture News* to comment: "This series is interesting and instructive to all ages." *Ebony Shrine* (1930), described by *Motion Pictures News* as "heavy stuff" because of its emphasis on religion, displays in reverent detail the Church of the Black Christ of Esquipulas in Guatemala, as well as the Cathedral of San Francisco, the oldest Christian church in the Americas (This film was originally scripted to focus on Ensenada in the Baja region, a stopover during the unit's trek from Mexico to Guatemala, but the church footage was deemed more compelling). *Gem of Agra* (1930) is an equally austere exploration of the Taj Mahal, with a lively discussion of its history; while the focus in *Sands of Egypt* (1930) is just as much on the sacred ruins of Karnak as on its "plot" concerning a centuries-old map found wrapped within a mummy. *Well of Fortaleza* (1931), though making the most of the inherent melodrama surrounding a poisoned Puerto Rican spring, also takes us on a guided tour of the island's decrepit but still-functioning prisons. *Hurricane Island*, (1931), constructed around harrowing footage of the aftermath of the 1930 Santo Domingo hurricane, cuts away from the devastation long enough for edifying glimpses of the tomb of Columbus. And *Through the Ages* (1931) virtually abandons sensationalism for an in-depth look at the remnants of the Toltec Civilization, here filmed for the first time.

As was the case with *Grantland Rice Sportlights* (see Chapter 6), the three main *Vagabond Adventure* units would film extensively in single locations to provide material for several separate shorts, staggering the release of these films to avoid repetition. Worthy of note are two 1931 episodes crafted from one solitary expedition to Haiti. *The Fallen Empire* devotes half its reel to a hyperbolic lecture on the bloody reign of "Slave King" Toussaint Louverture, while the camera glides around and through the ruins of the despot's Haitian palace. *Song of the Voodoo*, regarded as the better of the two films by trade reviewers, manages to keep adventure-movie fans titillated with scenes of forbidden voodoo rituals (a comparatively benign sequence for this series) while satisfying the aesthetes in the crowd with lingering views of Port-au-Prince, the "babble of the marketplace" contrasted with the silence and solitude of the native jewelry workshops. The film also dabbles in social commentary, showing the work of sculptor Charles Normil depicting the cultural and educational advancements of the Haitian people in the past century, and closing with narrator Terriss' plaintive yearning for a future in which "the races will better understand each other." In its November 1931 edition, *National Board of Review* magazine rated *Song of the Voodoo* "one of the best of the series," adding "These pictures avoid the silliness that so often goes with films of this sort." (Well, *this* time, anyway.)

Scene from *Song of the Voodoo* (1931)

After 1930's *Mystic Isles*, the series dropped its studio-filmed dramatic interpolations, relying solely upon the carefully edited travel footage and Tom Terriss' mellifluous narration to carry the day. Coinciding with this format tweak was the departure of co-supervisor Alfred T. Mannon, who shifted attention to his executive duties with the Independent Motion Pictures Producers Association, as well as his own new production firm Supreme Pictures. In 1935 he organized another outfit called Resolute Picture to produce B westerns, but this enterprise lasted only four films. When last heard from, Mannon was busily promoting his 1936 quasi-documentary feature *I Was a Captive of Nazi Germany*, based on the memoirs of Isobel Lillian Steele (who played herself on screen). In spite of—or more likely because of—fierce opposition from various German-American organizations and the German Embassy itself, Alfred T. Mannon was able to retire comfortably off the profits of his final film, keeping it in healthy circulation throughout World War II.

Tom Terriss himself left *Vagabond Adventures* after 26 episodes; the narration was taken over by Elmer Clifton for 1931's *Through the Ages*, and thereafter by California-based radio actor Gayne Whitman, then famous for his portrayal of the title role in the syndicated radio series *Chandu the Magician*. Terriss went on to narrate other documentaries for other producers, and to star in a popular NBC radio program likewise titled *Vagabond Adventures*. The actor also showed up in caricature form (younger and with more hair) in a long-running newspaper comic strip, reprinted in the monthly periodical *Famous Funnies* until the early 1950s. Long retired, Tom Terriss died in 1964.

Without Terriss' screenwriting input *Vagabond Adventures* began leaning upon "funny" narration to hype the imagery, perhaps in emulation Walter Futter's *Travelaughs* in which humorist John P. Medbury sprinkled verbal wisecracks over otherwise straightforward travel footage. Only in a handful of post–Tom Terriss entries did narrator Gayne Whitman bypass the sniggering jests provided by the uncredited writing staff: For example, *Land of Gandhi* (1931) sustains audience interest via the time-honored *Vagabond Adventures* device of comparing modern manufacturing methods in India with traditional hand-crafted artisanship. But too many other efforts were along the lines of *Door of Asia* (1931), in which a potentially respectful overview of everyday life in China is constantly undercut by such derisive narration as Whitman claiming that a somber peasant funeral is the result of the decedent eating a 400-year-old egg; and *Drums of the Orient* (1932), with its compelling images of cultural life in Bangkok compromised by poking fun at the unisex mode of dress ("If it grows up and marries a man, it's a woman")—and more egregiously, describing two sacred statues outside a Buddhist temple as "the Siamese Amos 'n' Andy."

The series hit rock bottom with its final 1932 release *Malaysia*, in which narrator Gayne Whitman was for reasons unknown replaced by William Hanley. In addition to the anticipated quips about the male tribal leaders of the Orang Asli people heading off in an outrigger canoe for their "poker game" and resembling members of "the local stock company," the villagers' humble handmade clothing is ridiculed as "old pajamas with the legs cut off," while the distinctive headgear proudly worn by one young man is patronizingly dismissed as "the local color." To top it off, the narrator seems overjoyed when the film's camera crew introduces cigarettes to the village children.

In addition to its other offenses, *Malaysia* is perhaps the apotheosis of the several *Vagabond Adventures* which take advantage of a certain unofficial pre–Code censorship edict. To wit, that it is entirely acceptable to show bare-breasted women on screen so long as the film is a documentary and the topless damsels are non–Caucasian natives. While this semi-nudity is tastefully (and fleetingly) displayed in such earlier entries as *Mystic Isles* and *Wizard Land*, *Malaysia*'s emphasis upon unadorned female mammaries, accompanied by William Hanley's slavering narration, immediately brings to mind the Hollywood legend of Hunt Stromberg exhorting his fellow MGM producers to finance the 1928 tropical melodrama *White Shadows on the South Seas*: "Boys, I've got an idea. Let's fill the screen with tits!"

Not long before *Malaysia* Elmer Clifton had severed ties with *Vagabond Adventures*, accepting an offer to supervise his own general-interest "Elmer Clifton Subjects" for newly incorporated Beverly Hills Productions. Running anywhere from two to three reels, narrated by Clifton's longtime actor friend Wilfred Lucas, and bearing titles like *Man Eater, Mad Monarch, Priests of Painted Cave* and *War Debts*, the series lasted until 1934 and was highly rated by industryites and filmgoers alike. The shorts enabled Clifton to return full-time to features, with some worthwhile B westerns starring Buck Jones and Johnny Mack Brown on the plus side, and such grindhouse exploitationers as *City of Missing Girls, Marihuana: Assassin of Youth* and *Slaves of Bondage* in the minus column. Elmer Clifton's last directorial assignment was *Not Wanted* (1949), a cheap but serviceable location-filmed melodrama. Falling mortally ill early in the proceedings, Clifton was unable to finish the job, compelling the film's leading lady Ida Lupino to take over the direction herself—thereby launching one of the most impressive directorial careers of the 1950s and 1960s, with Lupino helming such *noir* masterpieces as *The Hitchhiker* (1952) and scores of episodes for TV series as varied as *Have Gun—Will Travel, The Untouchables, The Twilight Zone* and *Gilligan's Island*.

With Alfred Mannon and Elmer Clifton gone, *Vagabond Adventures* no longer carried any supervisor credits. In the absence of solid proof, it is reasonable to assume that the supervisory responsibilities had been inherited by the series' general manager Richard Heermance, recently risen from the ranks of Van Beuren's editing department, and who years later became one of the most prolific producers for Monogram/Allied Artists. No matter who was now calling the creative shots, *Vagabond Adventures* took a tremendous upswing in 1933 with the hiring of narrator Alois Havrilla and screenwriter Russell Spaulding. Havrilla's career is more thoroughly discussed in Chapter 24; Spaulding, a renowned world traveller who spoke several languages fluently, had risen to industry prominence by scripting the English versions of such prestigious foreign films as *Mädchen in Uniform*. Once engaged by Van Beuren, Spaulding spent a great deal of time researching each *Vagabond Adventure*, often taking his work with him on vacation. His narrative style, crammed with facts and erudition but easily accessible to the average moviegoer, was perfectly attuned to the breezy delivery and appealing mid–Atlantic accent of Alois Havrilla, who though occasionally heard to stifle a chuckle (usually borne of awe or surprise) never joked about nor condescended to the peoples and cultures onscreen. The improvement in the series was immediately noticed by the *Variety* reviewer of the first Havrilla-Spaulding collaboration *Holland Mosaics* (1933): "It's intelligent, factually correct (often not so in shorts), and yet down to earth enough for common audience consumption."

Though the later *Vagabond Adventures* still occasionally burrowed into the miles of documentary footage left behind by Tom Terriss, most of the shorts released between 1933 and 1935 were comprised of independently produced films purchased by Van Beuren. The combined expertise of Russell Spaulding and the studio editorial staff successfully managed to reshape the "outside" material to conform with the series' established format. The uncredited documentarian responsible for the images in *Cuba* (1933) provided just the right shots for Spaulding to weave a coherent narrative around glimpses of ex-Cuban president Machado going into exile, tourists enjoying the hospitality of Sloppy Joe's and the San Souci resort, native rope making, the plentiful Nuevitas berry trees, and (especially attractive for audiences just emerging from Prohibition) the Bacardi distillery. Complemented by Alois Havrilla's jaunty narration, *Cuba* adheres to the *Vagabond Adventures* credo of defining a faraway country not merely via architecture (the Presidential Palace in this one) but also the day-to-day lives, activities and pastimes of its people.

Four of the best entries of the 1933–34 season were provided by the Arcturus Pictures Corporation, formed in 1933 by prominent travel agent James W. Boring and filmmaker F. Herrick Herrick for the purpose of making promotional films for various Mediterranean tourist bureaus. Boring expanded his operation to include films made on an expedition to Africa, chartering the S.S. *Columbus* and other liners for that purpose and bringing along his own audio equipment to record authentic sounds and voices. Originally slated for release directly through RKO, the 40,000 feet of film shot by Arcturus was instead purchased by Van Beuren, with all hints of commercialism removed in the cutting room and the remaining footage deftly adapted to suit the purposes of *Vagabond Adventures*.

The first Arcturus effort in the Van Beuren series had initially borne the title *España Morisca*, but Russell Spaulding opted for the English translation *Moorish Spain*. It was the second Arcturus entry that made the biggest impact: *The Holy Land*, lovingly lensed in Palestine at such locations as the port of Jaffa, the sea of Galilee, and the narrow alleyways of Jerusalem. Though Christian hymns are heard on the soundtrack throughout, the film's inherent religious angle encompasses many faiths and creeds, appealing to as wide an audience as possible.

Russell Spaulding's manipulation of the footage at hand in *The Holy Land* is masterful. The film warms up the audience with such light touches as narrator Havrilla pretending to recognize a Brooklyn deli owner of his acquaintance, now running a thriving Jerusalem stationery store thanks to the largesse of British General Allenby, whose World War I victory at Jaffa led to establishing the Palestine Mandate in 1922. Further humanizing the material are glimpses of lemonade and snow cone vendors in the streets, a brace of "stalwart Rebeccas" uncomplainingly bearing 60-pound water jugs on their heads, and children swimming in the waters of Galilee, sublimely ignorant of its historical significance. The script then shifts gears to the land itself; describing Palestine as "the unique blend of promise and fulfillment," Havrilla expresses admiration for a civilization that has survived 20 centuries by keeping its eyes fixed firmly on the future. The mood becomes more somber in an extended sequence at the Wailing Wall, focusing on worshippers "as they seek divine comfort" and "find also the spiritual strength that has given them the courage and patience to carry on through centuries of persecution." But no words are spoken—or needed—for the intimate closeup of a septuagenarian Jewish man chanting a prayer from memory just inches from the blessed wall. The climactic sequence in which pilgrims of all races and faiths are drawn to the temple of the Holy Sepulchre to celebrate the Resurrection occasionally editorializes by noting the "religious delirium" and intensity "to the point of fury," but Spaulding and Havrilla are careful not to cast these elements in a critical light. The only negative words are reserved for "the pagans and nonbelievers" who "seek profit at the expense of gullible pilgrims to whom they sell sacred relics that may or may not be genuine."

Most motion pictures of the era treaded softly on the subject of religion, worried that somewhere someone would be offended by a careless word. But Russell Spaulding knew exactly how far to go and when to pull back while describing the cosmopolitan spectacle of Holy Week in the land of its birth. Though officially released in New York and Los Angeles in February 1934, *The Holy Land* was held back in most regions until Easter Week in late March. Needless to say, the film was a box office smash.

Less reverent but no less entertaining were the two remaining Arcturus contributions: *Madeira, The Land of Wine* and *Gibraltar, Guardian of the Mediterranean*. Perhaps because Gibraltar and its history were comparatively familiar to audiences of the period (and of our period, for that matter), *Madeira* is the more fascinating of the two. James W. Boring and F. Herrick Herrick's original concept of using their films as enticement for the tourist trade pokes its head up more often than usual in this one, with picture-postcard views of the Portuguese Bay of Funchal, lengthy shots of tourists riding up mountains in hammocks and down cobblestone streets in sleighs, and the mouth-watering finale of a wine vault being opened for the first time in 50 years and the rare vintage therein sampled by the smiling Vagabond Adventurer (probably Mr. Boring or Mr. Herrick, enjoying the fringe benefits of moviemaking).

Other documentarians were content to contribute only one or two films to *Vagabond Adventures*. Earning a producer credit on *Roumania* (1935) was George Popovici, a Romanian-born photographer then living in Florida. The obligatory shots of churches, antiquities, peasant dances and local arts-and-crafts are pleasant if not outstanding, with Spaulding's script and guest narrator Jimmy Wallington working overtime to keep us engaged. What should have been the film's highlight, a cluster of candid-camera glimpses of the Romanian royal family, proved a bit disappointing back in 1935, especially since Popovici's highly-touted interview of Queen Marie was excised from the short before release.

Conversely, Van Beuren scored a real coup by acquiring the services (after a fashion) of legendary American photographer Margaret Bourke-White for two *Vagabond Adventures* in 1934, representing the only occasion in her career that she experimented with the medium of motion pictures. Then employed by magazine mogul Henry Luce—and still two years away from her iconic photo of the Fort Peck Dam on the inaugural cover of *Life* magazine—Margaret Bourke-White was like many Americans of the era fascinated by the remarkable industrial advances of Soviet Russia, especially in contrast with the stultification in the U.S. arising from the Depression. Between 1931 and 1933 Bourke-White made three trips to Russia, camera in hand, choosing (or being forced to choose) to concentrate on the country's progressivism while ignoring its poverty, repression and starvation. As she later explained, "I wanted to take the pictures of this astonishing development, because, whatever the outcome, whether success or failure, the effort of 150 million people is so gigantic, so unprecedented in all history, that I felt that these photographic records might have some historical value." In her 1931 book *Eyes on Russia*, she praised the nation as "the land of today after tomorrow," albeit admitting that every opportunity she had to offer a more balanced portrait was stymied by Soviet bureaucracy.

For her third Russian visit in 1933 Bourke-White opted to deploy motion picture cameras rather than her customary photographic equipment. "Having brought in the first photographs to be made by a non–Soviet citizen," she recalled in her autobiography *Portrait of Myself*, "I was ambitious to do the same with a newsreel or travelogue." Kodak donated 20,000 feet of film to this enterprise, assuming that the result would be an educational feature for schoolroom and other non-theatrical use. But Van Beuren trumped Kodak and purchased 2000 feet of celluloid from Bourke-White, to be edited into a brace of *Vagabond Adventure* one-reelers: *Eyes on Russia: From the Caucasus to Moscow*, and *Red Republic: From Baku to Dnieprostroi*—the first American documentaries sanctioned by the Soviet government.

The opening titles of both films proclaim that they were "photographed and produced under the personal direction of Margaret Bourke-White." Russell Spaulding prepared the continuities, and though Alois Havrilla was slated to narrate, Bourke-White provided her own offscreen commentary for the first release *Eyes on Russia*. The emphasis in the films was on such technological marvels as the Dnieper hydroelectric dam (engineered by an American named Hugh Cooper), but the audience was also treated to a few unique and unexpected highlights. For *Red Republic*, Bourke-White managed to get permission for an excursion into the Republic of Georgia, where she photographed the family of Soviet Premier Josef Stalin—including his mother.

Bourke-White herself felt the films were "not very good," lamenting in her autobiography: "I did all the wrong things: used big cameras, big films, big tripods. I composed each scene with lengthy care and took innumerable static views, forgetting that the important word in motion pictures is motion." Be that as it may, the remarkable images she managed to capture still hold the power to enthrall modern viewers. The same can be said of the films' fleeting "selfies" of Margaret Bourke-White, who looks exactly as we'd always imagined she'd look as she expertly sets up her equipment, braves the bone-chilling weather and treacherous terrain, and flashes a movie-star smile at everyone and everything, obviously enjoying her adventure to the hilt. While these behind-the-scenes vignettes were appreciated by reviewers of the period, *Motion Picture Daily* wasn't keen on one element of *Eyes of Russia* that would be of inestimable value to future generations: "The running commentary by Miss White could stand considerable improvement."

Margaret Bourke-White, photographer and star of two memorable *Vagabond Adventures*, 1934.

The final *Vagabond Adventure* release *Quebec* (1935) can be looked upon as a harbinger for the upcoming Van Beuren travelogue series *World on Parade* (see Chapter 24), what with its focus on North America. After this entry the series was cancelled—or, more precisely, absorbed. Van Beuren had decided to completely redress the format by harking back to the "humorous" narration of the last Mannon–Clifton offerings; this time, however, the narrators were professional funsters with a solid fan following. *Pharoahland* (1935) was shipped out under the *Vagabond Adventures* imprimatur, but was actually the pilot film for a new series starring radio humorists Goodman and Jane Ace. As will be noted in Chapter 21, by the time the fourth entry in this series came around in July of 1935, all vestiges of *Vagabond Adventures* had been removed from the introductory credits, never to return.

Chapter 11

Animated Cartoons, Part Two

Tom and Jerry, Cubby Bear, The Little King, Amos 'n' Andy

By 1930 the mainstay of the Van Beuren operation was its yearly manifest of animated cartoons. Amedee Van Beuren was doing just fine with such live-action franchises as *Grantland Rice Sportlights* and *Vagabond Adventures,* but in most interviews he emphasized that "animated cartoons in particular" had not only kept him afloat in both good times and bad, but also the entire short-subject industry. Virtually every major Hollywood studio of the early-talkie era was delivering cartoons to a panting public: Paramount had Max Fleischer, Universal Walter Lantz, MGM Ub Iwerks and Warner Bros. Leon Schlesinger (by 1932 Fox would join the club by taking over distribution of Educational Pictures' Terrytoons). Even second-string Columbia was cleaning up with *two* Hollywood-based cartoon properties, the Walt Disney product and the Charles Mintz efforts.

The newest "big" studio RKO entered the animation field in 1930 with a cartoon package produced by Charles Mintz and starring one Toby the Pup. Once Pathé was purchased by RKO, the studio added Van Beuren to its animated roster, part of a greater effort by RKO to emerge as the industry leader in the realm of short subjects. In addition to handling two cartoon concerns, by 1931 RKO was also distributing the combined two-reel comedy output of Pathé, Radio Pictures and independent producer Larry Darmour.

Alas, Toby the Pup had no staying power and the series was cancelled after 11 episodes. At the same time, Van Beuren had lost his live-action series *Floyd Gibbons Supreme Thrills* (see Chapter 12) and needed a new property to maintain his production quota for RKO. For their mutual benefit, RKO and Van Beuren quickly launched a companion cartoon series for the still-flourishing *Aesop's Fables.* Under the guidance of animation director John Foster, studio newcomers George Stallings and George Rufle developed a new series with a Mutt-and-Jeff team of funny human characters named Tom (the tall one) and Jerry (the short one), monikers possibly inspired by the popular 1821 stage comedy *Tom and Jerry, or Life in London,* but just as likely derived from the even more popular eggnog-brandy-rum cocktail of the same name. Tom and Jerry have been described as Van Beuren's first original cartoon characters, though in fact they had their roots an earlier tall-and-short duo who'd appeared in *Aesop's Sound Fables,* Waffles the Cat and Don Dog. (Tom and Jerry had also been the names of a black jockey and his goofy horse in a brief series of stop-motion animated shorts produced by miniature-model designer J.L. Roop in 1923 and 1924).

With an expanded staff of 131 artist-animators and assistants, and equipped with five modern cameras operated by seven cameramen working in two shifts, Van Beuren was certainly up to the challenge of augmenting his yearly supply of *Aesop's Fables* with an additional batch of *Tom and Jerry* cartoons. Beginning with *Wot a Night* (released August 1, 1931), 26 Tom and Jerry cartoons were produced in all, with animation head John Foster supervising all but six and George Stallings and George Rufle alternating direction for the bulk of the entries. Other directors included *Fables* veteran Frank Sherman and, for the 1933 entry *Hook and Ladder Hokum*, future Jerry Lewis and Jayne Mansfield director Frank Tashlin, then a Van Beuren gag man billed under his *nom de cinema* Tish Tash.

It has been claimed by cartoon historians that Tom and Jerry were a couple of empty suits without discernable personalities. This isn't quite true: In *Wot a Night* the basic characters are firmly established, and retained throughout several subsequent episodes. The arrow-narrow, rubber-limbed Tom fancies himself the leader of the pair but is invariably flustered by his own cowardice and excitability; the chubby, cheerful Jerry takes everything in stride and emerges as the braver and more resourceful of the two. These distinct characterizations had already been developed for Waffles the Cat and Don Dog, but Tom and Jerry make them all their own.

Unfortunately the *Tom and Jerry* cartoons are as inconsistent as the *Aesop's Fables*. After one watches a first-rate entry like *In the Bag* (1932) in which Tom and Jerry are sharply defined individuals with all-too-human strengths and frailties, it's

Another of Van Beuren's animated opening titles, 1932. Tom and Jerry tapped their feet in rhythm with the theme music.

both disheartening and tedious to wade through the lesser cartoons in which our heroes walk, move and react exactly alike, as if they were robots. And while the characters are immensely appealing, they're frequently too passive to carry their own cartoons. In some entries like *The Tuba Tooter* (1932) and *The Phantom Rocket* (1933) Tom and Jerry barely appear, leaving the best gags—and most of the screen time—to the supporting cast. Toward the end of the series it appears that the Van Beuren staff had run out of ideas to sustain interest in Tom and Jerry: In *Puzzled Pals* and *In the Park* (both 1933) there is a concerted effort to spin off a new star personality, a mischievous (and unnamed) baby—who never progresses any farther than the expected "ka-ka" jokes.

Overall, however, the batting average of *Tom and Jerry* was higher than that of the concurrently produced *Fables*. Series highlights include the skeleton minstrel show in *Wot a Night!*, Tom and Jerry eating too much Swiss cheese and breaking out in holes in *A Swiss Trick* (1932), the Texas Guinan mermaid ("Hello, suckers!") in *Rocketeers* (1932), the outrageous but rather endearing gay and Jewish stereotypes in *Doughnuts* (1933), and the most famous (or infamous) *Tom and Jerry* gag of all, Jerry "murdering" a sour musical note and flushing it down the toilet in *Piano Tooners* (1932). The series' best effort, and one of the best cartoons Van Beuren ever made, is *Pencil Mania* (1932), a ragged but rollicking precursor to the 1953 Chuck Jones classic *Duck Amuck*, with Jerry creating a whole new world with whole new rules using nothing more than his pencil. Few sound cartoons have ever captured the freewheeling spirit of silent animation as perfectly as *Pencil Mania*.

Most enjoyable are the musical scores arranged by Gene Rodemich. There is hardly a Tom and Jerry cartoon without at least one scene where the stars plunk out a tune on a piano or hammer away on a makeshift xylophone, giving Rodemich ample opportunity to trot out such bouncy ditties as "Nagasaki," "Business in F," "Dinah" "Schultz Is Back Again," "Yes, We Have No Bananas" and "Wabash Blues." Even those who are hostile toward the Van Beuren cartoons find it impossible to dislike those treasured moments when the boys drop whatever they're doing to go into a spirited song and dance to such toe-tappin' tunes as "Oh, How We'd Love to Run a Fish Store" and "We're Glad That We Are Plumbers."

History hasn't recorded who supplied the voices of Tom and Jerry (when they *had* voices, which wasn't often), but in the team's *Magic Mummy* (1933) and several other Van Beuren cartoons we hear a squeaky-voiced female singer who sounds exactly like Betty Boop. That's because she *is* Betty Boop—or rather, the first actress who provided Betty's voice in the Max Fleischer cartoons produced right across the street from Van Beuren Studios. The December 10, 1932, edition of *Film Daily* announced that Margie Hines, "well known radio artist and musical comedy star," had been signed to an exclusive contract by Van Beuren to provide cartoon voiceovers. Hines remained with the studio until 1934; four years later she returned to Fleischer, where she provided the voice of Olive Oyl in the *Popeye* cartoons. From 1939 to 1942 Margie Hines was married to Jack Mercer, the voice of Popeye himself.

And speaking of voices, there are a couple of odd ones in the oddest *Tom and Jerry* cartoon of all. After a conventional airborne opening, *Plane Dumb* (1932) abruptly switches gears and moods as Tom and Jerry disguise themselves in blackface and start trading dialogue in exaggerated Southern-black dialects, the better to avoid attracting attention while exploring the African coast. The characters also exchange personalities, with Jerry the coward and Tom the aggressor. As if this wasn't perplexing enough, *Plane Dumb*'s opening credits are superimposed over live-action footage of Niagara Falls.

But don't lose any sleep, folks, there's an explanation for all this. The cartoon's original title was *All Wet*, hence the mysterious waterfall. Also, the cartoon wasn't supposed to be a *Tom and Jerry* entry, but instead a one-shot featuring the voices and caricatures of popular black comedy team Flournoy Miller and Aubrey Lyles. It is not known whether Van Beuren was planning a Miller & Lyles series, or if this cartoon was designed as an adjunct for the team's vaudeville appearances. Nor do we know why *All Wet* was ultimately scrapped: Speculation that it was due to the death of Aubrey Lyles is unlikely, since Lyles passed away two months after the cartoon's release. For whatever reason, Van Beuren decided to retain the prerecorded Miller & Lyles voice track and the completed animation, then add an opening sequence with Tom and Jerry so that *All Wet* could be released as part of their series under the barely relevant title *Plane Dumb*. Now that *that*'s cleared up, you can get some sleep. Or keep reading.

Tom and Jerry set no box office records, but the series pleased the crowd and was well received by reviewers. Of *Tuba Tooter*, *Film Daily* observed: "John Foster and George Stallings, the animators, and Gene Rodemich, the musical director, have turned out a release that compares favorably with the best." But "compares favorably" wasn't good enough for Amedee Van Beuren, whose cartoons still fell far short of the popularity and prestige enjoyed by industry leader Walt Disney. Sometime in late 1932 or after John Foster had been fired in early 1933, Van Beuren summoned a group of his animators and directors for a conference over dinner at the New York Athletic Club. As Mannie Davis recalled to Leonard Maltin, "[W]e didn't know what it was about. There were about seven or eight of us. Seems that there was a need for a new character. And they wanted to get some new life into the pictures. And we were all told [to bring] our pads with us..." Davis' contribution was a sketch for a new character named Cubby Bear, which Van Buren immediately accepted, possibly because Cubby was short with round ears, round nose, expressive eyes and a pair of white trunks that made him almost resemble ... need we say the name?

Under Davis' (uncredited) direction, Cubby Bear made his debut in *Opening Night*. Since this cartoon was released nationally on February 10, 1933—"A new star appears in the pen-and-ink sky" trumpeted the trade ads—one might assume that the Athletic Club meeting took place early that same year. But in fact *Opening Night*'s world premiere was December 29, 1932—and the cartoon was initially intended exclusively for a New York audience. On that same day, the 3500-seat RKO Roxy Theater at Rockefeller Center, planned as the "sister" movie house of Radio City Music Hall, opened its doors. On the bill was the RKO feature *The Animal Kingdom*, and as an extra added attraction a Van Beuren cartoon created specifically for the occasion, which according to the souvenir program had been "hand-colored by Brock" (Gustav Brock, who later added color tints to the 1934 Van Beuren feature film *Adventure Girl*). In the spirit of Christmas week, the cartoon opens with Santa Claus merrily sprinkling stardust from his sleigh, stardust that promptly forms the letters "RKO ROXY" emblazoned on an art-deco tower. We first see "Cubby the Bear" (as he is billed) as a gate-crasher at the Big Premiere, which is attended by every form of talking-animal life in Manhattan, including a Jewish elephant who mutters

"Dis is a system?" into a radio mike. Cubby makes his way to the theater's projection booth, pulling a lever that opens a trap door and deposits him into the orchestra pit, where he obligingly assumes the role of conductor. The rest of the cartoon is an opera parody rife with John Foster–style gags, including a balloon-breasted soprano and the entire orchestra crashing through the floor for a finale. Cubby's resemblance to Mickey Mouse is more pronounced in *Opening Night* than in subsequent appearances, wherein the animators can't seem to make up their minds *what* he should look like from one cartoon to the next.

Mannie Davis would receive sole directorial credit for six additional *Cubby Bears*, but though Cubby was his "baby" Davis didn't do much in the way of making him memorable or distinctive. The second entry *Love's Labor Won* (1933), codirected by John Foster, introduces Cubby's girlfriend Honey Bear as well as a "plot" that would be repeated virtually verbatim in the next two cartoons: Cubby and Honey sing and dance until a villain either beats up Cubby or kidnaps Honey or both, whereupon the tables are turned and virtue triumphs. It was a formula that had already been worn threadbare by every other cartoon studio, and it does little to promote Cubby as a unique or proactive character. In fact, our hero frequently has to rely on outside help like the bald eagle in *The Last Mail* (1933) to foil the bad guy. Elsewhere, *Barking Dogs* (1933) and *Sinister Stuff* (1934) dredge up the moth-eaten "Mortgage on the farm/Me Proud Beauty" melodrama spoof that the earlier *Aesop's Fables* had effectively bled dry—perhaps with a few new and unusual gags, but otherwise the same old Same Old.

The series received a shot in the arm when Steve Muffati (later most closely associated with Max Fleischer and Paramount-Famous Studios) began sharing directorial credit with Mannie Davis. Their first collaboration *Fresh Ham* (1933) wrings one bulls-eye gag after another from the premise of Cubby auditioning various vaudeville acts, and though the leading character still hasn't assumed control of his own cartoons (in this one he plays straight to a feline janitor) the results are a lot more satisfactory than before. The highlight comes when a photo of Irving Berlin springs to life and whines "Oy Oy Oy!" over Cubby's ear-splitting piano rendition of "Alexander's Ragtime Band." Steve Muffati would earn solo credit for the series' best cartoon *Croon Crazy* (1933), a nonstop laugh parade in which radio singer Cubby, appearing over station R-K-O, is forced by circumstance to imitate Paul Whiteman, Kate Smith, Al Jolson, Bing Crosby and Mae West. As the broadcast progresses, we see its cathartic effect on listeners throughout the world: In India, Mahatma Gandhi dances so energetically that his shawl falls off, revealing a bra and panties underneath!

Two of the *Cubby Bears* stand out from the rest if only because Van Beuren had practically nothing to do with their production. Having recently left Warner Bros.' Leon Schlesinger cartoon unit, animation directors Hugh Harman and Rudolph Ising were shopping for a new distributor. In 1933 Harman and Ising were contracted by Van Beuren for a brace of Cubby cartoons, *World Flight* and *The Gay Gaucho*. If one hadn't seen the opening credits one could easily jump to the conclusion that these were actually Schlesinger-produced "Looney Tunes," and that Cubby Bear had morphed overnight into Harman-Ising's longtime star Bosko. Cubby bounces up and down rhythmically to the background music, rolls his wide eyes and takes furtive peeks at the camera, just like Bosko had been doing since 1930. Further evidence of

Cubby Bear (left) contemplates leaving the theatrical-agent business in this scene from 1933's *Fresh Ham*.

the Harman-Ising touch are the exaggerated spot gags and the effervescent music scores by the team's longtime orchestrator Frank Marsales, not to mention the "guest" appearances in *World Flight* of such caricatured celebrities as Maurice Chevalier, the Marx Brothers, Ed Wynn, Charles Lindbergh and even Adolf Hitler. (A third Harman-Ising Cubby Bear effort, *Mischievous Mice*, was not released by Van Beuren. Sometime in the late 1940s, Hugh Harman himself distributed the cartoon's work print with a new soundtrack.)

In November 1933 Gene Rodemich resigned as head of both the Van Beuren music and animation department. Rodemich's hand-picked successor Winston Sharples took over the musical scores, while George Stallings, who'd been with *Aesop's Fables* since 1927, was promoted to head animation director. Because of a dramatic price hike in music royalties, Sharples was unable to employ the popular dance numbers and ballads that had been Rodemich's *forte*, but his clever original scores were a welcome addition to the Van Beuren operation. Working in collaboration with Steve Muffati, George Stallings held the directorial reins for the last five *Cubby Bears*—which, since Cubby never officially had a separate series, were also the final entries in the venerable *Aesop's Fables*. Cubby Bear finally settled on a stable, workable character design, and the cartoons themselves were handsomely assembled with imaginative gags. Superior entries like *How's Crops?* and *Mild Cargo*—a takeoff of Van Beuren's own feature film *Wild Cargo* (see Chapter 13)—hinted at the positive direction Cubby might have taken had the character not been dropped by incoming animation director Burt Gillett (see Chapter 19) in mid–1934.

Harking back to Van Beuren's staff conference at the New York Athletic Club, one of the attending animators suggested that the studio purchase animation rights for magazine artist Otto Soglow's panel-cartoon character the Little King, which had appeared in *The New Yorker* since 1930. Though his previous foray into the funny pages with the live-action *Smitty* comedies (see Chapter 8) had not been a significant success, Van Beuren was intrigued by Soglow's streamlined, minimalist style and by the artist's captivating creation. The Little King was a cute, bell-shaped monarch with a semicircular pointed beard and a tiny crown which he never removed, even in bed. Enjoying the privileges of monarchy to the utmost, the King ignored pomp, circumstance and dignity, shocking and embarrassing his much-taller Queen and his courtiers by indulging in such plebeian pleasures as sliding down the staircase bannister, riding a merry-go-round, feeding monkeys at the zoo or sneaking behind his throne to share a box lunch with a common laborer. In a world of ruthless dictators and despots the Little King was a true democrat, possessing no class consciousness whatsoever and scoring laughs with the basic incongruity of a powerful regent behaving like an innocent schoolboy.

Whether or not the gentle, pantomimic Little King could be successfully adapted to animation was problematic, since not only did the Van Beuren staff have to worry about retaining Soglow's distinctive style but they also had to extract some momentum from a basically passive character. In the words of Leonard Maltin, "it's amazing that the animators succeeded as well as they did." To give his staff practical experience in nailing down Soglow's draftsmanship in animated form, animation head Gene Rodemich came up with two audition cartoons in March of 1933, released as part of the *Aesop's Fables* series and featuring another Soglow creation. By this time, Hearst's King Features syndicate had secured the daily and Sunday newspaper-strip rights to *The Little King*, but this version could not legally be launched until Soglow's ironclad contract with *The New Yorker* had run its course in September 1934. In the interim, the artist provided Hearst with a Sunday strip called *The Ambassador*, featuring an exact double for the King minus the crown, velvet robe and title. *The Ambassador*'s companion "topper" strip was *Sentinel Louie*, the wordless adventures of a plump palace guard. Rodemich chose Sentinel Louie (respelled "Louey") as a trial balloon for Van Beuren's *Little King* series, resulting in two beautifully designed *Fables* entries, *A Dizzy Day* and *A.M. to P.M.* (both 1933). Theme music for this miniseries was the Boswell Sisters hit "Crazy People," and while the cartoons were too leisurely to qualify as crazy they proved that the Soglow *oeuvre* could be successfully replicated on the moving screen.

Finally in September of 1933, the *Little King* series proper was launched with *The Fatal Note*, directed without credit by George Stallings, who helmed the rest of the series with the exceptions of *Marching Along* and *Pals* (1933), both credited to James Tyer (whose animation career would extend all the way to Ralph Bakshi's *Fritz the Cat* in 1972). RKO promoted *The Little King* with gusto, preparing full-page trade ads showing the magazine character shaking hands with his screen counterpart ("He lives and breathes and sneezes through his beard!") and licensing a line of toys and accessories like the "Little King" beauty compact. RKO also issued press releases indicating that Otto Soglow was personally writing gags for the cartoons, though he was reportedly displeased with the series.

The *Little King* cartoons are among Van Beuren's best animated and most attractive black-and-white efforts. The property's animators included such budding talents as Pete Burness, later the principal director of UPA's innovational *Mr. Magoo* cartoons. The series' pinnacle, and the one entry most often revived today, is the studio's Christmas 1933 release *Pals*, in which the jovial King, seized by the Yuletide spirit, opens his chamber doors—and his pile of Christmas presents—to a pair of scraggly hoboes. Though as a whole *The Little King* is not a terribly exciting property, its laid-back charm and good intentions shine through. Ten cartoons were produced in the series before its cancellation upon the departure of George Stallings and the arrival of Burt Gillett in 1934. The Little King would make one more (dismal) screen appearance in Max Fleischer's *Betty Boop* series before permanently returning to the printed page, where he remained a King Features staple until Otto Soglow's death in 1975.

The most ambitious project under the Stallings regime may have been launched during the Rodemich era at that aforementioned Athletic Club meeting, but more likely got under way at the behest of Van Beuren's distributor RKO. The studio's association with its sister radio network NBC's biggest attraction *Amos 'n' Andy* stretched back to the release of the radio stars' 1930 feature-film debut *Check and Double Check*. It's hardly a spoiler to reveal that Amos Jones and Andy Brown were two black men portrayed on radio by two white men, Freeman Gosden and Charles Correll. The phenomenal popularity of the radio series had prompted RKO to feature Gosden and Correll, in blackface makeup, as the stars of *Check and Double Check*, which ended up one of the studio's biggest hits of 1930 but was ultimately written off as a loss once the public's curiosity was satisfied and box office receipts plummeted. Since that time Gosden and Correll steered clear of the movies, but 1933 seemed to be the right year to return to the visual medium. Though still at the top of the ratings chart, the radio program had begun to lose listeners to such competitors as CBS' Bing Crosby, and to counter this dip Gosden and Correll embarked on a national vaudeville and personal appearance tour, wearing their *Amos 'n' Andy* costumes and makeup for the pleasure of their huge fan base (which included almost as many black listeners as white). In anticipation of the tour, the team struck a deal with Van Beuren, described as a "Family Affair" in the January 31, 1933, *Variety*: "With the NBC Artists Service acting as the radio act's rep, the Van Beuren Corp. has closed with Amos 'n' Andy for a series of 13 shorts. Each of the subjects will be in cartoon, with the voices of the blackface, team, playing all the parts, dubbed in. Van Beuren is affiliated with RKO, which in turn is a subsid with NBC of RCA."

There was also talk that the team would appear in a group of live-action two reel comedies for the same producer and distributor, but this came to nothing. Up until March of 1933 it appeared as if the cartoons themselves would never get under way, with the trade papers declaring that the project was a definite "go" one week, only to announce its premature demise the week after. But on March 9, virtually every industry periodical reported that Gosden and Correll had briefly left their Chicago headquarters for one day's worth of voice recording at Van Beuren's New York studio. On March 28 RKO sent out a statement that Van Beuren had assembled a 38-person staff to labor exclusively on the *Amos 'n' Andy* animated series.

Accustomed to controlling every creative aspect of their radio program, Gosden and Correll also exercised final approval of Van Beuren's character designs. These were reminiscent of those seen in the studio's abortive Miller & Lyles cartoon *All*

Wet: Instead of the standard pitch-black coloring used for African American caricatures, the screen version of Amos 'n' Andy would be rendered in gray tones. The usual minstrel-show white lips were retained, not so much out of showbiz tradition but in order to emphasize the lip movements, which according to RKO would be synchronized with a "new process." Judging from interviews granted years later by Van Beuren artist Bill Littlejohn (whose long animation career would culminate decades later with TV's *Peanuts* and *Garfield* specials), the "new" process was a variation of the time-honored rotoscope system, with the animators tracing live-action films of the voice artists. In keeping with the studio's promise that Amos 'n' Andy would look "just as their millions of fans imagined them," Littlejohn recalled: "There was nothing exaggerated or caricatured about the drawings of their faces. They were pretty much drawn to scale." The cartoons required far more individual drawings with far more meticulous attention to detail (right down to the vest buttons) than was typical at Van Beuren.

To prepare audiences for the radio-to-screen transition, RKO's advertisements featured photos of the "real" Amos 'n' Andy slowly morphing into their cartoon counterparts. RKO's ad copy assured fans that several of radio series' other beloved characters would show up onscreen, including the scheming Kingfish, industrious Brother Crawford, slow-as-molasses Lightnin' and Andy's erstwhile lady friend Madame Queen, drawn in the ads as a saucy young wench—rather at odds with the brash harpie described on radio. (Madame Queen was ultimately dropped from the cartoons).

Directed by George Stallings, the initial *Amos 'n' Andy* effort *The Rasslin' Match* was designed and promoted as a "special," with a prolonged 11-minute running time and a world premiere at Radio City Music Hall on January 4, 1934. As a bonus, the cartoon's plotline was based on a genuine *Amos 'n' Andy* radio continuity of 1932, in which Kingfish arranged a wrestling bout pitting Andy against the appropriately yclept Bullneck Mooseface. Before the story even gets under way, we hear the voice of the radio show's announcer John Hay over the opening credits informing us that we'd be hearing "the same voices that you hear on the air each night," adding "I hope that you will look forward to seeing the Amos 'n' Andy sound cartoons, and that you will enjoy them thoroughly." Hay signs off with his familiar catchphrase, "Here they are."

Here they are, all right. Though character movement and lip synchronization in *Rasslin' Match* are sharper and more convincing than usual in Van Beuren cartoons, the rest of the animation is surprisingly crude, well below the standards of the last *Cubby Bear* efforts. Whatever humor can be found is generated by the dialogue delivery and subtle vocal inflections of Freeman Gosden as Amos and the Kingfish (we know he's the Kingfish because there's a piscatorial charm on his watch chain) and Charles Correll as Andy and Mooseface; the sight gags are competent at best, clumsy at worst. And while no one could have realistically expected the animated Amos 'n' Andy to radiate the warmth and humanity of the radio characters, the two guys we see on screen aren't even as engaging as Tom and Jerry. The second cartoon in the series, *The Lion Tamer* (1934), is marginally better drawn and paced, relying on standard slapstick bearing little relation to Amos 'n' Andy beyond their presence, but amusing enough to keep us from rending our garments.

We'd love to discuss the remaining 11 episodes in Van Beuren's *Amos 'n' Andy* series, but two cartoons were all that were completed. On October 25, 1933, *Film Daily* had this to say: "Due to the impracticability of keeping the two famous

Trade ad for the first of Van Beuren's *Amos 'n' Andy* cartoons, from the January 2, 1934, *Motion Picture Daily*.

comedians in New York for voice dubbing, the Van Beuren Corp. has abandoned production of the 'Amos 'n' Andy' combination shorts-cartoon series scheduled for this season's release." That was the official story at the time, but in March 1935 a new narrative emerged when Van Beuren filed a breach of contract suit for $181,995 in the New York Supreme Court against Freeman Gosden, Charles Correll and NBC, alleging that the team's contract for 13 cartoons had been breached. The defendants countersued for $254.000, citing the studio's failure to fulfill its contract requirements.

Research has not revealed the outcome of this litigation. It can be said, however, than in 1935 any additional Amos 'n' Andy entries, or for that matter any other black and white cartoons, were the farthest things from the mind of the new man in charge of the Van Beuren animation factory. That man was Burt Gillett, and he's going to get a chapter of his own in due time.

Chapter 12

Floyd Gibbons Supreme Thrills

With *Grantland Rice Sportlights* (see Chapter 6) going full steam at the box office in 1931, Amedee Van Beuren was undoubtedly convinced that he'd cornered the market in colorful journalists when he signed Floyd Gibbons for a powerhouse series of 13 one-reelers. But what might have been one of the most successful properties in the history of the Van Beuren Corporation was abruptly terminated after only two entries—cut down in its prime by (prepare yourself for a shock) another lawsuit.

By 1931 Floyd Gibbons had survived enough thrills, chills and spills to fill three lifetimes. Born in Washington, D.C., in 1887, Gibbons had just been expelled from Georgetown University when he landed his first newspaper job as a crime reporter in Minneapolis, Minnesota, almost immediately making his mark in the world by interviewing a fugitive from justice during a shootout with the police. As a roving correspondent for the Chicago *Tribune* he interviewed both Mexican guerrilla leader Pancho Villa and U.S. Army General John J. Pershing while covering the bloody Villa Expedition of 1916. Dispatched to the battlefields of France in the months just prior to America's entry into World War I, Gibbons' assignment was nearly over before it began when on February 25, 1917, the British ocean liner *Laconia* was torpedoed right from under him. His impassioned account of the deaths of two American passengers helped stoke the flames of public demand for a declaration of war against Germany, and before long Gibbons was issuing colorfully detailed reports from the front lines.

While on patrol in Belleau Wood with the U.S. Marines in June of 1918, he was struck down by enemy machine-gun fire. "My fingers rested on something soft and wet," he later recalled. "I withdrew my hand and looked at it. It was covered with blood." Floyd Gibbons quickly came to the realization that he had just lost his left eye. Though he could have easily been fitted with a glass replacement at any point in his career, Gibbons chose instead to wear the white eyepatch which became his lifelong trademark, greatly enhancing his dashing, devil-may-care public persona.

After receiving the Croix de Guerre for courage on the battlefield, Gibbons cashed in on his celebrity by hitting the lecture and vaudeville circuits. He also covered the first year of Communist rule in Russia, repeatedly outscooping the competition with gruesomely graphic descriptions of the postwar Russian famine. Proceeding to invade the literary world with a biography of Germany's "Red Baron" Von Richtofen and several other bestsellers, Gibbons went on to conquer the new medium of radio, promptly establishing a reputation as the fastest talker on the air (217 words per minute). His first film assignment was as narrator of the 1930 feature-length documentary *With Byrd at the South Pole* (one of the rare occasions that he *didn't* go along for the ride), and soon after he was first seen by the moviegoing public in the trailer for the 1931 Oscar-winner *Cimarron*. Clearly the time was ripe for a Floyd Gibbons movie series, with Amedee Van Beuren first in line to secure Gibbons' services thanks to the firm familial bonds between the journalist's home radio network NBC and Van Beuren's distributor RKO.

This auspicious occasion was duly chronicled by *Motion Picture Herald* on April 18, 1931:

> The next point in Floyd Gibbons' furious career is the screen. The newspaper adventurer and radio journalist has been signed for a series of RKO-Pathé shorts to be released under the title "Floyd Gibbons Supreme Thrills." They will be produced under the immediate auspices of the Van Beuren Corporation. Gibbons will interview heroes of the World War, thus telling the stories of their greatest thrills in the conflict. Production will be in the East so as not to interfere with Gibbons' radio work as "Headline Hunter" for NBC.

It was, according to the June 1931 edition of *What's on the Air* magazine, the largest contract ever offered for a series of one-reel movie shorts, with Gibbons assured a total of $60,500, or $4654 per short—not to mention additional remuneration for writing and submitting story ideas. The line producers for the series were Hollywood press agent A.P. Waxman and prominent New York theater owner Michael Mindlin, both of whom knew a thing or three about blanket promotion. Unlike Grantland Rice, who generally avoided appearing in or narrating the Van Beuren shorts bearing his name, Gibbons would be an on-screen presence in each and every *Floyd Gibbons Supreme Thrills*, not only conducting interviews with the leading players of World War I but also narrating library footage of the conflict in his inimitable rat-a-tat-tat delivery. As an added showmanship flourish, the initial *Supreme Thrills* had its first press screening in an improvised theater on the 79th floor of the Empire State Building. (King Kong and Fay Wray sent their regrets).

Directed by Vitaphone alumnus Arthur Hurley, whose previous credits included Spencer Tracy's film debut *Hard Guy* (1930), the inaugural *Supreme Thrills* was *Woodrow Wilson's*

Floyd Gibbons in *Radio Digest*, July 1930.

Great Decision—said "decision" being the President's determination after several years of studied neutrality to enter the Great War. Through narration, illustrations, animated maps and stock footage of genuine and reconstructed historical highlights, Wilson's diplomatic activities were chronicled from the time he declared war in 1917 to his death in 1924. Bookending these scenes was Gibbons' interview with the late President's personal physician, Admiral Cary T. Grayson. Establishing and sustaining the exhausting pace of *Woodrow Wilson's Great Decision* was of course Floyd Gibbons himself, as noted by *Film Daily* on August 5, 1931. Labeling the new series "tabloid hot-shots," the periodical stated that the debut short "hits the high spots of the war and runs about ten minutes at express train speed.... If future releases live up to the promise of this first sample they should click handily." *Motion Picture Herald* agreed: "Gibbons' discourse is a fortissimo, bravisimo, recital of events and moods of the period. He maintains the high excitement of his typical radio delivery." Only the monthly *Motion Picture Review* magazine had reservations: "Children under ten may find the picture tiresome." Not to worry, though. Children over ten ate it up with a spoon and demanded seconds.

While this writer has been unable to view a print of *Woodrow Wilson's Great Decision*, a fair assessment of the style, substance and quality of *Floyd Gibbons Supreme Thrills* can be gauged by the series' second entry *Turn of the Tide* (1931), which focuses on the combined battles of Château-Thierry and Belleau Wood. As mentioned, Gibbons had provided eyewitness coverage (first with both eyes, then with one) of this pivotal campaign, which ended successfully for the Allies on July 18, 1918, all but guaranteeing total victory over Germany five months later. First seen with a golf club tucked under his arm (he's a Man of Action, remember), Floyd Gibbons opens the reel at the Rye, New York, estate of General James G. Harbord, former chief of staff for General Pershing—who in turn had commanded the Allied Expeditionary Force in concert with France's Marshall Foch. After exchanging pleasantries with Gibbons, Harbord describes Château-Thierry as (yes) the turning point of the war, drawing a map on the ground (frustratingly out of camera range) to illustrate his assertion. "This must have been the greatest thrill of your life, General" says Gibbons. Picking up his cue, the General invites Gibbons—who, after all, was also there—to take over the narration. And take over he does in patented rapid-fire fashion, his lightning words augmented with cartoon maps and vintage battle scenes (including a spectacular shot of a zeppelin exploding in midair) while the portentous strains of Beethoven's "Coriolan Overture" saw away in the background. Phrases essential to the action include "Nature favored our side," "the riddled ranks re-form" and "stern and grim and proud of the distinction, they march into the unknown." The victorious Allies are characterized as "YOUR sons and YOUR brothers and YOUR daddies," as well as "crusaders against all wars." In the spirit of fair play, Gibbons also heaps praise upon the bravery of the Germans and their gallantry in defeat.

"Gibbons at all times talks rapidly but never incoherently" insisted *Variety* on October 16, 1931. Modern viewers may encounter difficulty keeping up with Gibbons' verbal barrages and will probably require more than one viewing to digest all the information he hurls in our direction. Some may tend to agree with *Motion Picture Review*: "It smacks too strongly of the emotional football announcers' sensational methods to seem in the best taste." In light of the debates over the pointlessness of World War I that have raged during the past century, it's a bit off-putting to hear and see Floyd Gibbons treat the whole tragic affair as a glorious schoolboy adventure—though admittedly, it's also hard to resist being swept up by his unabashed enthusiasm.

A third short subject, *Pershing—The Kaiser's Last Stand*, was already in the works when Amedee Van Beuren had the temerity to complain about the budget for *Floyd Gibbons Supreme Thrills*, which ranged between $12,500 and $15,000 per reel—lofty indeed for what was essentially 1931's version of a power-point presentation. Would Gibbons please balance this expenditure by agreeing to take a salary cut? According to *Variety*, George Engels of NBC Artists' Management "derided" Van Beuren's counter-offer. In a pique, Van Beuren axed the series after a mere two episodes, only to learn the hard way that Floyd Gibbons was not a man to screw around with. In early 1932 Gibbons levied a $60,500 attachment against Van Beuren Productions, tying up the organization's bank accounts to the tune of over $52,000. Faced with a huge outstanding bill from Consolidated Laboratories, Van Beuren was forced to pay Consolidated all the profits from the two existing *Supreme Thrills*, and to put up his recently completed feature film *Bring 'Em Back Alive* (see Chapter 14) as collateral.

No one had more fun during the subsequent courtroom proceedings than Floyd Gibbons, who merrily signed autographs for admirers outside the courtroom and luxuriated in the publicity surrounding his first-ever lawsuit, which turned out to be a slam-dunk for the plaintiff. Adding to Van Beuren's financial woes was an additional $1000 judgment regarding the producer's refusal to pay for specially commissioned material written by Gibbons about Italian dictator Benito Mussolini's ongoing conflict with Pope Pius XI, which Van Beuren subsequently decided not to use. *Variety* explained that this contretemps with Gibbons "has to do with the legal precedent that a screen writer can collect on a work he had been commissioned to do." Gibbons' attorney Harold M. Goldblatt argued that the writer had to be compensated whether the material was used or not. The court agreed, and Van Beuren's association with Floyd Gibbons ended with the producer taking a $61,500 bath.

Though Floyd Gibbons was through with Van Beuren, he continued to pursue film stardom with a second and more enduring series of shorts for Vitaphone. Produced between 1937 and 1939, *Floyd Gibbons: Your Headline Hunter* dramatized prize-winning stories by fledgling journalists, with such New York–based actors as Harry Shannon (who played Orson Welles' father in *Citizen Kane*) and Harry Bellaver (later a costar on TV's *The Naked City*) in the casts. Not that this flurry of filmmaking impeded Gibbons' other activities one particle: He continued to headline his own NBC radio show, provided on-the-spot newspaper reports from the battlefields of China and Ethiopia, and covered the Spanish Civil War from both sides of the conflict. This author is not the first (and most likely not the last) to find it ironic that after a lifetime of death-defying exploits around the world, Floyd Gibbons succumbed peacefully to a heart attack at his Pennsylvania farm in 1939.

Chapter 13

The Liberty Short Short Stories

One of the more vexing aspects of chronicling Van Beuren's non-cartoon output is the present unavailability of many of the films. This is particularly true in the case of the company's *Liberty Short Short Stories* series, produced for the 1931–32 movie season. Prints do exist, but are apparently only in the possession of film collectors disinclined to share their bounty with the rest of the world. Even more frustrating is the lack of truly substantial documentation from such contemporary sources as newspapers, trade magazines and fan publications. And now that this writer is finished feeling sorry for himself, let's get down to the information we *do* have about the series.

It all began with *Liberty* magazine. Advertising itself as "A Weekly for Everybody," *Liberty* was launched in 1921 by the Colonels McCormick and Patterson of the Chicago *Tribune*-New York *Daily News* syndicate (which, as noted in Chapter 8, was also the source of the comic strip that spawned Van Beuren's *Smitty* comedy series). In 1931 the magazine was purchased by physical culturist and publishing mogul Bernarr Macfadden, then going full strength with such properties as *True Detective* and *Photoplay*. Backed by Macfadden's formidable promotion and publicity department, *Liberty* grew apace, and was soon second only to the *Saturday Evening Post* in popularity. The magazine specialized in human-interest articles, short stories and film reviews, flattering its audience by posting an average "reading time" at the beginning of each article (as in "Reading Time: 12 Minutes"), which only the most myopic and illiterate of readers could not match or beat. The list of contributing writers was stellar indeed, including F. Scott Fitzgerald, Agatha Christie, Robert Benchley, Budd Schulberg and even George Bernard Shaw. Occasional guest columns were penned by everyone from Winston Churchill to Leon Trotsky, and from Mae West to Al Capone. Illustrations were provided by the likes of James Montgomery Flagg, John Held, Jr., and young Theodore Geisel, already signing himself "Dr. Seuss."

The fiction appearing in the pages of *Liberty* proved to be a rich source of filmmaking material, with over 120 short stories and serialized novels adapted for the screen during the magazine's existence. In 1930 RKO's Radio Pictures secured the services of *Liberty* editor Fulton Oursler (aka Anthony Abbott) to write screenplays exclusively for the studio, making it a logical progression for RKO short-subject supplier Van Beuren to also delve into the *Liberty* story files. It was producer-director Nat Ross, best known at the time for his work on Universal's long-running *Collegians* two-reel series, who broached the idea with Van Beuren. In 1931 Ross negotiated a deal to not only utilize existing *Liberty* stories but also option film rights for the magazine's still-unpublished stories, allowing himself and Van Beuren to exercise editorial control over the material for the next five years. Plans were drawn to issue 13 shorts in the new series during the 1931–32 season; each story would be dramatic in nature, with comic undertones and a neat O. Henry twist at the finish.

The series was billed onscreen and in print ads as *Liberty Short Short Stories*, though the one-reel films themselves were copyrighted simply as *Liberty Short Stories* and the trade papers often listed them as either "Novelties" or "Van Beuren Miniatures." The property's production unit was set up at Van Beuren's longtime Hollywood facility Tec-Art studios, with Nat Ross as associate producer and Richard Heermance, newly promoted from Van Beuren's editorial staff, as general manager. William Cowan, a former DeMille assistant who'd previous megged the early RKO talkie feature *Half Marriage* and would later call the shots on Monogram's 1933 version of *Oliver Twist*, was assigned to direct the first series entry *Stung* (working title: *Fixed*), adapted by Cowan from a story by F.R. Buckley.

Setting the standards for the series, *Stung* boasted superior production values and a cast top-heavy with familiar Hollywood character actors. Stuttering comedian Roscoe Ates, then headlining his own two-reel series for RKO, starred as a dimwitted juror in a murder trial. Maurice Black played the defendant, a gangster accused of first degree murder. Warner Richmond was cast as Black's lawyer, who, knowing his client is guilty as hell, bribes Ates to persuade the other jurors to bring in a lesser charge of manslaughter, thus saving Black from the chair though still earning him a stiff prison sentence. The strategy is successful, but after sentence is passed Ates has the last laugh when he tells Richmond that the rest of the jury had been willing to let Black get off scot-free. "Unusually well directed for a short film," was the pithy critique in the normally hard-to-please *National Board of Review* magazine; the trade papers also liked *Stung*, though more than one reviewer failed to see the humor in the film's most irritating minor character, a drunken reporter played by Crauford Kent.

National Board of Review magazine found the series' second effort *Ether Talks* "handled with unusual imagination and effectiveness." Again directed by William Cowan and adapted by the director from a story by Houston Day, *Ether Talks* featured Jason Robards, Sr., Dorothy Revier and John Holland in the bizarre tale of a wounded man whose hallucinations while under the influence of ether turn out to be all too true. According to *Variety*, this ten-minute epic set something of record at the Tec-Art studio by being completed in a scant two days. Despite the haste in production, everyone was satisfied with *Ether Talks* except the New York Board of Censors. This august group of nervous nellies demanded that Van Beuren eliminate "all views of ether cone over patient's face, and all views of doctor administering ether"—thus neatly killing the point of both the film's title and plot.

Fred Newmeyer, a seasoned comedy director previously associated with Harold Lloyd, took over from William Cowan for the next two entries. *Double Decoy* (1931) was adapted for the screen by Dick Smith and Ruth Todd from a story by Robert Yates. Huntley Gordon headed the cast as a crooked businessman, who after squandering the life savings of his partner Jason Robards, Sr., schemes to frame Robards into a "gun trap" to murder the man and get away with it. What Gordon doesn't know is that his faithless wife Josephine Dunn is planning to run off with Robards, who in turn intends to use a scarecrow made up to look like himself to throw the cuckolded Gordon off the track. In his eagerness to kill Robards, Gordon shoots the scarecrow instead. Scared witless (to put it euphemistically), both men skedaddle off to parts unknown, leaving Josephine dazed, confused and utterly alone.

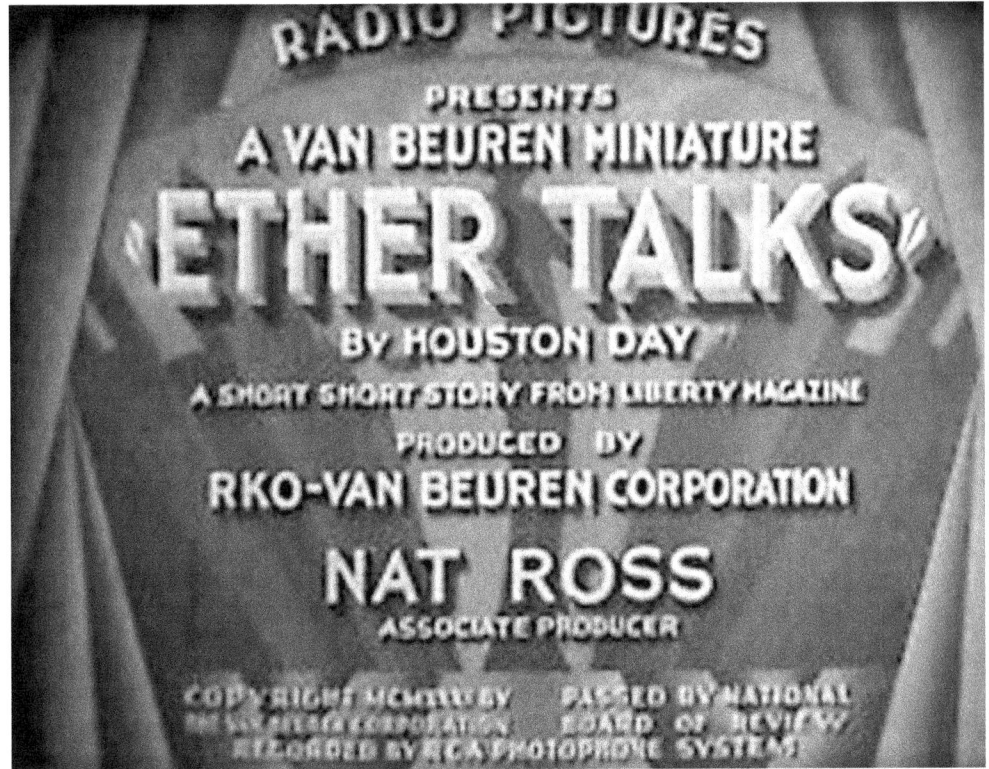

This title sequence from "Ether Talks," the second of Van Beuren's *Liberty Short Short Series* has been floating around the internet for some time. But neither the source nor the film itself has shown up, nor are any other series entries available.

What little we know for certain about the fourth entry *Endurance Flight* (working title *Round Heels*) includes the film's plot, wherein an aviator makes himself miserable—and puts his life in jeopardy—by wrongly suspecting his wife of infidelity. We also know that Ruth Todd and Dick Smith adapted a short story by Norman Anthony, who normally contributed illustrations to *Liberty*. *National Board of Review* magazine said only that this 1932 release was "well done and interesting of its type"—no help whatsoever for hapless film historians seeking out full synopses and cast credits.

William Cowan returned to the director's chair for *Secretary Preferred* (originally *The Feminine Touch*), with Ruth Todd and Dick Smith teamed once more, this time visualizing a story by Frederick Arnold Kummer. Familiar movie faces Selmer Jackson, Arthur Hoyt, Crauford Kent, Eleanor Hunt and Hazel Howell were featured in this trifle about a male con artist and his moll ordering a $10,000 emerald necklace from a jeweler, with the man claiming to be the secretary of a well-known playboy. The crooks' master plan is to show up at the playboy's office when the necklace is delivered, claim it was shipped by mistake, then shuffle off to Buffalo with the precious bauble in hand. Unfortunately the playboy's gold-digging secretary convinces her moonstruck boss to accept the necklace as a present for her. The defeated con man philosophically bows out of the picture with a cynical "Sister, your racket has mine beaten by a mile." *Variety* took notice of *Secretary Preferred*'s onscreen product-placement references to Chryson's, a Hollywood novelty-jewelry shop, opining: "The plug may be the answer to a new idea in meeting the production budget."

Filmed under the title *She Held Him*, the sixth and last *Liberty Short Short Stories* was *Beautiful and Dumb* (1932). Walter Marquiss wrote the original story; Ruth Todd and Dick Smith again handled the adaptation, in collaboration with director Emmett J. Flynn, whose prior credits included the lavish 1921 Fox adaptation of *A Connecticut Yankee* and the offbeat 1928 Laurel & Hardy short *Early to Bed*—and whose last film this was. Venerable screen cad-and-bounder Lew Cody starred as a jewel thief posing as a nobleman, who insinuates himself into the home of wealthy old Dot Farley. The lady's airheaded young niece Mary Nolan apparently assumes that Cody is a weekend house guest and "unwittingly" helps the man pilfer Auntie's diamond necklace. Only when Cody thinks he has made a clean getaway does realization dawn that the supposedly birdbrained Nolan has had his number from the get-go, and has been undermining his scheme all along. *Beautiful and Dumb* was generally regarded as the runt of the *Liberty Short Short Stories* litter, with *Film Daily* dismissing the subject as "flat and unfunny" in its April 17, 1932, review.

Another title, *Leading Citizen*, had been announced in the trade papers at the outset of the series, but Van Beuren ultimately made it official that *Beautiful and Dumb* would be the property's swan song. Barely promoted by either *Liberty* magazine or RKO, *Liberty Short Short Stories* made very little impression with filmgoers and was scuttled after only six of the announced 13 shorts. Other factors that may have contributed to the series' demise include Amedee Van Beuren's preoccupation with his upcoming feature-film debut *Bring 'Em Back Alive* (see Chapter 14), his time- and energy-consuming legal battles with former contractees Grantland Rice and Floyd Gibbons (see Chapters 6 and 12), and the fact that *Liberty* editor Fulton Oursler had left the RKO-Radio writing staff for a new contract with Columbia Pictures. Nat Ross, the man who'd made the original deal with *Liberty*, was supposed to have remained with Van Beuren to produce a series of two-reel musical comedies with zany vaudevillians Olsen and Johnson, but when this project fell through he moved his base of operations to Metropolitan Studios, hoping (but failing) to revitalize his old Universal *Collegians* series.

Unfazed by the cancellation of their Van Beuren contract, *Liberty* magazine continued to prosper through the 1930s and 1940s, and to supply story material to Hollywood; one of their most noteworthy literary contributions was a serialized novel by James M. Cain that matriculated into Billy Wilder's *film noir* masterpiece *Double Indemnity*. Purchased from Bernarr McFadden by Kimberly-Clark, *Liberty* began to falter in the postwar years and went out of business in 1950. Some twenty years later the property was briefly revived as a nostalgia magazine, sprinkling new articles among reprints of pieces from past issues. If *Liberty* is remembered at all today it is because of the reference to the magazine in one of Groucho Marx' best throwaway gags in *The Cocoanuts* (1929), and as the punchline to bandleader Alvino Rey's 1940s novelty tune "I Said No, No, No." And of course, no aging baby boomer can ever forget the incessantly repeated "Dad joke" of the 1950s and 1960s: "Give me Liberty—or give me my money back!"

Chapter 14

Frank Buck

Bring 'Em Back Alive *(1932)*; Wild Cargo *(1934)*; Fang and Claw *(1935)*

**To Begin With...

    For twenty years Frank Buck has been going down into the jungles of the world for the purpose of bringing back alive and in perfect condition the strange, wild animals, birds and reptiles which you see in zoos and menageries everywhere.

    He is the sole representative of this unique and romantic profession ... a hunter who uses no gun, except in self-defense. The man who brings 'em back alive.

    Frank Buck has handled so many wild jungle creatures that he naturally has had many thrilling experiences.

    Here's the picture with Frank Buck himself describing some of the thrills encountered during his most recent expedition into the Malayan jungle.

    This long-winded preamble was but a portion of the two-minute opening credit sequence for Amedee J. Van Beuren's first feature-length release *Bring 'Em Back Alive*. One might consider it an unnecessary mess of verbiage for movie audiences of 1932, who were already familiar with Frank Buck and his colorful adventures as extensively chronicled in the daily press, the weekly and monthly periodicals, and Buck's own 1930 best-selling memoirs, bearing the same title as the Van Beuren film. The introductory comments are undoubtedly of more value to present-day observers, to whom Frank Buck is only a distant (and not always accurate) memory. Let us fill in a few more blanks below:

    Born in Gainesville, Texas, in 1884, Frank Howard Buck was enraptured by stories of exotic animals in distant lands from an early age. Bored with traditional schooling Frank dropped out after the seventh grade, and with the assistance of his brother Walter found work as a cowpuncher at a cattle ranch, selling songs to vaudeville performers as a sideline. These activities brought him to Chicago, where after winning $3500 in a poker game Buck embarked upon his first overseas tour. By 1911 he was making regular treks deep into the jungles of Africa, Asia and South America, where he and his hearty band of assistants rounded up wild animals, birds and reptiles—not to kill or stuff as trophies in the manner of other hunters, but to ship them alive and kicking to the zoos and circuses of the world. In an era when big-game hunting was still politically correct and widely practiced, Buck shunned firearms unless the lives of himself, his assistants or his captured beasts were in danger. In the absence of modern-day stun guns and other such tranquilizers Buck became an expert in building intricate and ingenious traps to ensnare his quarry with a minimum of pain and bother. To ensure that his captures were brought back to civilization unharmed and well cared for, Buck would travel with them on the same vessels.

Because many of the species he brought back alive were endangered even back then, Buck regarded himself as a conservationist and humanitarian, though some of his methods to subdue and domesticate the beasts might be considered cruel and insensitive today. While employed as director of the San Diego Zoo in 1923 Buck was accused of such questionable practices as force-feeding snakes and oiling the skins of animals to keep their bodies porous; he in turn reprimanded the zoo's management for allegedly selling animals to experimental labs and clothing manufacturers. Buck's directorship was short and litigious; within a few years he relocated his headquarters to the Raffles Hotel in faraway Singapore, thereafter dividing his time between his hunting expeditions and his home in California. By the end of the 1920s Frank Buck was universally recognized as the world's foremost supplier of wild animals.

On the advice of friends he compiled several of his more thrilling exploits into a book titled *Bring 'Em Back Alive*, cowritten by Edward Anthony and published in 1930. The book sold like the proverbial hotcakes, and with the encouragement of journalist Floyd Gibbons—and also under the spell of the silent Merian C. Cooper-Ernest Schoedsack nature documentary *Grass*—Buck decided to adapt his book into a film, assembling a movie crew to accompany him on his next trip to Malaya.

But no major Hollywood studio was interested in a picturization of *Bring 'Em Back Alive*. Most industry moguls had been scared off by reports of the bloated budget and endless production problems attending MGM's recent jungle epic *Trader Horn*, and by the well-deserved accusations of fakery hurled at Walter Futter's 1930 "documentary" *Africa Speaks*. As Buck recalled in his 1941 autobiography *All in a Lifetime*:

> After exhausting the major studios without success, I began, as a last resort, on the makers of short film subjects. The Van Beuren Corporation, a subsidiary of R.K.O., was interested. Amedee Van Beuren, the president, read *Bring 'Em Back Alive* and immediately called me. We drew up a contract in which I agreed to make thirteen moving-picture shorts, and the Van Beuren Corporation agreed to pay the entire cost of my expedition to the jungle countries, from the salaries of cameramen down to the last cocktail I might buy en route. Instead of a salary or a guarantee, I was to receive a share of the profits of the pictures I would make, which was exactly what I wanted.

Exactly what Van Beuren wanted from the shorts is not clear. At first glance it appears that the producer envisioned another documentary series in the tradition of his self-contained *Vagabond Adventures* shorts (see Chapter 10), but Buck's literary collaborator Edward Anthony later claimed in a lawsuit (yep, another lawsuit) that he was instructed to script the series in the style of a serial, with each short segueing into the next. Whatever the case, Buck's contract stipulated that Van Beuren would neither view nor edit the project until all the film had been delivered to the producer's New York office, lest it emerge in a form contrary to the filmmaker's personal vision. Buck later stated that even he did not see a foot of completed film until after his return to the States: "Exposed film does not keep for long in the jungle humidity, so as fast as we ground out the reels they were sealed in air-tight tins along with a generous amount of drying powder and shipped back to the Van Beuren Corporation as often as we could get out to a shipping point."

The director hired to impose dramatic unity upon *Bring 'Em Back Alive* was Clyde E. Elliott, who back in 1919 had founded Post Pictures Corporation to make nature films for Paramount release. Elliott had been inactive for nearly a decade when he was hired by Buck to accompany cinematographers Nick Cavaliere and Carl Berger on the Malayan expedition. Flouting the tradition set by such earlier jungle documentarians as Martin and Osa Johnson, Elliott chose to never show the cameras or the cameramen in any scene, keeping them well in the background and thus providing viewers unencumbered views of wildlife in the raw.

Along for the ride to the Far East was Dahlam Ali, for years the head servant in the California household of Frank Buck and his wife (who also accompanied Frank to Malaya, at least as far as the Raffles Hotel). According to legend, Ali had been devoted to the family ever since Buck nursed him through a ravaging jungle illness. Though he spoke no English, Ali instinctively anticipated his employer's every instruction and desire, though he probably never imagined that he would be pressed into service as an actor. In the film, Ali is depicted as Buck's "Right Hand Man" for the expedition, and it is contrived to suggest that he'd been in Malaya awaiting Buck's arrival before the story began. In his narration, Buck describes Ali thusly: "Even though his body was brown, he was pure white inside." If you can get past this cringeworthy line, chances are you'll get through the rest of the show.

Bring 'Em Back Alive was shot silent to keep the budget down, which explains the film's sped-up, herky-jerky quality. With several years' experience on the lecture circuit under his belt, Frank Buck bypassed such traditional Van Beuren "announcers" as Tom Terriss and Gayne Whitman to serve as the film's narrator. The musical score was in the capable hands of studio stalwart Gene Rodemich, while the sounds of the jungle beasts were provided by radio actor Donald Bain, acknowledged by his peers as the finest animal impersonator in the business.

Rodemich and Bain's contributions to the post-production process might not have come to pass had Van Beuren acted upon his impulse to discontinue the project after the first 50,000 feet of unexposed film arrived in New York. Buck's agent George T. Bye appealed to the producer to at least pay for the unit's transportation back to America. Later, Buck would credit Van Beuren's general manager Jesse Goldburg (with the studio since 1929) for getting the project off the ground and having enough faith to see it through, even when Van Beuren didn't. The total negative cost was a trim $52,500, most of which was for post-production.

Buck had asked that the proposed 13 shorts not be advertised *as* shorts in the trade papers, hoping to talk Van Beuren into releasing the expedition footage as a feature film. Though the producer publicly stated as early as 1930 that he'd toyed with the idea of making features, going so far as to tell *Film Daily* that he planned six feature-length productions for the 1930–31 season, his heart remained in short subjects. Van Beuren ignored Buck's request and advertised *Bring 'Em Back Alive* as the blanket title for his newest short series—and intended to keep the property in that format right up to the moment that the unedited footage arrived at his New York screening room. But as Buck recalled in his autobiography: "After the first few thousand feet had flashed on the screen, there was no more doubt. It was a feature! Everyone agreed that, cut to the normal length of 7,000 feet [approximately 65 minutes], *Bring 'Em Back Alive* would be utterly different and would create a sensation in the movie world." Minus Buck's latter-day hyperbole, this was the revised announcement that Van Beuren issued to the trades.

As noted at the start of the chapter, *Bring 'Em Back Alive* takes its own sweet

Modest 1932 trade-paper advertisement (as it appeared in *Motion Picture Herald*) for Van Beuren's first Frank Buck feature film, *Bring 'Em Back Alive*.

time getting under way, opening with a short montage of wild-animal closeups which dissolves into the credits and introductory notes. The film is touted onscreen as the "official and authentic motion picture record of the RKO VAN BEUREN MALAYAN JUNGLE EXPEDITION," adding: "Every foot of this picture was actually photographed in the Malayan Jungle Country"—to be precise, the Malayan jungles of Johore, though some scenes were lensed at game preserves and on the estate of Buck's friend Sultan Ibrahim. Buck's narration is clipped, breathless, brimming over with hubris and occasional word flubs. A professional announcer he ain't, but he is perfectly cast for his self-appointed role. Clearly, Buck fervently hopes that the viewer will accept the film as being totally comprised of "reality footage," and that its sequence of events is precisely the order in which they actually occurred. You can do so if you like.

There follows a few establishing shots of the Suez Canal and Indian Ocean before we arrive in Singapore for a progression of smooth and seemingly endless tracking shots of Frank Buck riding in a rickshaw. Eventually he confesses "I was getting impatient," and he's not the only one at this point: Eight minutes pass before we even see so much as a rhesus monkey. Another thick slice of footage is devoted to Buck's assistants building his jungle compound (actually constructed several years earlier) and loading guns and supplies. We then get a few fleeting glimpses of such wildlife as the rhinoceros hornbill (that's a bird), and finally twelve minutes into the film Buck makes his first capture, of a drowsy-looking monitor lizard. We are also treated to the first of many sequences wherein Buck improvises a sturdy animal trap with the materials at hand—a sort of MacGyver of the Jungle.

The film's throughline is introduced by establishing the Bengal tiger as the villain of the piece: "The only animal in the world without a spark of good nature." The first tiger we see onscreen engages in an uneven "street-corner brawl" with a surly black leopard who has just emerged from a scrape with a python. A second tiger does battle with a water buffalo and is later shot to death (assuming it's the same tiger) while stalking a baby elephant that has strayed from its herd. Buck captures the puny pachyderm, but not without a struggle. Our hero is then shown fashioning bamboo tubes to feed the elephant milk taken from gourds growing in a tall tree, which are retrieved and brought to earth by a tame rhesus. Just an average working day in Frank Buck Land.

All this is mere prologue for the introduction of the most ferocious Bengal tiger in the film, who promptly engages in a thrill-packed sequence that through the magic of editing seems to occur within a single 12-minute timespan. First, the tiger takes on an alligator, who in turn is crushed to death by a 30-foot rock python. We've now arrived at the film's "money scene": A fierce and prolonged duel between python and tiger, which surprisingly ends in a draw. This is the true climax of the film, but before the fadeout some seven minutes later we're invited to appreciate anew Buck's meticulous construction of strong individual traps to snag first the python and then the tiger. All this activity is accompanied by one of Gene Rodemich's finest musical scores, featuring original themes that would do yeoman duty in scores of future Van Beuren shorts (one *mysterioso* would feature prominently in the studio's reissue of Chaplin's *Easy Street*) as well as such classical passages as Rimsky-Korsakov's "Scheherazade" suite (heard during the capture of the baby elephant).

The episodic nature of *Bring 'Em Back Alive* occasionally betrays its origin as a baker's dozen of separate shorts, though the flow of the narrative will appear seamless to those unaware that the movie was not initially conceived as a feature. Showman that he is, Frank Buck punctuates the action scenes with light comedy relief, mostly supplied by an adorable little honey bear who is captured by dauntless native boy Ahmed after his comrades have all run away, mistaking the bear for a more dangerous adversary; and by frequent cutaways to the compound's mascot, Percy the silvery gibbon, who dances a little jig every time a new animal is hauled into camp. (It's the same piece of footage—with the same piccolo music—over and over. We're not supposed to notice). For all its vaunted authenticity, portions of the film must have looked artificial even in 1932, never more obviously than in the scene where the honey bear escapes from his cage while the native boys are otherwise occupied: Lucky that there were cameras already set up to record both getaway and recapture. The contrivance of tying the various captures into a coherent narrative by adding "bridge" scenes that were obviously filmed separately and after the fact (one young native lass smiles broadly at the camera while supposedly fleeing a tiger) never mitigates the genuine perils recorded throughout the film, so we can forgive Frank Buck a dramatic flourish or two. We can also grant him the privilege of boosting the film's box-office value with a flash of voyeurism during a gratuitous scene in a native village, with the strapping young males flexing their pecs as they engage in a blowgun competition while the bare-breasted (and occasionally bare-bottomed) damsels enjoy their annual "bathing festival."

The much-publicized "battle royal" between the python and the tiger is cunningly edited but ultimately goes on too long, a minor defect that would be corrected in Buck's later films. Though it still retains its thrill value and basic credibility, it is the one sequence that in 1932 drew the most accusations of fakery from more jaundiced viewers, not only because the battle ends in a draw (which admittedly seems unlikely) but because it takes place in an artificially small clearing, suggesting that the fracas was totally stage-managed for the benefit of the cameras. This led to whispers that the bulk of the film was *not* shot in Malaya, but in a more safe and secure locale, possibly even California.

Terry Ramsaye, editor of *Motion Picture Herald*, issued an impassioned defense of Buck, assuring readers that the film was largely made "in a compound adjacent to the city of Singapore, in the Straits Settlements." It would later be revealed that while *Bring 'Em Back Alive* and its 1934 sequel *Wild Cargo* were indeed shot in the Far East as advertised, Buck's "heart of the jungle" compound was located only a few miles from the Raffles Hotel in Singapore, about 100 yards off a main highway. Terry Ramsaye doesn't specify this (he didn't know *all* the facts), but acknowledges, "The scenes staged and recorded in the compound may be accepted as dramatically reasonable reconstructions of what actually happens in the open jungle."

For his part, Frank Buck never denied staging certain scenes or rearranging events in the editing room, but was able to counter the more strident accusations of phoniness by endorsing a "behind the scenes" account of the tiger-python scene in an article by Alfred Abelli for the monthly magazine *Modern Mechanix and Inventions*. Photographer Nick Cavaliere, the article's main source, was particularly proud of the sequence and of his work in the film as a whole, telling Abelli:

> That was the first time I was ever in the jungle … and I found plenty to learn about photography in that zone. I hope that we brought back knowledge which will be of assistance to science in future work of a similar nature.
>
> I was told that I would have great difficulty in getting good quality in my photography after three o'clock in the afternoon. I found that point to be accurate. I was told too that I must not consider "shooting" anything between twelve o'clock noon and half past one.
>
> However, with my own ideas on this matter, I tried several exposures at the forbidden time, and the results were excellent. It became my suspicion that other cameramen had no desire to work in the intense heat of the tropical mid-day sun.

The article goes on to state that Buck, Clyde Elliott and the two cameramen set up their equipment near a waterhole where it was known that animals regularly congregated. Two days were spent arranging a clearing that was properly sized to allow for filming, its unnatural smallness leading to unfounded suspicions that the python-cobra duel was pre-planned and staged. Nick Cavaliere and co-photographer Carl Berger were planted in camouflaged nets high in the trees, hung against the wind so that the animals wouldn't pick up a human scent. A third unmanned camera, a DeVry automatic with a visual radius of ten feet, was installed in another tree.

These careful preparations enabled the cameramen to capture the bout between the cobra and the unfortunate crocodile—who might not have been given a second look had the cobra not been aroused by the vibration of the motors powering the cameras. Abelli's article explains that the noise from *this* battle attracted the tiger, whom the crew had originally intended to film by itself for a separate sequence. The tiger calmly drank from the waterhole for a few minutes, then finally noticed the python (which had fallen asleep), grabbing the snake by its jaw. As seen in the film, the python wrapped itself around the tiger, then relaxed and allowed the big cat to escape, walk away, and return to resume the battle. The engagement really *did* end in a tie, mainly because both python and tiger were worn out from their previous scrapes. As Nick Cavaliere noted, "The scenes are clear and, as we say, 'full of great definition.'" The dull parts of the fight were neatly excised in the editing process.

Milton Silver, director of advertising at Universal, was temporarily hired away by RKO and Van Beuren to promote *Bring 'Em Back Alive* as a "special assignment." RKO's own promotion expert Robert Sisk designed several splashy theater-lobby displays and advertising floats festooned with motor-animated animal models spewing forth fearsome jungle sounds. The picture opened to record business at the RKO-Mayfair in New York; for the initial run, Frank Buck himself appeared at each screening to deliver a stirring preshow lecture, a practice that may have inspired a similar scene in RKO's *King Kong*, wherein the character of intrepid documentary producer Carl Denham (Robert Armstrong) is blatantly based on Buck. Playing to sellout crowds all over the country, the film enjoyed a domestic gross of $2,000,000. For all its thrills and spills (actual and contrived), by universal concession the hit of *Bring 'Em Back Alive* was the lovable, scampish honey bear ("everything he did was funny") which Buck adopted early in the proceedings. The relationship did not end well, however: As reported by *Movie Classic* in September 1935, the bear later turned on Buck and severely clawed his knee, leaving the great white hunter with a slight limp.

Buck parlayed the film's success into an NBC radio series of the same name, which ran first as a weekly serialized version of the film from October 30 to December 18, 1932, under the sponsorship of toymaker A.C. Gilbert, then as a daily dramatized lecture from July 16 through November 16, 1934, sponsored by Pepsodent. More lasting and profitable was Frank Buck's Jungle Camp, a reproduction of the Buck's Malayan compound erected for Chicago's "Century of Progress" World's Fair in 1933, and later reassembled as a permanent exhibit in Amityville, New York. Director Clyde Elliott, suddenly a potent property after years of obscurity, was hired by Fox to helm the similar jungle opus *Devil Tiger* (1934), which came off as even hokier than *Bring 'Em Back Alive* by including a dramatic plot and a romance (Elliott's last effort, another love-in-the-rough romp involving tigers, was Paramount's *Booloo* [1938]). In addition to *Devil Tiger*, the Van Beuren film inspired Universal's *The Big Cage* (1933) starring Buck's biggest professional rival, lion tamer extraordinaire Clyde Beatty. The phrase "bring 'em back alive" instantly became part of American nomenclature, used frequently and sometimes appropriately to describe professional trackdowns of everything from criminals to lost children. Van Beuren capitalized on the drawing power of the film's title by building up his 1932–33 short subject program with the slogan "Bring 'Em Back with Quality Shorts." And of course the phrase was endlessly lampooned, as witness the 1933 Hal Roach comedy *Bring 'Em Back a Wife* and Van Beuren's own *Aesop's Fable* cartoon *Bring 'Em Back Half-Shot*. As late as the 1938 Laurel and Hardy feature *Block-Heads*, big game hunter Billy Gilbert could be heard boasting to reporters: "I don't bring 'em back alive. I bring 'em back dead. *I come back alive.*"

The whopping financial returns of his first feature encouraged Van Beuren to continue experimenting with longer-form films, first with the 12-part 1932 serial *The Last Frontier* (see Chapter 16), then with a 1934 sequel to *Bring 'Em Back Alive*. *Wild Cargo* was based on Buck's own follow-up book of 1932, again penned in collaboration with Edward Anthony. But Anthony would not be involved with the film version, having broken up with Buck and then suing Van Beuren to restrain future showings of *Bring 'Em Back Alive*, claiming he was engaged to write the planned 13 shorts as a serial but was not properly compensated or credited when the project emerged as feature. While Anthony was still acknowledged onscreen as cowriter of the literary source for *Wild Cargo*, the script and narration was attributed to Courtney Ryley Cooper, who'd previously written Van Beuren's *The Last Frontier*. The camera crew for *Bring 'Em Back Alive* was rehired for the new film, while Eugene Rodemich's successor Winston Sharples wrote the score, a job he'd retain for Van Beuren's third Frank Buck starrer *Fang and Claw*.

Replacing Clyde Elliott as director was Anglo-Belgian explorer and filmmaker Armand Denis, who'd risen to prominence with the 1932 featurette *Kris*, a Technicolor "docu-fantasy" lensed on location in Bali and codirected by Denis and his business partner Andre Roosevelt (They were still collaborating on such fine works as *Under the Southern Cross* and *Among the Headhunters* well into the 1950s). Armand Denis went into *Wild Cargo* as an admirer of Frank Buck, but disillusionment abruptly set in when he realized that Buck's jungle compound was not deep in the wilds as claimed, but a mere stone's throw from Singapore. Quoted in Derek Bousé's *Wildlife Films*, Denis recalled that the compound "consisted mainly of a few cages containing a variety of despondent-looking animals, and of a number of enclosures more or less ingeniously camouflaged and in which obviously the animals were to be placed for various scenes to be photographed. With a sinking heart I began to realize what was expected of me." Further vexing Denis was the discovery that most of the animals slated to be "captured" in the film had been rented from the Sultan of Ibrahim and other wealthy locals. It dawned on Denis that despite the many articles bragging of *Bring 'Em Back Alive's* unassailable authenticity, Frank Buck was willing to set up battles between otherwise fairly placid beasts. When Denis argued that animals "don't normally fight for nothing," Buck is supposed to have replied jauntily "Don't they, eh? When I'm around they do."

Again financed by Van Beuren with RKO handling distribution, *Wild Cargo*, "an official and authentic motion picture record of the Van Beuren-Buck Malayan jungle expedition," was partially filmed in Ceylon and India (mentioned in Buck's narration but not in the credits). Originally the film ran 96 minutes, half an hour longer than *Bring 'Em Back Alive*. The requisite padding isn't too obvious, limited to opening shots of the Tooth of Buddha ceremony in the Ceylonese city of Kandy and attenuated views of an elephant safari, but there's a noticeable increase in comedy relief and excess attention given to the more "lovable" animals, notably a brand-new honey bear described the June 1934 edition of *Screenland* as "more adorable than Janet Gaynor and more expressive than La Hepburn." Percy the dancing gibbon makes an encore appearance, in one closeup performing a double-take that rivals Jimmy Finlayson.

Here's the chronology of the film: Buck's expedition heads into the Salan jungle, where he oversees the building of a four-acre corral to capture an entire elephant herd, letting most of the beasts go and keeping only those that can be domesticated. He then nabs several golden gibbons, a king cobra and a Malayan tapir, whereupon an action sequence obviously intended to "top" *Bring 'Em Back Alive's* cobra-tiger donnybrook is introduced: A *duel à mort* between a 25-foot python and a leopard. The

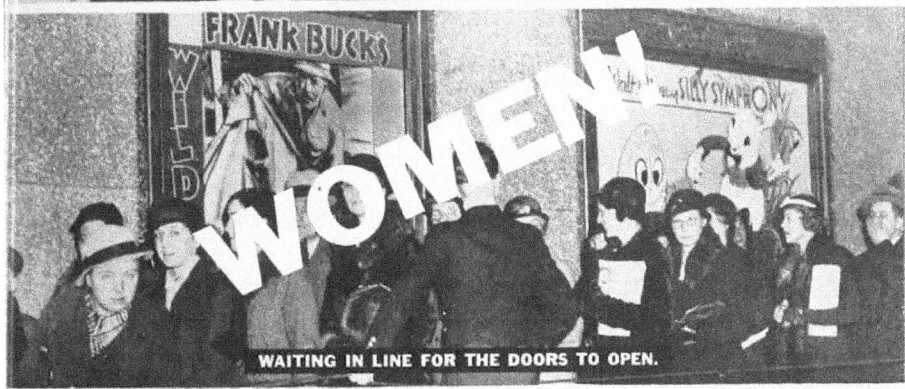

More trade-paper ballyhoo, this time for Frank Buck's second feature, *Wild Cargo*.

camera crew had camped out for two days awaiting this epic struggle, having previously seen the python on the premises before setting about to draw the leopard into camera range by beating drums. Sensitive to complaints from fans that the cobra-tiger scene from the first film ended disappointingly with both animals calling it quits, Buck was probably hoping that this new sequence would conclude with a definite kill—and it does, with the leopard dearly and most sincerely dead. The victorious cobra is summarily captured and shipped off to the Chicago zoo, where, according to narrator Buck, "mealtimes will be regular but less exciting."

There follows a sequence that many contemporary reviewers considered too frightening and gruesome for the kiddie trade. To fill a consignment, Buck rounds up a flock of "flying foxes," also known as "Dracula" bats. This he does in the daytime, when the bats are at their most myopic and vulnerable. Subsequent closeups of these oversized bloodsuckers are indeed enough to make the flesh creep, and are fortunately brief. Then it's off to Sumatra, where Buck entraps a group of speckled monkeys, luring them out of hiding with rice-filled cocoanuts. We're now counting down to the film's second "money scene," as Buck is asked by the Sultan of Ibrahim to capture a killer tiger that is menacing a local rubber plantation. The tiger is shown on the job in a cutaway scene featuring a native laborer peacefully sapping a rubber tree, only to scramble away in terror as the fearsome feline predator approaches—one of several vignettes that moved the *New York Mirror* to comment, "*Wild Cargo* bears the mark of careful staging."

Buck rises to the Sultan's challenge, explaining that "a dozen zoologists had asked me to catch a man-eater. This was my first real chance. I simply had to capture that monster." He orders his men to dig a pit baited with an animal carcass (which, he takes care to point out, *wasn't* killed by human hands), then to cut a hole in the fence of the compound in hopes that the tiger will stick its head through, jump towards the dead meat, and fall into the pit. Buck describes the process of assembling the trap with the precision of an architect, with its bamboo-chute camouflage his particular pride and joy. He adds that it took three days' patience for the tiger to make an appearance. The beast tumbles into the pit, his escape efforts retarded by the unforeseen circumstance of water trickling into his underground prison. The natives are reluctant to drag the snarling tiger out of the pit and into a specially built portable cage. "Someone had to guide that cat into the box we'd lowered," says Buck, and he appoints himself. This leads to several intense seconds-lasting shots of Buck wrestling the beast into submission. "I kept my promise to those dozen zoologists," declares the triumphant Buck as he and his helpers are shown lifting the tiger out of the pit with a derrick, then bearing it off to the compound. "It was a great feeling to carry that man-eater away to serve his life sentence ... for murder."

Anything would be anti-climactic after this, but with extra reels to go Buck proceeds to nab an orangutan and save a sweet little mouse-deer from a python; the writhing reptile later attacks Buck's arm, in a sequence crammed with low-key-lit closeups of both man and snake. For the "wow" finish, a white rhino is subdued after the hapless beast stumbles into an abandoned well. Studio publicists at the time would have had us believe that Buck brought back the rhino as a personal gift for Amedee Van Beuren. (It's not known if the gift was reciprocated).

It is perhaps best to watch *Wild Cargo* without being forearmed with the knowledge of how certain scenes were planned and staged—at least as recalled by the film's disgruntled director Armand Denis. According to Denis, Buck had originally hoped to juice up his capture of a orangutan by showing the beast battling a Bengal tiger, but was talked out of the idea when the director explained that the two animals were from different regions and thus would never logically meet in real life. But Denis was not able to dissuade Buck from ordering his assistants to mercilessly flog a captured elephant herd into obeisance before penning them up in a cage. This disturbing sequence was retained in the original 96-minute release version of *Wild Cargo*, with Buck explaining that the beatings didn't really hurt the elephants, but were administered just to show them "who's boss." After many objections from naturalists other than Denis, the harsh treatment of the elephants was removed from the much-shorter reissue version of the film, which concentrated on the capture.

As far as Armand Denis was concerned, the tiger-pit sequence was the last straw.

This widely circulated trade ad seems to be shouting, "Don't miss *Wild Cargo* (1934) if you know what's good for you!"

Modern viewers might be tipped off that the scene isn't entirely kosher by the blasé reactions of the supposedly frightened natives surrounding the entrapped tiger (one guy nonchalantly scratches his arm in mid-"fright"). In the film, it is made to appear that the trapping of the beast and the hauling-out process occur in the same day within minutes of each other. But as Denis later revealed, two days passed between the tiger's descent into the pit and its recovery by Buck and the natives—and between those two days a heavy rain flooded the pit and drowned the poor animal. Thus, what we see on screen is fearless Frank Buck sweating and straining as he wrestles with a dead tiger. The limp and dormant figure that is subsequently lifted out of the pit and borne away on a long stretcher is one animal that most definitely will not be brought back alive.

Blissfully ignorant of this ghoulishness, the public was willing to forgive the less fatal artifices attending *Wild Cargo*. Advertised on the streets of New York with "The S.S. RKO-Van Beuren," a 50-foot-long float bearing 19 mechanical animals, the film opened at RKO's premiere presentation house Radio City Music Hall, and like its predecessor played to turnaway crowds, not only in Manhattan but in all other major venues. Though not in the blockbuster class of *Bring 'Em Back Alive*, *Wild Cargo* still brought in a healthy $100,000 profit.

This time there would be no two-year gap between Frank Buck feature films. After first announcing plans to team the star with fellow globetrotter Joan Lowell (see Chapter 20), Van Beuren instead financed one more solo Buck foray into the Far East. The resultant 1935 film, originally titled *Jungle*, was renamed for its source book *Fang and Claw*, written by Buck and new collaborator Ferrin Fraser (who also served as scriptwriter). Nine months were spent in preparation for this third in the unofficial Frank Buck feature series, ostensibly directed by Buck himself—though one suspects that much of the film's pace and punch were provided by Van Beuren's new editing team of Horace and Stacy Woodard, fresh from an Oscar win for their *Battle for Life* nature shorts released by Educational Pictures. The Woodards' work on *Fang and Claw* so impressed Van Beuren that he wooed them away from Educational for a new short-subject project, *Struggle to Live* (see Chapter 22). Making his third trip overseas with Buck was cinematographer Nick Cavaliere, who brought along a new partner, Harry E. Squire. Mr. Squire would reluctantly make his acting debut in *Fang and Claw* with a re-enactment of his real-life injury during filming, when while helping Buck load a python into a box the cameraman suffered a four-inch arm wound.

Fang and Claw was the least sanguinary of the three Buck features, with no onscreen death struggles and lots of footage devoted to the mechanics of setting up traps and lures; some reviewers suggested that the downplaying of violence was reflective of the recently-strengthened Production Code. In addition to Buck's usual Malayan stamping grounds, the film was partially shot in Assam in the Northeast Sector of India, and was described in the opening credits as the "official and authentic motion picture record of Frank Buck's wild animal collecting expedition in the Asiatic jungles."

The 70-minute picture gets off to a brisk start with the capture of yet another python, this goomer weighing in at 300 pounds. The peaceful trapping of a resplendent bird of paradise is next on the bill, followed by the snaring of an armored rhino, whose life is saved when Buck kills a marauding tiger. Buck is forced to amputate the rhino's injured ear, further humiliating the poor beast by nicknaming her "Lucy," just as the film's by-now-obligatory honey bear is identified as "Hard Luck Harry." If you like monkeys, they're here in abundance as Buck lures them into captivity with several gallons of tapioca (What, no nutmeg?). A sixteen-foot crocodile is next on Buck's collar list, and then we must sit through a slightly risible scene of long-suffering Dahlam Ali encircled by and rescued from a python. Back in Malaya, Buck picks up some Asian antelopes, rescuing still more natives from still more tigers for good measure. In the comparatively sedate closing sequence, the captured animals are gathered together and safely packed up for the ocean voyage back to America (One shot of an elephant being hoisted onto a ship would somehow find its way into the "News on the March" sequence of RKO's 1941 classic *Citizen Kane*. Watch for it next time.)

When the big New York RKO movie houses took a pass on *Fang and Claw*, the film ended up as the opening attraction for publicist Arthur Mayer's legendary and newly-renovated Rialto Theater on 42nd St. and 7th Ave. Normally the home of such medium-budget films as the Laurel & Hardy and W.C. Fields features (and later the Big Apple home of the Universal horror pictures), the Rialto had a 65-cent limit on ticket prices, as opposed to the top-dollar roadshow admissions charged for *Bring 'Em Back Alive* and *Wild Cargo*. The theater relied upon multiple daily showings with large turnovers (especially kiddie matinees) to pack the seats. Thus, while the initial run of *Fang and Claw* played to the same full houses as its predecessors it did not accrue the same big profits. Elsewhere in the U.S., exhibitors complained that Buck was becoming "old stuff" and his new offering didn't come up to the bloodthirsty

Fang and Claw **was the third and last of the Frank Buck-Van Beuren collaborations (***Film Daily***, 1935).**

standards of the earlier features. In most towns the film was shown on a double bill, sharing its profits with the co-feature. Only in those houses where Frank Buck made personal appearances in conjunction with *Fang and Claw* did the film really perform. The picture grossed only $65,000 and netted a comparatively meager $42,000; it would be Amedee Van Beuren's last feature film.

But that's not the end of the story. During a moment of financial crisis in 1941, RKO conjured up a surefire box-office success out of thin air, recycling footage from all three of Frank Buck's 1930s features—which with the demise of Van Beuren Productions in 1938 RKO now owned outright—into a compilation feature titled *Jungle Cavalcade*. The opening credits state flat out that the footage was culled from *Bring 'Em Back Alive, Wild Cargo* and *Fang and Claw*, crediting the directors of the first two films and the cinematographers of all three. While a separate title card notes that the "new" film's narration is by "Frank Buck himself," credit for writing that narration is bestowed upon Phil H. Reisman Jr., thereby launching a prolific film career that lasted until 1984, mostly in the documentary field. (Reisman was also the creator of the 1955 TV anthology *I Spy*, no relation to the later Cosby-Culp series).

It fell to Reisman and staff editor Jay Bonafield to weave excerpts from three separate films into a single narrative, as if all the highlights occurred during the same Far Eastern expedition. The scenes lifted from the earlier films are seldom presented in their original order, and sometimes two different sequences are combined into one: For example, the leopard-tiger fight from *Bring 'Em Back Alive* is spliced together with scenes of another leopard falling prey to a python in *Wild Cargo*, creating the illusion that one battle led to another. Most of the vignettes are drawn from the first two films, with token representation from *Fang and Claw* (the bird of paradise and tapioca-monkey captures, animals prepared for shipment, and other snippets). Buck's new narration incorporates several of the quips and witticisms from the original films, with a handful of updates referencing World War II—the armor of a rhino is described as being as strong as a panzer tank—and such minor alterations as renaming Percy the gibbon "Goldie." Nat Shilkret's musical score has a larger, roomier sound than the Rodemich-Sharples compositions, spiced up a with a few jazzy riffs more appropriate to the 1940s—though like Rodemich and Sharples before him, Shilkret isn't above swiping whole passages from such classics as Liszt's "Les Préludes."

Costing next to nothing, *Jungle Cavalcade* could not help but make money, and would have been a fitting *adieu* to films for Frank Buck if he hadn't kept trying to recapture the old glory with new cinematic endeavors throughout the late 1930s and early 1940s. Given the popularity of his 1941 biography and other bestsellers, his lucrative lecture tours, and such successful enterprises as the 1939 World's Fair attraction "Frank Buck's Jungleland" he hardly needed movies to keep solvent. Still, Buck continued appearing before the cameras to ever-diminishing returns. He starred in the 1937 Columbia serial *Jungle Menace*, where as "Frank Hardy" his acting (if you can call it that) paled in comparison with his more polished costars Reginald Denny, Esther Ralston, William Bakewell, Charlotte Henry and Clarence Muse. 1942's *Jacaré* was a return to form, a documentary feature filmed on location in the Amazons, but the rehearsed quality of the picture was more pronounced than ever before, and distribution (by United Artists) was spotty and nonprofitable. One year later Buck starred in *Tiger Fangs*, an ultra-cheapie from that ultracheapest of studios PRC, wherein the big-game hunter journeys to Malaya (courtesy of stock footage and cramped interior sets) to prevent the Nazis and Japanese from plundering Allied-controlled rubber supplies. Fortunately Buck's film career ended on a high note when he and his old "friendly enemy" Clyde Beatty amusingly portrayed themselves in the 1949 Abbott and Costello comedy *Africa Screams*. Frank Buck died of lung cancer the following year in his home state of Texas, aged 66.

Chapter 15

The Charlie Chaplin Mutual Comedies

"Encouraged by reports of failure and abandonment of double feature policies in important situations throughout the country, an ambitious program has been set by the RKO Van Beuren Corp. for 1932–33 production." So declared *Film Daily* on March 27, 1932. The article went on to itemize Van Beuren's short-subject offerings for the coming season: 26 *Aesop's Fables*, 13 *Tom and Jerry* cartoons, 13 *Vagabond Adventures* and 13 *Liberty Short Short Stories* (the latter a project that would soon be axed, as noted in Chapter 13).

The majority of print space was devoted to a new Van Beuren series that had already been reported in other trade papers as early as February 6: "In addition, Van Beuren will re-enter the two-reel comedy field with the re-issuing of 12 two-reel [Charlie] Chaplin comedies in sound.... Feeling that the majority of exhibitors are now seeking some plan whereby double features may be eliminated, it is felt that the Chaplin comedies will supply the necessary box-office draw to supplant the second feature picture in most cases. In fact, it is felt that the Chaplin name will be a greater pull than some of the features now on the market."

Van Beuren's luck with his earlier plunges into comedy production had ranged from variable (Mrs. and Mrs. Sidney Drew, *Smitty and His Pals*) to downright miserable (*Henry and Polly*). This time around he would minimize the risk of failure and maximize the profit potential by marketing an existing film property that was a guaranteed success—and best of all, one for which his own cash outlay would be minimal compared to the costs incurred by his previous forays into comedy. Sweetening the pot for Van Beuren was the fact that Charlie Chaplin was in 1932 a hotter commodity than he'd been in years thanks to the surprise success of his 1931 feature *City Lights*, in which the legendary filmmaker gambled—and won—that a well-made silent film was still capable of drawing crowds three years into the talking-picture era.

By the early 1930s it was generally conceded that Chaplin's greatest and most sustained period of comic creativity was concentrated in the 12 two-reelers he made for the Mutual Film Corporation from 1916 through 1917. With his own studio and production staff, total creative control, and a stellar coterie of supporting actors headed by Edna Purviance and Eric Campbell, the director-comedian's genius soared to hitherto unattained heights with such masterpieces as *The Vagabond, One A.M., The Pawnshop, The Rink, The Immigrant,* and especially *Easy Street*. Charlie's "golden dozen" was perfectly summed up by film historian William K. Everson as a "flawless welding of brilliant comedy and really moving pathos."

If one takes into consideration the plethora of duped, washed-out and mutilated prints of the Mutual Chaplins inflicted on the public over the past century, one might assume that the films had lapsed into public domain almost the instant that the series ended in 1917. In truth, the twelve comedies were licensed to, and strictly controlled by, several different legal owners right up to the moment the Van Beuren deal was closed—though this of course did not prevent fly-by-night entrepreneurs from palming off illegally copied prints to unwary exhibitors and home-movie enthusiasts. Less

Van Beuren trumpets its "new" series of vintage Charlie Chaplin two-reelers in *Film Daily*, 1932.

than a year after Chaplin and Mutual parted company, the films were legitimately reissued in the United Kingdom as the "Twelve Wonder Comedies" by J.D. Walker. In 1919 the Mutuals made their first U.S. reappearance courtesy of a firm called Chaplin Classics. Four years later, the two-reelers were acquired by Ben Blumenthal of the Export and Import Film Company, which controlled the world exhibition rights everywhere except the U.S. and Canada. In 1924 those two countries were added to the contract, with Blumenthal taking full-page trade ads declaring that Export and Import's subsidiary Mutual Chaplins Inc. was sole proprietor of "All rights and interests" and warning fast-buck promoters against distributing any illegally manufactured prints. To ensure that none of Mutual Chaplins Inc.'s authorized films would fall into the wrong hands, exhibitors were ordered to return all prints no later than 1927.

By the time that Pathé News president Courtland Smith and Hays Office general consul Charles C. Pettijohn brokered the 1932 arrangement between Ben Blumenthal (whose company had gone out of business) and Amedee Van Beuren to once more theatrically reissue the Chaplin Mutuals, the films had not been seen outside of private collections and archival screenings for nearly five years. During that period, only a handful of vintage silent films had been shown to the general public in the manner in which they were *supposed* to be shown. With such notable exceptions as *The Birth of a Nation*, *The Big Parade*, *Son of the Sheik* and *Ben-Hur*, most films of the silent era were shamefully misrepresented by chopped-up and gagged-up versions with silly sound effects and sarcastic narration, *a la* Pete Smith's *Goofy Movies* one-reelers. Audiences of the early 1930s were encouraged to regard these cinematic "relics" with derision and disrespect, as if there was nothing more ridiculous on earth than a old movie without sound. Given this cavalier industry attitude, Van Beuren's decision to exhibit the twelve Chaplins almost exactly as they'd originally been screened, *without* inviting audiences to mock the films, was downright radical.

It has been reported that each of the Mutual shorts cost Van Beuren $10,000. But according to contemporary sources, the whole package was priced at $60,000, or $5,000 per short, with an additional $5000 each allotted for added music and sound effects. All 12 films were not immediately purchased from Ben Blumenthal: Van Beuren chose to buy six at a time, to be released over a twelve-month period. If these reissues proved to be profitable, he had the option to buy the rest of the series. Further breaking down the process, Van Beuren prepared two of the best Chaplins, *Easy Street* and *The Cure* (the 9th and 10th of Mutuals), to be shown without prior notification before preview audiences—and if *these* went over with the crowd, the producer would then proceed to release the remaining four during the first twelve-month cycle, followed by the final six in Cycle Two. You got all that, or do you need a trail guide?

What Van Beuren got for his money were the best available prints at the time. None were entirely complete: Over the previous fifteen years a number of cuts had been made and several of the inter-titles (containing dialogue and exposition) removed. The picture quality was clear and focused but hardly pristine, since Van Beuren was only able to secure dupe negatives from Blumenthal. To accommodate the new sound tracks, the left side of the picture frame was slightly cropped; and with no technology then available to allow the films to be run at the "standard" 16 frames-per-second silent speed (Chaplin often instructed his ace photographer Rollie Totheroh to undercrank in order to juice up the action), the 24 f.p.s sound speed resulted in some *very* accelerated onscreen movement, so fast at times that several of Chaplin's throwaway gags failed to register with 1930s audiences. For all that, the sped-up movement was infinitely preferable to the alternate "stretch-framing" process in which every other frame was printed twice, causing the image to appear jerky and flickery. Despite the shortcomings of the available prints, they were vastly superior to the barely visible third-generation dupes that were being circulated by less reputable distributors. And though Van Beuren's editing staff made a handful of additional cuts in each film, denying contemporary audiences some of Chaplin's cleverest sight gags, at least the most important inter-titles were recreated and presented as original written, in lieu of the witless wisecracks and feeble puns imposed upon other Chaplin reissues of the time.

In charge of synchronizing the sound effects and writing the musical scores was old Van Beuren reliable Gene Rodemich, who at the same time was head of the studio's animation division, to say nothing of being responsible for scoring all of Van Beuren's other live-action releases. Never in the best of health, Rodemich found himself overwhelmed by the workload and began searching for an assistant composer. After reading a Walter Winchell newspaper column which heaped orchids upon a gifted young pianist in the Vincent Lopez Orchestra, Rodemich contacted and hired 23-year-old Winston Sharples.

Born in Fall River, Massachusetts, in 1909, Win Sharples was like Gene Rodemich a musical prodigy, playing piano in vaudeville at the tender age of eight. Obtaining a master's degree in music from Carnegie Institute and studying drama at Yale, Sharples played various spots with his own band before being hired by Vincent Lopez in 1930. Once safely ensconced at Van Beuren, Sharples quickly proved himself a worthy colleague of Rodemich, becoming head of the music department after his mentor retired in 1933. When Van Beuren folded four years later, Sharples moved to the Max Fleischer cartoon studio, where among other compositions he wrote the hit song "It's a Hap-Hap-Happy-Day," introduced in Fleischer's animated feature *Gulliver's Travels*. He remained with the Fleischer unit right through the firm's reorganization as Famous Studios, and in 1964 succeeded Sammy Timberg as musical supervisor. Sharples spent his final working years running his own stock-music service in partnership with animation producer Hal Seegar, supplying tunes for such made-for-TV cartoons as *Underdog* and *Milton the Monster*. He died in 1978.

The importance of Gene Rodemich and Win Sharples' musical contributions to the popularity of Van Beuren's Chaplin reissues cannot be overstressed. Though purists might grouse that the background music is occasionally anachronistic, using tunes that hadn't yet been composed when the films were originally made, not one of these tunes was ever inappropriate to the action onscreen. Deploying such popular songs as "Happy Feet," "Happy Days are Here Again" and "Auf Wiedersehen" to underscore *The Cure* not only contributes to the enjoyment of the film but actually enhances it. Similarly well and wisely chosen are the occasional passages from classical compositions: Utilizing Mendelssohn's Scherzo from *A Midsummer Night's Dream* to accompany the sequence in *Easy Street* wherein villain Eric Campbell pursues Charlie around a crumbling tenement building is sheer inspiration. According to Chaplin historians Michael Hayde and Richard Roberts, among the talented musicians heard in these lively Van Beuren musical tracks are such notables as Benny Goodman, Artie Shaw and Joe Venuti.

Latter-day viewers often express dissatisfaction with the cartoonish sound effects in the reissues. Responding to these come-lately carpers, Richard Roberts issued a strong defense of Van Beuren's aural repertoire of slide whistles, kettle drums, "boings" and the like in a 2007 post on the NitrateVille website: "I get tired of hearing people whine about the Van Beuren scores and sound effects; those sound effects are actually historically accurate in the type of sound effect utilized by silent film accompanists and orchestras during the Silent Era..." Roberts added that by invoking the *zeitgeist* of the silent picture palaces of yore, Van Beuren's staff pumped fresh blood into the old films: "They actually treat the Chaplin Mutuals as comedies rather than museum pieces or 'works of art.'"

Though the revamped *The Cure* was the first official release in the "new" Van Beuren Chaplin series (slated for August 9, 1932), the second scheduled release *Easy Street* was the film most often shown during the preview process. A particularly successful preview was staged in New Bedford, Massachusetts, with the theater patrons showering more praise on the Chaplin film than on the main feature, James Cagney's *The Crowd Roars*. The trade-paper revues were just as encouraging, with *Film Daily* gushing on October 8, 1932:

> The addition of sound puts some extra values into the short, but Chaplin's gift for combining genuine humor, slapstick, the right dash of sentiment, and the old reliable action climax, are still the main things. An audience at the Mayfair on Broadway applauded the comedy, and if the Broadway crowd does this, the folks in the hinterlands should go for it even more. Coming at a time when exhibs need items to bolster their bills, and costing less than a second feature though worth more in audience satisfaction, these comedies should be a cleanup. The faster they are released, the better.

Three months later *Variety* got around to reviewing *The Cure* with equal enthusiasm, not only for the film but also Van Beuren's method of presentation:

> The added sound effects are no deterrent and lend *The Cure* a very modern atmosphere, as Gene Rodemich's orchestra has dubbed in the musical background and the sound exclamations.... Chaplin has been analyzed time and again, so further commentary on Van Beuren's reissue of this short is extraneous. But one can't help but marvel anew at how much expression and business the comedian gets out of trivialities. This short, like any Chaplin, new or old, is b.o., and not merely a program rounder-outer.

As he'd occasionally done in conjunction with his cartoon shorts, Van Beuren tied in the release of *Easy Street* with an illustrated 32-page children's book, filled with frame blowups from the film rather than production stills due to the producer's inability to acquire those stills along with the two-reelers. The RKO-Van Beuren promotional packet suggested that in addition to selling the picture books, local theater managers would do well to hark back to the publicity ploys used when the Mutuals were originally released, such as placing life-size cardboard cutouts of The Little Tramp outside the theater and staging Chaplin lookalike contests. It was 1917 all over again.

On the strength of this positive feedback, Van Beuren went ahead with his plans to reissue four additional Chaplins during the 1932–33 season. *The Rink* and *The Floorwalker* came out respectively in November and December of 1932, while *The Vagabond* and *The Pawnshop* followed in February and March of 1933. Although a few exhibitors complained that the films only appealed to children, most others found this to be a major advantage during weekend showings packed with cheering youngsters. The new soundtracks were frequently singled out for praise, with more than one theater owner noting that the music and sound effects helped patrons "forget" the age

Lobby poster for *The Cure*, the first of Van Beuren's Chaplin reissues.

of the films. The series turned out to be a gold mine for exhibitors, for Van Beuren and for RKO—but not for Charlie Chaplin, who no longer owned the films and had no legal recourse to their being shown without his getting a piece of the action. But considering the boost that his reputation as a surefire laughmaker received from these venerable two-reelers, it's possible that Charlie didn't mind at all that he wasn't in on the gravy train.

Season Two of the Van Beuren Chaplins commenced in August of 1933 with the reissue of 1916's *The Fireman*. There are good and powerful reasons why this film (actually the second of Chaplin's twelve Mutuals) was held back so long by Van Beuren. In addition to being regarded by many Chaplin scholars as the weakest of his Mutuals, *The Fireman*'s photography was undercranked to the point that the action is nearly impossible to follow when projected at sound speed. Van Beuren didn't do much to make the picture any more presentable, outfitting it with a disappointingly lackluster musical score and having one scene with supporting player Leo White clumsily overladen with newly recorded shouts of "FIRE! FIRE!" in a lousy French accent.

The second season picked up tremendously with *The Count* in November 1933 and *The Immigrant* in December, followed by Chaplin's memorable solo turn *One A.M.* in March 1934. This last film, like others in the series, was missing a few scattered gags that were featured in the original release, notably the drunken Charlie's attempt to ascend a staircase in the manner of an Alpine mountain-climber, but unless the viewer knew that the gag had been there in the first place, nothing was really missed. (It has been claimed that a far more detrimental edit was made in *Easy Street*, namely the bit in which Charlie is galvanized into wreaking havoc on the heavies after sitting on a dope addict's hypodermic needle. But the rhythm of the existing music-and-sound track suggests that the gag *was* included in the 1932 reissue, then later removed once the Production Code went into effect). Closing out the 1933–34 manifest were *Behind the Screen* in May 1934, and Chaplin's final Mutual *The Adventurer* in July. The box-office returns had been so gratifying that Van Beuren would most likely have shipped out a third season had Chaplin had the foresight to make six more shorts back in 1917.

And now for the inevitable courtroom capers. In 1935 Amedee Van Beuren filed suit against Charles Pettijohn and Courtland Smith, whom you'll remember had arranged the deal to purchase the Mutuals from Ben Blumenthal. Van Beuren demanded $10,000 on the account of the purchase price in the transfer of the films to his organization, prompting Pettijohn and Smith's attorney Louis Nizer to countersue for $20,000, and to demand that Van Beuren's books be examined. Whatever decision was reached in court became a moot point after Van Beuren's studio closed in 1937 and the exhibition rights for the Chaplins were picked up by Commonwealth Productions, whose parent company Guaranteed Pictures specialized in reissues and American distribution of foreign films. In 1938 the twelve comedies were withdrawn from theaters as separate entities and reorganized into a trio of compilation features, all released by Guaranteed. *Chaplin Carnival* was made up of *Behind the Screen*, *The Count*, *The Fireman* and *The Immigrant*; *The Charlie Chaplin Cavalcade* was comprised of *One A.M.*, *The Rink*, *The Pawnshop* and *The Floorwalker*; and *The Charlie Chaplin Festival* featured *The Adventurer*, *The Cure*, *Easy Street* and *The Immigrant*. To maintain a uniform running time of 75 minutes for each ersatz feature, the already shortened Van Beuren reissue prints were pared down even farther. And while Van Beuren's refilmed intertitles were replaced with newly shot title cards featuring the now-familiar Chaplin silhouette design, the Rodemich-Sharples scores and sound effects were retained with only minor variations.

In the past two decades the Chaplin Mutuals have all been restored to near-perfection, with magnificent picture quality, correctly adjusted projection speed (generally 20 f.p.s.) and meticulous recreations of how the original main and inter-titles (long considered lost) likely appeared when first seen back in 1916–17. There is still some question as to whether the Mutual films exist precisely as originally shown to pre–World War I audiences. Many modern examples are a combination of footage from the Van Beuren releases and additional negative material from internationally distributed prints, which sometimes included bits of business and alternate takes that never appeared in the North American versions.

More recently, a variety of freshly written and orchestrated musical scores have been added to the Mutuals. While some of these compositions can be deafeningly pretentious, others are quite entertaining and occasionally even appropriate to the era in which the films were made. But even after eight decades, the Van Beuren scores written by Gene Rodemich and Win Sharples in 1932 and 1933 are regarded by the majority of Chaplin buffs as "definitive"—perfect as they stand, and not to be tampered with. Certainly this was the attitude of David Shepard and Bill Lindholm, who used the Van Beuren soundtracks to accompany their painstaking and widely admired restorations of the Mutuals for Blackhawk Films in the mid–1970s.

Amedee Van Beuren undoubtedly figured that adding up-to-date soundtracks to pep up a group of old silent films was nothing more than a logical and expedient business move back in 1932. He probably never imagined that he was establishing a musical legacy that would endure well into the next century.

Chapter 16

The Last Frontier (1932)

As mentioned in Chapter 14, Van Beuren's first feature film *Bring 'Em Back Alive* was at one time conceived as a serialized group of one-reel shorts. The studio may have decided to transfer this concept to its first and only official serial *The Last Frontier*, but the guiding force of that project might also have been Van Beuren's distributor, RKO Radio Pictures. In 1932 RKO was in another of its periodic slumps, which the studio's executives—and a few trade papers—attributed to its overabundance of "women's pictures" starring Constance Bennett, Ann Harding and other high-strung actresses. There was an industry-wide theory that male moviegoers were largely brought into the theaters at the request of their female companions, thus RKO's films were principally aimed at female tastes.

To stem the flow of red ink on their ledgers, RKO decided to radically alter their policy and aim their product at the menfolk. Lou Brock, associate producer of the studio's short subject division, spelled out the new strategy in a 1932 *Film Daily* article: "The time is past when productions can be made to please women alone, trusting that men will follow them into the theater as a matter of course and of courtesy. The emancipation of women has emancipated men as well—they won't sit through features they don't like unless there is something else on the bill to attract them." RKO's two-reel comedies had for several seasons set their sights on male audiences, especially Edgar Kennedy's popular "Average Man" series. In compliance with the shorts unit, the studio bore down on the "action crowd" (another phrase used by the industry to identify the men in the stalls) in its feature-film product as well: More than half of the 62 features planned for the 1932–33 season were adventure or mystery pictures.

This left one last, rich audience demographic untapped: The youngsters, whom rumor had it were also fond of adventure and mystery films, albeit on a less sophisticated scale. And that's where serials came in. Though throughout the teens and twenties such cliffhanging chapter plays as *Peg O' The Ring* and *The House Without a Key* were produced with adult viewers in mind, once talkies came in and the basic unreality of serials was made more obvious with dialogue and sound effects the genre lowered its sights by truckling to the kiddie trade. This is likely the reason that with the exception of Universal Pictures, the major studios, more interested in grown-up audiences paying higher admission fees, steered clear of serials, leaving the genre in the hands of minor companies like Mascot and Syndicate. But in keeping with its avowed mission to leave no potential audience group unexploited, in 1932 RKO took the plunge and drew up plans for not one but three 12-chapter serials, the first of which would be *The Last Frontier*.

The property had its roots in a 1923 novel by newspaperman and former war correspondent Courtney Ryley Cooper, chronicling the efforts of a 19th century Indian scout to aid settlers and the military in the Wild West by halting the activities of gun runners who sold rifles to hostile Native Americans. Movie mogul Thomas H. Ince was in the early stages of converting the novel into a screen epic intended to rival Paramount's 1923 blockbuster *The Covered Wagon* when he died in 1924. Ince's Culver City studio was subsequently taken over by Cecil B. DeMille's Producers Distributing Corporation (PDC), which also inherited a number of unfilmed projects including *The Last Frontier*. Produced by Hunt Stromberg, directed by George Seitz, and considerably scaled down from its original concept, the film finally emerged in 1926, starring future "Hopalong Cassidy" William Boyd in his first western role, along with leading lady Marguerite De La Motte and child actor Junior Coghlan. The slightly altered storyline concerned frontier newspaper editor Tom Kirby (Boyd), who like the Indian scout in the novel was bent upon smashing the gunrunning racket and revealing the identity of the scoundrel behind the operation; meanwhile, the nefarious villain hoped to foment an Indian war and drive the settlers out of the territory so he could grab up all the land himself. Pathé acquired the story rights of both the novel and film versions of *The Last Frontier* when the company merged with PDC in 1927, sharing those rights with RKO when that studio absorbed Pathé in 1930.

Although a serialized version of *The Last Frontier* would technically have a longer running time (nearly four hours) than any feature, the fact that it was essentially comprised of twelve short subjects consigned its production to RKO's shorts unit. Since that division was already overloaded with product, one of RKO's independent shorts suppliers would have to take over production—and Van Beuren, then supplying more "outside" shorts to RKO than anyone else, was the logical candidate. With his customary efficiency in delegating authority, Amedee Van Beuren enlisted Fred J. McConnell as the serial's producer. McConnell had previously overseen silent chapter plays at Universal and Pathé, a job he obviously enjoyed. Quoted in *Film Daily*, McConnell described serials as "pullers," creating "a continuity in the mind of the moviegoer that he does not want disturbed."

Once on the job, Fred McConnell assembled a team of like-minded professionals, beginning with director Spencer Gordon Bennet (1893–1987), known to action-film aficionados everywhere as "King of the Serials." Bennet was four years into his Hollywood career when he helmed his first cliffhanger, 1925's *Sunken Silver*. A natural-born organizer whose skill at getting top-dollar results from nickel-and-dime budgets was uncanny, he went on make over 100 serials in his long career, with such noteworthy credits as Republic's *Secret Service in Darkest Africa* (1943) and *Zorro's Black Whip* (1944), and Columbia's *Superman* (1948) and *Batman and Robin* (1949). Bennet managed to give each of his serials a distinctive *auteur* stamp, usually via his fondness for thrusting the action *into* the camera with flying fists, leaping stuntmen and smashed furniture. In 1956 he had the distinction of megging the very last two Hollywood serials, Columbia's *Blazing the Overland Trail* and *Perils of the Wilderness*. Also prolific in the Western field, Bennet would hang up his professional spurs at age 71 with the above-average 1964 Dan Duryea oater *The Bounty Killer*, which nostalgically featured a roundup of veteran sagebrush stars including Rod Cameron, Buster Crabbe, Johnny Mack Brown, Bob Steele, Edmund Cobb and even Broncho Billy Anderson, the man who literally invented the western-movie genre back in

1908—and who was likely the only man on the set older and more experienced than Spencer Gordon Bennet. (For *Last Frontier*, Bennet shared onscreen credit with second-unit director Tom Storey.)

While Courtney Ryley Cooper was on hand to help reshape his novel for movie purposes, the screen adaptation was credited to George Plympton and Robert F. Hill, both of whom had previously worked with producer McConnell at Pathé, as had cinematographers Edward Snyder and Gilbert Warren. Credit for the serial's one major digression from the original novel, that of having hero Tom Kirby periodically assume the Zorro-like identity of a masked vigilante known as The Black Ghost, can be logically bestowed upon Fred J. McConnell. According to film historian Jerry Blake, McConnell likely borrowed the dual-identity gimmick from the silent serial *The Return of the Riddle Rider*, which he'd coscripted for Universal in 1927.

For the starring role of Tom Kirby, McConnell selected a recently-signed RKO contractee, 26-year-old Creighton Chaney. The fact that the young actor was the son of the late "Man of a Thousand Faces" Lon Chaney was not lost on the RKO publicity department, which played it up big in the serial's "deluxe" 12-page pressbook. The younger Chaney resented this, hoping to succeed in films on his own merits, but as his career regressed from RKO to independent productions he was "starved" (his own word) into rechristening himself Lon Chaney, Jr.—though it would not be until his breakthrough role as Lenny in 1939's *Of Mice and Men* and his subsequent tenure as Universal's reigning all-purpose horror star in such films as *The Wolfman*, *Son of Dracula*, *The Mummy's Ghost* and *House of Frankenstein* that he would attain true stardom. Though he had far less screen experience than his *Last Frontier* costars, Chaney registered well with a forceful, virile performance—except whenever he was saddled with a painfully unconvincing Mexican accent in his guise as the Black Ghost (which in itself was the serial's weakest aspect, a totally gratuitous and unnecessary plot contrivance).

Spunky, self-resourceful heroine Betty Halliday, daughter of the film's nominal military authority figure Colonel Halliday (Claude Payton), was portrayed by freelance actress Dorothy Gulliver, who'd risen to prominence in the late 1920s in Universal's popular two-reel comedy series *The Collegians*. These had been produced by Nat Ross, who just before wrapping up

This suave young actor is none other than future horror icon Lon Chaney, Jr., billed as Creighton Chaney for his starring role in the Van Beuren serial *The Last Frontier* (from *Motion Picture Herald*, July 19, 1932).

his work on Van Beuren's *Liberty Short Short Stories* one-reelers (see Chapter 13) was briefly on the production staff of *The Last Frontier*, and thus probably recommended Gulliver to McConnell. Or probably not, since the 24-year-old actress was already a serial veteran, having costarred in 1931's *The Phantom of the West* and *The Galloping Ghost*, and 1932's *The Shadow of the Eagle*. Far from the traditional damsel in distress (though she did spend an inordinate amount of time tied up and/or facing Certain Death), Betty Halliday—and for that matter the actress portraying her—was clearly able to take care of herself, and as the serial progressed she rescued the hero just as often as he rescued her. Dorothy Gulliver remained active in films and TV until the 1950s, emerging from retirement for a key role in John Cassavetes' experimental *Faces* (1968).

In a departure from standard serial-casting formula, *The Last Frontier* boasts a second set of romantic leads, married couple Jeff and Rose Maitland. Their presence adds an extra layer of tension to the proceedings, with the essentially decent Jeff collaborating with the gun-runners in order to provide for himself and his wife, while long-suffering Rose prays that Jeff will ultimately straighten up and fly right. Though Francis X. Bushman Jr., was obviously cast as Jeff to give RKO even more publicity ammunition by featuring the sons of *two* important silent-film actors in the cast, the young Bushman is outstanding in his difficult role, well matched by the equally talented Judith Barrie as Rose.

Beyond the Maitlands, the character breakdown adheres faithfully to serial tradition: A sneering "brains" heavy, backed up by a squad of brutal henchmen. As the outwardly respectable but inwardly reprehensible land agent-cum-gunrunner Lige Morris, Richard Neill, who in happier days had essayed major roles in such silents as *Tumbleweeds* and *Wanderer of the Wasteland*, proves beyond question that he was not suitable for talkies. His breast-beating, eye-rolling, hyperventilating performance is so blatant that it's surprising none of the extra players placed him under citizen's arrest on general principles. More convincing are Morris' trio of musclemen, played by former western hero and rodeo star Pete Morrison, perennial sidekick Ben Corbett, and sharkishly handsome LeRoy Mason (in the first of many serial appearances). Joe Bonomo, one of Hollywood's premier stuntmen and silent-serial stars, is cast as a secondary heavy listed in the onscreen credits as Kit Gordon but identified in the dialogue as Joe Burke. Bonomo's big fistic set-to with hero Chaney is one of the film's highlights, though the star is doubled in most shots by the great Yakima Canutt (who also doubles for heroine Dorothy Gulliver!)

The obligatory (and ritualistically unfunny) comedy relief is supplied by obscure vaudeville entertainer Slim "King" Cole, whose specialty was performing vocal sound effects, not unlike Michael Winslow in the *Police Academy* movies (an unfair comparison, since Winslow has talent). Also struggling to raise a chuckle or two is child actress Mary Jo Desmond as precocious Aggie Kirby, the hero's foster daughter. While suffering through Mary Jo's inept kindergarten-pageant emoting, one might wonder how she ever landed the part—until one glances at the cast list and notes that the role of General Custer is played by the girl's real-life father, silent leading man William Desmond, whose last appearance for Van Beuren was as "guest star" in the 1928 *Smitty* two-reeler *No Children* (see Chapter 8). But there should be no question as to why leathery Syrian character actor Frank Lackteen was cast as Indian chieftain

Pawnee Blood. Lackteen, you see, had played the same role in the 1926 version of *The Last Frontier*, and was rehired to match up stock footage from the earlier film, which as a cost-trimming measure was used extensively throughout the serial (notably a thrillingly staged buffalo stampede, filmed on location in Alberta).

Fred McConnell spent three months in pre-production for *The Last Frontier*. It would not only be Van Beuren's highest-budgeted effort, but also the costliest talkie serial to date—though still below the budget of an average RKO programmer. Most exteriors were filmed in Kernville, California, 180 miles from Hollywood, where local entrepreneur George Brown had built an authentic-looking "western" street that was regularly rented by other film producers. Brown charged a daily rental rate of $75 as opposed to the standard $100 per day, a discount explained in the June 14, 1932, edition of *Variety* as a strategy "to help out the town's unemployed. Every time a film troupe arrives Kernville's residents, 100 of 'em, get jobs as extras." Interiors were filmed at RKO-Pathé back in Culver City.

Completed in a fast four weeks, the serial was ready for release on September 2, 1932. Around the same time, producer McConnell told *Film Daily*:

> My judgment is that the principal difficulty in putting serials over is that the showman today is passing up this product. A good serial does not need outstanding showmanship to put it over. It has the natural exploitation angles that lend themselves admirably to any type of campaign and bring hundreds of children into the theater to see each episode—children that do not ordinarily go to that theater at all, many of them that do not go to shows at all.

Van Beuren wasted no time devising the best angle to promote the serial. In direct opposition to the dire warnings of contemporary sociologists who felt that action movies "over-stimulated" children, leading them to random acts of violence and law-breaking, Van Beuren stressed the positive values of *The Last Frontier*, going so far as to label the plotline "timely" despite its 19th century ambience. With considerable prodding from the Van Beuren and RKO publicists, *Film Daily* told its readers that the serial

> tells the story of the building of the west in those pioneer days immediately following the Civil War. There was a depression following that war much the same as there is a depression now following the World War. The people in populated centers of the east were compelled to spread out and seek new lands, new means of earning a livelihood.... There were good and bad in the lot, as anyone who has read American history knows and the good eventually won out. There is a lesson and moral portrayed in The Last Frontier that is bound to appeal to anyone interested in child welfare or education. Parent-teacher organizations, school boards, chambers of commerce, community workers of whatever name, are more than willing to sanction films of this kind that not only entertain, but educate as well.

Seen today, *The Last Frontier* is a mixed bag. One tends to agree with serial historian Alan G. Barbour that the production is "pedestrian" in spots, and often downright ludicrous *vis-a-vis* the Armour Star villainy of Richard Neill, the excessive comedy relief and the pointless "secret identity" schtick. The serial also suffers from a lack of background music, a common failing of chapter plays from this period. That said, *Last Frontier* is several notches above the usual early-talkie serial. The first seven episodes are virtually non-stop action, beautifully staged by the director and vigorously performed by the stars and their overworked stunt doubles. While the narrative begins to lag around Chapter Eight ("Facing Death") with a wearisome flashback explaining how Tom Kirby came to adopt the orphaned Aggie, things pick

Motion Picture Daily advertising spread for *The Last Frontier* (1932).

up tremendously thereafter as the narrative shifts from chasing the gunrunners to forestalling an all-out war between settlers and Indians.

Best of all, the serial never "cheats" with its chapter endings. The usual pattern was to show the hero or heroine in an inescapable death trap at the climax of one chapter, then reveal at the beginning of the next installment that the hero or heroine has avoided disaster via a method that had not been revealed the previous week. There was no such bait-and-switch here, however: When, for example, the heroine accidentally shoots the hero at the end of Chapter Four ("The Fatal Shot"), we see him crumpling to the ground with a nasty wound in his shoulder at the outset of Chapter Five ("Clutching Hands")—no near-miss, no Bible in his pocket.

According to the January 28, 1933, *Film Daily*, RKO's sales on *The Last Frontier* exceeded all expectations: "Hundreds of theaters that have not run serials in years are trying them out again." Quoted in the article, Van Beuren declared exuberantly:

> I am satisfied there is a distinct market for serials. There is no use talking, the theaters must consider the children, not only for the money they actually bring in, but for their influence in bringing their parents and older people with them to the theater.... Sex and horror are almost taboo with children. It is a case today where the theater manager must realize that the child market must be considered and give them that fast, moving, melodramatic type of entertainment that really has a wholesome appeal. Serials have this appeal.

The success of *The Last Frontier* emboldened Van Beuren to announce that he would proceed with two additional serials: *Lost in the Malaysian Jungle*, which was to be built around leftover footage from the 1932 Van Beuren feature *Bring 'Em Back Alive*, and another cliffhanger tentatively titled *Airplane Express*. Unfortunately, Van Beuren's distributor RKO was embroiled in yet another financial crisis and attendant regime change, with Merian C. Cooper taking over from David O. Selznick while the company went into receivership. Someone in the upper RKO echelons decided that the studio wasn't going in the direction of serial production, and as a result there were no follow-ups to *The Last Frontier*, save for a 55-minute feature adaptation titled *The Black Ghost*.

Van Beuren and RKO's one-and-only serial continued to make money throughout the 1930s and 1940s, though not for its original creators. Beginning in 1938 *The Last Frontier* was redistributed by Commonwealth Films, and later by Goodwill Films. On both occasions the opening titles were refilmed and Creighton Chaney prominently billed as Lon Chaney, Jr., a name that would mean more and more at the box office as the years rolled on, long after Van Beuren himself had been largely forgotten.

Chapter 17

The Van Beuren Musical Comedies

With his operation going full blast with such ambitious projects as the feature film *Bring 'Em Back Alive* (see Chapter 14) and the serial *The Last Frontier* (see Chapter 16), not to mention his usual quota of animated cartoons and *Vagabond Adventures* one-reelers, no one would have blamed Amedee Van Beuren if he'd chosen to rest on his laurels in the summer and fall of 1933. But Van Beuren was bent upon revitalizing two planned but abandoned properties: A series of one-reel musical shorts featuring top NBC radio performers, and a group of two-reel musical comedies starring the whacky vaudeville team Olsen & Johnson. When both projects fell through, Van Beuren decided to codify the two into a single new series of comedies with music, headlining a variety of major stage and radio talents other than Olsen & Johnson. Chosen to guide this series was Meyer Davis, an entrepreneur after Van Beuren's own heart.

The saga of Meyer Davis extends from the pre–World War I years to the era of rock 'n' roll and the Beatles. While still in his teens in 1912, Davis was a fiddle player with the Marine Band, not a military unit but a quintet of red-coated musicians who provided dance tunes for the Willard Hotel ballroom in Washington, D.C. At first the Marine Band was one of several units hired by the hotel, but Davis suggested to the managers that the Band be made a permanent and exclusive fixture of the establishment. After several successful seasons at the Willard, Davis broke away to form his own eponymous dance orchestra in 1915. Playing such prestigious gigs as the annual horse show in Bar Harbor, Maine, the Meyer Davis Orchestra was one of the leading purveyors of what was known as "refined" jazz, lining up far more engagements than the group could possibly fulfill. Setting up offices in DC, New York, Philadelphia and Boston, Davis expanded his operation by hiring numerous other musical units, and by 1928 he'd accumulated 105 bands bearing his name with 1000 musicians on his payroll, playing in hotels and dance emporiums all over the country as well as the orchestra pits of the nation's premier silent-movie palaces. In the tradition of Amedee Van Beuren (with whom he had undoubtedly crossed paths over the years), Davis also invested heavily in such non-musical concerns as bowling alleys and amusement parks. Once network radio gained a foothold Davis aligned himself with both NBC and CBS. Throughout all this managerial activity, Meyer Davis continued to wield the baton with his original orchestra, raking in enormous profits via his remarkable acumen for anticipating the public's ever-changing musical tastes.

Branching out into films, Davis became an associate producer at the Fox Movietone studio in New York City, and it is at this point in the narrative that he joined forces with Van Beuren. It is not recorded who first came up with the idea for a series

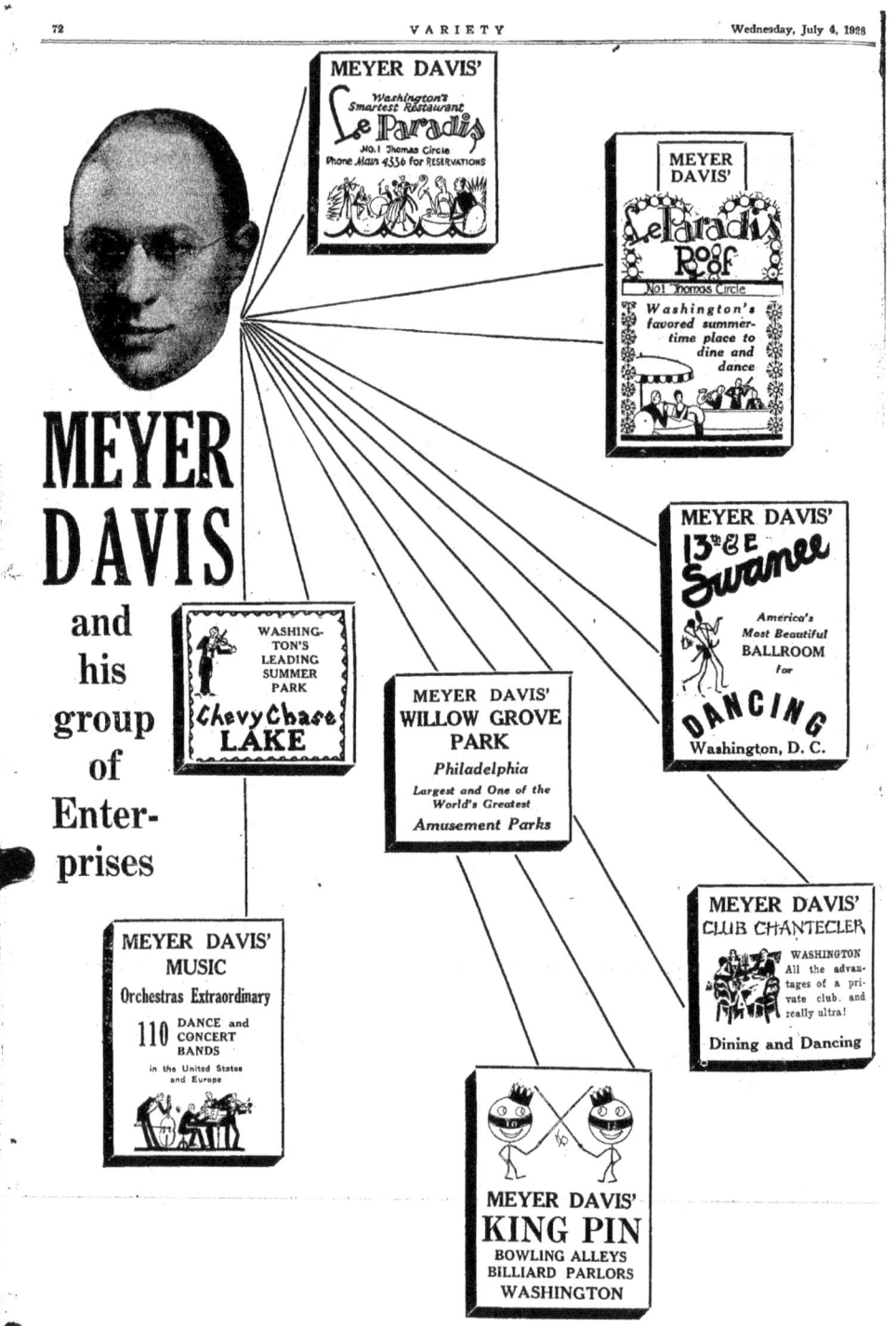

Variety ad for the Meyer Davis entertainment empire.

of musical shorts featuring stage and radio luminaries, but in any case the earliest announcements were sent out to the trade papers in the fall of 1933. Davis had formed a film company called Magna Pictures, soon to be rechristened the Meyer Davis-Van Beuren Corporation. The new operation's contract to produce 13 two-reel shorts for RKO release was finalized in October, just before production began. Fred McConnell, late of the Van Beuren serial *The Last Frontier* and the intended producer for the aborted Olsen & Johnson series, took charge of production for the Van Beuren half of the corporation (though his name never appeared onscreen). Monroe Schaff of Movietone was appointed supervising producer, while the film-processing work was handled by Consolidated Labs, who'd taken over printing of all Van Beuren product from Pathé in October of 1932, and whose president Herbert J. Yates was given a financial piece of Davis-Van Beuren. The Irving Berlin Publishing company, a longtime customer of Davis, agreed to issue sheet music for the original songs heard in the shorts. These fresh new tunes were penned by the fresh new team of Johnny Burke and Harold Spina, respectively 24 and 25 years old. (Burke would later cowrite "Pennies from Heaven" with Arthur Johnston, and the Oscar-winning "Swingin' on a Star" with his longest-lasting collaborator Jimmy Van Heusen). Davis' own orchestra would be heard performing the songs on the soundtrack.

Lining up the onscreen talent was Davis' responsibility, and he certainly didn't shirk his duties. The earliest published cast roster included such Broadway and airwave favorites as Bert Lahr, The Mills Brothers, Ethel Waters, Ray Perkins, Arthur Tracy, the Sisters of the Skillet (a radio comedy duo consisting of Ed East and Ralph Dumke), Baby Rose Marie, Jimmy Wallington, the Boswell Sisters, "Singin' Sam" (aka Harry Frankel), James Melton and Harry Richman. Over half of the above-named performers would ultimately appear in the shorts, with Bert Lahr and Ethel Waters signing long-term contracts with Davis-Van Beuren. (Comedian Joe Penner signed a similar contract, but terminated the agreement before making a single film).

Industry anticipation was high for what would be blanket-titled *The Van Beuren Musical Comedies*. While musical shorts were hardly a novelty—every major studio had been grinding them out since talkies began—most of them were dreary, unimaginative star vehicles weighed down with unfunny badinage and banal storylines (when they actually *had* storylines). Standout shorts like RKO's brilliant, innovative Phil Harris vehicle *So This is Harris* (1933) were few and far between, and by 1933 audiences were inclined to groan in unison whenever a "new" musical one- or two-reeler flashed on the screen. But as the pseudonymous "Phil M. Daly" wrote in his "On the Rialto" column for the October 30, 1933, *Film Daily*, bigger and better things were expected from the Van Beuren shorts.

As reported by Mr. Daly, RKO's general manager Jules Levey had decreed that the new series "will set the style for the latest model in 1933–34 screen entertainment." In his standard technique of separating his comments with ellipses, the columnist added: "The big thought in planning this series of short musicals had been to eschew ... a story built around a worn-out musical setting ... every pix will be cast with stars who fit the various roles...." The correspondent further commented "So this series of Van Beuren Musical Comedies bids fair to administer the final kick in the pants to those terrible alleged musical comedy shorts ... salvaged from the outworn debris of ham vaude acts of the late '90's dressed up with modern studio sets ... it's the

New Deal in musical shorts." With "Real Plots, Class Music, Big Names," concluded Mr. Daly, "how can they miss?"

Scripted by actor-bandleader Art Jarrett and Broadway special-material writer Bert Granet—later a top producer at RKO and its successor Desilu—the first of the *Van Beuren Musical Comedies* to go before Joe Ruttenberg and Sam Leavitt's cameras was *Hizzoner*, starring Bert Lahr in his first screen appearance since the 1931 feature *Flying High*. Although his three Van Beuren shorts are never specifically mentioned in Lahr's biography *Notes on a Cowardly Lion* (written by his son John), the book goes into some detail tallying the reasons why, with the spectacular exception of *The Wizard of Oz* (1939), Bert's sporadic film career was never as satisfying as his stage work. For some contemporary viewers, Lahr comes on much too strong in his Van Beuren appearances, seemingly unable or unwilling to scale down his performances for the camera. John Lahr has revealed that the fault was less Lahr's than his directors, who were inclined to let the comedian do whatever he wanted onscreen, figuring that he knew his business and could essentially direct himself. Bert admitted in later years that his manic movie performances were far over the top: "Different movements which got laughs on stage came out overplayed, 'funny-funny' on the screen.... The camera made every reaction twice as large. Instead of underplaying, I was way over. I was a caricature. In moving pictures, I learned that the audience subsconsciously expects everything to be *real* ... if it wasn't, the audience wouldn't believe your story."

And yet, many modern comedy *aficionados* are of the opinion that what we see in his Van Beuren shorts is the *real* Bert Lahr: The broad, brazen, buffoonish force of nature who held three generations of Broadway first-nighters in the palm of his hand. Lahr's gargoyle-like grimaces, seismic double-takes, aggressive pawing of male and female costars alike, and periodic bursts of his trademark lament "*Gnaang-gnaag-gnaag!*" are treasured moments for those too young to have witnessed firsthand such glorious musical-comedy grotesques as Ed Wynn, Clark &McCullough, the Marx Brothers et. al. These comedy buffs are grateful indeed that the director of *Hizzoner* was Leo McCarey's prolific but less talented brother Ray McCarey, who having recently megged a brace of Laurel & Hardy comedies knew darn well that the best way to handle powerhouse comic talents was to yell "Action!" and then just sit back and enjoy the show. (Joe Nadel, supervising director for the first two Van Beuren shorts, was evidently just as hands-off as McCarey.)

Bert Lahr needn't have worried that his performance was unrealistic, since not for one nano-second is *Hizzoner* remotely believable. The film opens with corrupt, flea-brained Mayor Little (played by radio tenor James Melton) answering his fan mail in rhyme as we cut away to his adoring female constituents—including the termagant wife of illiterate, imbecilic traffic cop Lahr. While bragging about capturing a nest of gangsters, Bert has his patrol car stolen right under his nose; he then compounds his klutziness by arresting Mayor Little and his campaign manager (Jimmy Wallington) for a traffic violation. The opposing political party concludes that if a dufus like Little can be elected, a stupider specimen like Lahr would make an even better candidate for City Hall. Lahr and Little's subsequent radio debate consists primarily of the current mayor warbling the Burke-Spina ballad "With All My Heart," which like all the songs in the Van Beuren Musical Comedies is charmingly performed "live" without post-dubbing. Lahr's campaign manager (Fred Hildebrand) hires a gay ventriloquist to do Bert's talking for him ("just like a puss in the corner"), but our hero insists on giving his own speech, scoring laughs with such non-jokes as "Let's get the wimmen outta politics—the battleaxes!" through sheer lung power. The opposing manager's mistress (Loretta Sayers) figures the only way to get Bert out of the running is to frame him in a compromising situation, which she does with the help of her big number "Oh, Gee What You Do to Me." Not exactly George Bernard Shaw, but undeniably entertaining.

An encouraging start to the new series, *Hizzoner* more than paid its way at the box office, performing better in big cities where Lahr's name meant something than in the hinterlands where he was barely recognized. *Film Daily* of November 29, 1933, rated the two-reeler "Okay," further commenting "Lahr uses all his laughmaking tricks and his followers should be more than satisfied." and singling out for special praise the "wow, surprise finish" (which most 21st century viewers will see coming a mile away). Less impressed was A.H. Edwards, manager of the Orpheum Theater in Orwigsburg Pennsylvania, who complained to *Motion Picture Herald* that Bert Lahr was "trying to imitate Joe E. Brown"—ironic, in that Lahr had earlier contemplated suing Brown for imitating *him* in the 1930 film version of Bert's Broadway hit *Hold Everything*.

The second of the *Van Beuren Musical Comedies* went into production as *Change Your Luck*, then was retitled *Hot 'n' Bothered* before finally settling on *Bubbling Over*. Black songstress Ethel Waters, fresh off her triumphant appearance in Irving Berlin's Broadway revue *Thousands Cheer*, was paid $3000 to star in this two-reeler, which featured such stellar African American performers as Hamtree Harrington (Waters' costar in her previous Vitaphone short *Rufus Jones for President*), Frank L. Wilson, Joe Byrd, the NBC Quartette and the Raymond Johnson Choir—as well as several long-stemmed Cotton Club chorines, if we are to believe the RKO publicists. Though top-heavy with black talent, the behind-the-scenes contributors to *Bubbling Over* were to a man as white as snow, including composers Burke & Spina, screenwriters Bert Granet and Burnett Hershey and director Leigh Jason, which pretty much explains the film's preponderance of stereotypical characters, minstrel-show humor and *Amos 'n' Andy*-style malaprops like "psych-annihilated"—though it fairness, *Bubbling Over* isn't as hard to endure as some of the other all-black short subjects from the same unenlightened era.

The story takes place in the Harlem Apartments, with Ethel Waters delivering an earthy, warm-hearted performance as Ethylene, long-suffering wife of indolent janitor Samson Peabody (Harrington). As if doing all the chores around the place isn't misery enough, Ethylene also must also put up with Samson's endless parade of mooching relatives. Enter phony mystic Swami River (Wilson), who worms his way into Ethylene's confidence by predicting that her millionaire uncle Frisby (Byrd) will soon drop in for a visit (information gleaned by peeking into the Peabodys' mailbox). Dreams of a life of luxury and ease are shattered when Uncle Frisby turns out to be an escaped lunatic with nary a dime to his name—and a kleptomaniac to boot. Songs in *Bubbling Over* include Ethel Waters' plaintive "Darkies Don't Dream" (an unfortunate title for an above-average ballad) and her lively "Takin' Your Time," sung in response to her husband's laziness; "When You Hang Your Hat in Harlem Flat," harmonized *a cappella* by the NBC Quartette (playing four of Samson's poor relations); the Rhythmaires' ensemble number "Company Is Comin' Tonight," full of sprightly rhythmic dialogue (a specialty of this series); and the closing spiritual "Bow

Down," performed by the Raymond Johnson Choir while dear old Uncle Frisby scampers about stealing everything that isn't nailed down.

Showcased at New York's Radio City Music Hall along with the RKO feature *If I Were Free*, *Bubbling Over* was hailed by *Variety* as "one of the pleasures of the current program." As was the case with Bert Lahr's *Hizzoner*, the film's success outside of Manhattan depended on the location of the theater and the audience's familiarity with the star. As chronicled in *Motion Picture Herald*, exhibitor reaction ranged from "Just what you need in musical two-reelers for any program. This colored girl and her bunch are extra good" (M.P. Foster, Granada Theater, Monte Vista, Colorado) to "A harmless two-reel so-called musical comedy. Nothing much in its favor or against it" (A.B. Jeffries, New Piedmont Theatre, Piedmont, Missouri); and, on the bottom rung, "These musical specials are a pain in the neck. This one has better recording than the previous numbers, but this story of Negro life in Harlem is a total loss to my town" (Roy W. Adams, Mason Theater, Mason, Michigan). Mixed reviews notwithstanding, *Bubbling Over* was one of the most popular Davis-Van Beuren offerings, enjoying numerous theatrical revivals courtesy of Official Films and Sack Amusements, the latter distributor catering specifically to black theaters. Curiously, despite the success of *Bubbling Over* Ethel Waters made no further films for Van Beuren, evidently nipping her long-term contract in the bud.

Filmed before *Bubbling Over* but released third in the series, *The Strange Case of Hennessy* (1933) was considered a lost film until a nearly complete print surfaced in the early 21st century, allowing one DVD distributor to promote the short as "so rare it isn't even listed on Internet Movie Database" (It is *now*). Directed by Ray McCarey, *Hennessy* is a labored spoof of "Old Dark House" murder mysteries, elevated by the atmospheric photography of future *film noir* specialist Joe Ruttenberg. The star is Cliff "Ukulele Ike" Edwards, twixt-and-tween his early-talkie MGM musical appearances and his most celebrated screen assignment as the voice of Jiminy Cricket in Disney's *Pinocchio*. Though Edwards is permitted a snatch of uke-plunking in an opening scene (missing from currently available prints), his customary effervescence is surprisingly absent here; as a result, his portrayal of Detective Silo Dance (a play on S.S. Van Dyne's urbane sleuth Philo Vance) is never as funny as it might have been, not even in the final scene where Inspector Dance, like Uncle Frisby in *Bubbling Over*, is exposed as a runaway lunatic. Better served in this insignificant outing are former *Our Gang* member Johnny Downs as a newlywed and Van Beuren contractee Margie Hines, then providing voices for the studio's animated-cartoon output (see Chapter 11), as Johnny's bride. Indicating that the filmmakers weren't persuaded that Cliff Edwards could carry a short subject by himself, the film features another pair of musical sweethearts, singer-songwriter Jack Fulton, Jr., then with the Paul Whiteman Orchestra, and Jean Sargent, who'd introduced the Schwartz-Dietz standard "Alone Together" in the Broadway hit *Flying Colors*. If Sargent's role seems unusually brief, it may be because she suffered a nervous breakdown just before shooting started and was nearly replaced.

Like its predecessors in the series, *Strange Case of Hennessy* makes extensive use of rhythmic dialogue, especially in Cliff Edward's "Make a Note of It" and the ensemble pieces "I Thought I'd Heard a Noise" and "He Thinks He Is Silo Vance." A metronome was used on the set to make certain that the "talking songs" be timed just right, requiring more rehearsals than usual for a two-reeler. The film's one straight ballad, "I

Knew I'd Find You," is lushly performed by Jack Fulton, Jr., and Jean Sargent, albeit cut short by a sudden plot development.

Adjudged "a nifty" by *Film Daily*, *The Strange Cast of Hennessy* was otherwise roundly panned by the true arbiters of public taste, the theater exhibitors of America—at least those cited in *Motion Picture Herald*. Here's a sampling: "I would never

A 1933 trade ad for the *Van Beuren Musical Comedies*. The Ethel Waters entry would be retitled *Bubbling Over*.

have believed that a producer would have the guts to offer such punk under the heading of musical comedies. Cliff Edwards sang about a half of a song and from then on not even a chord. The comedy is about a crazy man, if you can call such a sad affliction funny." (A.H. Edwards, Orpheum Theater, Orwigsburg PA); "This is supposed to be one of the special Van Beuren musicals, but the only evidence of that is in the opening titles. Rotten entertainment. Better left unplayed." (Walter Beymer, Lido Theatre, Providence KY); "A waste of good film. Did not even hear a giggle." (L.G. Tewksbury, Opera House, Stonington ME); and "Brother exhibitors, here are two reels of the worst entertainment ever produced. If Van Beuren cannot make a better comedy than this, he should stop making them." (J.J. Medford, Orpheum Theater, Oxford NC). Ignoring this final volley, Van Beuren continued making his comedies—but not with Cliff Edwards.

The fourth series entry, and the second to star Bert Lahr, *Henry the Ache* (1934) comes closest to successfully capturing Lahr's bombastic stage persona on film, and can even be considered a dry run for the comedian's burlesque of King Louis XV in his later Broadway success *DuBarry Was a Lady*. Per its title, *Henry the Ache* is a takeoff of the recent Charles Laughton film *The Private Life of Henry VIII*, focusing on the lusty monarch's boudoir escapades. Written in a devil's brew of Shakespearean prose and up-to-date slang by Burnett Hershey and Bert Granet and directed by Ray McCarey, the film opens with the portraits of Henry's three former wives—Catherine of Aragon, Anne Boleyn, Jane Seymour—coming to life and cynically bemoaning their fate in song. The story proper commences as Henry's latest spouse, the statuesque Anne of Cleves (Leni Stengel), commiserates with the king's trusted aide Thomas Culpepper (Monte Collins), complaining that her husband neglects her while Culpepper tries to make time with her. All this is prologue to the antic entrance of Henry (Bert Lahr) himself, attempting to sneak past his own guards as he rolls in from a night on the town. Once Henry casts his optics on gorgeous royal manicurist Catherine Howard (Janet Reade), whom he regards as a "hunk o' stuff," he tries to arrange for a quickie Reno divorce. When this fails, Henry orders "Annie" to be executed, an event covered on radio like a sports event by "Sir Walter Winchell" and capped with an impromptu chorus of Johnny Burke's hit song "Annie Doesn't Live Here Anymore." Once wed to Catherine, Henry's time is beaten by the amorous Culpepper, leading inexorably to the traditional climax of the no-longer-trusted aide hiding in the bedroom closet to avoid detection, and the classic "Come outta there!" bit in which Henry discovers several would-be suitors hiding in that same closet. "*Gnaang-gnaag-gnaag!*"

The Burke-Spina tunes on this occasion include "The King Has Had a Change of Heart," performed by Monte Collins, the Girl Friends trio and a bevy of leggy pagegirls; and "The Moment the King Turned His Back," with Collins accompanying himself on an anachronistic guitar. *Henry the Ache* has received a great deal of latter-day exposure due to the very brief appearance by Shemp Howard of "Three Stooges" fame as Artie the Lackey. But of course the emphasis is on Bert Lahr, making the most of his role with his Holbein costuming, patently false beard and leering verbal gags like "I was at a meetin' of the Knights of the Garter. It was Ladies' Night."

With *Henry the Ache*, the exhibitors who regularly contributed comments to *Motion Picture Herald* finally found an entry of *Van Beuren Musical Comedies* that they could thoroughly enjoy. The normally hypercritical J.J. Medford of the Orpheum in Oxford NC spoke for most of his brethren: "This is the best comedy we have played from RKO and hope there will be more of these. Our entire audience enjoyed this one and they laughed throughout the entire two reels. Come on, RKO, keep up the good work and gives us good shorts." Even before its release, *Henry the Ache* engendered goodwill amongst industryites: In December of 1933, Bert Lahr joined Amedee Van Beuren and Meyer Davis for a special appearance at the *Film Daily* Relief Fund luncheon, held at Sardi's in New York, where Bert aggressively auctioned off copies of a Henry VIII biography.

Scheduled to begin shooting the third week of December 1933 under the direction of musical-film specialist Leigh Jason, the fifth short *The Knife of the Party* was delayed until January. Following a four-day shooting schedule, the short was released three weeks after completion on February 16, 1934. Lillian Miles, the Broadway and Hollywood singer who was later showcased during the "Continental" number in the Astaire-Rogers epic *The Gay Divorcee* (and still later starred in the anti-marijuana cult classic *Reefer Madness*), was given star billing along with song-and-dance man Jack Good. But the real Life of the Party in *Knife of the Party* is Shemp Howard, who is the sole reason why this particular Van Beuren musical has received a wider latter-day circulation than any other series entry. An original member of comedian Ted Healy's Stooges along with brother Moe Howard and Larry Fine, Shemp had broken away from Healy in 1932 to solo in a series of two-reelers for Vitaphone. By 1934 Shemp had acquired a couple of stooges of his own named James Fox and Charles Senna, and in this film he and his new cohorts essentially duplicate Ted Healy's old act, replete with punches, kicks, eye-pokes and salty expletives like "I'm a little too quick for ya, ain't I?" and "Ya see *that*?" The short's highlight is a dining-room football game, with a frozen ham tossed hither and yon by Shemp, Fox, Senna, and the vaudeville team of Rogers & Anthony, all wearing Confederate uniforms for no discernable reason.

In case you're wondering, there *is* a plot. A stranded theatrical troupe, unable to pay their board bill, makes an arrangement with hotel owner Mr. Dora (Leo Kennedy) to work off their obligations by signing up as the domestic staff. This set-up permits Lillian Miles and the Girl Friends trio (remember them from *Henry the Ache*?) to go about their daily duties while singing "Whistle While You Work"—*not* the familiar Disney tune by any stretch of the imagination—and for Jack Good to romance Mrs. Dora (Gertrude Mudge) to distract the lady while Lillian makes a long-distance phone call, the better to audition for a big-time producer by singing the two-reeler's second big Burke-Spina tune "Why Am I in Love?" So why the title *Knife of the Party*? Well, it seems that the insanely jealous Mr. Dora is a former vaudeville knife-thrower and ... well, you can fill in the rest. And we weren't kidding about "Why Am I in Love" being a "big" tune. The song was quite popular in its day, especially after being performed over the NBC radio network by Ethel Shutta.

"This has names, a surprising variety of scenes and good looking girls as well as incidental music by Meyer Davis' orchestra," reported *Motion Picture Daily* on the topic of *Knife of the Party*. "The story is light—a traveling stage unit is stuck when the customers pay their admission in vegetables and they have to work out their hotel bill. Some of the gags are good." *Motion Picture Herald* rated the film "a fair comedy," observing, "A good portion of the comedy is supplied by Shemp Howard and his stooges, who are entertaining." The exhibitors also had their say in the *Herald*, with the difficult-to-please J.J. Medford displaying uncharacteristic effusion: "This is a very good comedy that will please your patrons. It is a musical comedy, with beautiful girls, good music and a few songs. This is one of the best of this series and I certainly hope there will be more like it."

As far as this writer can determine, the sixth Van Beuren musical *Everybody Likes Music*, originally titled *So You Won't Talk*, has seldom been exhibited since its March 9, 1934, release date (a little over a month after production wrapped). Until I'm able to secure a copy myself, I'll have to trust the contemporary reports. Tenor Donald Novis, who'd recently starred in his own series for Mack Sennett, appears as himself, as does singer Irene Taylor, who like *Henry the Ache*'s Jack Fulton, Jr., was associated with the Paul Whiteman orchestra. Set in the mythical country of Bullvania, the story finds Ms. Taylor throwing a party for the President (Jules Epaully) in hopes of cinching a cushy cabinet post for her husband. In the midst of the festivities the President is robbed of several important documents, meaning that war will be declared unless a goofy detective (Shemp Howard, who received $250 for three days' work) is able to locate the precious papers. Meyer Davis makes a rare screen appearance in *Everybody Likes Music*, fronting his own orchestra and backing up Donald Novis' rendition of "Cuban Serenade," Irene Taylor's performance of "Between You and Me," and Novis and Adelina Thomason (as "Mrs. Pennyfeather," a ditzy character

Shemp Howard, flanked by Adelina Thomason and Jules Epaully (right) in the long-missing Van Beuren musical comedy *Everybody Likes Music* (1934).

Thomason had introduced on the radio series *The Cuckoo Hour*) in the *sprechgesang* duet "What Will You Play?"

Art Jarrett and H.O.Kussell, the same team who'd previously cooked up *Knife of the Party*, shared responsibility for the script of *Everybody Likes Music*, with Leigh Jason directing. Our faithful correspondent J.J. Medford of Oxford NC felt that this short didn't live up to the standard set by *Knife of the Party*, informing *Motion Picture Herald*: "This is only fair entertainment of the slapstick variety. Donald Novis sings two selections and they are about the only part worth mentioning. The orchestra does very well, but the story is terrible and did not please our audience."

The seventh in the Van Beuren series was *Sea Sore* (1934), directed by Joe Nadel. The film was held back from release for a couple of months in favor of the eighth entry, Bert Lahr's *No More West*. Considering their quality, both shorts should have been held back as long as possible—say, until 2015, when the only surviving print of *Sea Sore* (owned by collector Ralph Celentano) was given its first public screening in decades at the Syracuse Cinefest. Monte Collins, who'd supported Lahr in *Henry the Ache*, wrote the script for *Sea Sore*, casting himself in the leading role: A fiddle-playing steward on an excursion boat who tries to impress his girlfriend (Mady Correll) during the annual Police Captain's Picnic by pretending to be the boat's skipper.

Guest stars in this outing are Baby Rose Marie—still an adolescent jazz singer, far removed from TV immortality on *The Dick Van Dyke Show*—Arthur "The Street Singer" Tracy, orchestra leader Freddie Martin (given a special superimposed cast credit) and the chubby radio comedy duo Sisters of the Skillet. These artists supposedly perform their musical specialties during a concert staged on a shipboard set constructed at Fox Movietone, but were actually filmed separately on the upper deck of an actual Hudson River dayliner (The deception does not go unnoticed). Another featured player is Emily Van Loesen, then the leading fan dancer in the floor show of New York's Paradis Restaurant, coincidentally owned by Meyer Davis. Emily doesn't dance, worse luck, but she's a mighty fetching sight clad in only a life preserver. Redoubtable North Carolina theater owner J.J. Medford, who for reasons that baffle science continued booking these shorts despite his obvious disdain for the series, complained to *Motion Picture Herald* that *Sea Sore* "is only fair entertainment and we had many walkouts while this was showing. Arthur Tracy sings one number, but the terrible recording spoils this."

Though ostensibly Meyer Davis was going through with his agreement to produce 13 *Van Beuren Musical Comedies*, short #8 *No More West* (1934) turned out to be the series finale. Prior to starting work on the film, star Bert Lahr joined writers Monte Collins, Bert Granet and H.O. Kussell, and unit cinematographer Sam Leavitt, on a motor trip to Florida, there to engage in a series of story conferences. From the looks of things, the boys didn't get much work done: *No More West* is by far the weakest of Lahr's Van Beuren efforts, so much so that in his otherwise reliable book on Hollywood short subjects, historian Leonard Maltin misidentifies *No More West* as one of the comedian's mediocre two-reelers made at Educational Pictures between 1935 and 1937. Despite this error, Maltin's assessment of the film is right on target: "[T]he most generous helping of Lahr's mannerisms and mugging were useless."

On this occasion, Meyer Davis determined that his unit had outgrown the Movietone facilities and thus moved into the newly renovated and wired-for-sound Biograph studios in the Bronx, where once D.W. Griffith had ruled the roost. Former

Griffith player Florence Auer appears in *No More West* as Lahr's battle-axe wife, while others in the cast include Bert's future *Wizard of Oz* costar Charley Grapewin, ubiquitous character actor Harry Shannon, the Rhythm Boys singing aggregation, and child performer Bixey Paumstead, whom Davis touted as a "discovery" but who would swiftly return to the ranks of the undiscovered. Nick Grinde, later a fixture of the Columbia Pictures B unit, wielded the megaphone for this one, doing as best he could with Burnett Hershey's sloppy screenplay.

Released precisely two weeks after completion, *No More West* finds Lahr swaggering around as "Gunpowder Bert," imagining himself a rootin' tootin' cowboy while running a Broadway shooting gallery. After accidentally foiling a pair of bank robbers, Bert is emboldened to don a ten-gallon hat and a pair of chaps and head out to what passes as the Wide Open Spaces in this studio-bound epic. Once again he crosses the path of the two bank bandits, who trick him into framing himself for a heist. Bert is nearly railroaded into the Big House by his lawyer—who happens to be one of the crooks in disguise (yes, Lahr is *that* dumb in this one)—but all ends happily except perhaps for the audience, not to mention those increasingly dissatisfied exhibitors like J.J. Medford, who apparently was so appalled that he couldn't bring himself to make a comment for *Motion Picture Herald*. Another theater owner, A.E. Hancock of Columbia City IN, took up Medford's cudgel with a critique of his own: "Terrible. This chap from Broadway with his horselaugh or what it is called (it is hard to identify just what noise he makes) is very unfunny. They can bury him deep down and no one will miss him. Never have we had anything that approached it for general no-goodness."

Though no formal announcement was made that the *Van Beuren Musical Comedies* would cease production after eight of the proposed 13 films, as early as the January 29, 1934, edition of *The Hollywood Reporter* Meyer Davis was indicating that he planned to forsake two-reelers in favor of a six-reel musical feature. Restoring the original "Magna Pictures" label to his unit, Davis announced that the upcoming feature would be filmed at Biograph studios under Nick Grinde's direction, with Bert Lahr starring in a spoof of beauty contests. The film would also serve as a comeback for nasal-voiced character actor Lee Tracy, who'd been blacklisted from Hollywood after an undiplomatic act of public indecency while in Mexico filming MGM's *Viva Villa*. But Davis' expansion plans proved too rich for the blood of Amedee Van Beuren, especially since the costly musical series had not performed at the box office as well as expected, despite the isolated success of such above-average shorts as *Bubbling Over* and *Henry the Ache*. Nor did Van Beuren evince any interest in Meyer Davis' alternate proposal of producing six two-reel comedies with radio favorite Phil Baker.

Thus it was that the *Van Beuren Musical Comedies* quietly folded in April of 1934, representing the last two-reelers ever produced by Amedee Van Beuren. Henceforth the only Van Beuren product to run any longer than one reel would be the producer's occasional documentary features like Frank Buck's *Wild Cargo* and *Fang and Claw*.

Chapter 18

The Dumb-Bell Letters

Rapidly mounting budgets and RKO-dictated cutbacks at Van Beuren Productions necessitated the hasty creation of a *really* inexpensive series to fill out the 1934–35 shorts season. Amedee Van Beuren chose a property that not only observed this cost-consciousness but also hearkened back to one of the company's most successful series of yore, *Topics of the Day* (see Chapter 2), which during the silent era consisted of nothing more than a series of written titles quoting choice headlines and interesting tidbits from the periodicals of the era. As the series wore on, *Topics* abandoned its "straight" commentary in favor of pure comedy, mostly supplied by Van Beuren's own writing staff. The producer's new series for 1934 would forego the gradual progression of the earlier shorts and aim straight for laughs from the get-go. The trade papers not only took immediate notice of the resemblance between the new project and the old *Topics*, but most of them applauded the nostalgic harkback. For his part, Van Beuren would describe the brand-new *Dumb-Bell Letters* series as "Another novelty unusual in its laugh-provoking merits" that "leaped into prominence in the short subject field immediately after the release of the first issue" (*Film Daily*, April 12, 1935).

You knew we'd get around to mentioning the title sometime, and we're going to do it again. *Dumb-Bell Letters* was the brainchild of newspaper humorist Juliet Lowell, (*née* Lowenthal), born in New York City in 1901. After graduating from Vassar, Lowell entered journalism and began collecting examples of foolish, unintentionally funny letters written by "regular folks" to newspapers, corporations, politicians and the like. These were trotted out in Lowell's regular column for the Hearst syndicate, "Dumb Belles-Lettres," a play on the French publishing firm "Les Belles Lettres." Several of the choicest missives were published in book form by Simon & Schuster in 1933, with illustrations by Otto Soglow of *The Little King* fame (see Chapter 11).

The ephemeral nature of Van Beuren's *Dumb-Bell Letters* shorts may be the reason that apparently none of them have been preserved for posterity. Since the early episodes were ostensibly reliant upon Lowell's first published collection, we can assume that the typical examples of correspondence listed below showed up at one time or another on the big screen. So, with grammatical and spelling errors intact, here goes:

The opening letter in the 1933 book is from "Margie L—" of Circleville, Indiana, written to the Mitchell Schneider Company of New York City: "Gentlemen: I am going to be married—I want to get a real nice nightgown for my wedding night. Please—don't send anything too fancy—I want to have all the attention."

"Charles S—," writing to the Mutual Telephone Company: "Gentlemen: I protest against check machines and telephone books that are chained to tables. Such distrust is an insult to the public. And furthermore it just about ruins a person's knife to cut one of those chains."

"Miss Christine A—" to the Model Brassiere Company of NYC: "Gentlemen: My busts are terrible. Last year they weighed 12 pounds each and this year the two weigh 30 pounds. They now hang as low as my waist. O, for goodness sakes, tell me what to do? Where will they go next? ... Enclosed find stamp. Hurry, hurry and write me at once, or send someone to see me."

"Miss P—C—" to an unidentified male Hollywood star: "Dear Sir: Please send me three of your autographed pictures. You see I am saving pictures of actors and we girls exchange them. So if I have three of yours I can exchange them for one of Douglas Fairbanks. Please send them right away."

"Caroline B—" to a Minneapolis advice-to-the-lovelorn columnist: "Dear Miss True: I invited a young man to dinner at my home. Having met him only once before, I was somewhat amazed when he called my mother a 'fat-fanny.' He apologized when I asked him to and behaved like a gentleman the rest of the evening. Should I invite him again?"

"Clarabelle D—" to the Bank of America, Beverly Hills: "Yesterday you returned my check for $30, marked 'no funds.' How come a big bank like yours should be so short of money?"

"Marvin D—" requesting a book titled *Treatment of Sexual Impotence* from Cosmopolitan Press, NYC: "I enclose money order for $5.50. Please send me your book Sexual Impatience."

"Alvin C—" to the Outdoor Advertising Company [and this one must have struck home with former bill-posting mogul Amedee Van Beuren]: "What do you think an abled body American of 40 odd years want to think about all day, ketchup? I'll bet you don't think of ketchup, but that's what you have plastered up outside my window and it's been there for three years. Three years, do you get it? Every time I gaze out of the window that is what I see. Ketchup! Ketchup! Ketchup! Now, how about a girl on the sign board for a change, at least for spring.... Let's have something hot on the landscape, after all pal, I havent got a steno, you know."

And this writer's personal favorite, from "Stella K—" to the advice columnist of the New Orleans *Times-Picayune*: "Dear Miss Solomon: We have been married for two month, but the trouble is starting already. My husband belongs to the Naval Reserves and is ever preparing for war. Not a family fight, I mean a war with Russia or Japan. I did nothing to prevent his readiness until he proposed cutting a hole in the bedroom floor and putting in a fire-man's pole. This is going too far, as we have a very lovely rug in the bedroom and I suppose he wants to cut that too. I have spoken to my mother-in-law about it, and she only remarked thus: 'Ralph was always a spoiled boy.'"

Also included were a few of what *Mad* magazine's Al Jaffee would later describe as "snappy answers to stupid questions," like this one from a big-city department of Health to the L.A. Bureau of Vital Statistics: "In reply to your question—our death rate is the same here as elsewhere—one death for every inhabitant."

To sum up, the humor was primarily based on the ignorance and shaky literary skills of the writers. On the negative side, a lot of *Dumb-Bell Letters* poked cruel fun at foreign-born writers and their difficulty with the English language; and there were too many tasteless jibes concerning religion, ethnicity, physical deformities, mental retardation and other categories in the "formerly funny."

Chapter 18—The Dumb-Bell Letters 171

Van Beuren Productions' Sam Jacobson supervised the film version of *Dumb-Bell Letters*, with former Van Beuren publicist Don Hancock, returning to the fold after four years on the editorial staff of *Film Daily*, as production manager. In half-reel doses running anywhere from 4 to 5 minutes. the series was launched on a monthly basis (at first) with *Dumb-Bell Letters No. 1* on June 22, 1934; the last short, *Dumb-Bell Letters No. 26*, came out in August of 1936. An average of nine letters per short

A 1934 trade ad for Van Beuren's *Dumb-Bell Letters*.

were flashed onscreen, or one every thirty seconds. There was no "live" footage, and nothing on the soundtrack save for background music.

Of the inaugural entry, which featured eight letters, *Motion Picture Daily* remarked:

> First issue of "Dumb Bell Letters," assembled by Juliet Lowell who authored the amusing book of the same name, got a helluva reaction from Music Hall audiences last week. They rollicked and they rolled, so funny were the purported facsimiles of communications sent by the intelligent public to manufacturers of this and that. Hollywood ought to study them for a slant on the populace it is trying to serve. Then watch the mentality of future product sink like a plumb line...

Catching on that some of the letters might not have been authentic [you *think*?] *Motion Picture Daily* added: "Whether they're real or not, they're funny."

In *Motion Picture Herald*'s weekly column of reactions from regional theater owners, the first and second *Dumb-Bell Letters* entries were commented upon by M.P. Foster, Granada Theatre, Monte Vista CA: "Very short but gets the laughs. Five minutes of photographed actual letters really received by stores, insurance companies, etc. The more intelligent your audience, the more laughs you'll get." Similarly, A. West Johnson of the Heilig Theatre, Eugene OR, noted: "A new type of subject, and one that audiences go for in a big way. From the opening moment until the last flicker there isn't a letdown." But A.N. Miles of Eminence Theater, Eminence KY groused: "Our first and last of this series. It did not go over with our folks at all." And Alice Simmons, Lyric Theater, Jefferson TX grumbled: "This series will have to beat the first one if they go over here. About the length of a trailer, and this one was just nothing."

Mr. Miles and Ms. Simmons notwithstanding, the series was an instant hit, as reported by *Motion Picture Daily* on November 5, 1934: "Nothing since the phenomenal success of the Mickey Mouse and Silly Symphony series hit the short subject field like the 'Dumb-Bell Letters' laugh-getters. That is, unless this doddering memory has gone completely to pot. The inside has it the entire negative cost returned itself to Van Beuren from first run rentals out the metropolitan area alone..."

Originally only 13 shorts were contracted by distributor RKO, but the immediate success of the property doubled the order within a few months. In the fall of 1935 Don Hancock told *Motion Picture Daily* that six second-season shorts were completed and ready for release with "the possibility they might be increased later," even though all 13 for the 1935–36 season had been completed (Why did he say this? Why are you asking *me*?) *Dumb-Bell Letters* was also widely distributed abroad, with separate foreign-language versions prepared. Examples of British correspondence were used exclusively in those shorts released in the United Kingdom, French correspondence was used in France, and so forth.

Inevitably, some observers began to grow dog-weary of the series' unyielding format. Commenting on *Dumb-Bell Letters No. 8*, the *Philadelphia Exhibitor* opined: "As the series grows longer, novelty becomes rare. Letters in this one don't provoke the chuckles of the first few." A few exhibitors were likewise growing restless: C.L. Niles of the Niles Theater, Anamosa IA, said of the sixth entry: "Why the exhibitor buys these reels I cannot understand." Likewise fed up was Phil Billiet of the Coliseum Theatre, Annawan, IL: "Too dumb to be good. This is one of RKO's weakest points, their shorts. Why don't they get some orchestra acts instead of wasting film on something of this nature?"

But in general, the series remained popular, with scores of filmgoers anxious to get in on the fun, as reported by *Film Daily* on April 12, 1935: "The daily mail bag coming into the Van Beuren offices invariably contains a number of 'dumb bell letters' sent in by fans who want to help along the compilation of these amusing entries. The contributions come from executives as well as underlings, and from various countries." *Dumb-Bell Letters* was also one of the highlights of the RKO sales convention held in Chicago on June 19, 1935, according to *Motion Picture Daily*: "Practically everyone at the convention got a chance to show whether or not he could 'take it' when a special reel of 'Dumb Bell Letters,' prepared especially for the occasion, was shown at the morning projection. Each one came in for a share of good natured ribbing."

The series' second complement of 13 shorts continued to reap profits for Van Beuren and RKO. Reviewing *Dumb-Bell Letters No. 16* (1936), *Film Daily* commented: "Juliet Lowell's nutty notes still provoke enough chuckles to make fans regret the brevity of the picture. Most of the letters exhibited for this issue are supposed to have been received by the Department of Internal Revenue and other government offices."

In contrast, during this same period *Motion Picture Herald* spoke up for those who were not amused by the series' premise and felt that it was truckling to the lowest common denominator. In a review titled "Rabble Bait," the trade publication sneered:

> Juliet Lowell, who makes a business of this sort of thing, has collected and here presents another dozen or so of letters written by unintelligent persons to various companies and individuals not above guffawing at ignorance and exhibiting the written evidence thereof to persons of equivalent intellectual stature for purposes of amusement. Possibly there are motion picture audiences capable of lusty response to this kind of thing and to these the present collection of items may be recommended as of especially low grade, therefore likely to evoke especially hilarious reactions.

Fascinating and enlightening though these contemporary comments may be, it is frustrating for film historians like myself that reviewers and exhibitors spoke of each new *Dumb-Bell Letters* in generalities, almost never bothering to specify their actual content. One of the few critique to actually give latter-day buffs a hint of the daffy correspondence seen in a typical entry is this one for *Dumb-Bell Letters No. 21* in the January 9, 1936, *Motion Picture Daily*: "Perhaps the best of the lot is one in which a woman writes to the Voice of Experience. She has two children and wants a third, but she has been informed that every third child is born Chinese." Rabble Bait indeed.

The reasons that *Dumb-Bell Letters* was discontinued by Van Beuren have been lost to the ages, though trade papers of the period indicate that Juliet Lowell had moved over to Educational Pictures to prepare a property called "Krazi-Inventions" for Educational's general-interest *Treasure Chest* series. While this resulted in only one short, Lowell certainly did not want for steady employment. A longtime fixture on the national lecture circuit, she was also a member of the board of the Heckscher Foundation for the Children of Idaho during World War II, and later served as chairman of the book committee of the New York-Tokyo Sister City Affiliations. Her other memberships included Authors League of America, International Platform Association and Vassar Alumnae Association.

Through it all, Juliet Lowell regarded the humor arising from goofy letters as her real life's work, compiling such books as *Dear Hollywood, Dear Mr. Congressman*, and *Dear Sir*, the latter a cross-section of military bureaucracy that placed second on 1945's list of nonfiction bestsellers. There was also an autobiography, *Dear*

Me. Hailed by fellow columnist Walter Winchell as "the female Mark Twain," Juliet Lowell parlayed her popularity into a regular panelist spot on the 1950 TV series *We the People*, and later collaborated on a record album of her most outrageous sample mail with eminent "blooper" expert Kermit Schaefer. Juliet Lowell remained active as a lecturer until her eighties, passing away at 97 in 1998.

If the gods should smile upon us and exhume a few examples of the long-unseen Van Beuren *Dumb-Bell Letters* series, we might be as entertained as filmgoers were eight decades ago. Or, given today's P.C. oversensitivity, we might have the same reaction as Roy W. Adams, manager of the Mason Theater in Mason Michigan, who commented on *Dumb-Bell Letters No. 3* in the February 9, 1935, *Motion Picture Herald*: "Some of these are funny but it seems in poor taste to publish some poor fellow's private correspondence who is trying to express himself on a matter of desperate importance to him."

Chapter 19

Animated Cartoons, Part Three

Burt Gillett and the Rainbow Parades

The year of 1934 was a watershed one for Van Beuren animation. In the early-talkie era Amedee Van Beuren was inclined to take a laissez-faire policy towards his animators so long as the cartoons made money. By late 1932, however, he'd grown displeased that the unit was not keeping apace with Walt Disney, the standard by which all other cartoonmakers were measured in the minds of the intelligentsia. Shaking up the studio personnel and attempting to create a star personality to rival Mickey Mouse's popularity fell short of expectations, while efforts to produce cartoons built around such popular presold commodities as The Little King and Amos 'n' Andy (see Chapter 11) likewise came a cropper.

There were also outside influences affecting the Van Beuren product. For many years the animation industry trafficked heavily in humor aimed at adults, resulting in growing resistance from exhibitors who considered cartoons strictly kiddie fare. Trade papers of the early 1930s were full of complaints from theater owners that cartoons had become too raw for their own good—one of several factors that led to the strengthening of the Motion Picture Production Code in 1934. No longer would Van Beuren's cartoons be permitted to crack wise about bootleg hootch, fallen women, homosexuals, bronx cheers or bowel movements. For the remainder of its existence, the cartoon unit trafficked almost exclusively in children's entertainment.

To prettify his product, make it more palatable for youngsters and (hopefully) elevate it to the Walt Disney plateau, Van Beuren hired one of Disney's top men. Born in Elmira, New York, Burt Gillett (1891–1981) had by 1913 matriculated from prize-winning teenage artist to professional newspaper cartoonist. Sometime between 1916 and 1918 he entered the animation field, working periodically for Hearst's cartoon division and more steadily on the venerable *Mutt and Jeff* silent shorts. Gillett went on to spend two years with Max Fleischer, briefly operate his own Associate Animators studio, and close out the silent era working on Pat Sullivan's brilliant *Felix the Cat* cartoons. In 1929 he talked himself into a job at Disney, joining such equally experienced directors as Ub Iwerks and Ben Sharpsteen. After proving his salt on the Mickey Mouse series he was given the honor of directing Disney's first three-strip Technicolor cartoon *Flowers and Trees* (1932), which earned the studio's first Academy Award. Gillett followed this triumph with *The Three Little Pigs* (1933), the most celebrated cartoon of its time.

On the strength of *Three Little Pigs*, Gillett was invited to relocate from California to New York as the new head of Van Beuren's animation department. After making a few preliminary tours of the studio in March of 1934, Gillett was officially installed in his new job at the annual RKO convention in June. It was then announced that Gillett's initial projects would be two new series, *Toddle Tales* and *Rainbow Parades*, the latter planned as Van Beuren's first color effort.

Immediately upon arrival, Gillett set about to make over Van Beuren in Disney's image. To an ageing staff accustomed to simply drawing pictures that would be copied on celluloid and then committed to film, the new animation chief introduced pencil tests, model sheets, storyboards and Moviolas. On weekends, Gillett conducted lectures indoctrinating the staff in the techniques, principles and goals he'd garnered at Disney. While old-timers who were steamed that Gillett had deposed their longtime colleague George Stallings as head man resented this arrogant Hollywood elitist telling them their business, the younger staffers, among them such future notables as Joseph Barbera and Alex Lovy, were stimulated and inspired by Gillett's enthusiasm and knowhow—at least at first.

For the inevitable transition to color, it was necessary to pare down the yearly number of cartoons, from 32 in 1933 to 19 in 1934 and 15 in 1935. This, however, did not translate to shorter hours or an easier workload. Gillett was a stern taskmaster, in the habit of summarily firing those who didn't immediately come up to his standards. For all his talent Gillett was no diplomat, and the air at Van Beuren was at times so thick one could cut it with a carving knife. Shamus Culhane and Izzy Klein were among the former studio employees who in later years opined that Gillett was bipolar, keeping everyone on edge with his violent mood swings; he also reportedly had an alcohol problem which exacerbated his mercurial behavior. Van Beuren was sympathetic to the animators' complaints but invariably backed up Gillett, feeling that all the *tsouris* was worth the price if the end product was superior to previous studio efforts.

But the results didn't bode well in the early months of the Gillett regime. Obliged to fill out Van Beuren's 1933–34 contract with RKO, Gillett quickly dashed off three black-and-white cartoons before the switchover to color. These were the *Toddle Tales*, and a sorry bunch they were indeed. Each entry was bookended with live-action scenes filmed at New York's Movietone studios and on the grounds of a rented Long Island estate. These sickly sequences featured obnoxious child actors indulging in misbehavior that would then segue into a cartoon segment, ostensibly designed to teach the kids a moral—though such life lessons as "alarm clocks have feelings too" in *Grandfather's Clock* or "never misjudge a frog" in *Along Came a Duck* were of negligible value in the real world. The cartoons themselves were feeble *faux* Disney at its stickiest, with the sole exception of *A Little Bird Told Me* (1934), a pungent parody of newspaper films replete with cigar-chomping city editor, flirtatious telephone operator and ace reporter "Walter Finchell," all employed by the *Birdville Daily Bugle* to get the lowdown on a jam-stealing youngster.

The *Toddle Tales* were the last black-and-white cartoons made by Van Beuren. As far back as 1931 the studio owner was musing over the potential of color film, but with reservations. As noted in *Motion Picture Herald*, Van Beuren

> sees color in cartoons as the next step to add novelty to cartoon entertainment, though he does not believe that color has been perfected sufficiently as yet, or that it has proven enough of a success from an audience standpoint in feature productions to merit serious consideration for the time being.

> It has taken long years of study and work, he says, to bring black and white cartoons to their present state of perfection and they will not be abandoned for the sake of novelty until color has been developed to an equally satisfactory degree and picture audiences definitely decide they want color on the screen.

Van Beuren further told the *Herald* that his studio's camera department had set up a special laboratory to prepare sample color cartoons "when the time is ripe and the process has been perfected to overcome the various technical difficulties that now present themselves." No mention was made of this mysterious lab—which may or may not have provided the brief (and now lost) color shot of an American flag in the 1932 *Tom and Jerry* cartoon *A Spanish Twist*—when Van Beuren officially adopted color in 1934, possibly because the equipment was on this occasion personally provided by the new studio employee responsible for the initial color efforts. Burt Gillett's first significant hire was independent animator Ted Eshbaugh (1906–1969), a Canadian import who made his mark on the industry with three noteworthy cartoons filmed in the two-color Cinecolor process: *Goofy Goat Antics* (1930), released by RKO; *The Snowman* (1931), distributed by Invincible Films; and best of all, *The Wizard of Oz* (1933), which unfortunately was not released theatrically. Though Eshbaugh was more concerned with pretty images than with characterization or story development, his sheer virtuosity was enough to secure him a spot in the revamped Van Beuren operation.

Released in July 1934, the first *Rainbow Parade* entry was Eshbaugh's *Pastry Town Wedding*, in which a village populated by cherubic chefs prepares a skyscraper-sized wedding cake for the diminutive hero and heroine. That's all the "story" there is, and though undeniably attractive in design and execution the cartoon doesn't really perk up until the climax wherein the leering master chef reads the wedding vows from his trusty cookbook. The cartoon's main virtues are the buoyant musical score by Winston Sharples and Eshbaugh's adroit manipulation of a limited two-color palate to create the illusion of a vast array of hues.

These positives were carried over into Eshbaugh's next and finest effort *The Sunshine Makers* (1935), not only a huge success when first released but also a cartoon that has since developed so fervent a cult following that it is unnecessary to recount its storyline, its gallery of unique elfin characters or its irresistible appeal. Suffice to say that *Sunshine Makers* is a big step up from *Pastry Town Wedding* if only because its premise—the forces of "Joy" vanquishing the agents of "Gloom"—gives the cartoon a narrative urgency that its predecessor lacks. Eshbaugh's third and final *Rainbow Parade* entry *Japanese Lanterns* (1935) is the most elaborate and colorful of all, albeit the least interesting. Still, the director warrants praise for depicting Asian characters without resorting to stereotype or caricature, undoubtedly the result of hiring a special staff of Japanese artists to collaborate on the model sheets.

Ted Eshbaugh left Van Beuren in 1935 to pursue a lucrative career in animation advertising. In 1940 he purchased the negatives of *Pastry Town Wedding* and *Sunshine Makers*, offering them as "new" cartoons to promote the wares of New York–based Cushman Bakeries and Borden's Dairy Products. *Pastry Town Wedding* was augmented with fresh animation inserting the Cushman name embossed on the cookbook used in the climactic marriage ceremony; and though Borden's name appears only in the reshot opening and closing titles of *Sunshine Makers*, the fact that the cheery dwarf protagonists distribute their sunshine in milk bottles was enough

CUSHMAN SON'S NEW CARTOON

♦ A new animated cartoon in color and sound has just been released for theatrical distribution by Cushman Son's, Inc., baking firm. Produced by Ted Eshbaugh Studios, Inc., the subject is a fanciful story of the pastry realm, cleverly etched with romance and a musical background. A Scene from "Pastry Town Wedding"

A 1941 *Business Screen* magazine blurb for Ted Eshbaugh's altered reissue of his 1935 *Rainbow Parade* cartoon *Pastry Town Wedding*.

to satisfy the sponsor. (Perhaps significantly, Burt Gillett's co-director credit was removed from both cartoons). *Japanese Lanterns* wouldn't see the light of day again until offered in a black-and-white version by Official Films in 1943, wartime sentiments dictating its reissue title *Chinese Lanterns*.

Burt Gillett's initial Eshbaugh-less cartoons included two more *Toddle Tales*, though they weren't billed as such. The live-action moppets, now filmed in Cinecolor, are just as repulsive as ever, while the first of two cartoons, *Spinning Mice* (1935), makes the worst of a bad situation by showing a batch of unappealing cartoon rodents released from a dollhouse by the kids and running amok. John McElwee of the *Greenbriar Picture Show* website offers this pungent summary of *Spinning Mice*: "I kept thinking [the children are] going to end up with rabies. A disquieting sense of impending crib death hovers over live-action at Van Beuren, this being very much an endorsement for those who like cartoons jagged around the edges."

Those who don't like jagged cartoons are referred to the last color *Toddle Tale*, 1935's *Picnic Panic*. It's easily the best of the series, and not just by default. The live-action footage is thankfully at a minimum, just long enough to establish that a trio of singing kettles are putting on a show to amuse some urchins stuck indoors on a rainy day. The titular picnic is held by an aggregation of humanized cups, saucers, pots, pans, bowls, utensils and condiments; small wonder that this captivating cartoon has been cited as a principal inspiration for Maja Moldenhauer's wonderful 30s-animation-style *Cuphead* video game. Adding to the fun is Winston Sharples' opening song "Rhythm of the Rain," one of many *Rainbow Parade* original tunes commissioned by Van Beuren in hopes of coming up with another "Who's Afraid of the Big Bad Wolf?" For many years *Picnic Panic* was available only in a faded reissue version minus the live-action bookends. It has since been restored to its original glory by cartoon historian and Van Beuren enthusiast Steve Stanchfield.

The final *Toddle Tales* were codirected by Burt Gillett's fellow Disney alumnus Tom Palmer, one of the few California-based animators to answer Gillett's call for new talent at Van Beuren. Palmer's less than distinguished resume included a very brief directorial job at Warner Bros.' Harman-Ising unit. His only screen credit during this period was *I've Got to Sing a Torch Song* (1933), one of several celebrity-caricature cartoons in the *Merrie Melodies* manifest. Warner executives were so displeased by this and Palmer's other efforts that they ordered them completely overhauled by Friz Freleng, Ben Hardaway and other animators. Thus Tom Palmer came to Van Beuren with a blot on his escutcheon that was only occasionally erased in his subsequent work. Palmer's one solo credit for the studio, *Cupid Gets His Man* (1936), is a cut above his other efforts, harking back to the Harman-Ising days by building the action around two movie-star caricatures, in this case W.C. Fields and Edna May Oliver.

Before discussing the three mini-series introduced under the *Rainbow Parade* banner by Burt Gillett, let's take a quick look at the more generic efforts. Most of these one-shots are barely worth mentioning: Things like *Bird Scouts* and *A Waif's Welcome* try so ruthlessly to emulate Disney that they seem to be force-feeding charm down our throats. One would like to believe that the legendary Shamus Culhane's first of two directorial credits at the studio, *Foxy Terrier* (1935), was a rose among thorns, but the cartoon apparently no longer exists. Another blossoming talent, Dan Gordon (later responsible for some of the best *Popeye* and *Superman* cartoons at Paramount-Famous Studios), made excellent use of his sole opportunity to direct. Gordon's *It's a Greek Life* (1936) is a refreshing departure from the sweetie-pie characters and cloying sentiment of the Gillett era. Set on Mount Olympus, this story of a centaur blacksmith who steals Mercury's winged sandals in hopes of learning to fly brims over with originality and hilarity, with one superb sight gag emulating the epic "waking lions" montage in Eisenstein's *Battleship Potemkin*. Sadly, *It's a Greek Life* was Van Beuren's next-to-last cartoon release.

Back to 1934, the year of Burt Gillett's first attempt to launch a new series with original characters. *The Parrotville Fire Department* is set in a small community populated entirely by anthropomorphic talking parrots, with a bird known as "The Captain" as town patriarch. A few minutes into the cartoon and one can understand why no other animator ever attempted to make stars out of parrots. The aviary protagonists are unattractive and mostly unfunny, and *Parrotville Fire Department* doesn't give this new menagerie much support with its repertoire of weary cartoon tropes. The 1935 follow-up *Parrotville Old Folks* is almost as deadly as its title, though redeemed by a deliciously bizarre closing gag. The series mercifully ended with *Parrotville Post Office* (1935), which at least boasts a colorful villain in the tradition of Disney's Peg-leg Pete.

Gillett collaborated with Tom Palmer on his second—and as it turned out, last—attempt at a studio-created star personality. Molly Moo Cow had first appeared as an obstreperous unnamed bovine in the *Toddle Tales* swan song *Picnic Panic*. The character was elevated to star status in *The Hunting Season* (1935), one of the last Van Beuren cartoons made in Cinecolor. Since we're now in Production Code territory, we shouldn't be surprised that Molly Moo Cow has no udder. And since we're also in Burt Gillett territory, it's no surprise the Molly is neither very funny nor particularly memorable. Nonetheless, the series received a box-office boost when in 1935 Disney's exclusivity contract with three-strip Technicolor expired and Burt Gillett was finally permitted to use every color of the rainbow in the *Rainbow Parades*. The vivid, vibrant hues in the remaining four *Molly Moo Cow* entries remain a feast for the eyes

Parrotville Fire Department **(1934).**

to this day, with *Molly Moo Cow and the Butterflies* (1935) a standout. Bowled over by the multi-tinted splendor of the whole enterprise, exhibitors raved over the new Van Beuren series. In certain locales, theater owners advised RKO not to ship out any other cartoons but the *Molly Moo Cows*.

The addition of Technicolor resulted in the largest budgets ever incurred by the animation unit. Van Beuren was less bothered by this than by Burt Gillett's tendency to go over budget due to indecision, lack of organizational skills and chronic inability to get along with his staff, whom he now ordered to put in extra hours without pay. The war of wills and words between Gillett and the animators escalated in early 1935, when a group of in-betweeners and inkers tried to organize a union. Gillett countered by threatening to fire all "troublemakers" and blacklist them in the industry. (Incidents like these would inspire Van Beuren artist Bill Littlejohn to co-found the Screen Cartoonists Guild in 1938, serving as the union's first president). Things became so volatile that Van Beuren had to intervene, making the curious statement that he was behind the animators 100 percent and behind Gillett 150 percent. More firings and resignations followed, but for the moment the crisis had abated.

One can sort of understand Van Beuren's attitude. Despite ever-mounting costs and dissention in the ranks, the *Rainbow Parades* were raking in the cartoon studio's biggest profits in years. Gillett was so emboldened that he incurred even more expense by securing the animation rights for two prize comic-strip properties. One of these had been in the newspapers since 1923, and four years

Molly Moo Cow and the Butterflies (1935).

prior to that on theater screens in animation form: Pat Sullivan and Otto Messmer's immortal *Felix the Cat*. The character had not survived the transition to sound, and by 1935 was known primarily for his comic strip adventures, as indicated by RKO's full-page trade ads hailing the character as "The favorite funnie [sic] of 190,000,000 readers of newspapers totalling a daily and Sunday circulation of more than 64,000,000!"

Inasmuch as Gillett had worked on Felix' silent cartoons from 1927 to 1929, one might assume that Van Beuren's Technicolor *Felix the Cat* revival would restore the spirit and energy of the original, with the iconoclastic Felix as fiercely independent and aggressively proactive as in his glory days. But once Gillett had closed the deal with the late Pat Sullivan's estate (namely, Pat's brother), it became painfully clear that the "new" Felix would be little more than Van Beuren's latest attempt to match the popularity of Mickey Mouse with a Mickey lookalike and sound-alike.

The inaugural entry *Felix the Cat and the Goose That Laid the Golden Egg* (1936) is resplendently colored, magnificently animated and superlatively scored by Win Sharples. Alas, the worldly, cynical Felix of the silent days has been supplanted by a childlike, relentlessly cheerful goodie-two-shoes with an irritating falsetto voice. (Some sources indicate that Felix' voice was supplied by 20-year-old Walter Tetley, who later played Leroy on radio's *The Great Gildersleeve*—and whose vocal timbre never changed due to a freak condition, enabling him to provide the voice of Sherman in Jay Ward's "Mr. Peabody" cartoons at the age of 44). Worse still, the silent

Felix' boundless resourcefulness, best demonstrated by using his detachable tail as a weapon or some other helpful implement, is here treated as a throwaway, as is the character's trademark "pensive walk." The other two Felix cartoons *Neptune Nonsense* and *Bold King Cole* (both 1936) are the mixture as before, lovely to look at but not delightful to know. Felix remains a shadow of his former self, repeatedly upstaged and

A 1936 *Motion Picture Herald* ad for Van Beuren's *Felix the Cat* revival.

out-gagged by the supportive characters (especially in *Bold King Cole*). In retrospect, it's unfortunate that Felix' creator Otto Messmer turned down Van Beuren's offer to let him supervise the new cartoons with a full free hand. Still and all, the *Felix* entries were just as successful with the public as the rest of the *Rainbow Parades*, justifying their extra expenditure so far as Van Beuren was concerned.

The other comic-strip property purchased by Gillett was Fontaine Fox's *Toonerville Folks*, which made its newspaper bow in 1908. Based on Fox's home town of Louisville, Kentucky, Toonerville was a close-knit community connected to the outside world by the ramshackle Toonerville Trolley, which "met all trains"—though seldom on schedule—under the guiding hand of its ancient conductor, known only as The Skipper. The best-remembered Toonerville denizens include the Powerful Katrinka, a hefty young lady of super strength; the Terrible Tempered Mr. Bang, who lived up to his name and then some; and surly sandlot bully Mickey "Himself" McGuire, who from 1927 through 1934 headlined a series of live-action comedy shorts produced by Larry Darmour and starring Mickey Rooney. *Toonerville Folks* itself had previously appeared in two-reel comedy form in a series filmed in Philadelphia between 1920 and 1922, featuring Dan Mason as the Skipper and Wilna Hervey as Katrinka. The property would not make its sound debut until the Van Beuren cartoons, all filmed in Technicolor and released during the 1935–36 season.

The series got off to a strong start with *Toonerville Trolley*, which manages to capture the essence of Fontaine Fox's deliberately sketchy and simplistic artwork while fleshing out the characters for animation purposes. The focus here is on the Skipper and the Powerful Katrinka, the latter repeatedly rescuing the Trolley from disaster with sheer muscle power and her endearing catchphrase "I fix." Performing box-office duty at mid-cartoon is Molly Moo Cow in a cameo appearance. After this promising opening, the series went south quickly with *Trolley Ahoy*, which tried and failed to build the comedy around the remorselessly non-comic Terrible Tempered Mr. Bang. Rounding out the series, and the last Van Beuren cartoon ever released, was the so-so *Toonerville Picnic*, which plays like one of RKO's Edgar Kennedy two-reelers as Mr. Bang struggles to control his anger by taking a vacation. It doesn't speak well of the Toonerville Folks to note that the cartoon scores its biggest laughs with a belligerent purple octopus.

Though the 1935–36 *Rainbow Parades* ran hot and cold (to say the least), the positive public and critical reaction to the cartoons was music to Van Beuren's ears. At long last it appeared that he had achieved the prestige and acclaim that would place his cartoons on the same lofty pedestal as Disney's. But all this changed on that dark day in March of 1936 when the trade papers made the unanticipated announcement that Disney had left his distributor United Artists and secured a more financially beneficial arrangement with RKO. Although this arrangement would not go into effect until January 1, 1937, there was immediate speculation that the Van Beuren animation unit was in jeopardy. Early reports that RKO would continue releasing both the Disney and Van Beuren product gave way to articles in which Van Beuren replied "I do not know" to the question of whether he would seek out a new distributor or remain with RKO on a picture-by-picture basis. But on April 10, 1936, Van Beuren officially announced that he would close his cartoon studio at the end of his present contract. Most of the studio's personnel had little trouble securing new jobs, several older hands realigning themselves with Van Beuren's original animation supplier Paul

Terry at Terrytoons. Burt Gillett briefly returned to Disney, made a briefer pit stop at MGM, and ended up with Walter Lantz, where he remained until his (voluntary?) retirement in 1940.

The trades were assured that the loss of the Van Beuren cartoons did not affect the producer's association with RKO in the field of live-action shorts, with the studio renewing his contract for the 1936–37 season. But the bell was already tolling in the distance for Amedee Van Beuren, and it sounded ominously like a dirge.

Chapter 20

Adventure Girl (1934)

The tremendous success of Van Beuren's first feature-length outing *Bring 'Em Back Alive* (1932), starring big-game hunter Frank Buck (see Chapter 14), undoubtedly impressed other real-life adventurers who hoped to enhance their public prestige via the motion picture medium. Trade papers of the period reported that a family of aviators known as the Flying Hutchinsons had contracted with an independent producer to finance a round-the-world flight in exchange for the exclusive picture rights. After the expedition went awry at considerable expense to the Hutchinsons and the producer, one of the "trades" erroneously reported in that it was Van Beuren who'd taken the financial bath, when in fact the unfortunate producer was William Pizor. This was an understandable and excusable error in that Pizor was responsible for a series of one-reel travelogues which closely resembled Van Beuren's *Vagabond Adventures* (see Chapter 10). In the same article, the Hutchinson debacle was compared to another failed filmic expedition to Guatemala, bankrolled by Van Beuren and spearheaded by a self-styled explorer-adventurer named Joan Lowell. This statement was *not* in error—though Van Beuren unquestionably erred big-time when he decided to pour additional money into a second Guatemalan expedition by the estimable Joan Lowell. But we're getting ahead of our story.

Joan Lowell's real name was Helen Wagner, and she was born in Berkeley, California, in 1902. Failing to qualify for the prestigious Berkeley High School, she dropped out and took on a succession of dead-end jobs for a perfume manufacturer, a canning factory and a car wash, at one juncture functioning as a scab during a telephone workers' strike. After attending a San Francisco business college she found work as a stenographer, then took acting lessons in order to break into the movies. Renaming herself Joan Lowell, she played inconsequential roles in films both large (*Souls for Sale, The Gold Rush*) and small (*Branded a Thief, Cold Nerve*), then in 1929 re-invented herself as a professional journalist. That same year she wrote her first book, *Cradle of the Deep*, published by the formidable firm of Simon & Schuster.

Advertised as an autobiography, *Cradle of the Deep* told the world that the infant Joan Lowell had been one month shy of a year old when her sea-captain father ripped her out of home and hearth to live with him on board the *Minnie A. Caine*, a four-masted schooner that sailed the trading routes between the South Seas and Australia. Learning to swear before she could walk, for the next 17 years Joan lived the life of a sailor under the care and tutelage of an elderly sailmaker named "Stitches." Wearing clothes fashioned from flower sacks and sleeping in a hammock like the rest of the hearty crew, she entered her teens as a seasoned seafarin' gal, surviving storms and typhoons, going along on dangerous excursions into islands populated by savages, witnessing a fellow tar being devoured by sharks, assisting in the amputation of another crewman's leg, and learning the facts of life while dissecting the carcass of a female shark. The book ended with Joan rescuing a litter of pet kittens while swimming away from her dad's ship as it burned to the waterline off the Australian coast.

To the amazement and delight of Simon & Schuster, *Cradle of the Deep* became a runaway best-seller, with 125,000 copies sold in its first month. The Book-of-the-Month Club honored it as their March 1929 selection, and at least two distinguished maritime experts staked their reputations on the book's authenticity. The public and most of the professional reviewers swallowed the story whole, while D.W. Griffith ponied up $75,000 to option the book for a big-budget movie adaptation. Only a few brave souls were willing to probe the manuscript and single out its absurdities and inconsistencies (described by one nitpicker as "a barefaced piece of nautical sham.")

One critic of note, Lincoln Colcord, was finally able to persuade reporters from the San Francisco *Chronicle* and the Berkeley *Gazette* to dig a bit deeper into Joan Lowell's colorful yarn. It soon became public knowledge that during the period Lowell claimed to have been living and working on the *Minnie A. Caine* she was actually attending Garfield Junior High School, and there were plenty of witnesses to back this up. Her father was indeed captain of the *Caine*, but only for one year; and instead of sharing its deck solely with Joan, he'd frequently taken his wife and other children aboard. The *coup de grâce* was the revelation that the *Minnie A. Caine*, which according to Lowell had burned to ashes, was still safely docked in Oakland Harbor.

Even when the truth came out there were a lot of people who wanted to believe that Lowell hadn't entirely fabricated her story, mostly out of fear that the literary integrity of all future "true-life adventure" memoirs would be automatically compromised. For her part, Joan Lowell refused

Joan Lowell shaves four years off her age in this studio head shot (*Exhibitors Herald*, July 7, 1923).

to back down from her claims—or, as *Pathé News* advertised when they interviewed her on camera, "It's her story and she's stuck with it." Lowell told Alma Chesnut in the March 17, 1930, *Pittsburgh Press*, "Eighty percent of it was true and the rest I made up," adding "I made some changes to protect people and the rest to make it better reading. That's an author's privilege." In later interviews she became downright belligerent, using language that couldn't be reproduced in mass-market publications as she chided her detractors for lacking her imagination and ingenuity ("Any damn fool can be accurate—and dull"). Meanwhile, Simon & Schuster shamefacedly reclassified *Cradle of the Deep* as fiction, and the Book-of-the-Month Club offered refunds to disgruntled readers.

Predictably, professional comedians and humorists had a field day with the Hoax of the Decade. Simon & Schuster's rival publisher G.M. Putnam & Sons went so far as to commission *Vanity Fair* critic and satirist Corey Ford to write a scalding (and best-selling) parody of the Lowell tome titled *Salt-Water Taffy*, in which "June Triplett" sailed the seven seas on the *Carrie L. Maine* accompanied by her dad and his loyal first mate "Old Britches." Putnam spared no expense skewering its competition, engaging such Algonquin Round Table habitués as journalist Heywood Broun, playwright Donald Ogden Stewart, magazine editors Harold Ross and Frank Crowninshield and artists Neysa McMein and Percy Crosby to pose for photographs depicting the book's characters (June Triplett was "played" by Chicago debutante Anne Laurie Jacques). Every highlight of *Cradle in the Deep* was fair game for Corey Ford's satiric harpoons: The "sailor talk" of the original book was translated into such pseudo-salty gibberish as "Strum the m'n'tch" and "Avast the poop!"; the sea gull that Joan Lowell claimed to have adopted as a childhood pet became in *Salt Water Daffy* a cute baby waterspout named Gladys; and the graphic sex education Joan received while cutting open a shark was rewritten so that June Triplett reached into the shark's bowels and pulled out a copy of Margaret Sanger's *What Every Girl Should Know*.

Bloody but unbowed, Joan Lowell followed up *Cradle of the Deep* by starring in a play cowritten by then-husband Thompson Buchanan, *Star of Bengal*, which folded almost as quickly as the marriage. In 1933 she once again tried to pass herself off as a globetrotting adventuress in another "memoir," *Gal Reporter*, supposedly inspired by her experiences as a staff writer for the Los Angeles *Examiner* and United Press (that she actually worked for these two concerns was the only verifiable fact). That same year she further exploited her own notoriety by persuading Amedee Van Beuren to finance a sailing expedition to the Rio Dulce region of Guatemala with her father and a small crew, for the purpose of making a quasi-documentary feature film with potentially the same box-office appeal of the producer's recent *Bring 'Em Back Alive*. She was also determined to prove to a skeptical world that, evidence to the contrary, she was not a complete and utter charlatan. In a December 1934 *Photoplay* article covering both the filming and its aftermath, Mildred Mastin described Lowell as "a real sailor who prided herself on being the only lady on the high seas could spit a curve in the wind." Joan was bent upon living up to that description and to confound her detractors by returning from Central America with irrefutable cinematic proof not only of her nautical prowess, but also her willingness to risk her life on both sea and land. "If there are any landlubber critics there," Joan told Mastin's readers, "you can all go plumb to ____"

After an initial plan to costar Lowell with *Bring 'Em Back Alive*'s protagonist

Frank Buck was quickly scotched (presumably at Buck's insistence), filming commenced on the proposed Lowell feature *Adventure Girl*, which was also the title of a book hastily written by Joan (and an uncredited ghost writer) to coincide with the production. The 45-foot two-master *Black Hawk* was commissioned for the expedition, its crew consisting of Lowell, her dad Captain Wagner, first mate Bill "Leatherneck" Sawyer (so named because he'd been a Marine), and deckhand Otto Siegler. Two of Frank Buck's future collaborators were also hired: Screenwriter Ferrin Fraser, charged with the task of making Lowell's scrambled storyline marginally believable; and cinematographer Harry Squire, who hadn't had a Hollywood screen credit since 1917's *Salt of the Earth*. Also brought back to the land of the living was the film's director Herman C. Raymaker, who though active throughout the silent era—his credits included several vehicles for canine star Rin Tin Tin—had previously helmed only one talkie, *Trailing the Killer*, starring another doggie thespian named Caesar. RKO's Guatemalan representative Ashton Dearholt arranged to secure locations in the town of Chichicastenango as well as Antigua in the West Indies—neither site anywhere near the Rio Dulce—and to hire local talent ahead of the expedition.

On June 15, 1933, the *Hollywood Reporter* announced that after six weeks of "hardships and setbacks" in Central America, the *Black Hawk* and its personnel had limped back to America with barely a foot of usable film. A second expedition seemed to be as doomed as the first when the show-business labor union IATSE banned its members from participating in any overseas Van Beuren project, leaving Lowell and her expedition "tied up in Gravesend Bay," as the *Reporter* noted on August 15. Once this dispute was settled the production crew was reassembled and the company again set sail for the Southern hemisphere. The second voyage was successful to the extent that the picture was actually completed; additionally, Joan brought back two souvenirs of her voyage that would prove beyond doubt to those _____ landlubber critics that this time around she'd lived her adventures instead of just making them up. One souvenir was a six-year-old adopted son named Mario, whom she had found wandering in a Guatemalan slum. The other was a deep bite on her shoulder from an alligator, which had forced her to spend considerable time convalescing at Nuthall Memorial Hospital in Kingston, Jamaica.

On August 4, 1934, *Film Daily*'s pseudonymous gossip columnist "Phil M. Daly" recounted the August 1 world premiere of *Adventure Girl* aboard the South American steamer S.S. *Colombia*, with Joan and Capt. Wagner in attendance along with Amedee J. Van Beuren and his production manager Sam Jacobson, Jules Levey of the RKO executive staff, Arthur Mayer representing the Rialto Theater where the film would have its New York premiere, Actors Equity officer Bert Lytell, and newspaper critic Margaret Talezaar. "Another comer is the Joan Lowell expedition to South America and sech places" reported Daly, under the impression that colloquial misspellings were funny. "In a card from Joan we are cheerfully told that she successfully rode the Roaring Falls, Jamaica, in her 30-foot sloop and secured some grand footage for the feature.... It's another Van Beuren scoop." Mr. Daly had obviously not seen the film.

With Van Beuren touting Joan Lowell as "The Most Publicized Girl in the World," *Adventure Girl* received general release on August 17, 1934. Superficially, the film adheres to the pattern established by Frank Buck's *Bring 'Em Back Alive*. The opening credits give way to a verbose foreword, beginning "A year ago, Joan Lowell returned from a trip to the vastnesses of central America, with a tale of well-nigh incredible adventures." The film proper is shot silent, narrated by Lowell herself, while the evocative background music is supplied by Van Beuren's house orchestrator, in this case Winston Sharples. But here all resemblances between the Buck and the Lowell films come to an end. Though it was never denied that some of the thrills in *Bring 'Em Back Alive* were hoked up with clever editing, rearrangement of events and the occasional re-enactment of a specific event, *Adventure Girl* states outright that the film restages *all* the highlights of Lowell's Guatemalan expedition. While this may appear to be unprecedented honesty and frankness on the part of Joan Lowell, a woman who'd achieved her greatest fame as a literary humbug, it really isn't, since the implication remains that the events restaged herein are entirely factual.

Not even Mildred Mastin's 1934 *Photoplay* article, which was sympathetic to Lowell and written with Joan's full cooperation, could accept this implication with a straight face. Remarking upon the film's opening sequence in which Lowell and the *Black Hawk* crew barely survive a tempestuous storm in the "West Indies" (actually just off Cape Hatteras in North Carolina), wherein the vessel's mainmast snaps and Joan is compelled to rescue Bill Sawyer when he's washed overboard, Mastin deadpanned: "On the screen, the scene is exciting. The storm is thrilling. The rescue amazing. But the most impressive thing (especially to the feminine mind) is that Cameraman Harry Squire apparently stood calmly at the rail grinding his camera—catching each detail of the storm, the struggle, the rescue." Ignoring Mastin's inference that not only was the sequence faked but that the storm itself was likely the screenwriter's invention, Joan Lowell brazened it out: "That's why I think Harry is a wonderful cameraman. He stays with his camera. He'll risk any discomfort to get a picture! Why, I've seen him stand waist-deep in a mosquito-infested swamp along the Rio Dulce, just to get a good shot." Note than Joan never mentions director Herman Raymaker, who by any stretch of logic should have been in the vicinity as well.

The article further touches upon the miraculous good fortune of Harry Squire being right on hand during the allegedly unexpected moment when Joan was prevented from entering a jungle cave by a boa constrictor, which suddenly dropped from a tree and wrapped around her neck. This time Lowell fessed up that the scene had been staged, albeit insisting the danger posed by the snake was very real. She explained that the crew had found the boa hanging in a tree, whereupon she was positioned to stand just beneath it in hopes that the serpent would take the cue and drop, while Joan made certain that "Harry [was] near me, with the camera" and "Bill, of course, was there to assist in my rescue." Again: where was the director?

According to the article, "the most distressing experience" during filming in Guatemala—as opposed to earlier "genuine" events that purportedly inspired the re-enactments—occurred aboard the *Black Hawk* in calm weather. The water tank had sprung a leak and all on board were in danger of dying of thirst—except Joan's pet bulldog "Jack," who'd been given the last drops of water from a ginger ale bottle. At this point Joan and Bill decided to row to an island forty miles away in search of liquid replenishment, reaching the shores in the nick of time and returning to rescue Joan's father in an equally timely fashion. Correspondent Mildred Mastin allows that this is all "thrilling and impressive": That said, "it is difficult not to keep thinking of the cameraman and imagining him following Bill and Joan on their forty mile row, exhausted, dying of thirst, but grinding his camera valiantly. It does seem that Cameraman

Joan Lowell is clearly a force to contend with as she sets up a location shot for *Adventure Girl* (from the December 1934 *Photoplay*).

Harry, and not the bulldog, deserved the last of that drinking water." Mastin does, however, confirm that Lowell *did* suffer an alligator bite—which strangely enough is never alluded to in the film, nor is Joan's adopted son, who also escapes mention in future biographies of the Adventure Girl.

I guess we have to get around to a synopsis of the film sometime, so fasten your seat belts. In a flat, toneless voice belying her claim that she'd received acting lessons from the niece of Sarah Bernhardt, Joan Lowell tells us in the first scene that her voyage on the *Black Hawk* was a 76th birthday present for her father. After the aforementioned Caribbean hurricane (not visualized in currently available prints, which run about 4 minutes shy of the official 65-minute running time) blows the vessel into the treacherous Sargasso sea, the crew comes across a derelict ship, inspiring Joan and Bill Sawyer to go on a treasure hunt in the ruined hull. They chance upon an ancient map guiding them to a priceless "square emerald," imbedded in a statue within a religious shrine in a tiny Central American village ruled over by statuesque Indian queen Maya, played in the film by 19-year-old Ula Holt (*née* Florence Eugene Watson of Los Angeles). Arriving in this secluded kingdom, Joan has a few scrapes with local animal life as she searches for the sacred shrine. Outraged that Joan has the cojones to steal the emerald, Queen Maya orders our heroine to be burned alive. The last-minute arrival of "Leatherneck" Bill saves Joan from a fiery finish, and as the sun slowly sinks in the west, the *Black Hawk* returns to Civilization As We Know It.

If it is true, as she claimed, that Joan Lowell made *Adventure Girl* to redeem herself and her reputation in the eyes of the public, it's puzzling indeed that she goes out of her way to make herself unsympathetic and thoroughly unlikable throughout the film. After deliberately risking the lives of her elderly father and his hapless crew by embarking on what is guaranteed to be a dangerous cruise, she insists upon plundering a wrecked ship for possible treasure despite the fact that she and her cohorts are exhausted and nearly out of provisions. Upon reaching the domain of Queen Maya, Joan flat-out lies that she wants to explore the sacred temple to find precious minerals that will improve the lives of Maya's native subjects—whom she has mercilessly ridiculed in her narration during the previous reel. A few hours before exploring the region, Joan witnesses a battle to the death between a snake and a mongoose, a gruesome scene so obviously staged for the camera that, in a perfect world, the ASPCA would have had the film's star drawn and quartered.

After grabbing the emerald that she has no right to possess, Joan is caught red-handed by Maya and a fistic battle ensues, with the obviously stronger Lowell adamantly refusing to play fair. Once she is captured and borne off to the execution pyre, Joan finds herself center of attention at a gala event for which the entire countryside gathers to dance, sing, play musical instruments and sell wares. (Is it possible that these festive scenes were filmed at an actual native celebration where no white woman was scheduled for execution?) Everybody seems to be having such a good time that it's a big letdown when Joan is rescued and whisked off to the *Black Hawk* by her loyal compadres.

In the original prints, this climax was enhanced by hand-coloring each frame, a specialty of artist Gustav F.O. Brock; as the film now stands, all we have left are the fuzzy monochrome hues of a worn television print. Which is a shame, since the one

An imaginative ad for *Adventure Girl* ran in the *Motion Picture Herald*, September 15, 1934.

saving grace of *Adventure Girl* is the splendid photography of Harry Squire—when you can properly see it. But for all his cinematic knowhow, Squire seems incapable of making Joan Lowell any more physically attractive than she is morally appealing. To anyone in 1934 who attended the film in hopes of seeing a ravishing, thinly-clad damsel in various kinky predicaments *a la* the concurrently produced *Tarzan* films, *Adventure Girl* was a total washout, unable to spark any sort of sensual arousal whatsoever out of such normally surefire devices as a nude bathing scene, a sweaty hair-tugging girlfight, the "heroine" bound hand and foot as she writhes before her captors, and no fewer than two protracted shots of Lowell immersed in water while wearing a torn blouse. To paraphrase S.J. Perelman, the film's erotic content has about as much punch as a seed catalogue.

Even the kindest reviews for *Adventure Girl* were mixed. *Motion Picture Herald* praised the "several outstanding scenic shots," but qualified this with "It's frankly melodramatic," advising exhibitors "The end of the week is possibly the better booking allocation for lesser situations"—a nice way of saying "Strictly for kids." *National Board of Review* magazine summed up the film as "supposedly authentic but seemingly improbable," concluding: "Whether truth or fiction it is an entertaining yarn."

The public, understandably anticipating an epic of the caliber of *Bring 'Em Back Alive*, wanted no part of *Adventure Girl*. The film lost $300,000, compelling Van Beuren to shun any future association with Joan Lowell, explaining to both the lady and the trade papers that her acting performance was inadequate. Lowell responded by (you're way ahead of us) suing Van Beuren, not for maligning her talent but for the 15 percent of the film's profits she'd been promised. In September 1935, over a year after the film's release, Lowell was given permission by New York judge Charles McLaughlin to examine Van Beuren's account books against their claim that there'd been no profits, while Van Beuren countersued her for losses suffered at the box office. For the next two years she kept her legal complaint alive but never made a move to proceed with her suit in court. Finally in December 1938 the case against Van Beuren was dismissed, thanks to Lowell's failure to prosecute.

The only person to reap any benefits from his association with the *Adventure Girl* fiasco was RKO's Guatemalan representative Ashton Dearholt, whose brief taste of active filmmaking had inspired him to remain in the country to produce a profitable independent serial, *The New Adventures of Tarzan* (1936), distributed by "Tarzan" creator Edgar Rice Burroughs and starring Olympic champion Herman Brix (a.k.a. Bruce Bennett). At the same time Dearholt left his wife to have an affair with Ula Holt, *Adventure Girl*'s Queen Maya, who also played the non–Jane heroine in the serial.

Joan Lowell left the United States a few months after *Adventure Girl*, not by popular demand as one might suspect, but to manage a successful Brazilian coffee plantation with her second husband. In 1952 she wrote a remarkably (for her) authentic account of her life and work in Brazil, *Promised Land*—and just to prove that there was nothing Hollywood loved more than a cheerful fraud (how else would "Prince" Mike Romanoff have been able to parlay his unproven claims of noble Russian birth into establishing a popular high-priced restaurant?), *Promised Land* was promptly optioned by a major studio, just as if *Adventure Girl* had never happened. The proposed film was never made, but at least this time Joan Lowell got her percentage, adding to the considerable fortune she would accumulate before her death in her adopted country in 1967.

Chapter 21

Easy Aces

Goodman Ace (1899–1982), "Goody" to his friends, was born Goodman Aiskowitz in Kansas City, Missouri. After studying journalism at Kansas City Polytech, he held down various eating-money jobs until becoming a reporter for his home town paper the *Journal-Post*. In 1922 he married his high school sweetheart Jane Epstein, a union that lasted until Jane's death at age 77 in 1974. By 1930 Ace was working at Kansas City radio station KMBC, reading the Sunday comics and his own theater reviews at the behest of his editor, who hoped thereby to increasing the *Journal-Post*'s circulation. Though not a professional announcer, Ace's charmingly grumpy personality earned him a considerable fan following throughout the midwest.

One night in 1930 the recorded program that regularly followed Ace's nightly fifteen-minute broadcast proved unavailable, prompting Goody to fill the timeslot with a recap of a recent bridge game. Jane happened to be in the studio and was invited to join the conversation, which drifted into a discussion of a recent real-life case in which a husband had killed his wife over an argument about bridge (unusual but not surprising: At that time bridge was a national obsession, sparking hundreds and thousands of domestic and professional quarrels over the proper playing of the game). Advised off-mike by her husband to "be dumb" for the amusement of the audience, Jane began to prattle on in a nasally sing-song voice—not her real speaking voice, which was warm and expressive—about her peculiar bridge technique, peppering her conversation with impromptu malapropisms. The off-the-cuff program scored a hit with the public, whereupon KMBC set up Goodman and Jane in their own twice-weekly comedy series (for which they received $30 per week) about a bridge-playing couple with the double-pun title *Easy Aces*. Subsequent episodes in which the Aces squabbled over card strategy were not entirely fictional: Though Ace was devoted to his wife he genuinely considered her an inept player and told her so on the air, prompting Jane to frequently storm off the program and even threaten divorce.

The Aces moved to Chicago in October 1931 when *Easy Aces* was picked up by the CBS network. The series became a three-per-week attraction (the broadcast days varied) emanating from New York beginning in 1932, by which time Ace was both writing and directing the show, gradually moving away from bridge to a wider variety of domestic-comedy situations. Though she refused to consider herself an actress and turned down several lucrative offers to appear on stage, Jane agreed to maintain her "dumb blonde" persona for the airwaves, spouting such scripted malaprops as "working my head to the bone," "you hit the nail on the thumb," "familiarity breeds attempts" and "I hate to monotonize the conversation." For his part, Goodman essentially played his own acerbic self, often reacting to his wife's scatterbrained pronouncements with a resigned "Isn't that awful?" (For reasons undocumented, he was never referred to by his first name: Even Jane called him "Ace" before the mike). Although old-time-radio enthusiasts—this writer included—have eagerly scooped up existing recordings of the 13-year *Easy Aces* run over both CBS and NBC, the couple's dry humor leaves many uninitiated listeners cold: Expecting the belly laughs engendered by the likes of Burns and Allen, many contemporary comedy fans come away unsatisfied with the quiet chuckles arising from the Aces' various escapades.

Like most radio favorites of the 1930s, the Aces were invited to appear in one-reel comedies filmed in New York City. Although their faces matched their voices and radio characterizations perfectly, neither Goody nor Jane was especially enthused over appearing on-camera, but the money—"in short supply at the time," as he later noted—was too good to pass up. Filmed at Vitaphone's Brooklyn studio, their debut short *Easy Aces* (1933) was like their earliest broadcasts set up in the form of a bridge game, with the Aces partnered against a couple played by Lucille Sears and Fred Harper, whom they proceeded to drive crazy (not so much a drive as a short putt). Nobody expected this forgettable one-reeler to lead to any subsequent film work, but within a year Educational Pictures dangled a contract in front of the Aces for a group of two-reel comedies, likewise to be lensed in New York. The first and last short in this "series," *Dumb Luck* (1935), was like the Vitaphone one-reeler directed by Joseph Henabery and scripted by Mr. Ace. A moderately amusing update of O. Henry's "The Ransom of Red Chief," the story is set in motion when Jane wins a $50 lottery. A pair of criminals, led to believe that the prize was much larger, decide to kidnap Jane and hold her for ransom. Jane's wacky behavior quickly renders her captives helpless, and by film's end, as expected, the villains are not only willing to return her to Mr. Ace for free, but also turn themselves over to the cops rather than endure her imbecilic behavior and nonstop prattle one second longer. Both Aces are noticeably uncomfortable playing "characters" (Jane comes off best by a slim margin), while the funniest performance is delivered by veteran movie heavy Richard Cramer as one of the crooks.

Not long after completing *Dumb Luck*, Goody and Jane responded to a better movie offer from Amedee Van Beuren, signing on to provide comic narration for the producer's *Vagabond Adventures* one-reelers (see Chapter 10). Van Beuren had been making good coin on his short-comedy series *Dumb-Bell Letters* (see Chapter 18), and figured that a second package of mirth-provokers would go over equally well. The team's salary would be higher than at Educational; the Aces would be obliged to play no characters other than themselves; and best of all, each short would require only one day's shooting at Biograph studios in the Bronx. The film's copyright registration, "Vagabond Easy Aces No. 1," was proof enough that Van Beuren expected a lot more of the same.

Released February 22, 1935, "right on the heels of those cockeyed *Dumb-Bell Letters*" (according to RKO publicity), *Pharoahland* was heralded onscreen as "A Vagabond Adventure" with the Aces given equal-sized billing. Rather than open on the expected travelogue footage of modern Egypt, the short begins in a movie-theater set, with the Aces taking their seats in the audience and Jane making loud and inappropriate comments while Goody does his best to shut her up. But she doesn't, and throughout *Pharoahland* Jane stymies her husband's attempts to deliver a straightforward narration about the Pyramids et. al. with silly comments and sillier malaprops—some of which actually make sense, but not on purpose. The short ends with the theater's house lights going up and the Aces settling down for the main feature.

This formula was followed by the Aces' second Van Beuren outing *Topnotchers*, advertised (and copyrighted) as part of the "Vagabond-Ace High Series." The team stamps the short as their exclusive property when, as the opening credits appear, Jane

A 1934 trade ad for Van Beuren's *Easy Aces* one-reelers.

reads them out loud: "'Van Beuren Productions present the Easy Aces in *Topnotchers* ... oh, is this another short subject?" Not quite, Jane. Any other short subject dealing with the nation's top sports champions would allow them to go through their filmed paces backed up by respectful narration. But though Goody tries hard to show admiration and enthusiasm for the onscreen athletes, Jane is clearly not a sports fan and isn't afraid to say so. Hopefully the personalities seen in *Topnotchers*—including Willie Hoppe, Babe Ruth, pro bowler Mort Lindsey and champion race horse Twenty Grand—were in on the joke.

Interviewed in the April 12, 1935, edition of *Film Daily*, Van Beuren expressed confidence in the new property's continued success: "In the Ace High series can be seen the application of what I think will definitely develop into one of the most unusual ideas presented during the past season. A well established team of radio artists is brought to the screen in a way that retains all the entertainment and comedy value developed during hundreds of broadcasts on the air." With the pattern established on the once-per-month series, short #3 *Little New New York* came out on June 14, 1935. This time around the Aces describe several points of interest within Greater New York City, Goody providing cogent background information while Jane says whatever comes off the top of her head. By now the series was an acknowledged hit, with *Film Daily* commenting: "Van Beuren has moved forward a mile with this innovation, and left the rest of the funny picture commentators in the rear."

With the fourth entry *Six-Day Grind*, the "Vagabond Adventures" and "Ace High" designations were abandoned. The opening titles—which don't show up until 30 seconds into the film—indicate that the series' name has been streamlined to "Easy Aces," with the words spelled out on playing cards. In the pre-credit sequence Goody and Jane get into a hassle with a haughty movie patron who refuses to change seats and let the couple sit together. Thus as the "Van Beuren" logo zooms towards the camera in traditional fashion, Jane mutters "Notice the way *that* moves out? I wish some people woud take the hint and move." The documentary footage on this occasion consists of highlights from the 58th International Six-Day Bicycle Race at Madison Square Garden; for the first time in history, the event had been filmed in its entirety under the direction of Van Beuren producer Don Hancock. Reggie McNamara, Cecil Walker, Freddie Spencer, Franco Georgetti, Alfred Letour and Franz Duelberg are among the world-famous cyclists featured "at work," at rest, and even dining between laps. The reality footage is almost as entertaining as the narration, which contains the usual quota of lamebrained observations from Mrs. Ace: Upon witnessing a three-bike collision, Jane frets over the "torn liniments" suffered by the riders.

Unusualities, again heralded onscreen as part of the "Easy Aces Series"—minus the animated deck of cards—was the fifth release. Once past the obligatory gag opening, the viewer is treated to glimpses of such odd professions as fashioning threads and needles from a cactus plant, manicuring an elephant, setting up portable bath houses and operating one-man flying machines. Incidentally, this was the first series entry for which reviewers complained that the Aces' commentary was intrusive.

In mid–1935 Van Beuren financed a location jaunt to London where his camera crew shot thousands of feet of documentary footage, to be distributed amongst several future short subjects. The main beneficiary of this project was the sixth "Easy Aces" short *Jolly Ol' London*. If Van Beuren harbored any pretensions about his costly journey to the British capital, he was quickly brought down to earth by the Aces: As

Goody remarks that "London has a population of three million people," Jane spots a bobby nonchalantly strolling past the camera and chirps "There's one of them now." Curiously, this delightful reel was one of the few *Easy Aces* efforts to be negatively reviewed by *Film Daily*, who after dismissing the film as "trite, unfunny, and no credit to the Easy Aces" concludes: "They've got to write witty dialogue to get by in these travel pix, and there are few Lew Lehrs who can turn the trick." For the record, Lew Lehr narrated Fox Movietone's "Monkeys is de Cwaziest People" novelty films in a burlesque German accent, a nails-on-the-blackboard act that is virtually impossible to stomach today.

With six shorts completed and distributed, *Easy Aces* entered its second season with *Tricks of the Trade*, released September 6, 1935. Goody and Jane spent their requisite one day filming their standard "bookend" scenes for the film, the body of which consists of dramatized scenes showing how disreputable businessmen endeavor to outsmart their customers. On this occasion Jane's snide remarks were aimed at the dishonest merchants, leaving Goody little choice but to agree with her. The next entry, *A Capitol Idea* (1935), is comprised mostly of stock shots of Washington, D.C. While there was plenty to satirize in the political year of 1935, the Aces' barbs are relatively benign.

A World Within (1935) is a follow-up to the previous season's *Little New New York*, as the Aces crack wise (but not offensively) about the different nationalities and races in various selected sections of New York—subject matter that would seem to have been better suited to another Van Beuren shorts series, *World on Parade* (see Chapter 24), and possibly was originally slated for that series. But the next entry *Etiquette* (1935) was well within the established parameters of *Easy Aces*, with Goody and Jane quibbling over proper social behavior as examples of such appear on screen. Continuing their off-and-on exploration of inner New York, the Aces' January 1936 offering *Winter at the Zoo* features scenes from New York Zoological Park (better known as the Bronx Zoo), which was open the year round.

The series' second 1936 entry *An Old-Fashioned Movie* was a total departure from the usual formula. Instead of highlighting modern-day documentary footage, this one features excerpts from a one-reel silent melodrama filmed in 1912. Rated as "among the better offerings of the Aces under the Van Beuren insignia" by the *Philadelphia Exhibitor*, the short's narration gently sends up the "film techniques and weighty dramatics" of 1912 and "should provide a chuckle or two for today's screen audience" (these last two quotes from *Motion Picture Daily*). One of the best verbal gags, cited by Leonard Maltin in his landmark book on movie shorts, finds Goody commenting on the romance between the ancient movie's hero and heroine: "It was love at first sight." Whereupon Jane deadpans "She must have been nearsighted."

It was back to the "scenic" format with *Debonair New Orleans* (1936), which in addition to spotlighting the Mardi Gras and above-the-ground graves usually seen in documentaries about the Big Easy also features shots of the new Huey Long airport. None of which has as much impact on Jane Ace as her inability to see the movie screen. It's only when the house lights go up in the epilogue that we find Jane stuck on the floor underneath a broken theater seat.

Jane was able to secure a better view in *A Job's a Job* (1936), which a few years later would have fit comfortably into Paramount's "Unusual Occupations" shorts series. With "the girl making her goofy comments and her partner trying to set her straight" (according to *Film Daily*), this one-reeler features such offbeat pursuits as knife-throwing, manufacturing glass eyes, salmon catching, reconstructing fossils and administering first aid to a sea cow. *Film Daily*'s summary: "The newsreel collection of subjects are ordinary, and the comedy comments of the Aces fit them perfectly."

The fifteenth and final "Easy Aces" short, *Fool Your Friends* (1936), is essentially a showcase for professional magician and card manipulator David Allisen. In the manner of MGM's concurrently produced *Pete Smith Specialties*, Allisen uses his expertise to expose the mechanics of the "old shell game" and other such sleight-of-hand standbys; when he seems to make a coin appear out of nowhere, Jane declares patriotically "It's against the law to have gold!" For the grand finale, Allisen makes a bird cage disappear by clapping his hands. Back in the theater audience, Goody takes a long look at Jane and claps *his* hands—but alas, she remains visible.

The *Easy Aces* film series was dropped at the end of the 1935–36 season as part of an economy drive by Van Beuren. Goodman and Jane Ace thereafter focused their energy on their radio program, keeping the show alive after its cancellation by NBC in 1945 with a syndicated version comprised of old network transcriptions. Retitled *mr. ace & JANE*, the series returned in a half-hour format for CBS in 1948, then left the radio airwaves for good, though a TV adaptation briefly popped up in 1949. After Jane Ace's retirement, Goodman Ace successfully sustained his career as one of show business' best and most highly regarded comedy writers, turning out top-drawer material for Danny Kaye, Robert Q. Lewis, Milton Berle, Perry Como, Groucho Marx, Bob Newhart and many others. Among his most conspicuous latter-day credits was as head writer for *The Big Show*, NBC's mammoth 1950–51 attempt to keep network radio alive via a star-studded variety program headlined by Tallulah Bankhead. One cannot help but feel that there were times during this troubled assignment that Goodman Ace would liked to have left the temperamental Tallulah to her own devices and return to the relative tranquility of his long-forgotten Van Beuren one-reelers.

Chapter 22

Struggle to Live

Filling the gap left by the cancellation of *Vagabond Adventures* (or rather, the absorption of that property by the *Easy Aces* shorts), Van Beuren launched a new series of live-action, one-reel documentaries, *Struggle to Live*, beginning with the August 16, 1935, release *Neptune Mysteries*. As was usually the case, the property did not originate with Van Beuren but was developed by an independent production firm, this one headed by two highly creative siblings with an established movie track record.

Born in Salt Lake City in 1902 and 1904 respectively, Stacy and Horace Woodard both evinced a fascination with nature photography from boyhood. While studying biology at the University of Arizona, Stacy began submitting still photographs to various magazines. Horace, a chemist by profession, took up cinematography as a sideline while designing and constructing chemical plants in the Amazon basin of South America. In the late 1920s the brothers formed a professional partnership with two other film enthusiasts: Manny Nathan, a product of the California radio industry who would go on to produce the novelty-short series *Strange as It Seems* for both Universal and Columbia; and Jerry Fairbanks, later to achieve fame for his Paramount short-subject series *Popular Science, Unusual Occupations* and *Speaking of Animals*—and still later as producer of the pioneering TV cartoon project *Crusader Rabbit* as well as several live-action series deploying his patented multi-camera process.

The Woodards, Nathan and Fairbanks first attracted industry attention with *Battle for Life*, a nature series released by Educational Pictures. Given special consideration by critics and audiences of the period was the series' razor-sharp microscopic photography of animal, fish and insect life, made possible by Stacy Woodard's own handmade (and trademarked) camera, an enormous contraption set up in the brothers' Santa Monica, California, garage and weighing 4000 pounds. In 1932 Stacy severed ties with Nathan and Fairbanks and set up his own independent company with brother Horace. Their first commission was for producer B.F. Zeidman, lensing the wildlife encountered on a Central American expedition as part of a two-picture deal with Universal. The brothers also continued laboring on Educational's *Battle for Life* series, winning an Academy Award for "best short novelty film" with *City of Wax* (1934), an enduringly impressive up-close-and-personal study of the life and labors of a honeybee.

Despite this honor, Educational president E.W. Hammons admitted to the trade papers that shorts like *City of Wax* were worth more in prestige than box-office returns, which the Woodards took as a subtle hint that their days with *Battle for Life* were numbered. To keep busy before the inevitable fall of the axe, Horace and Stacy signed on with Van Beuren as editors of the producer's third Frank Buck documentary feature *Fang and Claw* (see Chapter 14). Van Beuren was so impressed by the Woodards' efforts that he offered them a contract to produce a new series of one-reel nature studies not unlike *Battle for Life*, with the similar blanket title *Struggle to Live*.

The inaugural short *Neptune Mysteries* was like all subsequent *Struggle to Live* entries narrated by radio announcer-actor Gayne Whitman, in a straightforward fashion totally unlike the mocking tone he'd used in his previous assignments for *Vagabond Adventures*. The musical score was largely (and sagaciously) drawn from the stock-theme library used in poverty-row melodramas and westerns, with a few appropriate classical passages thrown in. The short's main attraction was the eye-popping microscopic photography of such sea life as the snail and (especially) the octopus. The scholarly magazine *Educational Screen* noted: "Many stories have been told of the terrible octopi, but here the octopus is seen to be a kindly creature ready to defend its young with its very life." This humanization of non-human creatures would become a series trademark, with Whitman's narration pointing out the ancient habits of industrialization and self-preservation that animals, fish and insects performed instinctively and perfectly—as opposed to Mankind, which had to learn these traits through trial and error. Most trade critiques of *Neptune Mysteries* were in lockstep with the non-industry publication *Motion Picture Reviews*, "Fine for family or children"—though there were a few dissenters, such as one theater owner who complained to *Motion Picture Herald* that the film's squiggly octopi were "too gruesome" for the women in the audience.

By the time *Struggle to Live* had released *Beach Masters* (1935), the third of its ten one-reel episodes, the February 1936 *Educational Screen* was able to summarize the series as "splendid," adding: "Each of the three subjects produced to date is really an intense lesson in natural history given in the greatest detail." *Beach Masters* focused on what the magazine called "one of nature's most mystifying phenomena," the yearly migration of seals from Canada's Mist Island to the Bering Sea. In a closing shot typical of the Woodards, thousands of seals were shown at the end of their journey, an epic panorama worthy of DeMille. This time the local exhibitors quoted in *Motion Picture Herald* were united in their praise, with C.L. Niles of Anamosa, Iowa's Niles Theater declaring: "One of the finest reels of its kind on the market."

The present unavailability of most live-action Van Beuren films would normally make it difficult to assess the *Struggle to Live* series as whole. Fortunately, three of the existing shorts, released one after the other in 1936, offer a fine representative cross-section of the series—and if contemporary reviews can be trusted, are among the best of the batch. *Winged Pageantry*, like others in the series, opens with a printed foreword, describing the great spectacle of "the countless thousands of birds that abandon the freedom of the open sea and migrate to their place of birth to give rise to colonies and bring forth their young." The film made its biggest impression with critics and moviegoers with its extensive coverage of the pelican, "an impossible-looking creature" with an ungainly beak and faulty landing equipment which had somehow survived and flourished throughout the eons. The scenes of mother pelicans providing tender loving care for their young were uniquely entertaining, as were the glimpses of the migration patterns, breeding habits and "love rituals" of such species as Northern gulls, cormorants, sea parrots (a.k.a. puffins), gannets (shown standing

Chapter 22—Struggle to Live 201

Mr. Gannet goes a-courting in *Winged Pageantry* (1936).

in endless parallel rows at a New Zealand landing spot) and murres, which resemble penguins but have the power of flight—and in one of the short's highlights are seen depositing their yearly single egg at Walrus Island in the Bering Sea. Though the *Philadelphia Exhibitor* suspected that many of the sequences in *Winged Pageantry* were comprised of library footage, most of what was seen in these shorts was personally lensed by the Woodards, listed in the credits as associate producers.

Winged Pageantry was followed by *Underground Farmers* (1936), which was clearly conceived by the Woodards as the Van Beuren equivalent to their Oscar-winning Educational release *City of Wax*. The printed foreword on this occasion states: "Ages before man proclaimed himself a superior being, the tiny ant had developed the art of agriculture—a practice which was later to be the backbone of human society." Through their microscopic study of a typical ant colony in Equatorial South America, the Woodards reveal the organization and efficiency of the six-legged denizens, with their regimented division of labor and responsibilities among the "cultivators," "distributors" and of course the outsized "warriors" and "sentries." Despite the modern-day viewer's overfamiliarity with such scenes via the many TV nature programs now available, the film's images of building and sustaining subterranean ant farms (this particular colony cultivates mushrooms), all done instinctually, can still take one's breath away. The Woodards display their own instinct for showmanship at the climax, underscored by militaristic music, in which the tiny colonists battle another group of ants over possession of their farm—the editing making it appear at one point that the soldier ants are actually drawing up war plans. *Film Daily* rated *Underground*

Farmers "a pip," while the more guarded *Motion Picture Daily* described the closing scenes as "exciting and almost thrilling," as if the two were mutually exclusive.

The third of the "golden trio," *Living Jewels* (1936), would be memorable if only for its musical score, comprised *in toto* of Strauss' overture to "Die Fledermaus." The composition is supremely appropriate for the film's magnificent visuals, depicting unusual sea creatures which appear at first glance to be lovely and harmless gems and flowers, but can be dangerous when disturbed—"stinging paralyzing weapons" that fend off predators and trap unsuspecting fish (shown being eaten alive) with equal aplomb. In addition to various sea anemones and "colonial" underwater plants which house and nourish millions of tiny creatures while sustaining the great coral reefs of the world, we are treated to too-close-for-comfort shots of sharks, wolf fish and other bad actors. Unfortunately many of the species depicted are not identified, and some of those that are remain a mystery thanks to Gayne Whitman's curiously garbled articulation, leading Iowa theater manager C.L. Niles to inform *Motion Picture Herald*: "These reels would be a knockout if they would get an announcer they could understand."

Others in the series include *Hermits of Crab Land* (1935), charting the evolution of crustaceans by showing such examples as the mantis shrimp at various stages of maturity; *Swampland* (1936), focusing on the primitive life forms dwelling unseen in the swamps of Louisiana, and highlighted by two battles, one between a pair of snapping turtles and another a brace of alligators ("This is of an educational nature, but at the same time there are gripping struggle-for-life scenes that will thrill the

A wily sea anemone traps an unwary fish in *Living Jewels* (1936).

audience.... It is different, and should be exploited for its realistic punch"—*Motion Picture Daily*); *Deadly Females* (1936), featuring two male scorpions battling over a female, who promptly mates with and kills the winner ("One of the best in the series"—*Philadelphia Exhibitor*); *Forest Gangsters* (1937), filmed in the American West, where a cattle-killing mountain lion and a pesky wildcat prove worthy adversaries for two hunters on horseback; and the series finale *Desert Land* (1937), offering sundry reptiles and insects in their eternal search for food (L.A. Irwin of the Palace Theater in Penacook, New Hampshire, disagreed with the aforementioned *Exhibitor* assessment of *Deadly Females*, choosing *this* one as the "best in this series to date and that means plenty good.")

A few months before Van Beuren folded his tents in 1937, the Woodards signed on with famed documentarian Pare Lorentz to help photograph Lorentz' feature film *The River* (1938), a riveting history of the Mississippi and the devastating floods caused by human misuse of the mighty river. The job proved too time-consuming for Horace Woodard, who left the project early on; Stacy stayed with Lorentz almost to the end, sharing on-screen photography credit with Floyd Crosby and Willard Van Dyke. On their own, the Woodards journeyed to Northern Mexico to produce the critically acclaimed independent feature *The Adventures of Chico* (1938), which in addition to its other merits offered tantalizing peeks of what *Time* magazine described as "a long-beaked, shaggy-feathered bird about the size of a partridge": The Mexican road runner. (Please refrain from making references to coyotes, anvils, and the Acme company.)

Stacy and Horace Woodard continued to produce documentary features and industrial shorts in tandem until Stacy died suddenly of heart failure in 1942. Horace carried on alone throughout the 1940s and 1950s, lensing Frank Capra's wartime documentary *The Negro Soldier* and contributing remarkable scenes of insect life to the 1951 French-made dramatic feature *Monsieur Fabre*, among other assignments. He died in 1973.

Chapter 23

Sports with Bill Corum

Three years after the acrimonious parting of the ways between Amedee Van Beuren and sports columnist Grantland Rice (see Chapter 8), the Hollywood trade papers announced that the producer was about to return to the field of sports-oriented short subjects, featuring another prominent journalist—and not just any ink-stained wretch, but the man known to posterity as "Mr. Churchill Downs."

Born in Speed, Missouri, in 1895, Marlene Windsor Corum was apt to punch out anyone who referred to him by his given name and not by his chosen moniker Bill Corum. After serving as the youngest U.S. Army major in World War I, he launched his newspaper career, one of the few professional sportswriters who had actually studied journalism on a college level (Columbia University's Pulitzer School). Hired for the copy desk of the *New York Times* in 1921, Corum began covering the activities of the Brooklyn Dodgers in 1924, and two years later started chronicling the New York Giants for the *Times*' rival paper the *Evening Journal*. Of more significance to the history of sports reporting, Corum presided over the first network radio broadcast of the Kentucky Derby in 1925. In the course of this broadcast Corum referred to the Derby as "The Run for the Roses," not only assuring himself immortality but also cementing a lifelong association with Churchill Downs in Louisville, Kentucky.

If Grantland Rice can be regarded as the champagne of sportscasters, Bill Corum was the beer and chaser. In contrast with the clean-living and clean-minded Rice, to whom the "love of the game" was far more important than winning or losing, Corum was a heavy smoker, drinker and gambler to whom victory was all—especially when he had money on the outcome. The essential character and philosophy of Mr. Corum can be crystalized in the story of the day in 1949 when Bill was asked to become president of Churchill Downs and head of the Kentucky Derby, succeeding the colorful Matt T. Winn. Moral crusaders throughout the country had for years denigrated Louisville in general and the Derby in particular as a glorified clip joint, where out-of-town patrons of the annual event were habitually separated from their bankrolls by crooked entrepreneurs, gin joints and scarlet women. Rather than make any effort to counteract this negative publicity, Corum seemed to revel in it: "This is great. There is nothing better for a championship event than a treacherous woman. If a guy from North Dakota goes home from here after the race and has to be met because he doesn't even have cab fare left, that guy is going to say to himself, 'Wow. I must have had a hell of a time. I can't wait for next year.' But if that same guy goes home and he still has half his money, he is going to say 'I guess I didn't have such a great time at the Kentucky Derby after all.'

"Because, gentlemen, this is the rule. A sucker has to get screwed."

Unlike Van Beuren's wide-ranging *Grantland Rice Sportlights*, the subject matter in the Bill Corum one-reelers was limited to those sports in which Corum had a personal or wagering interest. Also unlike *Sportlights*, which Rice himself seldom narrated, Corum's "great, gravel voice" (as described by Jimmy Breslin) was heard on all the shorts bearing his name. The new Van Beuren series was launched in 1935 under the supervision of Don Hancock, with rousing background music supplied by house composer Win Sharples, who remained with the series even after leaving Van Beuren and joining the new firm Filmusic Inc.

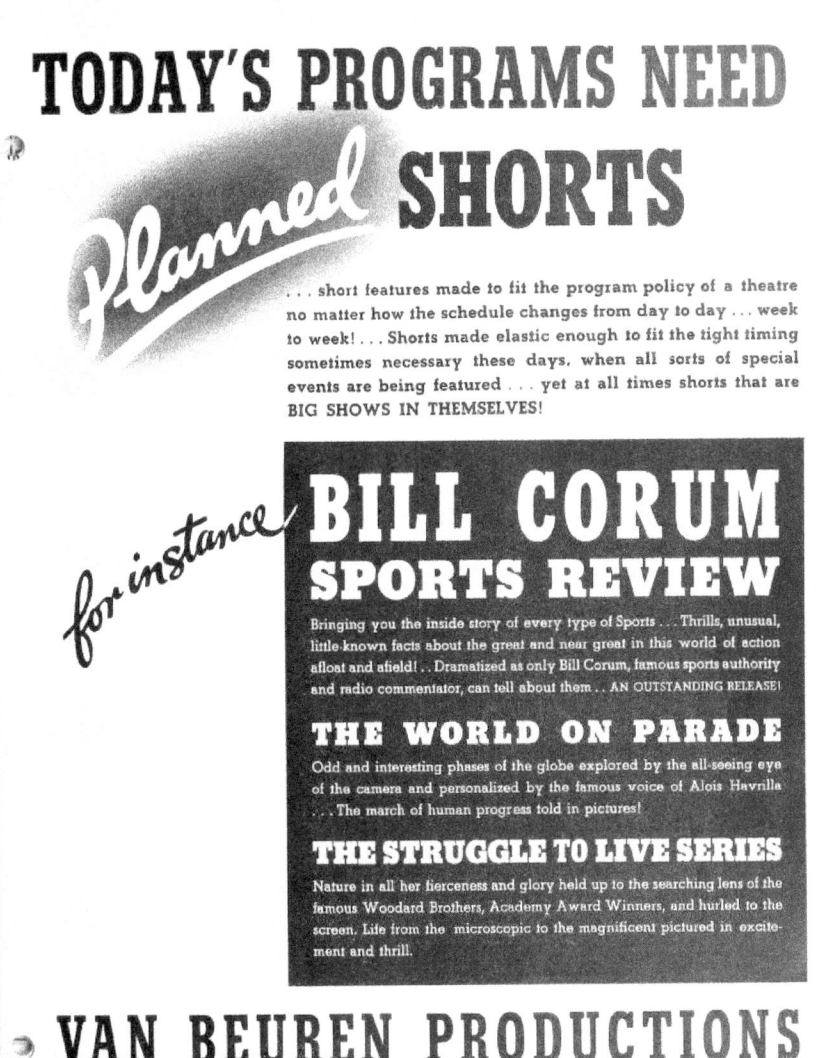

This 1937 Van Beuren trade ad bills the shorts series *Sports with Bill Corum* by one of its alternate titles.

Variously titled *Sports with Bill Corum, Inside Sports with Bill Corum* and *The Bill Corum Sports Review*, and advertised with the tagline "the human side of sports," the series got under way with the August 16, 1935, release *Inside the Ropes*. Originally titled simply *Boxing*, the ten-minute short focused on outstanding heavyweights past and present, including Jack Dempsey, Jim Braddock, Max Baer, Jack Sharkey and Benny Leonard. The film garnered extra publicity for its exclusive glimpses of up-and-coming champion Joe Louis, in training at his camp at Pompton Lake, New Jersey. The adulation afforded Louis in *Inside the Ropes* is a bit ironic in that Bill Corum, in standard white-supremacist fashion of the 1930s, had previously described the Brown Bomber in print as "born to be a singing cotton picker" and "a big, superbly built Negro youth who was born to listen to jazz music, eat a lot of fried chicken, play ball with the gang on the corner and never do a lick of heavy work if he could escape."

Though technically the second short in the series, *Inside the Ropes'* release date was moved forward by dint of Joe Louis' burgeoning celebrity, scoring big at the box office. More typical of the turf-loving Bill Corum was the first completed series entry (but the second released), *Bugles from the Blue Grass* (1935), which featured generous helpings of library footage to celebrate the more famous winners of the Kentucky Derby. An obligatory snippet of the great Man-o-War was especially appreciated by fans and film reviewers of the period.

Entry #3 *Gentlemen's Sports* (1935) chronicled such recreational activities as billiards, trap and skeet shooting, speed boating and polo. The film opened with Corum stating that if he had a million dollars to invest in any sport of his choice, his greatest desire would be to own a "string of race horses and travel around the country with them." Featured in the one-reeler were such wealthy sportsmen (many of them captains of industry) as Gar Wood, Richard DuPont, Eltinge F. Warner, Woolworth Donahue, G.H. "Pete" Bostwick and Francis and Edgar T. Appleby, while major events pictured included the Hambletonian at Goshen, New York, and the polo championship at Old Westbury, Long Island. This short was followed in January 1936 by *Tomorrow's Halfback*, (originally *The Happiest Boy in Town*) delineating the coaching systems and significant plays of various teams with leading football personalities acting them out, emphasizing the difference between college and pro football. The short's throughline involved a gridiron-happy youngster being given instructions by the great Lou Little, head coach at Corum's alma mater Columbia University from 1930 through 1956.

Filmed in Canada, the March 1936 entry *Winter Sports* offered ski jumping, curling, and sledding with Siberian huskies. Of a somewhat warmer nature was *Never Catch the Rabbit* (1936), lensed at the dog-racing tracks of Miami and St. Petersburg, Florida, with special attention given the late sports promoter Tex Rickard's kennel club. Curiously for a series that emphasized sportsmanship, this film demonstrated how races could be "fixed" by clipping a dog's toenails or putting chewing gum between its toes. The 1935–36 season of shorts concluded with *Row, Mister, Row* (June 19, 1936), a mini-tribute to the "Grand Old Man of Rowing," U.S. Naval Academy and Syracuse University crew coach A. Ten Eyck, here still going strong at age 88.

With Van Beuren general manager Don Hancock continuing to supervise the series, the 1936–37 season began with *High, Wide and Dashing* (1936), spotlighting such track and field stars as sprinter-long jumper Jesse Owens (fresh from his triumph at the Berlin Olympics), long-distance runner Glenn Cunningham, two-milers

J.T. McClusky and Donald R. Lask, 120-yard hurdler Philip G. Good, quarter-miler John Hoffstetter, high jumpers Walter Marty and Cornelius Johnson, and pole vaulters Fred Stein and Boyd Childs (I'm out of breath just listing their names). The Larchmont Yacht Club's participation in various annual regattas at Long Island Sound was the topic of the next episode *Pardon My Spray* (1936), featuring sea-sporters old, young, male and female, not to mention spectacular scenes of 300 yachts participating in a single competition. Timed for release at the beginning of football season, *Goals for Gold and Glory* (1936), like the earlier *Tomorrow's Halfbacks*, dealt with the game plans and coaching systems of professional and college gridiron teams, underlining the major differences of same between the amateur teams at Rutgers, Fordham, Penn State, and the pros of the Giants, Dodgers, and other top-drawer organizations.

Originally titled *Checkered Flag*, the November 1936 offering *Singing Wheels* was another "then and now" opus concentrating on auto races ranging from the annual Soapbox Derby to the Vanderbilt Cup, and from dirt tracks to asphalt lanes. Old-timers in the audience were delighted to see such enduring favorites as Barney Oldfield, Ralph de Palma and Tommy Milton. The distaff side of sports was given its due in December 1936's *Ladies Day*, with comely young female athletes participating in polo, fencing, surf swimming, diving, tennis, basketball, and a popular fad of the era, "archery golf." The participants in the January 1937 release *The Iceman* wore more clothes and sported more whiskers than those in *Ladies Day*; this time the sport of preference was ice hockey.

Putting on the Dog (1937), originally titled *Sportsman's Dogs*, was all about bird hunting and bird-dogging. *Saratoga Summers* (1937) combined the requisite stock shots of the famous New York spa's mineral springs and casinos with fresh footage of several celebrated racetrack thoroughbreds, concluding the reel with a water carnival staged by vacationing society kids. *Foreign Sports* (1937), found Bill Corum narrating footage of athletic events in Japan (jiu-jitsu), Mexico and Cuba (jai-alai), Spain and London. Released in the early weeks of baseball season, *Big League* (1937) followed the game from training camps in Florida and California to "the show" in Chicago, Boston, and New York, with piquant glimpses of such star players as Babe Ruth, Lefty Gomez, Big Bill Dickey and Guy Lazzeri—and a few none-too-subtle plugs for that popular chewing gum manufactured by the owners of Wrigley Field.

After the self-explanatory *Beach Sports* and *Royal Steeds* (both 1937), the second and final season of Van Beuren's Bill Corum series closed with the July 23, 1937, offering *Golf Timing*. This time the audience was whisked to Old Greenwich, Connecticut, home of the practice range owned by "rhythm and timing" golf expert Ira Miner. As Miner and his son showed viewers how easy it was to play their game of choice via a "group system," a line of underclad chorus girls appeared from nowhere to join in on the fun. No doubt about it: Bill Corum understood his core audience.

Despite the fact that Van Beuren Productions had gone out of business by mid–1937, Bill Corum renewed his contract for the 1937–38 season, moving over to Amedee Van Beuren's new venture Condor Productions. Promising higher budgets and bigger sports thrills for the proposed third season, Van Beuren and Corum reportedly completed the first two of 13 planned one-reelers, *Water Polo* and *One Man Team*. But as far as this writer can determine, neither short was ever released, and the series was among the many casualties of Condor's collapse in the fall of 1937.

His career slowed down not one whit by the termination of his film series (though a curious incident on May 12, 1937, in which he was shot and wounded by an unknown assailant on the streets of Los Angeles, *did* sideline him for a while), Bill Corum continued writing his daily newspaper column, even during his eight-year tenure as president of Churchill Downs. In 1939 Corum managed to raise the hackles of midwestern football fans with a column suggesting that the NFL drop the Green Bay Packers as "too small" a franchise for big-league consideration, though he reversed himself when the Pack scored a 27–0 victory over the New York Giants in the year's championship game. Corum also kept busy on radio, usually in tandem with fellow sportscaster Don Dunphy, as color commentator for major boxing events beginning with the first Joe Louis-Billy Conn fight in 1941. In addition, Corum served as chairman of the USO's sports division during World War II, and in 1952 engineered and announced the first national telecast of the Kentucky Derby, installing extra seating boxes and a sprinkler system at Churchill Downs and organizing a "film patrol" to shoot replays of dead heats—a celluloid precursor to the TV's instant replay. Bill Corum remained in harness, as it were, until his death from lung cancer in 1958.

Chapter 24

World on Parade

If Amedee Van Beuren had any worries in 1935 that the double-feature policy was the beginning of the end of quality short subjects in American movie theaters, you'd never know it from the confidence with which he launched three new series that year—all of them still healthy and thriving as he was preparing to close down his production company in mid–1937. The last of three turned out to be one of Van Beuren's finest offerings: *World on Parade*, which yielded twenty popular one-reel entries over a two year period.

With his previous long-distance runner *Vagabond Adventures* (see Chapter 10) having been absorbed and supplanted by *Easy Aces* (see Chapter 21), Van Beuren opted to continue the travel-film format, with a bit of *Easy Aces'* human-interest hook, in a new series with a new title. As had happened so often in past years, the perfect vehicle was delivered to him by an outside source. Colorado-born and Idaho-raised Harold McCracken (1894–1983) was a noted explorer and nature photographer, long associated with New York's Museum of Natural History. His fascination with other lands and peoples began in his youth, when he spent many happy months living amongst the Cree Indians and learning their methods of outdoor survival. While he was attending Columbia University in 1916, the Museum Board of Columbus Ohio sponsored the first of McCracken's many expeditions to Alaska. An extended 1928 journey to the Aleutians, during which he searched for remnants of the prehistoric Bering land bridge between Alaska and Russia (and nearly lost all his toes to frostbite), resulted in his illustrated best-seller *Beyond the Frozen Frontier*. McCracken was also a recognized expert on the American grizzly bear, a biplane stunt flyer, a cameraman for Pathé news, a prolific biographer of the great sculptors and painters of the American West, and the creator (in 1939) of Wyoming's Buffalo Bill Historical Center. Harold McCracken came up with the idea for his Van Beuren film series to raise money for his other, non-cinematic pursuits.

Though McCracken was a competent lecturer, he deferred the narration of *World on Parade* to a radio announcer who had previously worked on *Vagabond Adventures*. Born in 1891 to Slovakian parents in Austria-Hungary, Alois Havrila emigrated to the U.S. at age four. An early talent for singing led to several professional engagements before he switched interests to civil engineering. Exempted from service during World War I because of poor eyesight, Havrila attended New York University, jump-starting his singing career with a 1923 Carnegie Hall concert. Fellow singer Elliot Shaw and sportscaster-emcee Graham McNamee introduced Havrila to radio, first as a staff announcer at New York's WJZ and eventually securing such high-paying NBC network announcing gigs as *The Ford Fred Waring Hour, Paul Whiteman's*

Varieties, the Chevrolet Hour with Jack Benny and *The American Can Hour with Ben Bernie*. In 1935, the same year he began work on *World on Parade*, he won the annual diction award from the American Academy of Arts and Letters. In addition to his many lucrative radio assignments (including announcing all GOP Presidential campaigns from Hoover to Eisenhower), his 1928 marriage to wealthy Marion Munson enabled Havrilla to maintain a splendiferous Englewood, New Jersey, mansion and indulge his hobbies of travelling the world and collecting rare 19th century furniture. After leaving Van Beuren in 1937, Havrilla did some narrating for the Paramount shorts unit, then moved to Universal's *Stranger Than Fiction* series. At the time of his death in 1952, Alois Havrilla was back in local radio at Newark, New Jersey's WNJR.

Van Beuren's publicists heralded *The World on Parade* as "a new series of travel films glorified with the songs and music of the lands they picture.... The odd and interesting nooks and crannies of this great globe brought before your eyes." Subsequent trade-paper coverage indicated that Harold McCracken and his crew handled most of the cinematography on his short subjects. While this was true enough in the episodes covering the Western Hemisphere and especially the United States, at times it was necessary to burrow into Van Beuren's existing film library for material. Case in point: The first in the series, *Land of the Eagle* (released August 23, 1935) took advantage of footage previously filmed during Van Beuren's expedition to the tropical lowlands of Guatemala for his feature *Adventure Girl* (see Chapter 20). In the humanistic tradition of *Vagabond Adventures*, the short focused on local agricultural life (coffee and bananas mostly), bustling market places, churches, and native craftsmanship such as pottery-making and weaving. Upholding the standards set by *Vagabond Adventures*, the new series avoided the static, lifeless "picture postcards" typical of MGM's yawn-provoking *Fitzpatrick Traveltalks*, utilizing quick editing and constantly roving camerawork while recording the vestiges of Spanish and Aztec architecture still standing in Guatemala. *National Board of Review* magazine summed up *Land of the Eagle* as "Suggested for schools and libraries"—which might have

Alois Havrilla, narrator of Van Beuren's *World on Parade*, in the 1933 edition of *Radio Announcers Annual*.

been the kiss of death at the box office were it not for the more enticing reviews from *Motion Picture Daily* ("It is an interesting reel, splendidly photographed") and *Film Daily* ("skillfully presented.... A very superior travel picture that is different").

The next two *World on Parade* entries were to have been *Mr. Athos in Greece* and a one-reeler built around footage recently lensed during a Van Beuren-financed trip to London. The former was apparently never completed, while the latter was reworked and provided with comic narration as the *Easy Aces* entry *Jolly Ol' London*. The actual second short in the series was *Spain's Romantic Isle* (1935)—namely, Majorca. The *Film Daily* reviewer was pleased that the film focused on an exotic locale "that hadn't been done to death" in other travelogue series, adding that the cameraman "used good taste in his choice of scenes"—most likely a reference to the abundance of exposed female bosoms in the South Seas-centric *Vagabond Adventures* of a couple of seasons back.

World on Parade paid the first of many visits to North America with its last 1935 release *Land of Evangeline*. In the spirit of the titular Longfellow narrative poem ("This is the forest primeval..."), the film dwelled upon the French Acadian people still residing in Nova Scotia, beginning at the Bay of Fundy and progressing to Grand Pre. Narrator Alois Harvilla recounted the tragic historical background of the poem, while also emphasizing such positives of the region as its farming and fishing, not to mention the copacetic blend of Acadian, French and Scottish cultures. Virtually every review of *Land of Evangeline* cited its "beautiful photography." *Film Daily* also praised the picture as "A very peaceful and restful subject that will prove a boon to tired theater patrons," while *Motion Picture Herald* felt that the spoken commentary represented "Narrator Havrilla at his best." The film was chosen as one of *Philadelphia Exhibitor*'s Grand Shorts Award winners for 1936, along with MGM's 3-D novelty reel *Audioscopiks*, Universal's *Flash Gordon* serial and Disney's *Donald Duck* cartoons.

World on Parade's 1936 crop began with *Morocco*, one of a handful of series entries still available for viewing. As with several of the earlier shorts, this one begins with live-action footage of Alois Havrilla standing before a map as if prepared to deliver a lecture to a live audience. The image dissolves to travel footage of Casablanca, then settles for a long spell in Marrakech just outside the Atlas mountains, the remains of an ancient paved road inviting us to start our journey. After a few brief glances of the Koutoubia Mosque, built by Islamic Moors in 1157, we are treated to a typical business day in the "jamilas," or street-merchant district, as Berbers, Arabs, Moors, Jews and Sudanese peacefully go about their affairs. Among the individuals given special attention are a public scribe who whittles his pen from bamboo and children playing marbles in the dirt just like Jimmy, Johnny and Billy in your own neighborhood. Then, more craftsmen and artisans, including a harness maker rigging a goatskin belt and dyemakers using pomegranates and other vegetables for their colors and swirling silk around the dye to squeeze out excess liquid and dust. The film proceeds with a stopover in the farmlands, where the locals demonstrate various methods of killing the dreaded locust, and a visit to a snail farm, where the slimy li'l critters are harvested and packed up for consumption in Europe and the U.S. We end our stay in Morocco by observing proper etiquette during a tea ceremony. Unlike so many other travelogues of the 1930s, which for modern audiences cannot end quickly enough, *Morocco* actually leaves the viewer hungry for more.

The next episode *Prominent Personalities* was reviewed by *Film Daily* as "an attempt to do something different." Indeed, the film represented a deliberate departure from the *World on Parade* format, intended by Van Beuren as the pilot short for a spinoff series—which despite the film's better-than-average performance at the box office (verified by an item in the July 11, 1936, *Motion Picture Herald*) never came to pass. *Prominent Personalities* celebrated a group of what would now be called B-list celebrities, who'd achieved fame not with good looks or overwhelming popularity but because of their individual achievements. Included were attorney and football-kicking expert Leroy N. Mills; Helen Ritchey, America's first and (at the time) only transport pilot; musical prodigy Grischa Goluboff; and two members of the Van Beuren film family, past and present: Photographer Margaret Bourke-White, responsible for a brace of the best *Vagabond Adventures* entries (see Chapter 10), and *World on Parade*'s very own narrator Alois Havrilla, here described as "an engineer, actor, singer, radio and screen announcer." (He probably also juggled in the afterpiece).

Film Daily also liked the next, more traditional offering: *Coral Island of the Atlantic*, which featured the spider bridges and crystal caves of Bermuda, an island built on coral formations: "The narrative is of the dulcet, poetic variety but not so much so that it irritates." *Motion Picture Herald* rated this one "among the best of the World on Parade Series to date."

Another of the presently available series shorts is the May 1936 release *Venice of the North*, photographed by famed maritime expert Captain Warrick M. Tompkins. Narrating in the first person *a la* Tom Terriss of *Vagabond Adventures*, Alois Havrilla recounts a fogbound journey across the sea in Capt. Tompkins' 85-foot square rigger *Wanderbird* to the Swedish port of Stockholm. Described as a "city between bridges" built on 30 separate islands, the Stockholm of 1936 harbors one of the last commercial sailing fleets on earth—and, justifying the film's title, a large contingent of ferryboats to navigate the local canals. As Havrilla contrasts the modern metropolis with its "old town" district, we drop in on a china factory where employees wear earphones to listen to the radio while they work—a gesture of courtesy from a generous management that would not gain traction in America for another 40 years. Similarly, Havrilla praises Sweden's forward-looking laws against smoking while driving ("Something to think about") as well as the country's pro-ecological clean canals and pollution-eradicating sewage system. Stockholm's Tivoli Park is likewise environment-friendly, its ferris wheel propelled not by engines but by the customers; and traffic is kept under control and safely flowing by equipping the city's 27 main roads with roundabouts ("Something *else* to think about"). As pleasing as *Venice of the North* is to modern eyes, *Philadelphia Exhibitor* considered it only "fair," commenting dismissively: "Photography is interesting but not too striking."

After the first seven shorts, *World on Parade* was renewed for 13 additional entries, to be released throughout the 1936–37 season. The second manifest began with *Trinidad* (1936), which concentrated on the East Indian Hindu population of Port-of-Spain; highlights included the annual Hosein festival, in which tiny temples are thrown into the sea to carry prayers to Mohammed. The next three offerings were economically filmed in the U.S.A. *Washington in Virginia* (1936) was a tour of the locations in the state that held significance in the life of the Father of Our Country (*Philadelphia Exhibitor* suggested that it be rebooked for Washington's birthday in February of 1937). The still-extant *Heart of the Sierras* (1936) is a high-class chamber of commerce-style outing with excellent views of the "majestic cathedrals" created by nature at Yosemite National Park, along with flashes of the Sequoia tunnel trees, Mirror Lake, Hanging Rock, and the Yosemite, Vernal and Bridal Veil falls (in that order). A remarkable shot of a rainbow caused by the mist of cascading water serves to emphasize the one big shortcoming of *World on Parade*: Its budget did not extend to color film, thus the aforementioned rainbow is immortalized in not-so-glorious monochrome. Roy C. Irving, manager of the Ritz Theater in Washington State, told *Motion Picture Herald*: "In color [*Heart of the Sierras*] would have been outstanding, but worth running time even in black and white." Other exhibitors weren't so easily satisfied, certainly not C.L. Niles of Anamosa, Iowa: "A good black and white travel, but with everybody making excellent colored shorts, RKO might just as well get in the wagon or quit."

The last of the "United States trilogy" of 1936, *Graveyard of Ships* was filmed off Cape Hatteras, North Carolina, with attention lavished on the abandoned lighthouse, the skeletons of wrecked vessels and the Coast Guard going through a drill at sea. *Motion Picture Daily* was impressed by the "stark, forbidding atmosphere" of the film. The final 1936 release may have been shot in America, but with no physical evidence at hand we can't at present be sure. *Gold Fever* follows an "old-time prospector" and his dog and mule as they fruitlessly dig around various water holes and streams in search of the elusive yellow ore. Though obviously staged and rehearsed, *Gold Fever* was according to *Film Daily* pulled off "without any theatrical effects."

Romantic Mexico, the first 1937 release (and another that has survived in good condition to this day), offers views of the remnants of the Aztec civilization still intact within the architecture of modern Mexico City. This is one of the more pleasingly "cinematic" entries: One sequence in a public park is introduced with a balloon vendor's wares filling the screen and then receding into the background. Pyramids that predate the Aztecs are also featured, again avoiding the filmic sterility of most travelogues. We also see the indigenous people of the region tending their sheep and carrying their farm produce to market along ancient highways, with the cameraman's panchromatic film stock providing a dramatic backdrop of billowing clouds. *Romantic Mexico* was filmed on location in tandem with Van Beuren's *Sports with Bill Corum* reel *Foreign Sports*, under the supervision of Don Hancock and Al Wetzel.

The next release was widely regarded at the time as the best of the series, and remains impressive today. Filmed in January of 1937 and shipped to theaters one month later, *Manhattan Waterfront* is introduced with majestic theme music lifted from Liszt's "Les Préludes," underscoring its awe-inspiring images of the Hudson, East and Harlem rivers, the Battery, the Brooklyn Bridge and its recently erected "sister" the Triborough, the Hellgate train bridge, the Seaman's Church Institute, Fulton Fish Market, the stockyards, the waterfront's many ship terminals, and vessels ranging from tugboats to ocean liners. But before we're lulled into thinking that what will follow is merely another cinematic paean to the glories of American industry and ingenuity, Alois Havrilla's narration takes a somber and sour turn, contrasting glamour and progress with squalor and retrogression, and counteracting shots of lofty riverside apartment towers with the "jungles of the less fortunate" who scrape out a miserable existence along the waterfront.

The tone of the narration (written by Harold McCracken) is in no way radical or reactionary. Instead, it is a reflection of how the majority of more fortunate New Yorkers of 1937 felt towards the shabby down-and-outers vegetating in the "dead end

Title card of the best of the best entry in the *World on Parade* series.

of Manhattan," describing these pitiful wretches as "unholy ghosts of men who have failed at every opportunity." As if to deliberately undercut these conformist sentiments, *Manhattan Waterfront* overflows with unforgettable images of the extreme gaps between the privileged and the underprivileged. Particularly striking is the editorial decision to juxtapose glimpses of expensive yachts housed in private wharves with disturbingly protracted views of derelict barges that have been converted into shacks.

Boxoffice magazine gave *Manhattan Waterfront* a rave review in its March 28, 1937, edition, singling it out as "Short of the Week." Amedee Van Beuren offered a personal response to this review in the April 10 issue: "We appreciate the distinction given this reel. Recognition of this nature by a nationally known trade paper serves as an inspiration in continuing to make the better grade of pictures for the present day discriminating audience." These were mighty strong words for a man who was on the verge of closing down his operation, almost as strong as his published statements in the April 1, 1937, *Film Daily*: "The improvement in conditions generally and the many other indications that are apparent in the future of shorts justifies our faith in them and it is the reason for our recent announcement of additional budgets for our three main series." *Manhattan Waterfront* was without question one of the main beneficiaries of the producer's burst of optimism.

Though no subsequent *World on Parade* entries scaled the heights of *Manhattan Waterfront*, there was no discernable slackening of quality in the remaining shorts. *Mt. Vernon* (1937), a follow-up to the earlier historical jaunt *Washington in Virginia*, was filmed in the titular New York town "Through the courtesy of the Mount Vernon Ladies' Association." *California Missions* (1937) was a tip of the hat to the good works left behind by the old Franciscan Friars in and around Los Angeles. *Circus Winter Quarters (1937)*, lensed in Sarasota, gave us a peek at rehearsals for that year's mammoth "India" grand parade, and also featured a pair of curvaceous aerial artists working out their new routines, as well as the breaking in of upcoming animal acts. *Florida Cowboy* (1937), an "excellent photographic job" (*Film Daily*), chronicled a day in the life of a Florida cattleman headquartered in Seminole swamp country—and watch out for rattlers, mister! The penultimate release *Workshops of Old Mexico* (1937) featured glass blowing, pottery molding, toymaking and rope manufacturing, with Alois Havrilla's narration emphasizing the pride felt by the artisans in lieu of large financial returns. "Tastefully delivered" was *Film Daily*'s verdict this time out.

The final short in the series, and the last-ever theatrical release by Van Beuren Productions, was *Jungle Playmates*, originally distributed on July 30, 1937. The focus herein was on the many animal farms in California where jungle felines were raised for exhibition purposes. *Jungle Playmates* was deemed worthy of selection by Broadway's Criterion Theater to be showcased with two other RKO shorts, the musical comedy *Swing Fever* and the Van Beuren *Sports with Bill Corum* episode *Golf Timing*—comprising nearly half of the Criterion's nightly bill.

Anyone laboring under the misapprehension that Amedee Van Beuren would terminate his final season of independent film production with a sorry batch of cheap quickies, carelessly slapped together merely to fulfill his RKO contract as rapidly as possible, were in for a surprise as his three remaining live-action series brought forth their last offerings to the American public in the spring and summer of 1937. *Struggle to Live*'s *Desert Land*, *Sports with Bill Corum*'s *Golf Timing* and *World on Parade*'s *Jungle Playmates* were not only representative of the producer in his prime, but also head and shoulders above the majority of potboilers spewed out by the other Hollywood short-subject factories of the period. So permit us overlook the calamitous results of Amedee Van Beuren's effort to relaunch his activities with the foredoomed Condor Film Corporation in late 1937, and leave him at this high point.

The Van Beuren Filmography

(Unless otherwise indicated, all films are black & white)

I. Live-Action Short Subjects

THE PARAMOUNT-DREW COMEDIES

V.B.K Productions, Released by the Paramount Pictures Division of Famous Players–Lasky. Two reels each (unless otherwise indicated); silent

1918—

*September: *Financing the Fourth* (a Liberty Loan short: one reel)

1919—

Feb. 2: *Romance and Rings*
March 16: *Once a Mason*
Apr. 10: *The Amateur Liar*
May 4: *Harold, Last of the Saxons*
June 5: *Squared*
July 13: *Bunkered*
Aug. 24: *A Sisterly Scheme*

TOPICS OF THE DAY

This filmography lists only the films produced by Amedee Van Beuren. It does not list the "Topics of the Day" shorts released on a state's-rights basis between 1918 and 1919.

Timely Films Inc., released by Pathé. 300–400 ft. each; silent.

(Released one per week.)

May 4, 1919–Jan. 2, 1922: no. 1 through no. 140

(New numbering policy begins with the 141st entry, returning to no. 1 at the beginning of each year)

Jan. 7, 1922–Dec. 31, 1922: no. 1 through no. 52 [141–192]

Jan. 7, 1923–Dec. 30, 1923: no. 1 through no. 52 [193–244]

Jan. 6, 1924–Dec. 28, 1924: no. 1 through no. 52 [245–296]

Jan. 4, 1925–Dec. 27, 1925: no. 1 through no. 52 [297–348]

Jan. 4, 1926–Dec. 27, 1926: no. 1 through no. 52 [349–400]

Jan. 6, 1927–Dec. 29, 1927: no. 1 through no. 53 [401–453]

Jan. 5, 1928–Dec. 27, 1928: no. 1 through no. 52 [454–505]

Van Beuren Productions, released by Pathé. 300–400 ft. each.

Silent Shorts

1928—

Dec. 31: No. 1

1929—

Jan. 7: No. 2
Jan. 14: No. 3
Jan. 21: No. 4
Jan. 28: No. 5
Feb. 3: No. 6
Feb. 10: No. 7
Feb. 17: No. 8
Feb. 24: No. 9

Sound Shorts (Retitled Talking Topics of the Day)

Where a release date is in question, possible dates, based on trade paper information, are listed.

1929—

Apr. 2: *Topical Hits*
Apr. 16: *Topical Tips*
Apr. 30: *Topical Bits*
May 11 or May 18: *Pressing His Suit*
June 2: *Topical Nips*

June 16: *Topical Clips*
June 30: *Topical Pips*
July 14: *Topical Flips*
July 28: *Topical Slips*
Aug. 11?: *The Petters*
Aug. 25: *Topical Fits*
Sept. 8 or Sept. 22: *Topical Wits*
Oct. 19 or Oct. 25: *Topical Kicks*
Nov. 1: *Topical Sips* [title in doubt: may be a reissue of *Topical Slips*]
Nov. 15: *Topical Kicks*
Nov. 29: *Topical Ticks*
Dec. 13: *Topical Hicks*
Dec. 27: *Topical Nicks*

1930—
Jan. 12: *On the Air*
Jan. 19: *In the Park*
Feb. 29: *Cover Charge*
Mar. 9: *What No Bait?*
Mar. 23: *Home Sweet Home*
Apr. 4?: *Van Beuren News*

Ernest Truex

Ayveebee Films, released by the Paramount Pictures Division of Famous Players–Lasky. Two reels each; silent.

1919—
Nov. 30: *The Night of the Dub*
Dec. 28: *Too Good to be True*

Ayeveebee Films, released by Pathé. Two reels each; silent.

1921—
Nov. 20: *Little, But Oh My!*
Dec. 18: *Stick Around*

1922—
Jan. 15: *The Bashful Lover*

Henry and Polly

Gaiety Films, released by Pathé. Two reels each; silent.

1927—
Sept. 28: *Should a Mason Tell?*
Oct. 16: *Their Second Honeymoon*
Nov. 11: *King Harold*

The Grantland Rice Sportlight

This filmography lists only the films produced by Amedee Van Beuren. It does not list the "Sport Pictorial" shorts released by Arrow Films between 1920 and 1921; the "Sportlights" shorts released by Artclass Pictures between 1921 and 1932; the "Grantland Rice Sportlights" produced by John L. Hawkinson and released by Pathé between 1923 and 1928; nor the "Grantland Rice Sportlights" released by Paramount between 1933 and 1955.

Silent Shorts

Van Beuren Productions, released by Pathé. One reel each.

1928—
Aug. 28: *Canned Thrills*
Sept. 16: *Covering Ground*
Sept. 22: *South Sea Sagas*
Sept. 30: *A Gridiron Cocktail*
Oct. 14: *Muscle Marvels*
Oct. 28: *Getting Together*
Nov. 11: *Spartan Diet*
Nov. 25: *Targets*
Dec. 9: *School Days*
Dec. 23: *Amateur Antics*

1929—
Jan. 8: *Knowing the Ropes*
Jan. 20: *Players at Play*
Feb. 3: *Mild or Mighty*
Feb. 17: *Girls Will Be Boys*
Mar. 3: *Close Figuring*
Mar. 17: *Dogging It*
Mar. 31: *Bridle Byways*
Apr. 14: *Water Wonders*
Apr. 28: *Young Hopefuls*
May 12: *Surf and Sail*
May 26: *Fish and Feathers*
June 23: *Footwork*
July 7: *Sport Afloat*
July 21: *The Right Technique*
Aug. 4: *Rhythm* (title in question: this may be the silent version of the sound short *Modern Rhythm*).

Sound Shorts

Van Beuren Productions, released by Pathé between 1929 and 1930; and RKO–Pathé and RKO Radio between 1931 and 1932. One reel each.

The Van Beuren Filmography

1929—
March 10: *Winning Patterns*
Apr. 7: *Three Aces*
May 5: *Crystal Champions*
June 2: *Clowning the Game*
June 16: *Conditioning*
June 30: *Sport Almanac*
July 28: *Modern Rhythm*
Aug. 18: *The River Drivers*
Aug. 25: *Hook, Line and Melody*
Sept. 1: *Running the Scales*
Sept. 8: *Duffers and Champs*
Sept. 22: *Boyhood Memories*
Sept. 29: *Follow the Leader*
Oct. 6: *Gridiron Glory*
Oct. 20: *Boby Building Stamina*
Nov. 17: *Feminine Fitness*
Dec. 7: *Sports A-La-Carte*
Dec. 15: *Carolina Capers*
Dec, 29: *Interesting Tails*

1930—
Jan. 12: *Bows and Arrows*
Jan. 26: *Happy Golf*
Feb. 9: *The Feline Fighter*
Feb. 23: *Splashing Through*
Mar. 9: *Dogging It*
Mar. 23: *Big Top Champions*
Apr. 6: *Spills and Thrills*
Apr. 20: *Fish, Fowl and Fun*
May 4: *Fairway Favorites*
May 18: *Hooked*
June 1: *Sporting Brothers*
June 15: *Champion Makers*
June 29: *Campus Favorites*
July 13: *Somewhere Out*
July 27: *Let 'Er Buck*
Aug. 10: *Chasing Rainbows*
Aug. 24: *Ski Hi Frolics*
Sept. 7: *Self Defense*
Sept. 21: *Dude Ranching*
Sept. 21: *Gliding*
Oct. 5: *Cobb Goes Fishing*
Oct. 19: *Racqueteers*
Nov. 2: *Par and Double Par*
Nov. 16: *High Steppers*
Nov. 30: *Dixie Chase*
Dec. 14: *Monarchs of the Field*
Dec. 28: *Angles of Angling*

1931—
Jan. 11: *Under Cover*
Jan. 25: *Rough and Tumble*
Feb. 8: *Ski Pilot*
Feb. 22: *Tigers of the Deep*
Mar. 8: *The Speed Limit*
Mar. 22: *Swim or Sink*
Apr. 4: *Tennis Topnotchers*
Apr. 21: *Hunting Thrills*
May 3: *Outboard Stunting*
May 17: *Diamond Experts*
May 31: *Water Bugs*
June 15: *Blue Grass Kings*
June 29: *Younger Years*
July 12: *Battling Silver Kings*
July 26: *Poise*
Aug. 10: *Olympic Talent* (also listed as *Olympic Talents*)
Aug. 24: *Manhattan Mariners*
Sept. 7: *Floating Fun*
Sept. 21: *Pigskin Progress*
Oct. 10: *Timing*
Oct. 24: *Pack and Saddle*
Nov. 2: *Riders of Riley*
Nov. 16: *Canine Champions*
Nov. 30: *"Uncrowned Champions"*
Dec. 14: *Ducks and Drakes*

1932—
Jan. 27: *College Grapplers*
Feb. 6: *Slim Figuring*
Feb. 20: *Bob-White*
Mar. 3: *Flying Leather*
Mar. 17: *Take Your Pick*

WALTER FUTTER'S CURIOSITIES

This filmography lists only the films produced by Amedee Van Beuren. It does not list the "Walter Futter's Curiosities" shorts released by Educational Pictures between 1926 and 1928 nor the same-named shorts released by Columbia between 1930 and 1932.

Van Beuren Productions, released by FBO in 1928 and by RKO in 1929. One reel each.

Note: Research has not revealed with certainty whether the individual "Curiosities" released in 1929 were silent or sound (with narration). Those verified to be sound shorts are indicated by an asterisk.

1928—
- Sept. 26: *Believe It or Not*
- Oct. 10: *Fishing and How*
- Oct. 24: *Pets*
- Nov. 7: *Facts or Fancies*
- Nov. 28: *The Grab Bag*
- Dec. 5: *The Landlord Blues* (also listed as *Back Home*)
- Dec. 21: *Cash and Carry*

1929—
- Jan. 2: *Seeing's Believing**
- Jan. 17: *Potpourri*
- Feb. 13: *Birds and Beasts*
- Feb. 27: *Novelties*
- Mar. 13: *Orienta*
- Mar. 27: *Nifties*
- Apr. 10: *Odd Facts*
- Apr. 24: *Faces*
- May 8: *Here and There*
- May 22: *Follies of Fashion**
- June 4: *Odds and Ends*
- June 24: *Far and Near*
- July 28: *Gleanings* (copyrighted by Record Pictures Inc.)*
- Aug. 11: *Women Only* (copyrighted by Record Pictures Inc.)*
- Aug. 29: *Pedal Power* (copyrighted by Record Pictures Inc.)*
- Sept. 11: *This and That*

SMITTY AND HIS PALS

Van Beuren Enterprises, released by Pathé. Two reels each; silent.

1928—
- Oct. 7: *No Picnic*
- Nov. 18: *No Sale*
- Dec. 16: *Camping Out*

1929—
- Jan. 13: *All Aboard*
- Feb. 10: *Circus Time*
- Mar. 10: *No Children*
- Apr. 7: *Watch My Smoke*
- May 5: *Tomato Omelette*
- June 2: *Puckered Success*
- June 30: *Uncle's Visit*

SONG SKETCHES

Van Beuren Productions, released by Pathé. One reel each; sound.

1930—
- Jan. 5: *Mandalay* (copyright title: *The Road to Mandalay*)
- Jan. 19: *The Trumpeter*
- Feb. 2: *Songs of Mother*
- Feb. 16: *Love's Memories*
- Apr. 20: *Deep South*
- May 4: *Voices of the Sea*

VAGABOND ADVENTURES

Van Beuren Productions; released by Pathé in 1930, by RKO–Pathé in 1931, and RKO Radio between 1931 and 1935. One reel each; sound.

1930—
- May 5: *The Golden Pagoda*
- May 19: *The Glacier's Secret*
- June 2: *Streets of Mystery*
- June 15: *Lair of Chang-Ow* [also listed as *Lair of Chang-How*]
- June 29: *Drums of Fear*
- July 12: *Temple of Silence*
- July 27: *Sacred Fires*
- Aug. 10: *Venetian Nights*
- Aug. 24: *Love That Kills*
- Sept. 7: *Satan's Fury*
- Sept. 21: *Ebony Shrine*
- Oct. 5: *Jungle Terror*
- Oct. 19: *Gem of Agra*
- Nov. 2: *Sands of Egypt*
- Nov. 18: *Glory of Spain*
- Nov. 30: *Mystic Isles*
- Dec. 14: *Wizard Land*
- Dec. 28: *Spirit of Sho-Gun*

1931—
- Jan. 25: *Tale of Tutulia*
- Feb. 6: *Days of Solitude*
- Feb. 28: *The Well of Fortaleza*
- Mar. 8: *In the Shadow of the Dragon* (also listed as *Shadow of the Dragon*)

Mar. 22: *Thom the Unknown*
Apr. 7: *Call of Mohammed*
Apr. 21: *Hurricane Island*
July 27: *The Fallen Empire*
Aug. 24: *Beneath the Southern Cross*
Sept. 21: *Utmost Isle*
Oct. 19: *Song of the Voodoo*
Nov. 16: *Through the Age*
Dec. 21: *Children of the Sun*

1932—
Jan. 18: *The Land of Gandhi*
Feb. 22: *The Door of Asia*
Mar. 19: *Second Paradise*
Apr. 25: *Empire of the Sun*
May 23: *Shanghai*
June 18: *Drums of the Orient*
July 23: *Wild New Guinea*
Aug. 5: *Singapore*
Sept. 30: *Paris*
Nov. 25: *Malaysia*

1933—
Jan. 20: *Holland Mosaics*
Feb. 3: *Bali*
May 12: *Contrast in China*
Sept. 8: *Antwerp*
Nov. 10: *Cuba*

1934—
Jan. 12: *Moorish Spain* (Arcturus Pictures Corp.)
Feb. 16: *The Holy Land* (Arcturus Pictures Corp.)
Mar. 30: *Madeira, the Land of Wine* (Arcturus Pictures Corp.)
Apr. 2: *Gilbralatar, Guardian of the Mediterranean* (Arcturus Pictures Corp.)
June 8: *Damascus*
Aug. 9: *Eyes on Russia: From the Caucasus to Moscow*
Sept. 21: *Red Republic: From Baku to Dnieprostroi*
Dec. 7: *Fakeers of the East*

1935—
Jan. 11: *Isle of Spice*
Mar. 22: *The Saar*
May 17: *Jamaica*
Jun. 28: *Roumania*
Aug. 9: *Quebec*

Floyd Gibbons Supreme Thrills

Van Beuren Productions, released by RKO–Pathé. One reel each; sound.

1931—
Aug. 17: *Woodrow Wilson's Great Decision*
Sept. 14: *The Turn of the Tide*

Liberty Short Short Stories

Van Beuren Productions, released by RKO Radio. One reel each; sound.

1931—
Nov. 15: *Stung*
Dec. 12: *Ether Talks*
Dec. 16: *Double Decoy*

1932—
Feb. 13: *Endurance Flight*
Mar. 26: *Secretary Preferred*
Apr. 16: *Beautiful and Dumb*

Charlie Chaplin

Originally produced by Lone Star Productions and released by Mutual. Sound reissue versions produced by Van Beuren and released by RKO Radio. Two reels each; music and sound effects.

1932—
Aug. 19: *The Cure* (original release: Apr. 16, 1917)
Sept. 30: *Easy Street* (original release: Jan. 22, 1917)
Nov. 11: *The Rink* (original release: Dec. 4, 1916)
Dec. 30: *The Floorwalker* (original release: May 15, 1916)

1933—
Feb. 2: *The Vagabond* (original release: July 10, 1916)
Mar. 17: *The Pawnshop* (original release: Oct. 10, 1916)
Aug. 25: *The Fireman* (original release: June 12, 1916)
Nov. 17: *The Count* (original release: Sept. 4, 1916)

1934—
Jan. 19: *The Immigrant* (original release: June 17, 1917)
Mar. 23: *One A.M.* (original release: Aug. 7, 1916)

May 25: *Behind the Screen* (original release: Nov. 13, 1916)

July 5: *The Adventurer* (original release: Oct. 22, 1917)

THE VAN BEUREN MUSICAL COMEDIES

Produced by Meyer Davis–Van Beuren Productions, released by RKO Radio. Two reels; sound.

1933—
Nov. 17: *Hizzoner*
Dec. 8: *Strange Case of Hennessy*

1934—
Jan. 5: *Bubbling Over*
Jan. 26: *Henry the Ache*
Feb. 16: *Knife of the Party*
Mar. 9: *Everybody Likes Music*
Mar. 30: *No More West*
Apr. 20: *Sea Sore*

DUMB-BELL LETTERS

Van Beuren Productions, released by RKO Radio. 400–600 feet each; sound.

1934—
June 22: *Dumb-Bell Letters No. 1*
July 20: *Dumb-Bell Letters No. 2*
Aug. 17: *Dumb-Bell Letters No. 3*
Sept. 28: *Dumb-Bell Letters No. 4*
Oct. 26: *Dumb-Bell Letters No. 5*
Nov. 23: *Dumb-Bell Letters No. 6*
Dec. 21: *Dumb-Bell Letters No. 7*

1935—
Jan. 4: *Dumb-Bell Letters No. 8*
Jan. 18: *Dumb-Bell Letters No. 9*
Feb. 1: *Dumb-Bell Letters No. 10*
Feb. 15: *Dumb-Bell Letters No. 11*
Mar. 1: *Dumb-Bell Letters No. 12*
Mar. 15: *Dumb-Bell Letters No. 13*
Mar. 29: *Dumb-Bell Letters No. 14*
Apr. 12: *Dumb-Bell Letters No. 15*
Apr. 26: *Dumb-Bell Letters No. 16*
May 10: *Dumb-Bell Letters No. 17*
May 24: *Dumb-Bell Letters No. 18*
June 7: *Dumb-Bell Letters No. 19*
June 20: *Dumb-Bell Letters No. 20*

1936—
Jan. 3: *Dumb-Bell Letters No. 21*
Feb. 21: *Dumb-Bell Letters No. 22*
Apr. 3: *Dumb-Bell Letters No. 23*
May 29: *Dumb-Bell Letters No. 24*
July 10: *Dumb-Bell Letters No. 25*
July 18 [Copyright Date]: *Dumb-Bell Letters No. 26*

EASY ACES

Van Beuren Productions, released by RKO Radio. One reel each; sound.

1935—
Feb. 22: *Pharoahland* (Vagabond-Easy Aces Series #1)
Apr. 19: *Topnotchers* (Vagabond-Ace High Series #2)
June 14: *Little New New York* (Vagabond-Ace High Series #3)
July 26: *Six-Day Grand* (this and all subsequent entries are billed onscreen as part of the "Easy Aces" series)
Aug. 16: *Unusualities*
Aug. 30: *Jolly Ol' London*
Sept. 6: *Tricks of the Trade*
Oct. 4: *A Capitol Idea*
Nov. 1: *A World Within*
Nov. 29: *Etiquette*

1936—
Jan. 31: *Winter at the Zoo*
Feb. 28: *An Old-Fashioned Movie*
Mar. 27: *Debonair New Orleans*
May 22: *A Job's a Job*
June 9: *Fool Your Friends*

STRUGGLE TO LIVE

Van Beuren Productions, released by RKO Radio. One reel each; sound.

1935—
Aug. 16: *Neptune Mysteries*
Sept. 27: *Hermits of Crab-Land*
Nov. 8: *Beach Masters*

1936—
Feb. 14: *Winged Pageantry*
Apr. 17: *Underground Farmers*
June 12: *Living Jewels*

Sept. 18: *Swamp Land*
Nov. 13: *Deadly Females*
1937—
Jan. 8: *Forest Gangsters*
Apr. 16: *Desert Land*

Sports with Bill Corum

Van Beuren Productions, released by RKO Radio. One reel each; sound.

1935—
Aug. 16: *Inside the Ropes*
Oct. 11: *Bugles from the Blue Grass*
Dec. 13: *Gentlemen's Sports*
1936—
Jan. 24: *Tomorrow's Halfback*
Mar. 13: *Winter Sports*
Apr. 24: *Never Catch the Rabbit*
June 19: *Row, Mister, Row*
Sept. 4: *High, Wide and Dashing*
Oct. 2: *Pardon My Spray*
Oct. 29: *Goals for Gold and Glory*
Nov. 20: *Singing Wheels*
Dec. 18: *Ladies Day*
1937—
Jan. 15: *The Iceman*
Feb. 12: *Putting on the Dog*
Mar. 12: *Saratoga Summers*
Apr. 9: *Foreign Sports*
May 7: *Big League*
June 4: *Beach Sports*
July 2: *Royal Steeds*
July 23: *Golf Timing*

World on Parade

Van Beuren Productions, released by RKO Radio. One reel each; sound.

1935—
Aug. 23: *Land of the Eagle*
Oct. 18: *Spain's Romantic Isle*
Nov. 22: *Land of Evangeline*
1936—
Jan. 10: *Morocco*
Feb. 21: *Prominent Personalities*
Mar. 27: *Coral Isle of the Atlantic*
May 15: *Venice of the North*
Sept. 11: *Trinidad*
Oct. 9: *Washington in Virginia*
Nov. 6: *Heart of the Sierras*
Nov. 27: *Graveyard of Ships*
Dec. 25: *Gold Mania*
1937—
Jan. 22: *Romantic Mexico*
Feb. 19: *Manhattan Waterfront*
Mar. 19: *Mt. Vernon*
Apr. 16: *California Missions*
May 14: *Circus Winter Quarters* (reportedly the last entry filmed)
June 11: *Florida Cowboy*
July 9: *Workshops of Old Mexico*
July 30: *Jungle Playmates*

Miscellaneous

Van Beuren Productions for RCA-Photophone. One reel each; sound.

1929—
April: *The Swan* ("Walter Futter Overtures" series; originally tinted green)
[Release Date Unknown]: *Four in a Flat*

II. Animated Cartoons

(All dates are release dates, when known.)

Aesop's Fables

This series was also known as *Aesop's Modernized Fables*, *Aesop's Film Fables* and *Aesop's Sound Fables*. For the purposes of economy, the blanket title *Aesop's Fables* will apply to this filmography.

Fables Pictures Inc., for Pathé Release. Each cartoon runs 600–900 feet, or approximately 7–10 min. at sound speed. All entries are silent.

1921—
June 19: *The Goose That Laid the Golden Egg*
June 26: *Mice in Council*
July 3: *The Rooster and the Eagle*
July 10: *The Ants and the Grasshopper*
July 17: *Cats at Law*
July 24: *The Lioness and the Bugs*
July 31: *The Country Mouse and the City Mouse*
Aug. 7: *The Cat and the Canary*

Aug. 14: *The Fox and the Crow*
Aug. 21: *The Donkey and the Lion King*
Aug. 28: *Mice at War*
Sept. 4: *The Hare and the Frogs*
Sept. 11: *The Fashionable Fox*
Sept. 18: *The Hermit and the Bear*
Sept. 25: *The Hare and the Tortoise*
Oct. 2: *The Wolf and the Crane*
Oct. 9: *Venus and the Cat*
Oct. 16: *The Frog and the Ox*
Oct. 23: *The Dog and the Bone*
Oct. 30: *The Cat and the Monkey*
Nov. 6: *The Fox and the Goat*
Nov. 13: *The Owl and the Grasshopper*
Nov. 20: *The Woman and the Hen*
Nov. 27: *The Frogs That Wanted a King*
Dec. 4: *The Fly and the Ants*
Dec. 11: *The Conceited Donkey*
Dec. 18: *The Wolf and the Kid*
Dec. 25: *The Wayward Dog*

1922—
Jan. 1: *The Cat and the Mice*
Jan. 8: *The Dog and the Mosquito*
Jan. 15: *The Dog and the Flea*
Jan. 22: *The Bear and the Bees*
Jan. 29: *The Miller and the Donkey*
Feb. 5: *The Fox and the Grapes*
Feb. 12: *The Villain in Disguise*
Feb. 19: *The Dog and the Thief*
Feb. 26: *The Cat and the Swordfish*
Mar. 5: *The Tiger and the Donkey*
Mar. 12: *The Spendthrift*
Mar. 19: *The Farmer and the Ostrich*
Mar. 26: *The Dissatisfied Cobbler*
Mar. 30: *The Wolf in Sheep's Clothing*
Apr. 2: *The Lion and the Mouse*
Apr. 9: *The Rich Cat—and the Poor Cat*
Apr. 16: *The Wolf in Sheep's Clothing*
Apr. 23: *The Wicked Cat*
Apr. 30: *The Boy and His Dog*
May 5: *The Eternal Triangle*
May 14: *The Model Dairy*
May 21: *Love at First Sight*
May 28: *The Hunter and His Dog*
June 4: *The Dog and the Wolves*
June 11: *The Maid and the Millionaire*

June 18: *The Farmer and His Cat*
June 25: *The Cat and the Pig*
July 2: *The Country Mouse and the City Cat*
July 9: *Crime in a Big City*
July 16: *Brewing Trouble*
July 23: *The Mischievous Cat*
July 30: *The Worm That Turned*
Aug. 6: *The Boastful Cat*
Aug. 13: *The Dog and the Fish*
Aug. 20: *The Farmer and the Mice*
Aug. 27: *The Mechanical Horse*
Sept. 3: *Fearless Fido*
Sept. 10: *The Boy and the Bear*
Sept. 17: *The Two Explorers*
Sept. 24: *The Two Slick Traders*
Oct. 1: *The Big Flood*
Oct. 8: *The Fable of the Hated Rivals*
Oct. 15: *Two of a Trade*
Oct. 22: *The Romantic Mouse*
Oct. 29: *Henpecked Harry*
Nov. 5: *The Elephant's Trunk*
Nov. 12: *The Enchanted Fiddle*
Nov. 19: *A Rolling Stone*
Nov. 26: *The Fortune Hunter*
Dec. 3: *Friday The 13th*
Dec. 10: *The Man Who Laughs*
Dec. 17: *Henry's Busted Romance*
Dec. 24: *A Dog's Paradise*
Dec. 31: *The Two Trappers*

1923—
Jan. 7: *The Frog and the Catfish*
Jan. 14: *A Stone Age Romeo*
Jan. 21: *Cheating the Cheaters*
Jan. 28: *A Fisherman's Jinx*
Feb. 4: *A Raisin and a Cake of Yeast*
Feb. 11: *The Gliders*
Feb. 18: *Troubles on the Ark*
Feb. 25: *The Mysterious Hat*
Mar. 4: *The Spider and the Fly*
Mar. 11: *The Travelling Salesman*
Mar. 18: *The Sheik*
Mar. 25: *Farmer Al Falfa's Bride*
Apr. 8: *Day By Day—In Every Way*
Apr. 15: *One Hard Pull*
Apr. 22: *The Gamblers*

Apr. 29: *The Jolly Rounders*
May 6: *Pharoah's Tomb*
May 13: *The Mouse Catcher*
May 20: *A Fish Story*
May 27: *Amateur Night on the Ark*
June 3: *Spooks*
June 10: *The Stork's Mistake*
June 17: *Springtime*
June 24: *The Burglar Alarm*
July 1: *The Beauty Parlor*
July 8: *The Covered Push-Cart*
July 15: *The Pace That Kills*
July 22: *Mysteries of the Sea*
July 29: *The Thoroughbred*
Aug. 2: *Nine of Spades*
Aug. 5: *The Marathon Dancers*
Aug. 12: *The Pearl Divers*
Aug. 19: *The Bad Bandit*
Aug. 26: *The Great Explorers*
Sept. 2: *The Cat That Failed*
Sept. 9: *Walrus Hunters*
Sept. 16: *The Cat's Revenge*
Sept. 23: *Derby Day*
Sept. 30: *Love in a Cottage*
Oct. 7: *The Cat's Whiskers*
Oct. 14: *High Fliers*
Oct. 21: *Aged in the Wood*
Oct. 28: *The Circus*
Nov. 4: *Barnyard Romeo*
Nov. 11: *Do Women Pay?*
Nov. 18: *Farmer Al Falfa's Pet Cat*
Nov. 25: *Happy Go Luckies*
Dec. 2: *The Five Fifteen*
Dec. 9: *The Dark Horse*
Dec. 16: *The Cat Came Back*
Dec. 23: *The Good Old Days*
Dec. 30: *The Best Man Wins*

1924—
Jan. 6: *Five Orphans of the Storm*
Jan. 13: *Animals Fair*
Jan. 20: *The Black Sheep*
Jan. 27: *The Morning After*
Feb. 3: *A Rat's Revenge*
Feb. 10: *Good Old College Days*
Feb. 17: *A Rural Romance*
Feb. 24: *Captain Kidder*

Mar. 2: *Herman the Great Mouse*
Mar. 9: *An All Star Cast*
Mar. 16: *Why Mice Leave Home*
Mar. 23: *From Rags to Riches and Back Again*
Mar. 30: *The Champion*
Apr. 6: *Running Wild*
Apr. 13: *If Noah Lived Today*
Apr. 20: *A Trip to the Pole*
Apr. 27: *An Ideal Farm*
May 5: *Homeless Pups*
May 11: *When Winter Comes*
May 18: *The Jealous Fisherman*
May 25: *The Jolly Jail-Bird*
June 1: *One Good Turn*
June 8: *The Flying Carpet*
June 15: *That Old Can of Mine*
June 22: *The Organ Grinder*
June 29: *Home Talent*
July 6: *The Body in the Bag*
July 13: *Desert Sheiks*
July 20: *A Woman's Honor*
July 27: *The Sport of Kings*
Aug. 3: *Flying Fever*
Aug. 10: *Amelia Comes Back*
Aug.17: *House Cleaner*
Aug. 24: *The Prodigal Pup*
Aug. 31: *A Message from the Sea*
Sept. 7: *Barnyard Olympics*
Sept. 14: *In The Good Old Summertime*
Sept. 21: *The Mouse that Turned*
Sept. 28: *Hawks of the Sea*
Oct. 5: *Noah's Outing*
Oct. 12: *Lighthouse by the Sea*
Oct. 19: *Black Magic*
Oct. 26: *Monkey Business*
Nov. 2: *The Cat and the Magnet*
Nov. 9: *Sharp Shooters*
Nov. 16: *She Knew Her Man*
Nov. 23: *Good Old Circus Days*
Nov. 30: *Lumber Jacks*
Dec. 7: *She's in Again*
Dec. 14: *Noah's Athletic Club*
Dec. 21: *Mysteries of Old Chinatown*
Dec. 28: *Down on the Farm*

1925—

Jan. 4: *On the Ice*
Jan. 11: *One Game Pup*
Jan. 18: *African Huntsmen*
Jan. 25: *Hold That Thought*
Feb. 1: *Biting the Dust*
Feb. 8: *Transatlantic Flight*
Feb. 15: *Bigger and Better Jails*
Feb. 22: *Fisherman's Luck*
Mar. 1: *Clean-Up Week*
Mar. 8: *In Dutch*
Mar. 15: *Jungle Bike Riders*
Mar. 22: *The Pie Man*
Mar. 29: *Housing Shortage*
Apr. 5: *At the Zoo*
Apr. 12: *S.O.S.*
Apr. 19: *The Adventures of Adenoid*
Apr. 26: *Deep Stuff*
May 3: *Permanent Waves*
May 10: *Darkest Africa*
May 17: *A Fast Worker*
May 24: *Echoes from the Alps*
May 31: *Hot Times in Iceland*
June 7: *The Runt*
June 14: *The End of the World*
June 21: *Runaway Balloon*
June 28: *Office Help*
July 5: *Wine, Women and Song*
July 12: *When Men Were Men*
July 19: *For the Love of a Gal*
July 26: *Bugville Field Day*
Aug. 2: *Yarn about Yarn*
Aug. 9: *Bubbles*
Aug. 16: *Soap*
Aug. 23: *Over the Plate*
Aug. 30: *Window Washers*
Sept. 6: *Barnyard Follies*
Sept. 13: *The Ugly Duckling*
Sept. 20: *Nuts and Squirrels*
Sept. 27: *Hungry Hounds*
Oct. 4: *The Lion and the Monkey*
Oct. 11: *The Hero Wins*
Oct. 18: *Air-Cooled*
Oct. 25: *Closer Than a Brother*
Nov. 1: *Wild Cats of Paris*
Nov. 8: *The Honor System*
Nov. 15: *More Mice Than Brains*
Nov. 22: *The Great Open Spaces*
Nov. 29: *A Day's Outing*
Dec. 6: *The Bonehead Age*
Dec. 13: *The Haunted House*
Dec. 20: *The English Channel Swim*
Dec. 27: *Noah Had His Troubles*

1926—

Jan. 3: *The Gold Push*
Jan. 10: *Three Blind Mice*
Jan. 17: *Lighter Than Air*
Jan. 24: *The Little Brown Jug*
Jan. 31: *The June Bride*
Feb. 7: *The Wind Jammers*
Feb. 14: *Hunting in 1950*
Feb. 21: *The Wicked City*
Feb. 28: *The Mail Coach*
Mar. 7: *Spanish Love*
Mar. 14: *The Fire Fighters*
Mar. 28: *Fly Time*
Apr. 4: *The Merry Blacksmiths*
Apr. 11: *The Big Hearted Fish*
Apr. 18: *Hearts and Showers*
Apr. 25: *Rough and Ready Romeo*
May 2: *Farm Hands*
May 9: *The Shootin' Fool*
May 16: *The Alpine Flapper*
May 23: *Liquid Dynamite*
May 30: *The Bumper Crop*
June 6: *The Big Retreat*
June 13: *The Little Parade*
June 20: *The Land Boom*
June 27: *A Plumber's Life*
July 4: *Jungle Sports*
July 11: *Chop Suey and Noodles*
July 18: *Pirates Bold*
July 25: *Her Ben*
Aug. 1: *Venus of Venice*
Aug. 8: *Dough Boys*
Aug. 15: *The Last Ha Ha*
Aug. 22: *Scrambled Eggs*
Aug. 29: *A Knight Out*
Sept. 5: *Pests*
Sept. 11: *A Buggy Ride*
Sept. 19: *The Charleston Queen*
Sept. 26: *Watered Stock*

Oct. 3: *Why Argue?*
Oct. 10: *The Road House*
Oct. 17: *Phoney Express*
Oct. 24: *Gun Shy*
Oct. 31: *Home Sweet Home*
Nov. 7: *Thru Thick and Thin*
Nov. 14: *In Vaudeville*
Nov. 21: *Radio Controlled*
Nov. 28: *Buck Fever*
Dec. 5: *Hitting the Rails*
Dec. 12: *Bars and Stripes*
Dec. 19: *School Days*
Dec. 26: *Where Friendship Ceases*

1927—
Jan. 2: *The Musical Parrot*
Jan. 9: *Sink or Swim*
Jan. 16: *Chasing Rainbows*
Jan. 23: *The Plow Boy's Revenge*
Jan. 30: *Tit for Tat*
Feb. 6: *In the Rough*
Feb. 13: *The Crawl Stroke Kid*
Feb. 20: *The Mail Pilot*
Feb. 27: *Cracked Ice*
Mar. 6: *Taking the Air*
Mar. 13: *All for a Bride*
Mar. 20: *The Magician*
Mar. 27: *Keep Off the Grass*
Apr. 3: *The Medicine Man*
Apr. 10: *The Honor Man*
Apr. 17: *Anti-Fat*
Apr. 24: *Pie-Eyed Piper*
May 1: *A Fair Exchange*
May 10: *Bubbling Over*
May 17: *When Snow Flies*
May 24: *Horses, Horses, Horses*
May 31: *Digging for Gold*
June 7: *A Dog's Day*
June 14: *Hard Cider*
June 21: *Died in the Wool*
June 28: *One Man Dog*
July 3: *Big Reward*
July 10: *Riding High*
July 17: *The Love Nest*
July 24: *Subway Sally*
July 31: *The Bully*
Aug. 7: *Ant Life as It Isn't*

Aug. 14: *Red Hot Sands*
Aug. 21: *A Hole in One*
Aug. 28: *Hook, Line and Sinker*
Sept. 4: *Small Town Sheriff*
Sept. 11: *Cutting a Melon*
Sept. 18: *In Again, Out Agin*
Sept. 25: *Human Fly*
Oct. 2: *River of Doubt*
Oct. 9: *All Bull and a Yard Wide*
Oct. 16: *Lindy's Cat*
Oct. 23: *The Big Tent*
Oct. 30: *Brave Heart*
Nov. 6: *Signs of Spring*
Nov. 13: *Saved by a Keyhole*
Nov. 20: *The Fox Hunt*
Nov. 27: *Flying Fishers*
Dec. 4: *Carnival Week*
Dec. 11: *Rats in His Garrett*
Dec. 18: *Christmas Cheer*
Dec. 25: *The Junk Man*

1928—
Jan. 1: *The Broncho Buster*
Jan. 8: *A Short Circuit*
Jan. 15: *High Stakes*
Jan. 22: *The Boy Friend*
Jan. 29: *The Wandering Minstrel*
Feb. 5: *The Good Ship Nellie*
Feb. 12: *Everybody's Flying*
Feb. 19: *The Spider's Lair*
Feb. 26: *A Blaze of Glory*
Mar. 4: *The County Fair*
Mar. 11: *On the Ice*
Mar. 18: *The Son Shower*
Mar. 25: *Jungle Days*
Apr. 1: *Scaling the Alps*
Apr. 8: *Barnyard Lodge Number One*
Apr. 15: *A Battling Duet*
Apr. 22: *The Flying Age*
Apr. 29: *Barnyard Artists*
May 6: *A Jungle Triangle*
May 13: *Coast to Coast*
May 20: *War Bride*
May 27: *Happy Days*
June 3: *The Flight That Failed*
June 10: *Puppy Love*
June 17: *Ride 'Em Cowboy*

June 24: *The Mouse's Bride*
July 1: *City Slickers*
July 8: *The Huntsman*
July 15: *The Baby Show*
July 22: *The Early Bird*
July 29: *Outnumbered*
Aug. 5: *Our Little Nell*
Aug. 12: *Sunny Italy*
Aug. 19: *A Cross Country Run*
Aug. 26: *In the Bag*
Sept. 9: *Alaska or Bust*
Sept. 16: *Sunday on the Farm*
Sept. 23: *High Seas*
Sept. 30: *The Magnetic Bat*
Oct. 7: *Kill or Cure*
Oct. 14: *Monkey Love*
Oct. 21: *Big Game*
Oct. 28: *Gridiron Demons*
Nov. 4: *Laundry Man*
Nov. 11: *Caught in the Draft*
Nov. 18: *A Polar Flight*
Nov. 25: *On the Links*
Dec. 2: *The Fishing Fool*
Dec. 9: *Day Off*
Dec. 16: *Barnyard Politics*
Dec. 23: *Flying Hoofs*
Dec. 30: *Mail Man*

1929—
Jan. 6: *Land O' Cotton*
Jan. 13: *A White Elephant*
Jan. 20: *Snapping the Whip*
Jan. 27: *The Break of Day*
Feb. 3: *Sweet Adeline*
Feb. 10: *Wooden Money*
Feb. 17: *The Queen Bee*
Feb. 24: *Grandma's House*
Mar. 3: *Back to the Soil*
Mar. 10: *A Lad and His Lamp*
Mar. 17: *The Black Duck*
Mar. 24: *The Big Burg* (also listed as *The Big City*)
Mar. 31: *The Under Dog*
Apr. 7: *The Cop's Bride*
Apr. 14: *The Water Cure*
Apr. 21: *The Big Shot*
Apr. 28: *The Fight Game*

May 5: *The Little Game Hunter*
May 19: *The Ball Park*
May 26: *Fish Day*
June 2: *The Polo Match*
June 9: *Snow Birds*
June 15: *April Showers*
June 23: *Kidnapped*
June 30: *In His Cups*
July 7: *Cold Steel*
July 28: *A Midsummer's Day Dream*
Aug. 4: *Three Game Guys*
Aug. 11: *The Enchanted Flute*
Aug. 14: *The Cabaret*
Aug. 22: *The Fruitful Farm*

Van Beuren Productions, released by Pathé between 1928 and 1930, and by RKO-Pathé and RKO Radio between 1931 and 1934. Each cartoon runs 600–900 feet, or approximately 7–10 min. All entries are sound.

1928—
Oct. 14: *Dinner Time*
Dec. 23: *Stage Struck*

1929—
Apr. 14: *Presto-Chango*
Apr. 28: *Skating Hounds*
May 12: *Faithful Pup*
May 26: *Custard Pies*
June 9: *Wood Choppers*
June 21: *Concentrate*
June 22: *The Jail Breakers*
July 4: *Bug House College Days*
July 21: *House Cleaning Time*
Aug. 18: *A Stone Age Romance*
Sept. 1: *The Big Scare* (last Aesop's Fable crediting Paul Terry)
Sept. 15: *Jungle Fool* (first Aesop's Fable produced solely by Van Beuren)
Sept. 29: *The Fly's Bride*
Oct. 13: *Summer Time*
Oct. 27: *Mill Pond*
Nov. 1: *Barnyard Melody*
Nov. 10: *Tuning In*
Dec. 8: *Night Club*
Dec. 21: *A Close Call*

1930—
- Jan. 5: *Ship Ahoy*
- Jan. 19: *The Iron Man*
- Feb. 2: *Singing Saps*
- Feb. 16: *Sky Skippers*
- Mar. 2: *Good Old School Days*
- Mar. 16: *Foolish Follies*
- Mar. 30: *Dixie Days*
- Apr. 13: *Western Whoopee*
- Apr. 27: *The Haunted Ship*
- May 11: *Oom Pah Pah*
- May 25: *Noah Knew His Ark*
- June 8: *Bugville Romance*
- June 22: *A Romeo Robin*
- July 6: *Jungle Jazz*
- July 20: *Snow Time*
- Aug. 3: *Hot Tamale*
- Aug. 17: *Laundry Blues*
- Aug. 31: *Frozen Frolics*
- Sept. 14: *Farm Foolery*
- Sept. 28: *Circus Capers*
- Oct. 12: *Midnight*
- Oct. 26: *The Big Cheeze*
- Nov. 9: *Gypped in Egypt*
- Nov. 22: *The Office Boy*
- Dec. 7: *Stone Age Stunts*
- Dec. 21: *King of Bugs*

1931—
- Jan. 4: *A Toy Town Tale* (reissued as *A Toyland Adventure*)
- Jan. 18: *Red Riding Hood*
- Feb. 1: *The Animal Fair*
- Feb. 15: *Cowboy Blues*
- Mar. 1: *The Radio Racket*
- Mar. 15: *College Capers*
- Mar. 29: *Old Hokum Bucket*
- Apr. 12: *Cinderella Blues*
- Apr. 26: *Mad Melody*
- May 10: *The Fly Guy*
- May 24: *Play Ball*
- June 13: *Fisherman's Luck*
- June 27: *False Face Pup*
- July 5: *Making 'Em Move* (reissued as *In a Cartoon Studio*)
- July 19: *Fun On the Ice*
- Aug. 3: *Big Game*
- Aug. 17: *Love in a Pond*
- Aug. 31: *Fly High*
- Sept. 14: *The Family Shoe* (reissued as *The Golden Goose*)
- Sept. 28: *Fairyland Follies*
- Oct. 12: *Horse Cops*
- Oct. 26: *Cowboy Cabaret*
- Nov. 9: *In Dutch*
- Nov. 23: *The Last Dance*

1932—
- Jan. 27: *Toy Time*
- Feb. 20: *A Romeo Monk*
- Mar. 5: *Fly Frolic*
- Mar. 26: *The Cat's Canary*
- Apr. 25: *Magic Art*
- May 14: *Happy Polo*
- May 21: *Spring Antics*
- June 11: *The Farmerette*
- June 25: *Circus Romance*
- July 9: *Stone Age Error*
- July 23: *Chinese Jinks*
- July 30: *The Ball Game*
- Aug. 12: *Wild Goose Chase*
- Aug. 23: *Nursery Scandal*
- Sept. 9: *Bring 'Em Back Half-Shot*
- Sept. 23: *Down in Dixie*
- Oct. 7: *Catfish Romance*
- Oct. 21: *Feathered Follies*
- Nov. 4: *Venice Vamp*
- Dec. 2: *Pickaninny Blues* (reissued as *Uncle Tom and Little Eva*)
- Dec. 16: *A Yarn of Wool*
- Dec. 30: *Bugs and Books*

1933—
- Jan. 13: *Silvery Moon* (reissued as *Candy Town*)
- Jan. 27: *Tumble Down Town*
- Feb. 10: *Opening Night* (first appearance of Cubby Bear. Originally filmed to run exclusively at New York's Roxy Theater as part of its opening-night program on Dec. 29, 1932. Hand-colored sequence.)
- Feb. 24: *Panicky Pup*
- Mar. 10: *Love's Labor Won* (starring Cubby Bear)
- Mar. 24: *The Last Mail* (starring Cubby Bear)
- Apr. 17: *Runaway Blackie*

Apr. 28: *Bubbles and Troubles* (starring Cubby Bear)

May 5: *A Busy Day* (starring Sentinel Louey)

May 18: *Barking Dogs* (starring Cubby Bear)

June 16: *The Bully's End*

July 7: *Indian Whoopee* (starring Cubby Bear)

July 12: *Fresh Ham* (starring Cubby Bear)

July 14: *Rough on Rats* (reissued as *Scat Cats*)

July 28: *A.M. to P.M.* (starring Sentinel Louey)

Aug. 11: *The Nut Factory* (starring Cubby Bear)

Aug. 25: *Cubby's World Flight* (starring Cubby Bear. Produced by Harman-Ising. Also listed as *World Flight*.)

Oct. 6: *Cubby's Picnic* (starring Cubby Bear. Reissued as *Picnic Problems*)

Nov. 3: *The Gay Gaucho* (starring Cubby Bear. Produced by Harman-Ising)

Dec. 1: *Galloping Fanny* (starring Cubby Bear. Reissued as *Galloping Hooves*)

Dec. 29: *Croon Crazy* (starring Cubby Bear)

1934—

Jan. 26: *Sinister Stuff* (starring Cubby Bear. Reissued as *Villain Pursues Her*)

Feb. 23: *Goode Knight* (starring Cubby Bear)

Mar. 23: *How's Crops?* (starring Cubby Bear. Reissued as *Brownie's Victory Garden*)

Apr. 20: *Cubby's Stratospheric Flight*

May 18: *Mild Cargo* (starring Cubby Bear. Reissued as *Brownie Bucks the Jungle*)

June 15: *Fiddlin' Fun* (starring Cubby Bear)

Tom and Jerry
Van Beuren Productions, released by RKO-Pathé and RKO Radio. 600–900 feet each; sound.

1931—

Aug. 1: *Wot a Night!*
Sept. 5: *Polar Pals*
Oct. 10: *Trouble*
Nov. 14: *Jungle Jam*
Dec. 19: *A Swiss Trick*

1932—

Jan. 30: *Rocketeers*
Feb. 27: *Rabid Hunters*
Mar. 26: *In the Bag*
Apr. 23: *Joint Wipers*
May 14: *Pots and Pans*
June 4: *The Tuba Tooter*
June 25: *Plane Dumb*
July 23: *Redskin Blues*
Aug. 19: *Jolly Fish*
Sept. 16: *Barnyard Bunk*
Oct. 7: *A Spanish Twist* (brief color sequence)
Nov. 11: *Piano Tooners*
Dec. 9: *Pencil Mania*

1933—

Jan. 6: *Tight Rope Tricks*
Feb. 7: *The Magic Mummy*
Mar. 31: *Happy Hoboes*
Apr. 14: *Puzzled Pals*
Apr. 28: *Hook & Ladder Hokum* (reissued as *Fire Fire*)
May 26: *In the Park*
July 10: *Doughnuts*
July 31: *The Phantom Rocket*

The Little King
Van Beuren Productions, released by RKO Radio. 600–900 feet each; sound.

1933—

Sept. 29: *The Fatal Note*
Oct. 27: *Marching Along*
Nov. 24: *On the Pan*
Dec. 22: *Pals* (reissued as *Christmas Night*)

1934—

Jan. 19: *Jest of Honor*
Feb. 16: *Jolly Good Felons*
Mar. 16: *Sultan Pepper*
Apr. 13: *A Royal Good Time*
May 11: *Art for Art's Sake*
June 8: *Cactus King*

Amos 'n' Andy
Van Beuren Productions, released by RKO Radio. One reel each; sound.

1934—

Jan. 5: *The Rasslin' Match*
Feb. 2: *The Lion Tamer*

TODDLE TALES

Van Beuren Productions, released by RKO Radio. One reel each; sound.

1934—

June 29: *Grandfather's Clock*

Aug. 10: *Along Came a Duck*

Sept. 7: *A Little Bird Told Me* (last black-and-white cartoon)

THE RAINBOW PARADES

Van Beuren Productions, released by RKO Radio. 600–900 feet each; sound. All cartoons listed are in color.

1934—

July 27: *Pastry Town Wedding* (first Cinecolor Cartoon)

Sept. 14: *The Parrotville Fire Department*

1935—

Jan. 11: *The Sunshine Makers*

Jan. 25: *Parrotville Old Folks*

Mar. 8: *Japanese Lanterns* (reissued as *Chinese Lanterns*)

Apr. 5: *Spinning Mice* (originally produced as a "Toddle Tale")

May 3: *Picnic Panic* (originally produced as a "Toddle Tale")

May 31: *The Foxy Terrier*

May 31: *The Merry Kittens*

June 28: *Parrotville Post Office*

July 19: *Rag Dog* (reissued as the *Three Little Kittens*)

Aug. 19: *The Hunting Season* (starring Molly Moo Cow)

Aug. 23: *Scottie Finds a Home*

Sept. 20: *Bird Scouts* (last Cinecolor Cartoon)

Nov. 15: *Molly Moo Cow and the Indians* (first Technicolor Cartoon)

Nov. 15: *Molly Moo Cow and the Butterflies*

Dec. 17: *Molly Moo Cow and Rip Van Winkle*

1936—

Jan. 17: *Toonerville Trolley*

Feb. 7: *Felix the Cat and The Goose That Laid the Golden Eggs*

Feb. 28: *Molly Moo Cow and Robinson Crusoe*

Mar. 20: *Neptune Nonsense* (starring Felix the Cat)

May 29: *Bold King Cole* (starring Felix the Cat)

June 19: *A Waif's Welcome*

July 3: *Troller Ahoy* (Toonerville Folks)

July 24: *Cupid Gets His Man*

Aug. 2: *It's a Greek Life*

Oct. 2: *Toonerville Picnic*

III. Feature Films

BRING 'EM BACK ALIVE

A Van Beuren Production, released Aug. 19, 1932, by RKO. Directed by Clyde E. Elliott. Screenplay by Frank Buck and Edward S. Anthony, from their book of the same name. Cinematography by Carl Berger and Nicholas Cavaliere. Music by Gene Rodemich. Sound engineer, Paul M. Robillard. Sound effects, Leonard Mitchell and Donald Bain. 65 minutes. Sound.

Cast: Frank Buck, Dahlam Ali (Themselves).

WILD CARGO

A Van Beuren Production, released Apr. 6, 1934, by RKO. Directed by Armand Denis. Adapted From their book by Frank Buck and Edward S. Anthony. Dialogue and Narration by Courtney Ryley Cooper. Cinematography by Nicholas Cavaliere and Leroy G. Phelps. Editorial supervision by Sam B. Jacobson. Music by Winston Sharples. 96 minutes (original release). Sound.

Cast: Frank Buck, Dahlam Ali, The Sultan of Ibrahim (Themselves).

ADVENTURE GIRL

A Van Beuren Production, released Aug. 17, 1934, by RKO. Directed by Herman C. Raymaker. Narration script by Ferrin Frazier, from the novel by Joan Lowell. Cinematography by Harry E. Squire. Editorial supervision by Sam B. Jacobson. Music by Winston Sharples. Sound engineers, Larry Lynn and Al Sinton. Fire sequence tinted by Gustav Brock. "Grateful Acknowledgment" to Gen. Jorge Ubico, President of the Republic of Guatemala. 65 minutes (original release). Sound.

Cast: Joan Lowell, Capt. Nicholas Wagner, Bill "Leatherneck" Sawyer, Otto Siegler (Themselves); Ula Holt (Princess Maya).

FANG AND CLAW

A Van Beuren Production, released Dec. 20, 1935, by RKO. Directed by Frank Buck. Adapted from the book by Frank Buck and Ferrin Frazer. Cinematography by Nicholas Cavaliere and Harry E. Squire. Edited by Horace and Stacy Woodard. Music by Winston Sharples. 73 Minutes. Sound.

Cast: Frank Buck, Dahlam Ali, Harry E. Squire (Themselves).

IV. Serial

THE LAST FRONTIER

A Van Beuren Production, released Sept. 5, 1932, by RKO. Produced by Fred J. McConnell. Directed by Spencer Gordon Bennet and Thomas L. Story. Screenplay by George Plympton, Robert F. Hill and Carl Coolidge, from the novel by Courtney Ryley Cooper. Dialogue by Arthur Rohlsfel. Cinematography by Edward Snyder and Gil Warrenton. Edited by Thomas Malloy. Art direction by E.E. Sheeler. Assistant Director, Theodore Joos. 213 minutes; 12 chapters, each between 16 and 20 minutes. Also released in a 55-minute feature version titled *The Black Ghost*.

Chapter Titles: *The Black Ghost Rides, The Thundering Herd, The Black Ghost Strikes, The Fatal Shot, Clutching Hands, The Terror Trail, Doomed, Facing Death, Thundering Doom, The Life Line, Driving Danger, The Black Ghost's Last Ride.*

Cast: Creighton Chaney [Lon Chaney, Jr.] (Tom Kirby, a.k.a. The Black Ghost); Dorothy Gulliver (Betty Halliday); Francis X. Bushman, Jr. (Jeff Maitland); William Desmond (Gen. Custer); Joe Bonomo (Henchman Joe/Stunts); Pete Morrison (Henchman Hank); Leroy Mason (Henchman Buck); Yakima Canutt (Wild Bill/Stunts); Mary Jo Desmond (Aggie Kirby); King Cole (Uncle Happy); Richard Neill (Lige Morris); Judith Barrie (Rose Maitland); Claude Peyton (Col. Halliday); Ben Corbett (Bad Ben/Stunts); Frank Lackteen (Chief Pawnee Blood); Fritzi Fern (Mariah); Bob Burns (Doctor); Fred Burns (Fred); Tommy Coats (Jake/Stunts); Bill Nestell (Tex); Black Jack Ward, Wes Warner (Miners); Leo Cooper, Walt Robbins, Ray Steel (Riders);Thomas L Story (Irishman); Jack Evans (Henchman); Ken Cooper, Francis Walker (Stunts).

Selected Bibliography

Books

Andrews, Craig L. *Broken Toys: A Man's Dream, a Company's Mystery*. Bloomington, IN: AuthorHouse, 2002.

Ankerich, Michael G. *Broken Silence: Conversations with 23 Silent Film Stars*. Jefferson, NC: McFarland, 1993.

Barbour, Alan G. *Days of Thrills and Adventure*. Introduction by William K. Everson. New York: Collier Books, 1970.

Becker, Stephen. *Comic Art in America: A Social History of the Funnies, the Political Cartoons, Magazine Humor, Sporting Cartoons, and Animated Cartoons*. Introduction by Rube Goldberg. New York: Simon & Schuster, 1959.

Bogle, Donald. *Heat Wave: The Life and Career of Ethel Waters*. New York: HarperCollins, 2011.

Bourke-White, Margaret. *Portrait of Myself*. New York: Simon & Schuster, 1963.

Bousé, Derek. *Wildlife Films*. Philadelphia: University of Pennsylvania Press, 2000.

Brownlow, Kevin. *The War, the West and the Wilderness*. New York: Knopf, 1979.

Buck, Frank. *Bring 'Em Back Alive: The Best of Frank Buck*. Edited and with an introduction by Steven Lehrer. Lubbock: Texas Tech University Press, 2000.

_____, and Ferrin L. Fraser. *All in a Lifetime*. New York: R.M. McBride & Co, 1941.

Crawford, Richard W. *The Way We Were in San Diego*. Charleston, SC: The History Press, 2011.

Dunning, John. *On the Air: The Encyclopedia of Old-Time Radio*. New York: Oxford University Press, 1998.

Ford, Corey. *The Time of Laughter*. Introduction by Frank Sullivan. Boston: Little, Brown, 1967.

Fountain, Charles. *Sportswriter: The Life and Times of Grantland Rice*. New York: Oxford University Press, 1993.

Franklin, Joe. *Classics of the Silent Screen: A Pictorial History*. Research assistant, William K. Everson. New York: Citadel, 1959.

Gibbons, Floyd. *And They Thought We Wouldn't Fight*. New York: George H. Doran Co., 1918.

Goulart, Ron, editor. *The Encyclopedia of American Comics: From 1897 to the Present*. New York: Facts on File Inc., 1990.

Gudis, Catherine. *Buyways, Billboards, Automobiles and the American Landscape*. New York: Routledge, 2005.

Hampton, Benjamin. *A History of the Movies*. New York: Covici-Friede, 1931.

Hayde, Michael. *Chaplin's Vintage Year: The History of the Mutual-Chaplin Specials*. Orlando, FL: BearManor Media, 2016.

Horn, Maurice, editor. *100 Years of American Newspaper Comics*. New York: Random House, 1996.

Inabinett, Mark. *Grantland Rice and His Heroes: The Sportswriter as Mythmaker in the 1920s*. Knoxville: University of Tennessee Press, 1994.

Jewell, Richard B. with Vernon Harbin. *The RKO Story*. New York: Arlington House, 1982.

Lahr, John. *Notes on a Cowardly Lion*. New York: Knopf, 1969.

Lowell, Joan. *The Cradle of the Deep*. New York: Simon & Schuster, 1929.

Lowell, Juliet. *Dumb Belles-Lettres: Lallapaloozas from the Morning Mails*. Illustrations by [Otto] Soglow. New York: Simon and Schuster, 1933.

Maltin, Leonard. *The Great Movie Shorts: Those Wonderful One- and Two-Reelers of the Thirties and Forties*. Foreword by Pete Smith. New York: Crown Publishing, 1972.

_____. *Of Mice and Magic: A History of American Animated Cartoons, Revised and Updated Edition*. New York: Plume, 1987.

Mitchell, Glenn. *A-Z of Film Comedy: An Illustrated Companion*. Foreword by Kevin Brownlow. London: B.T. Batsford Ltd., 1998.

_____. *The Chaplin Encyclopedia*. London: B.T. Batsford Ltd. 1997.

Pitts, Michael R. *Poverty Row Studios, 1929–1940*. Jefferson, NC: McFarland, 1997.

_____. *RKO Radio Pictures Horror, Science Fiction and Fantasy Films, 1929–1956*. Jefferson, NC: McFarland, 2015.

Rice, Grantland. *The Tumult and the Shouting: My Life in Sport*. New York: A.S. Barnes, 1954.

Roberts, Randy. *Joe Louis*. New Haven: Yale University Press, 2010.

Temple, Olivia and Robert Temple (translators). *Aesop, The Complete Fables*. New York: Penguin Classics, 1998.

Magazine and Newspaper Articles

Abelli, Albert. "How Frank Buck Filmed His Tiger-Python Battle." *Modern Mechanix*, November 1932.

Beauchamp, Cari. "The Mogul Mr. Kennedy." *Vanity Fair*, April 2002.

Breslin, Jimmy. "The Art of the Trump: Call It Corum's Law." *Newsday*, June 7, 1990.

Cacho, Shannel. "The History of the Kentucky Derby," Horse Racing Radio Network website, May 2019. http://horseracingradio.net/post/history-kentucky-derby

Chesnut, Alma. "Joan Lowell, Ex-Sailor, Running Farm in Pennsylvania." *Pittsburgh Press*, March 17, 1930.

Clark, Bill. "History Forgets Bill Corum, Sports/Radio Personality." *Columbia [MO] Tribune*, December 17, 2008.

Colby, Anne. "Meet the Grandmother of Memoir Fabricators." *Los Angeles Times*, March 14, 2008.

French, Brett. "First Director of Wyoming Museum was a Wild Adventurer, Well-Known Western Art Scholar." *Billings [MT] Gazette*, July 5, 2017.

Klein, Isadore. "Cartooning Down Broadway." *Film Comment* XI, No. 1. January–February 1975.

Simkin, John. "Floyd Gibbons." Spartacus Educational website. No date. https://spartacus-educational.com/Jgibbons.htm

Skorobogatov, Yana. "How a Photographer Captured the USSR's Dramatic Rise as the US Economy Tanked." *Time*, August 28, 2015.

Dissertation

Harmonic, Wynn Gerald (Doctor of Philosophy): "'Disney Is the Tiffany's and I Am the Woolworth's of the Business': A Critical Re-Analysis of the Business Philosophies, Production Values and Studio Practices of Animator-Producer Paul Houlton Terry." School of Arts, Brunel University. June 2011.

Newspapers, Periodicals, In-House Publications, Yearbooks, Catalogs

Advertising: An Illustrated Monthly for Business Men, Vol. 9 (1896)
American Cinematographer
The Billboard
Boxoffice
Broadcasting
Business Screen
Cinematographic Annual
The Educational Screen
Entertainment Films 16mm Sound: Walter O. Gutlohn.
Exhibitors Daily Review
Exhibitors Herald-World
Exhibitors Trade Review
Film Daily
Film Mercury
Greater New York
Harrison's Reports
Harvard Business Review (1930)
Heinl Radio Business Letter (1935)
The Hollywood Reporter
Kodascope Library (various editions)
Larchmont [NY] Times
The Literary Digest
Motion Picture Daily
Motion Picture News
Motion Picture Reviews
Motography
Moving Picture World
National Board of Review magazine
The New Movie magazine
New York Clipper
The New York Exhibitor
Nitrateville
Ocala (FL) Star-Banner
Paramount Exhibitor's Pressbooks (1919)
Patent and Trade Mark Review Vol. XXI (1923)
Pathé Club Yearbook of 1927
The Pathé Sun
The Philadelphia Exhibitor
Photoplay
Polk's New York Copartnership and Corporation Directory: Vol 63 (1915)
The Poster
Radio Digest
San Diego (CA) Union-Tribune
Variety
What's on the Air
Wid's Daily

Internet Sources

British Pathé Historical Collection https://www.britishpathe.com/
Cartoon Research https://cartoonresearch.com/
Don Markstein's Toonopedia http://www.toonopedia.com/
The Files of Jerry Blake https://filesofjerryblake.com/
Greenbriar Picture Shows http://greenbriarpictureshows.blogspot.com/
Internet Archive https://archive.org/
Internet Movie Database https://www.imdb.com/
MousePlanet https://www.mouseplanet.com/
New-York Historical Society https://www.nyhistory.org/
1939 World's Fair Website http://www.1939nyworldsfair.com/worlds_fair/wf_tour/zone-7/jungle_land.htm
Nitrateville https://www.nitrateville.com/
The Retro Set http://theretroset.com/
ThreeStoogesNet https://www.threestooges.net/
Tralfaz https://tralfaz.blogspot.com/

Index

Numbers in *bold italics* indicate pages with illustrations

A. Van Beuren & Company 5
A. Van Beuren Bill Posters *and* Van Beuren & Pratt *see* A. Van Beuren & Company 5
Abbott and Costello 141
Abelli, Alfred 132
Ace, Goodman 17, 107, 193–195, *195*, 196
Ace, Jane 17, 107, 193, 193–195, *195*, 196
Ace High and *Vagabond-Ace High* (film series) see *Easy Aces* (Van Beuren film series)
Adventure Girl see Lowell, Joan
The Adventures of Chico (film) 203; see also Woodard, Horace; Woodard, Stacy
Aesop 47
Aesop's Film Fables (silent): 10, *11*, 12, *15*, 36, 43, 45, 47–49, 52, 53, 57, 95; individual film titles (in release order): *The Goose That Laid the Golden Egg* 48, 49, *50–51*; *The Lioness and the Bugs* 48; *The Mice in Council* 48; *The Rooster and the Eagle* 48; *The Frogs That Wanted a King* 48; *Day by Day—In Every Way* 52; *The Covered Pushcart* 52; *The Land Boom* 52; *The Last Ha-Ha* 52; *Bronco Buster* 54
Aesop's Sound Fables (sound): 14, 15, *15*, 17, 55, 57, 58, 60, 95, 108, 109, 113, 114, 133, 142 Individual film titles (in release order): *Dinner Time* 14, 53; *Jungle Fools* 15, 55; *A Close Call* 56; *The Haunted Ship* 57; *Jungle Jazz* 57; *Circus Capers* *56*; *Gypped in Egypt* 57; *The Office Boy* 56; *Red Riding Hood* 58; *Making 'Em Move* 58; *Happy Polo* 58; *The Ball Game* 58; *Bring 'Em Back Half-Shot* 133; *Silvery Moon* *59*, 60; *Rough on Rats* 60; starring Cubby Bear (in release order): *Opening Night* 111–112; *Love's Labor Won* 112; *The Last Mail* 112; *Barking Dogs* 112; *Fresh Ham* 112, *113*; *World Flight* 112, 113; *The Gay Gaucho* 112; *Croon Crazy* 113; *Sinister Stuff* 112; *How's Crops?* 113; *Mild Cargo* 113; *Fiddlin' Fun* 60; starring Sentinel Louey (in release order): *A Dizzy Day* 114; *A.M. to P.M.* 114
Africa Speaks (film) 78, 128
Aitken, Harry A. 7
Albee, Edward Franklin 9, 10, 12, *13*, 14, 61, 81
Albee, Reed 81
Ali, Dahlam 129, 139
All in a Lifetime (book) 128; see also Buck, Frank
Allen, Ross 69
Allisen, David 198
The Ambassador (comic strip) see *The Little King* (comic strip)
American Cinematographer magazine 96–97
The Americans Come (film) 96
Amos 'n' Andy: Radio series) 115, 116, 175; cartoon series 115–116, 118; individual film titles (in release order): *The Rasslin' Match* 116, *117*; *The Lion Tamer* 116
Anderson, Broncho Billy 151–152
Andrews, Frank 38
Anthony, Edward 127, 134
Anthony, Norman 125
Appleby, Edgar T. 206
Arcturus Pictures Corporation 104, 105; see also *Vagabond Adventures*
Armstrong, Robert 66
Arrow Films 65
Artclass Pictures 65
Associate Animators 175
Ates, Roscoe 124
Audioscopiks (film) 211
Auer, Florence 168
AyVeeBee Productions 9, 11, 41, 61, 80, 81; *see also* Van Beuren Corporation

Baby Rose Marie 159, 167
Baer, Max 206
Bailey, Harry 54, 55
Bain, Donald 129
Baird, Leah 62, *63*
Baker, Phil 168
Bakewell, William 140
Bankhead, Tallulah 198
Barbera, Joseph 176
Barbour, Alan G. 154
"Barney Google" (comic strip) 74
Barré, Raoul 54
Barrett, Alfred M. 7
Barrie, Judith 153
Barron, John Francis 92
Barrymore family 23
Barty, Billy 85
Battle for Life (film series) 138, 199–200; see also *Struggle to Live* (film series)
Beatty, Clyde 133, 141
Becker, Stephen 79
Beery, Noah 66
Bellaver, Harry 122
Belmont, Joseph "Baldy" 82, 88
Bennet, Spencer Gordon 151–152
Bennett, Lois 93, 94
Bergen, Edgar 81
Berger, Carl 129, 132
Berkeley Gazette 186
Berndt, Walter 14, 79, 80, 82, 83
Betty Boop 110, 115
Bevan, Billy 85, 88
Beverly Hills Productions 103
Beyond the Frozen Frontier (book) 209; see also McCracken, Harold
The Big Show (radio series) 198
Bill Corum Sports Review and *Inside Sports with Bill Corum* see *Sports with Bill Corum*
"Bill the Office Boy" see *Smitty* (comic strip)
The Billboard 5
Biograph Studios 26, 167, 168, 194
Black, Frank 68, 91, 94
Black, Maurice 124
The Black Ghost (film) see *The Last Frontier* (serial)
Black Hawk (schooner) see Lowell, Joan
Blackhawk Films 149

235

Blumenthal, Ben 144, 148
Bonafield, Jay 140
Bonomo, Joe 153
Borden's Dairy Products 177
Boring, James W. 104, 105
Bosko 112; *see also* Harman-Ising
Boston Globe 31
Bostwick, G.H. "Pete" 206
The Bounty Killer 151
Bourke-White, Margaret 106–107, ***107***, 212
Bousé, Derek 134
Bow, Clara 96
Bowers, Charlie 54
Boxoffice magazine 214
Boyd, William 151
Braddock, Jim 206
Bray, John R. 46, 47, 52, 53, 55
Breslin, Jimmy 205
Bring 'Em Back Alive (film) *see* Buck, Frank
British Pathé Historical Collection 75
Brix, Herman [aka Bruce Bennett] 192
Brock, Gustav F.O. 111, 191
Brock, Lou 150
Broun, Heywood 187
Brown, Beth 75
Brown, George 154
Brown, Joe E. 161
Brown, Johnny Mack 103, 151
Brunet, Andre 33
Buchanan, Thompson 187
Buck, Frank 17, 127–128, 129, 130, ***130***, 131, 132, 133–137, ***137***, 138–139, ***139***, 140, 185, 188, 189, 200; starring films produced by Van Beuren: *Bring 'Em Back Alive* 17, 122, 126, 127, 129–130, ***130***, 131–133, 134, 138, 139, 140, 150, 155, 185, 187, 188, 189, 192; *Wild Cargo* 17, 113, 133–135, ***135***, 136–137, ***137***, 138, 139, 140; *Fang and Claw* 17, 134, 138–139, ***139***, 140, 200; other starring films (in release order): *Jungle Menace* (serial) 140; *Jungle Cavalcade* (compilation) 140; *Jacaré* (documentary feature) 140; *Tiger Fangs* (feature) 140–141; *Africa Screams* (feature) 141
Buck, Walter 127
Buckley, F.R. 124
Burke, Johnny (actor) 87
Burke, Johnny (composer) 159, 160, 161, 164, 165
Burness, Pete 115
Burroughs, Edgar Rice 192
Bushman, Francis X., Jr. 153
Bye, George T. 129
Byrd, Joe 161

Cameron, Rod 151
Camp, Ruth Elder 70
Campbell, Eric 142, 145
Canutt, Yakima 153
Capra, Frank 203
Carle, Richard 88
Carr, Mary 88
Carruth, Milton 82
Cavaliere, Nick 129, 132, 133, 138
Celentano, Ralph 167
Chaney, Lon, Jr. [aka Creighton Chaney] 152, ***152***, 153, 156
Chaplin, Charles "Charlie" 7, 17, 21, 142, ***143***, 144–145, 146, ***147***, 148–149; Mutual comedies reissued by Van Beuren (in order of reissue date): *The Cure* 144, 145, 146, ***147***, 148; *Easy Street* 144, 145, 146, 148; *The Rink* 142, 146; *The Floorwalker* 146, 148; *The Vagabond* 142, 146; *The Pawnshop* 142, 146, 148; *The Fireman* 148; *The Count* 148; *The Immigrant* 142, 148; *One A.M.* 142, 148; *Behind the Screen* 148; *The Adventurer* 148 Compilation features released by Commonwealth (*Chaplin Carnival, The Charlie Chaplin Cavalcade, The Charlie Chaplin Festival*) 148; other Chaplin films referenced in text: *The Bond* 26; *City Lights* 142
Chaplin Classics 144
Check and Double Check (film) 115
Chesnut, Alma 187
Chicago Tribune 119
Chicago Tribune-New York Daily News Syndicate 79, 123
Childs, Boyd 207
Cimarron 120
Cinema Corporation 12
Citizen Kane 139
City of Wax (film) 199, 201; *see also Battle for Life* (film series)
Clark, Alexander 6
Clifton, Elmer 16, 39, 96–97, 102, 103, 104
Cobb, Edmund 151
Cobb, Irvin S. 71
Cobb, Ty 64, 65, 71
Cody, Lew 126
Coghlan, Frank, Jr. 66, 151
Colcord, Lincoln 186
Cole, Slim "King" 153
The Collegians (film series) 123, 126, 152
Collett, Glenna 71
Collier's magazine 74
Collins, Monte 164, 167
Colony, Beatrice 43
Columbia Broadcasting System (CBS) 157, 193, 194, 198
Columbia Pictures 78, 89, 108, 126, 140, 168
Commonwealth Productions 148, 156
The Condor Musicales (individual titles: *A Frozen Affair, Murder in Swing*) 20
Condor Pictures 20, 207
Consolidated Laboratories 122, 159
Cooke, Al 74
Coogan, Jackie 66
Coolidge, Calvin 83
Coombs, Jackie 82, 89
Cooper, Courtney Ryley 134, 151, 152
Cooper, Hugh 106
Cooper, Jackie 89
Cooper, Merian C. 156
Corbett, Ben 153
Correll, Charles 115, 116, 118
Correll, Mady 167
Corts, Ernest 65, 68, ***70***
Corum, Bill 17, 20, 21, 204–208
Cosmopolitan Pictures 74
The Covered Wagon (film) 151
Cowan, Lester 20
Cowan, William 124, 125
Crabbe, Buster 151
Cradle of the Deep (book) 185–187; *see also* Lowell, Joan
Cramer, Richard 194
Crawford, Merritt 75
Crosby, Floyd 203
Crosby, Percy 187
Crowninshield, Frank 187
Crumit, Frank 71
Cubby Bear 58, 111–113, ***113***, 114; *Mischievous Mice* (starring cartoon not released by Van Beuren) 113; *see also Aesop's Sound Fables*
Culhane, Shamus 176, 179
Cumberland, John 30
Cunningham, Glenn 206
Cunningham, James 72
Cuphead (video game) 178
Curiosities *see Walter Futter's Curiosities*
Cushman Bakeries 177
Cypress Gardens [FL] 69

Daly, Blythe 43
Dark Sands (film) 78
Darmour, Larry 74, 89, 108, 183
Davenport, Harry 61
Davis, Mannie 54, 55, 58, 111, 112
Davis, Meyer 157, ***158***, 159, 165, 166, 167, 168
Day, Houston 124
Dearholt, Ashton 188, 192
DeBeck, Billy 74
de Cordova, Leander 61
de la Fontaine, Jean 47
De La Motte, Marguerite 151
DeMille, Cecil B. 12, ***13***, 61, 66, 88, 124, 151
Dempsey, Jack 64, 71, 83, 84, ***84***, 206
Denis, Armand 134, 136, 137, 138

Index

Denny, Reginald 140
de Palma, Ralph 207
Desjardines, Peter 68
Desmond, Mary Jo 153
Desmond, William 85, 153
Devil Tiger (film) 133
Dickey, Big Bill 207
Disney, Roy 56
Disney, Walt 18, 19, 49, 53, 56, 58, 108, 111, 175, 176, 178, 179, 183–184, 211; character infringement suit against Van Beuren 56–57
Diversion Pictures 78; see also Futter, Walter
Dix, J. Airley 92
Donahue, Woolworth 206
Donald Duck 211
Douglas, Gilbert 43
Down to the Sea in Ships (film) 96
Downs, Johnny 81, 162
Drew, Louisa Lane 23
Drew, S. Rankin 24
Drew, Sidney 8, 9, 12, 23–24, *24*, 25–27, *27*, 28, 30, 41, 42, 62; solo films: *A Florida Enchantment*; *Goodness Gracious* 23
Drew, Mrs. Sidney (I) (Gladys Rankin) 23
Drew, Mrs. Sidney (II) (Lucille McVey, aka Jane Morrow) 8, 12, 23–24, *24*, 25–27, *27*, 28–29, *29*, 30, 41, 42
Duck Amuck (cartoon) 110
Duelberg, Franz 196
Dumb-Bell Letters (film series) 17, 40, 169–171, *171*, 172–174, 194
Dumb Luck (film) 194; see also *Easy Aces*
Duncan, Bud 74
Dunn, Josephine 124
Dunphy, Don 208
DuPont, Richard 206
Duryea, Dan 151

East Side Kids (film series) 89
Easy Aces: radio series 193; Vitaphone short film 194; Van Beuren film series 17, 107, 194–195, *195*, 196–198, 199, 209, 211; individual titles (in release order); *Pharoahland* 107, 194–195; *Topnotchers* 195–196; *Little New York* 196, 197; *Six-Day Grind* 196; *Unusualities* 196; *Jolly Ol' London* 196–197, 211; *Tricks of the Trade* 197; *A Capitol Idea* 197; *A World Within* 197; *Etiquette* 197; *Winter at the Zoo* 197; *An Old-Fashioned Movie* 197; *Debonair New Orleans* 197; *A Job's a Job* 197–198; *Fool Your Friends* 198; see also Ace, Goodman; Ace, Jane

Eaton, Jack 65, 66, 68, 70, 72, 73, 93
Educational Pictures 14, 17, 74, 75, 81, 84, 89, 108, 138, 167, 173, 194, 199, 201
Educational Screen magazine 200
Eduoarde, Carl 55, 58
Edwards, Cliff 162, *163*, 164
Edwards, Harry 87, 89
Elliott, Clyde E. 128–129, 132, 133, 134
Ellsworth, Van Beuren & Street 5
Engels, George 122
Ennis, Bert 82
Epaully, Jules 166, *166*
Equity magazine 81
Ernest, Georgie 82
Ervin, Russell T. 70
Eshbaugh, Ted 177–178
Estabrook, Howard 47, 49
Everson, William K. 142
Exhibitors Herald [aka *Exhibitors Herald-World*] 28, 36, 37, 39, 48, 49, 52, 53, 55, 72, 79, 85, 92, 98
Exhibitors Trade Review 44, 75
Export and Import Film Company 144
Eyes on Russia (book) 106; see also Bourke-White, Margaret

Fairbanks, Douglas, Sr. 83
Fairbanks, Jerry 199
Famous Players [aka Famous Players-Lasky] 8, 24, 25, 41, 43; see also Paramount Pictures
Fables Pictures Inc. [aka Fables Studios] 10, 46, 47, 48, 49, 53, 55; see also *Aesop's Film Fables*
Farley, Dot 126
Farmer Al Falfa 46, 49, 53, *54*, 55, 57; see also *Aesop's Film Fables*; *Aesop's Sound Fables*
Farrell, Johnny 71
Fay, W.P. 6
Fazenda, Louise 66
Felix the Cat see *Rainbow Parades*
Ferguson, Marietta [aka Marietta Van Beuren; aka Marietta Vignot] 4
Ferguson, William 56
Field, Sylvia 45
Fields, Harry 41, 43
Fighting for the Fatherland (film) 78
Film Booking Offices (FBO) 12, 14, 16, 74, 75, 76
Film Daily 16, 19, 38, 39, 45, 63, 71, 72, 73, 76, 92, 93, 98, 101, 110, 111, 116, 118, 121, 126, 129, 142, 146, 150, 151, 154, 155, 159, 160, 163, 165, 171, 173, 188, 196, 197, 198, 201–202, 211–212, 213, 214, 215

Fine, Larry 165
Finlayson, James 88
First National Pictures 66, 87
Fitch, Art 38
Fitch, Kay 38
Flash Gordon (serial) 211
Fleischer, Max 52, 108, 110, 112, 115, 145, 175
Fletcher, Charles Leonard 31, 32, 33
Fletchergrams 31, 32, 33
Flynn, Emmett J. 126
Flowers and Trees (cartoon) 175
Floyd Gibbons' Supreme Thrills (film series) 17, 108, 119–122; individual film titles (in release order): *Woodrow Wilson's Great Decision* 120–121; *Turn of the Tide* 121; see also Gibbons, Floyd
The Flying Hutchinsons 185
Floyd Gibbons: Your Headline Hunter (film series) 122
Folz, Artye 82
Ford, Corey 187
Forster, Viola 63
Foster, John 54–55, 57, 58, 60, 108, 109, 111, 112
Four in a Flat (film) 16; see also Van Beuren Corporation
Fox, Fontaine 74, 183
Fox, James 165
Fox Animals (film series) 82
Fox Film Corporation 84, 108, 133
Fox Movietone Studios 157, 159, 167, 176, 197
Fox Sunshine Comedies 82
Franey, Billy 87, 88
Fraser, Ferrin 138, 188
Freedman, Herman B. 32, 36
Freuler, John R. 7
Fries, Otto 84
Fulton, Jack, Jr. 162, 163, 166
Funk, Isaac Kaufmann 31
Funk & Wagnalls 31, 35, 36
Futter, Fred 74
Futter, Walter 14, 16, 74, 75, 76, 78, 103, 128

Gaiety Films 12, 61; see also Van Beuren Corporation
Gal Reporter (book) 187; see also Lowell, Joan
Ganley, Raymond 75, 83, 87, 88, 89
Garland, Judy 89
Georgetti, Franco 196
Gibbons, Floyd 119–120, *120*, 121–122, 126, 128
Gibson, Hoot 78
Gilbert, Billy 133
Giles, Cyprian 42
Gillett, Burt 18, 114, 115, 118, 175–176, 177, 178, 179, 180, 181, 182, 183, 184
The Girl Friends 164, 165
Goldberg, Rube 71

238 Index

Goldblatt, Harold M. 122
Goldburg, Jesse 129
Goldwyn Pictures 65
Goluboff, Grischa 212
Good, Jack 165
Goodman, Benny 145
Goodwill Films 156
Goofy Goat Antics (cartoon) 177
Gorcey, Leo 89
Gordon, Dan 179
Gordon, Huntley 124
Gosden, Freeman 115, 116, 118
Graham, Betty Jane 82, 84, 89
Granet, Bert 160, 161, 164, 167
Grange, Red 64
Grantland Rice Sportlights (film series) 16, 17, 66–67, 68–69, **69**, 70–71, 72, 91, 92, 93, 95, 101, 108, 119, 205; individual titles (in release order): for Pathé: *Wild and Wooly* 66; for Van Beuren: *Canned Thrills* 66; *Players at Play* 66; *Three Aces* 68; *Water Wonders* 68; *Crystal Champions* 68, 91; *Surf and Sail* 66; *Girls Will Be Boys* 66; *Winning Patterns* 66–68; *Footwork* 66; *Modern Rhythm* 70; *Sport Afloat* 71; *The River Drivers* 71; *Hook, Line and Melody* 69–70; *Gridiron Glory* **67**, 70; *Body Building Stamina* 71; *Feminine Fitness* 71; *Carolina Capers* 71; *Interesting Tails* 71; *Dogging It* 71; *Big Top Champions* 71; *Spills and Thrills* 69; *Fairway Favorites* 71; *Campus Favorites* 71; *Ski Hi Frolics* 70; *Dude Ranching* 70; *Gliding* 70; *Cobb Goes Fishing* 71; *Racqueteers* 71; *Par and Double Par* 71; *Dixie Chase* 71; *Swim or Sink* 69; *Hunting Thrills* 71; *Outdoor Stunting* 69; *Uncrowned Champions* 71; for Paramount: *Amphibious Fighters* 73; see also Rice, Grantland
Grantland Rice's Sports-Eye View 72, 73; see also *Grantland Rice Sportlights*
Grapewin, Charley 168
Grayson, Admiral Cary T. 121
Greenbriar Picture Show 178
Griffith, D.W. 96, 167, 186
Grinde, Nick 168
Guaranteed Pictures 148
Gude, O.J. 6
Guedel, John 85
Gulliver, Dorothy 152–153
Gulliver's Travels (cartoon feature) 145

Haines, Donald 82, *84*, 85, 89
Hall, Huntz 89
Hamilton, Lloyd 84
Hamilton, Neil 66
Hamilton, Reed 42

Hammond, Len 65
Hammons, E.W. 17, 199
Hampton, Benjamin 17
Hancock, Don 35, 171, 172, 196, 205, 206, 213
Hanley, William 103
Harbord, James G. 121
Harman-Ising [Hugh Harman, Rudolph Ising] 112–113, 179
Harper, Fred 194
Harrington, Hamtree 161
Harvey, John Joseph 42
Haskins, Charles 42
Haver, Phyllis 66
Havrilla, Alois 17, 104, 105, 106, 209–210, **210**, 211, 212, 213, 215
Hawkinson, John L. 65, 66
Hay, John 116
Hayde, Michael 145
Healy, Ted 165
Heermance, Clayton 25, 46
Heermance, Richard 25, 104, 124
Hellum, Barney 74
Henabery, Joseph 194
Hennecke, Clarence 82
Henry, Charlotte 140
Henry and Polly (film series) 12, 14, 62–63, 79, 81; individual film titles (in release order): *Should a Mason Tell?* 62, 63, **63**; *Their Second Honeymoon* 63; *King Harold* 62, 63
Herrick, F. Herrick 104, 105
Hershey, Burnett 161, 164, 168
Hervey, Wilna 183
Hicks, Tommy 85
Hildebrand, Fred 160
Hill, Robert F. 152
Hill, Thelma 74
Hines, Margie 110, 162
Hirliman, George 20
A History of the Movies (book) 17
Hitchcock, Tommy 64, 68
Hite, Les 20
Hoefler, Paul L. 78
Hoffman, M.H. 20
Hoffstetter, John 207
Holland, John 124
Hollywood Pictures 20–21
Hollywood Reporter 168, 188
Holmes, Taylor 61, 62, **63**
Holt, Ula 190, 192
Hoppe, Willie 71, 196
Hoskins, Robert 84
House, Judson 90
Howard, Moe 165
Howard, Shemp 164, 165, **166**
Howell, Hazel 125
Hoyt, Arthur 125
Hunt, Cyprian C. 27–28
Hunt, Eleanor 125
Hunt, Fary 38
Hunter, Ruth 38
Hurd, Earl 46, 47, 52, 53, 55
Hurley, Arthur 120
Hutchinson, W.G. 20

I Was a Captive of Nazi Germany (film) 102
Ince, Thomas H. 151
Invincible Films 177
Irving Berlin Publishing Co. 159
I've Got to Sing a Torch Song (cartoon) 179
Iwerks, Ub 108

Jackson, Eugene "Pineapple" 82
Jackson, Mary Ann 89
Jackson, Selmer 125
Jacobson, Sam 171, 188
Jacques, Annie Laurie 187
"The Jarr Family" (newspaper column) 12, 61–62, 81
Jarrett, Art 160, 167
Jarvis, Anna 93
Jason, Leigh 161, 165, 167
Jocko the Monk 82–83. 85
Johnson, Cornelius 207
Johnston, Arthur 159
Jones, Bobby 64, 68
Jones, Buck 103
Jones, Chuck 110
Jordan, Bobby 89

Kansas City [MO] *Journal-Post* 193
Keep Smiling (play) 24, 28
Keith, Benjamin Franklin 9, 12, 61
Keith-Albee 9, 10, 11, 12, 14, 17, 31, 32, 36, 46, 47, 49, 52, 53, 61, 66, 81
Keith-Albee-Orpheum (K-A-O) 12, 14, 36, 53, 61, 62, 63, 66, 74, 81
Kelly, Paul 61
Kelly, Walter C. 36
Kelton, Dr. Harry "Doc" 7, 8, 9, 17, 24, 25, 30, 41
Kennedy, Joseph P. 12, 14, 74
Kennedy, Leo 165
Kent, Crauford 124, 125
KFI (Los Angeles radio station) 96
Kimberly-Clark 126
King Features syndicate 114, 115
Kipling, Rudyard 90, 91
Kirsme, Margaret 71
Klein, Izzy 176
KMBC (Kansas City MO radio station) 193
Knapp, Evalyn 93
Kodak 106
Kodascope Library 43
Korkis, Jim 57
Kris (film) 134
Kruger, Stubby 69
Kummer, Frederick Arnold 125
Kussell, H.O. 167

LaBelle, Rupert 38
Lackteen, Frank 153–154
Lahr, Bert 159, 160–161, 162, *163*, 164, 165, 167–168
Lahr, John 160

Langdon, Harry 81, 87, 89
Lantz, Walter 108, 184
Larchmont [NY] Times 46
Lask, Donald R. 207
The Last Frontier (1926 film) 151, 154
The Last Frontier (Van Beuren serial) 17, 133, 134, 150–155, *155*, 159
Lauder, Ted 10, 14
Laurel and Hardy 133, 160
Lazerri, Guy 207
Leavitt, Sam 160, 167
Lehr, Lew 197
Lenox, Elizabeth 93
Leonard, Benny 83, 206
LeSaint, Edward J. 38
Letour, Alfred 196
Levey, Jules 188
Liberty magazine 123, 125, 126
Liberty Short Short Stories (film series) 17, 123–126, 142, 153; individual film titles (in release order): *Stung* 124; *Ether Talks* 124, *125*; *Double Decoy* 124; *Endurance Flight* 125; *Secretary Preferred* 125; *Beautiful and Dumb* 126
Liebman, Albert H. 20
Life magazine 106
Lindholm, Bill 149
Lindsey, Mort 196
Link, Barney 6
Literary Digest (magazine) 31, 32, 33, 35, 36
Littau, Joseph 76
Little, Lou 206
Little Herman (cartoon) 46; *see also* Terry, Paul
The Little King (cartoon series) 114–115; individual film titles (in release order): *The Fatal Note* 114; *Marching Along* 114; *Pals* 114, 115
The Little King (comic panel and strip) 114, 115, 169, 175
Littlejohn, Bill 116, 180
Lloyd, Harold 124
Longfellow, Henry Wadsworth 211
Lopez, Vincent 145
Lorentz, Pare 203
Louis, Joe 206
Louverture, Toussaint 101
Lovy, Alex 176
Lowe, Bert 38
Lowell, Juliet 17, 169, 172, 173–174
Lowell, Joan 17, 138, 185–186, *186*, 187–190, *190*, 191, *191*, 192; starring film for Van Beuren: *Adventure Girl* 17, 111, 188–190, *190*, 191, *191*, 192, 210
Lucas, Wilfred 103
Luce, Henry 106
Lund, Oscar 91, 93
Lupino, Ida 103–104
Luther, Frank 16, 93

Lyons, Frank 42
Lytell, Bert 188

MacBride, Donald 29–30
Macfadden, Bernarr 123, 126
Mack, Joseph P. 43
Magna Pictures *see* Meyer Davis-Van Beuren Corporation
Main, Marjorie 38
Maltin, Leonard 111, 114, 167, 197
Man-o-War (race horse) 206
Manne, Maurice 53
Mannon, Alfred T. 16, 39, 96, 98, 102
Mansfield, Martha 96
Marquiss, Walter 126
Marsales, Frank 113
Marshall, George 82, 83, 84, 85, 87
Martin, Freddie 167
Martin, Valerie Belasco 42
Marty, Walter 207
Marx, Groucho 81
Mason, Dan 183
Mason, LeRoy 153
Mastin, Mildred 187, 189
Mayer, Arthur 139, 188
McCardell, Roy 61, 62
McCarey, Leo 160
McCarey, Ray 160, 162, 164
McClusky, J.T. 207
McComas, Kendall "Breezy Brisbane" 82
McConnell, Fred J. 151, 152, 154, 159
McCracken, Harold 17, 209, 210, 213
McCutcheon, Wallace 43
McDonald, Charles D. 32, 35, 37, *37*, 38, 39, 46, 78
McElwee, John 178
McLaughlin, Judge Charles 192
McMein, Neysa 187
McNamara, Reggie 196
McNamee, Graham 70
McNutt, Ruth 38
Meaney, Helen 68
Medbury, John P. 103
Meehan, James 82
Melton, James 159, 160
Mercer, Jack 110
Messmer, Otto 49, 181, 183
Metro-Goldwyn-Mayer (MGM) 14, 69, 81, 103, 108, 128, 162, 184, 211
Metropolitan Studios 61, 126
Meyer Davis-Van Beuren Corporation 159, 162; *see also* Davis, Meyer; Van Beuren, Amedee James
Mickey "Himself" McGuire 74, 183; *see also* Fox, Fontaine
Mickey McGuire (film series) 89
Miles, Lillian 165
Milland, Ray 81
Miller & Lyles [Flournoy Miller, Aubrey Lyles] 111, 115

Mills, Julia 43, 45
Mills, Leroy N. 212
Milton, Tommy 207
Milton Mouse (Van Beuren's Mickey Mouse lookalike) 49, 56–57; *see also Aesop's Film Fables, Aesop's Sound Fables*; Disney, Walt
Mindlin, Michael 120
Miner, Ira 207
Minnie A. Caine (schooner) 185, 186; *see also* Lowell, Joan
Mintz, Charles 60, 108
mr. ace & JANE (radio series) 198; *see also Easy Aces* (radio series)
Mr. and Mrs. Sidney Drew (film series): at Kalem 23; at Vitagraph: 23–24 at Metro 24; at V.B.K. 8–9, 12, 24–29, *29*, 30, 31, 41, 62; individual film titles (by company, in release order): US 4th Liberty Loan Drive: *Financing the Fourth* 26 V.B.K.: *Romance and Rings* 26. *27*; *Once a Mason* 26–27, 62; *The Amateur Liar* 26, 28; *Harold, Last of the Saxons* 28, 62; *Squared* 28; *Bunkered* [Mrs. Drew solo] 29–30; *A Sisterly Scheme* [Mrs. Drew solo] *29*, 30; *see also* Drew, Sidney; Drew, Mrs. Sidney (I) and (II)
Moldenhauer, Maja 178
Monogram Pictures 89
Monsieur Fabre (film) 203; *see also* Woodard, Horace
Montana, Bull 87
Moorish Gardens 7, *8*
Morrison, Pete 153
Moser, Frank 47, 53, 54
Motion Picture Daily 39, 63, 93, 107, 165, 172, 173, 197, 202–203, 211, 213
Motion Picture Herald 72, 121, 132, 161, 162, 163–166, 167, 168, 172, 173, 174, 176–177, 192, 200, 202, 211, 212, 213
Motion Picture News 8, 10, 25–26, 32, 38, 48, 52–53, 75, 83, 85, 87, 88, 91, 100, 101
Motion Picture Review 121, 200
Motography 10
Movie Classic magazine 133
Moving Picture World 7, 8, 10, 23, 25, 26
Mudge, Gertrude 165
Muffati, Steve 112, 113
Munson, Henry 5
Munson, Marion 210
Murdock, John J. 9, 10, 12, 14, 61, 62
Murphy, Jimmy 74
Muse, Clarence 140
Mutual Chaplins Inc. 144
Mutual Film Corporation 7, 17, 142, 144, 146, 148, 149

Nadel, Joe 160, 167
Nathan, Manny 199
National Board of Review magazine 58, 101, 124, 125, 192, 210
National Broadcasting Company (NBC) 12–13, 38, 90, 98, 102, 115, 118, 120, 122, 133, 157, 165, 194, 198, 209
National Vaudeville Artists 9, 81
NBC Artists Management 122
NBC Artists Service 115
NBC Quartette 161
The Negro Soldier (film) 203
Neilan, Marshall 35
Neill, Richard 153, 154
Neville, George 38
New York Billposting Company 6
New York Board of Censors 124
New York Evening Herald 42
New York Evening Sun 42
New York Mirror 136
New York Morning Telegraph 42
New York State Exhibitor 72, 73
New York Times 42
New York Weekly 5
New Yorker magazine 114
Newmeyer, Fred 124
NitrateVille website 146
Nizer, Louis 72, 73
Nolan, Mary 126
Norelius, Martha 68, 71
Normil, Charles 101
North, Tom 92
Not Wanted (film) 103
Notes on a Cowardly Lion (book) 160; see also Lahr, Bert; Lahr, John
Notlek Amusement Company 7, 25
Notlek Amusement Park 7
Novis, Donald 166, 167
Nurmi, Paavo 66

Ober, Robert 16
O'Brien, George 20–21
O'Brien, Lawrence G. 38
O'Connor, Eddie 38
Official Films 162, 178
Oldfield, Barney 207
Ollendorf, Julian 36
Olsen and Johnson 126, 157, 159
Olson, Margaret 94
Orpheum Circuit 9, 10, 32, 53, 61; see also Keith-Albee-Orpheum; Radio-Keith-Orpheum
 Gang (film series) 14, 81, 82, 89, 162
  Fulton [aka Anthony] 123, 126
  ge 87
  206
  –179
  8
  Studios 112,

Paramount Pictures 8, 9, 17, 26, 28, 41, 43, 47, 52, 65, 72, 108, 151
Parrish, Helen 84–85
Pathé Club Yearbook of 1927 35, 64
Pathé News 144, 187, 209
Pathé Pictures Corporation [aka Pathé Exchange] 9, 10, 11, 12, 14, 16, 17, 32, 33, 37, 38, 39, 40, 43, 45, 46, 47, 48, 49, 52, 53, 54, 57. 61, 62, 63, 65, 66, 69, 70, 72, 73, 79, 81, 82, 83, 92, 93, 94, 98, 108, 151, 152, 159
The Pathé Sun (company newsletter) 90–91, 92, 98
Patterson, Captain Joseph 79
Paumstead, Bixey 168
Payton, Claude 152
Pemberton, Harvey 43
Perry, Newton 68, 69
Pettijohn, Charles C. 144, 148
"Phil M. Daly" 159–160, 188
Philadelphia Exhibitor 172, 197, 201, 203, 211, 212
Photoplay 187, 189
Pinocchio (cartoon feature) 162
Pittsburgh Press 187
Pizor, William 185
Plummer, Lincoln 43
Plympton, George 152
Pope, Dick 69
Popeye 110
Popovici, George 106
Portrait of Myself (book) 106; see also Bourke-White, Margaret
Pratt, Samuel 5, 6
PRC Pictures 141
Preston, Walter 90
Prevost, Marie 66
The Private Life of Henry VIII (film) 164
Producers Distributing Corporation (PDC) [aka DeMille Corporation] 12, 53, 61, 66, 81, 151
Promised Land (book) 192; see also Lowell, Joan
Prosser, Seward 72
Purviance, Edna 142
Putnam, G.M. 187

Racing Blood (film series) 74
Radio Corporation of America (RCA) 13, 55, 90, 115
Radio-Keith-Orpheum (RKO) 14, 16, 17, 19, 20, 21, 53, 57, 72, 75, 87, 98, 104, 108, 111, 114, 115, 116, 120, 123, 124, 126, 128, 133, 134, 139, 140, 142, 146, 148, 150, 151, 152, 153, 154, 155, 156, 159, 160, 162, 165, 169, 172, 173, 176, 177, 180, 181, 183, 184, 188, 192, 194, 213, 215
Radio Pictures 16, 108, 123, 126, 150; see also Radio-Keith-Orpheum
Rainbow Parades (cartoon series) 18, 176, 177, 179, 180–181, 183; individual film titles (in release order): *Pastry Town Wedding* 177, **178**; *The Sunshine Makers* 18, 177; *Japanese Lanterns* 177, 178; *Spinning Mice* 178; *Picnic Panic* 178, 179; *The Foxy Terrier* 179; *Bird Scouts* 179; *A Waif's Welcome* 179; *Cupid Gets His Man* 179; *It's a Greek Life* 179; *Parrotville* cartoons (in release order): *The Parrotville Fire Department* 179, **180**; *Parrotville Old Folks* 179; *Parrotville Post Office* 179 Molly Moo Cow (character) 179, 180, 181, **181**; individual films (in release order): *The Hunting Season* 179; *Molly Moo Cow and the Butterflies* 180, **181**; *Toonerville Folks*: comic strip and characters 183; cartoon series 183; individual titles (in release order): *Toonerville Trolley* 183; *Trolley Ahoy* 183; *Toonerville Picnic* 183 *Felix the Cat* (cartoon series) 181–182, **182**, 183; non–Van Beuren silent films 49, 175, 181–182; Van Beuren film titles (in release order): *Felix the Cat and the Goose That Laid the Golden Egg* 181–182; *Neptune Nonsense* 182; *Bold King Cole* 182, 183
Ralston, Esther 140
Ramsaye, Terry 132
Raymaker, Herman C. 188, 189
Raymond Johnson Choir 161, 162
RCA *see* Radio Corporation of America
RCA Photophone 13, 16, 36, 37, 38, 53, 90, 91
Reade, Janet 164
Record Films 76; see also Futter, Walter
Reddy, George J. 85
Reid, Laurence 48
Reisman, Phil H. 140
Resolute Pictures 102; see also Mannon, Alfred T.
The Return of the Riddle Rider (serial) 152
Revier, Dorothy 124
Rhythm Boys 168
Rhythmaires 161
Rice, Grantland 64–65, **65**, 66–67, **67**, 68, 69, 70, 71–72, 73, 91–92, 94, 120, 126, 204. 205
Richmond, Warner 124
Rickard, Tex 68, 83, 206
"Ripley's Believe It or Not" (newspaper feature) 75
Ritchey, Helen 212
The River (film) 203
RKO *see* Radio-Keith-Orpheum
RKO-Pathé 16, 120, 154; see also

Index

Pathé Pictures Corporation; Radio-Keith-Orpheum
RKO-Radio Pictures 16; *see also* Radio-Keith-Orpheum; Radio Pictures
Roach, Hal 3, 9, 10, 12, 14, 17, 81, 82, 83, 87, 89
Robards, Jason, Sr. 124
Roberts, Richard 145, 146
Roberts, Theodore 88
Robeson, Paul 78
Rock, Joe 74
Rockne, Knute 64
Rodemich, Eugene (Gene) 58, 70, 91, 94, 110, 111, 113, 114, 115, 129, 131, 134, 140, 145, 146, 149
Rogers & Anthony 165
Rooney, Mickey 89, 183
Roop, J.L. 108
Roosevelt, Andre 134
Ross, Harold 187
Ross, Nat 123, 124, 126, 152–153
Rothafel, Samuel "Roxy" 55
Rufle, George 55, 57, 108, 109
Ruth, Babe 64, 71, 83, 196, 207
Ruttenberg, Joe 160, 162
Ryerson, Florence 28

Sack Amusements 162
Saeger, Roy 82
Saint-Saëns, Camille 76, 78
Salt-Water Taffy (book) 187; *see also Cradle of the Deep* (book); Ford, Corey
San Francisco Chronicle 186
Sargent, Jean 162, 163
Sarnoff, David 12
Sawyer, Bill "Leatherneck" 188, 189, 190
Sayers, Loretta 161
Schaefer, Kermit 174
Schaff, Monroe 159
Schenck, Joseph M. 96
Schlesinger, Leon 108, 112
Schuyler Securities Corporation 20
Screen Cartoonists Guild 180
Screenland magazine 134
Searl, Jackie 88
Sears, Lucille 194
Seegar, Hal 145
Seitz, George 151
Selznick, David O. 156
Senna, Charles 165
Sennett, Mack 3, 7, 9, 17, 26, 81, 82, 85, 87, 166
"Sentinel Louie" (comic strip) and Sentinel Louey (cartoon character) *see Aesop's Sound Fables; The Little King* (cartoon series)
Service, T.O. 37
Shannon, Harry 122, 168
Sharkey, Jack 206
Sharples, Winston 113, 134, 140, 145, 149, 177, 178, 189, 205
Shaw, Artie 145

Shepard, David 149
Sherman, Frank 109
Shields, Jerry 47
Shilkret, Nat 140
Shope, Henry 90
Showmen's Association 5
Shutta, Ethel 165
Sidney, Jess 38
Siegel, Abe E. 10, 31–32, 33, 36, 46
Siegel, Lena 32
Siegler, Otto 188
Silver, Milton 133
Silver Springs, Florida 68, 69
Silverman, Sime 14, 53
Simon & Schuster 169, 185, 186, 187
Sisk, Robert 133
Sisters of the Skillet [Ed East, Ralph Dumke] 159, 167
Six Cylinder Love (play and film) 43, 96
Smith, Courtland 144, 148
Smith, Dick 124, 125, 126
The Smith Family (film series) 82
Smitty (comic strip) 14, 79, 83
Smitty and His Pals (film series) 14, 16, *80*, 81, 82, 83, 85, **86**, 87–89, 114, 123, 153; individual film titles (in release order): *No Picnic* 83, **84**, 87; *No Sale* 83–84; *Camping Out* 84; *All Aboard* 84–85; *Circus Time* 85, 88; *No Children* 85, 87, 88, 153; *Watch My Smoke* 87, *Tomato Omelette* 87–88; *Puckered Success* 88; *Uncle's Visit* 88–89
Snell, Frank 20, 73
The Snowman (cartoon) 177
Snyder, Edward 152
Soglow, Otto 114, 115, 169
Song Sketches (film series) 16, 70, 72, 90–94, 98; individual film titles (in release order): *Mandalay* 91–92, 94; *The Trumpeter* 92, 94; *Songs of Mother* 93; *Love's Memories* 93; *Deep South* 93, 94; *Voice of the Sea* 93, 94
Sono Art-World Wide Pictures 78
Spargo, John S. 75
Spaulding, Russell 104, 105, 106
Spaulding, William H. 71
Speaks, Oley 90
Spencer, Freddie 196
Spina, Harold 159, 160, 161, 164, 165
Sport Pictorial (film series) 65; *see also Grantland Rice Sportlights*
The Sportlight (film series) 65; *see also Grantland Rice Sportlights*
Sports Pictorials Inc. 66; *see also Grantland Rice Sportlights*
Sports with Bill Corum (film series) 17, 19, 20, **205**, 206–207, 213, 215; individual film

titles (in release order): *Inside the Ropes* 206; *Bugles from the Blue Grass* 206; *Gentlemen's Sports* 206; *Tomorrow's Halfback* 206, 207; *Winter Sports* 206; *Never Catch the Rabbit* 206; *Row, Mister, Row* 206; *High, Wide and Dashing* 206–207; *Pardon My Spray* 207; *Goals for Gold and Glory* 207; *Singing Wheels* 207; *Ladies Day* 207; *The Iceman* 207; *Putting on the Dog* 207; *Saratoga Summers* 207; *Foreign Sports* 207, 213; *Big League* 207; *Beach Sports* 207; *Royal Steeds* 207; *Golf Timing* 207, 215; *see also* Corum, Bill
Sportslights Corporation [Grantland Rice Sportlights Inc.] 72, 73; *see also Grantland Rice Sportlights*
Squire, Harry E. 138, 188, 189, 190, 192
Stalin, Josef 106
Stallings, George 57, 108, 109, 111, 113, 114, 115, 116, 176
Stanchfield, Steve 178
Stanley, James 16, **16**, 70, 90–91, 92, 93, 94
Star of Bengal (play) 187; *see also* Lowell, Joan
Steamboat Willie (cartoon) 53
Steele, Bob 151
Steele, Isobel Lillian 102
Stein, Fred 207
Stengel, Leni 164
Stewart, Donald Ogden 187
Storey, Tom 152
Street, E.V. 4, 5
Street & Smith 4–5
Strenge, Walter 38
Stromberg, Hunt 103, 151
Struggle to Live (film series) 17, 19, 138, 199–203, 215; individual film titles (in release order): *Neptune Mysteries* 199, 200; *Hermits of Crab-Land* 200; *Beach Masters* 200; *Winged Pageantry* 200–201, **201**, *Underground Farmers* 201–202; *Living Jewels* 202, **202**; *Swampland* 202–203; *Deadly Females* 203; *Forest Gangsters* 203; *Desert Land* 203, 215; see also Woodard, Horace; Woodard, Stacy
Sullivan, Pat 49, 175, 181
Sultan of Ibrahim 130, 134. 136
Sunken Silver (serial) 151
Supreme Pictures 102; *see also* Mannon, Alfred T.
The Swan (film) 16, 76, 78; *see also* Futter, Walter; Van Beuren Corporation

Talezaar, Margaret 188
Talking Topics of the Day (film

series) 15, 16, 37–40, 57, 78, 95, 96 Individual film titles (in release order): *The Petters* 37, 39; *Pressing His Suit* 37, 39; *Topical Hits* 38; *Topical Bits* 38; *Topical Nips* 38; *On the Air* 39; *In the Park* 39; *Cover Charge* 39; *What No Bait?* 39; *Home Sweet Home* 39; *Van Beuren News* 39; see also *Topics of the Day*
Tanguay, Eva 81
Tapley, Rose 61
Tashlin, Frank [aka Tish Tash] 109
Taylor, Irene 166
Tec-Art Studios 14, 39, 81, 87, 96, 97, 124
Ten Eyck, A. 206
Terhune, Albert Payson 26, 42
Terriss, Tom 16, 68, 96, 97, **97**, 98, 100, 102, 103, 104, 212
Terry, John 47, 54
Terry, Paul 10, 14, 15, 46–47, 48, 49, 52, 53, 54, 55–56, 183–184
"Terry Burlesques" (cartoon parodies) 47
Terrytoons 56, 108, 184
Tetley, Walter 181
Thanhouser Films 46
Thomason, Adelina 166, **166**, 167
The Three Little Pigs (cartoon) 175
Tiffany-Stahl Productions 96
Tilden, Bill 64, 68
Timberg, Sammy 145
Timely Films Inc. 32, 33, 36, 46, 47; see also Topics of the Day Inc.
Timely Topics Inc. 32; see also *Topics of the Day*
Toby the Pup 108
Todd, Ruth 124, 125, 126
Todd, Thelma 66
Toddle Tales (cartoon series) 176, 178; individual film titles (in release order): *Grandfather's Clock* 176; *Along Came a Duck* 176; *A Little Bird Told Me* 176; see also Gillett, Burt; *Rainbow Parades*
Tom and Jerry (Van Beuren cartoon series) **18**, 57, 108–109, **109**, 110–111, 142, 177; individual titles (in release order): *'Vot a Night!* 109, 110; *A Swiss 'ck* 110; *Rocketeers* 110; *In ‸g* 109; *The Tuba Tooter ‸: Plane Dumb* 110- 111; *‸lues* **109**; *A Span- ‸7; Piano Toon- ‸l Mania* 18, 110; *‸my* 110; *Hook ‸n* 109; *Puz- ‸Park* 110; *‸antom*

Tom and Jerry, or Life in London (play) 108
Tompkins, Captain Warrick M. 212
Toonerville Folks (comic strip and live-action silent films) see *Rainbow Parades*
"Toots and Casper" (comic strip) 74
Topics of the Day (film series) 10, **11**, 12, 31–34, **34**, 35–36, 37, **37**, 43, 45, 46, 47, 52, 95, 169; see also *Talking Topics of the Day*
Topics of the Day Inc. 10, 14, 36, 46, 47
Torrence, David 42
Totheroh, Rollie 144
Town and Country Films 16, 65; see also *Grantland Rice Sportlights*
Tracy, Arthur 159, 167
Tracy, Lee 168
Tracy, Nell 30
Trader Horn (film) 128
Travelaughs (film series) 103
Treasure Chest (film series) 173
Truax, Maude 82
Truex, Ernest 9, 11, 30, 41–44, **44**, 45, 61, 96; starring films for AyVeeBee: *The Night of the Dub* 30, 42; *Too Good to Be True* 42; *Little, But Oh My!* 43–44, **44**, 45; *Stick Around* 44–45; *The Bashful Lover* 45
The Tumult and the Shouting (book) 66; see also Rice, Grantland
Tunney, Gene 64, 68, 93
Twenty Grand (race horse) 196
Tyer, James 114
Tynan, James J. 82, 83, 87

United Artists 96, 140, 183
United Booking Office 9, 81
Universal Pictures 108, 123, 126, 133, 150, 151, 152, 199, 211

Vagabond Adventures (film series) 16, 17, 39, 95, 96, 97, 98, **99**, 100–103, 104–106, 107, 108, 128, 142, 185, 194, 199, 209, 210, 211, 212; individual film titles (in release order): *The Golden Pagoda* 98; *The Glacier's Secret* 98; *Streets of Mystery* 98; *Land of Chang-Ow* 98, 99; *Drums of Fear* 100; *Temple of Silence* 100; *Sacred Fires* 100; *Venetian Nights* 101; *Love That Kills* 100; *Satan's Fury* 100; *Ebony Shrine* 101; *Jungle Terror* 100; *Gem of Agra* 101; *Sands of Egypt* 101; *Mystic Isles* 100, 102; *Days of Solitude* 100; *The Well of Fortaleza* 101; *Hurricane Island* 101; *The Fallen Empire* 101; *Hurricane Island* 101; *Song of the Voodoo* 101, **102**; *Through the Ages* 101, 102; *The Land of Gandhi* 103; *The Door of Asia* 103; *Drums of the Orient* 103; *Malaysia* 103; *Holland Mosaics* 104; *Cuba* 104; *Moorish Spain* 105; *The Holy Land* 105; *Madeira, The Land of Wine* 105; *Gilbraltar, Guardian of the Mediterranean* 105; *Eyes on Russia: From the Caucasus to Moscow* 106, 107; *Red Republic: From Baku to Dnieprostroi* 106; *Roumania* 106; *Quebec* 107
Van Beuren, Alfred 4, 5–6, 7
Van Beuren, Amedee James [né Amedee James Vignot] 3–4, **4**, 5, 6, **6**, 7–9, 10, 11–12, 14, 15, 16–17, 18, 19–21, 23, 24, 25–26, 28, 30, 31, 32, 35, 36, 37, 38–39, 40, 41, 42, 43, 45, 46, 47, 48, 49, 52, 53, 54, 56-57, 58, 61, 62–63, 66, 71, 72, 73, 74, 75, 76, 78, 79–81, 83, 89, 90–91, 93, 95, 96, 98, 107, 111, 114, 118, 119, 120, 122, 126, 127, 128, 129, 133, 134, 136, 138, 140, 142, 144, 145, 146, 148, 149, 151, 154, 155, 157, 164, 165, 168, 169, 170, 175, 176–177, 180, 183, 184, 185, 187, 188, 192, 194, 196, 199, 200, 204, 207, 208, 210, 214, 215
Van Beuren, Blanche 7
Van Beuren, Harriet (née Ethel Anderson) 15
Van Beuren & New York Billposting Company 6, 7; see also A. Van Beuren & Company; New York Billposting Company
Van Beuren Corporation [aka Van Beuren Productions] 14, 16, 17–19, **19**, 20, 21, 68, 69, 70, 72, 73, 75, 78, 90, 92, 94, 95, 96, 100, 104, 105, 106, 107, 108, 110, 113, 115, 118, 119, 120, 122, 123, 124, 126, 128, 129, 131, 133, 140, 142, 143, 146, 149, 150, 151, 154, 156, 159, 160, 162, 165, 169, 171, 172, 173, 175, 185, 189, 196, 197, 198, 199, 200, 201, 205, 206, 207, 210, 212, 213
Van Beuren Enterprises 14, 36, 66, 81; see also Van Beuren Corporation
The Van Beuren Musical Comedies (film series) 159–161, **163**, 164, 167, 168 Individual film titles (in release order): *Hizzoner* 160–161, 162; *Bubbling Over* 161–162, 168; *The Strange Case of Hennessy* 162–164; *Henry the Ache* 164–165, 167, 168; *The Knife of the Party* 165–166, 167; *Everybody Likes*

Music 166, **166**, 167; *No More West* 167–168; *Sea Sore* 167; *see also* Davis, Meyer
Van Beuren Studios (animation studio) 14, 15, 17–19, 54, 55, 57, 60, 110, 111, 112, 113, 114, 115, 116, 175–176, 177, 178, 179, 183; *see also* Fables Pictures Inc.; Van Beuren Corporation
Van Dyke, Willard 203
Van Heusen, Jimmy 159
Van-Kelton Stadium 7
Van-Kelton Tennis Club 7
Van Loesen, Emily 167
Variety 10, 14. 20, 36, 38, 53, 62, 71, 72, 76, 81, 85, 93, 98, 100, 115, 121, 122, 124, 125–126, 146, 154, 162
V.B.K. Productions 8, 25, 26,30, 31, 32, 41; *see also* Van Beuren Corporation
Venuti, Joe 145
Vernon, Isobel 38
Vignot, Alfred 4
Vignot, Amédée 4
Vignot, Amedee James *see* Van Beuren, Amedee James
Vitagraph Pictures 23, 24, 27, 29, 30, 42, 61, 62
Vitaphone Corporation 87, 122, 165, 194

WAFilms 74; *see also* Futter, Walter
Waffles the Cat [aka Tom, aka Henry] 52, 57, 60; teamed with Don Dog 57, 108, 109; *see also Aesop's Film Fables*; *Aesop's Sound Fables*; *Tom and Jerry* (Van Beuren cartoon series)
Wagner, Captain 188
Walker, Cecil 196
Walker, J.D. 144
Wallington, Jimmy 106, 159, 160
Walter Futter's Curiosities 14, 16, 74–76, 78 Individual film titles (in release order): *Believe It or Not* 75; *Pets* 75; *Facts or Fancies* 75; *Seeing's Believing* 75–76, **77**; *Nifties* 76; *Faces* 76; *Here and There* 76; *Follies of Fashion* 76; *Gleanings* 76; *Women Only* 76; *Pedal Power* 76; *see also* Futter, Walter
Walters, J. Henry 10, 14
Ward, Jack 55
Warner, Eltinge F. 206
Warner Bros. 108, 112, 179
Warren, Gilbert 152
The Warrens of Virginia (film) 96
Waters, Ethel 159, 161, 162, **163**
Watkins, Mildred 62
Waxman, A.P. 120
We the People (TV series) 174
Webb, Kenneth 42
Weber, Harry 14, 81–82, 83, 87, 89, 96
Weber, Muriel 81
Weiss, Louis 65
Weissmuller, Johnny 64, 68, 69
Wetzel, Al 213
What's on the Air magazine 90, 120
White, Alice 66
White, Jules 89
White, Leo 148
Whitman, Emma Anderson 26
Whitman, Gayne 102, 103, 200, 202
Whitney, C.V. 71
Wid's Daily 30, 43
Wildlife Films (book) 134
Williams, William 82
Wills, Helen 71
Wilson, Don 21
Wilson, Frank L. 161
Winchell, Walter 145, 174
Windom, Lawrence 61
Winn, Matt T. 204
With Byrd at the South Pole (film) 119

Witwer, H.C. 74
The Wizard of Oz (cartoon) 177
WJZ (New York City radio station) 209
WNJR (Newark NJ radio station) 210
Wodehouse, P.G. 44
Wood, Gar 206
Woodard, Horace 17, 138, 199–200, 201, 203
Woodard, Stacy 17, 138, 199–200, 201, 203
World on Parade (film series) 17, 19, 20, 107, 197, 209, 210–215; individual film titles (in release order): *Land of the Eagle* 210–211; *Spain's Romantic Isle* 211; *Land of Evangeline* 211; *Morocco* 211; *Prominent Personalities* 211–212; *Coral Islands of the Atlantic* 212; *Venice of the North* 212; *Trinidad* 212; *Washington in Virginia* 212, 214; *Heart of the Sierras* 212–213; *Graveyard of Ships* 213; *Gold Fever* 213; *Romantic Mexico* 213; *Manhattan Waterfront* 213–214, **214**, *Mt. Vernon* 214–215, *California Missions* 215; *Circus Winter Quarters* 215; *Florida Cowboy* 215; *Workshops of Old California* 215; *Jungle Playmates* 215; *see also* McCracken, Harold
Wragge, Little Eddie 38

Yates, Herbert J. 159
Yates, Robert 124
Young, Clara Kimball 23, 62
Young, James 23

Zaharias, Babe Didrickson 64
Zeidman, B.F. 199
Zuro, Josiah 53, 55, 68

product-compliance
W, UK

932